REALITY • SENSE PERCEPTION AND VOLITION •
CONCEPT-FORMATION • OBJECTIVITY • REASON •
MAN • THE GOOD • VIRTUE • HAPPINESS •
GOVERNMENT • CAPITALISM • ART

A best-selling novelist, prolific writer, and world-renowned philosopher, Ayn Rand defined and developed Objectivism: the powerful system of thought which holds that human beings can and should live by the guidance of reason. In this epochal book, leading Rand scholar Leonard Peikoff presents the first comprehensive statement of her philosophy. Here is the definitive guide to Ayn Rand's brilliantly reasoned thought on all the crucial philosophical issues of our day.

OBJECTIVISM:
THE PHILOSOPHY OF AYN RAND

LEONARD PEIKOFF is universally recognized as the pre-eminent Rand scholar writing today. He worked closely with Ayn Rand for thirty years and was designated by her as heir to her estate. He has taught philosophy at Hunter College, Long Island University, and New York University and lectures on Rand's philosophy throughout the country. He is the author of *The Ominous Parallels* and editor of *The Early Ayn Rand*. He lives in southern California.

LEONARD PEIKOFF

OBJECTIVISM:
THE PHILOSOPHY OF
AYN RAND

A MERIDIAN BOOK

MERIDIAN
Published by the Penguin Group
Penguin Books USA Inc., 375 Hudson Street, New York, New York 10014, U.S.A.
Penguin Books Ltd, 27 Wrights Lane, London W8 5TZ, England
Penguin Books Australia Ltd, Ringwood, Victoria, Australia
Penguin Books Canada Ltd, 10 Alcorn Avenue, Toronto, Ontario, Canada M4V 3B2
Penguin Books (N.Z.) Ltd, 182–190 Wairau Road, Auckland 10, New Zealand

Penguin Books Ltd, Registered Offices: Harmondsworth, Middlesex, England

Published by Meridian, an imprint of Dutton Signet, a division of Penguin Books USA Inc.
Previously published in a Dutton edition.

First Meridian Printing, December, 1993
10 9 8 7 6 5 4 3 2 1

 REGISTERED TRADEMARK—MARCA REGISTRADA

LIBRARY OF CONGRESS CATALOGING-IN-PUBLICATION DATA
Peikoff, Leonard.
    Objectivism : the philosophy of Ayn Rand / Leonard Peikoff
        p.   cm.
    Originally published: New York : Dutton, 1991.
    ISBN 0-452-01101-9
    1. Rand, Ayn.   2. Objectivism (Philosophy)   I. Title.
[B945.R234P44   1993]
191—dc20   93–27923
                                                  CIP

Printed in the United States of America
Original hardcover designed by Steven N. Stathakis

To Kira
With the hope that this philosophy
will guide your life as it does
your mother's and mine

CONTENTS

ACKNOWLEDGMENTS

I want to thank Dr. Harry Binswanger, who was always eager for discussion and who helped me to clarify several important points.

Peter Schwartz and Steve Jolivette dedicated themselves to understanding the Objectivist ethics thoroughly. Their conscientious, persistent questions led me to some of the formulations in chapters 7 and 8.

Dr. Edith Packer got the project started. She was the first to argue at the time that a book on Objectivism had to be written. Linda Reardan helped complete the project, by preparing the index.

Besides the above, hundreds of Objectivists (including my present "Class of '91") have heard or read part of the material in the past six years. Their enthusiastic response has been heartening.

Diane LeMont, as cheerful as she is efficient, has done a superb job preparing the manuscript for the press, often in the face of an unusually difficult schedule.

Most of all, I want to acknowledge the help of Cynthia Peikoff, who encouraged me during the hard times of the writing, and who was the manuscript's exquisitely sensitive first editor. She has a rare ability to keep abstractions connected to reality—and a firm grasp of the difference between presenting Objectivism and refuting its enemies, i.e., between the positive and the negative. Our conversations led me to restructure several key chapters, including, most importantly, chapter 4. Thank you, Cynthia, for having done so much.

PREFACE

Ayn Rand's philosophy has changed thousands of lives, including my own, and has the power to change the course of history. Her views, however, are spread across more than a dozen books and hundreds of articles and speeches. The present book is the first comprehensive statement of her philosophy.

I have presented the ideas of Objectivism, their validation, and their interrelationships. I have arranged the ideas hierarchically; each chapter, and within the chapters each section, builds on earlier material.

I have covered every branch of philosophy recognized by Miss Rand and every philosophic topic—from certainty to money, logic to art, measurement to sex—which she regarded as important; this has led me to include abundant new material which she herself treated only in private discussion. But I have covered the ideas in conceptual form. That is: I have digested them, for myself and thereby for the reader. I offer not a heap of concretes, polemics, quotes, and random elaborations, but a progression of *essentials*. In every contest between the forest and the trees, I have chosen the forest: I have omitted every nonessential that might cause the reader to lose sight of Ayn Rand's system of thought as a whole.

With the present book to serve as a broad integrating context, future scholars can turn to study specialized aspects of Ayn Rand's work and to present them with an appropriately greater level of detail.

Like any proper work of general philosophy, this book is written not for academics, but for human beings (including any academics who qualify). In essence, the text can be understood by the general reader, although an individual will have an easier time if he first reads Ayn Rand's *Atlas Shrugged* and *Introduction to Objectivist Epistemology.*

This book was initially planned as an edited version of a lecture course, "The Philosophy of Objectivism," which I gave in New York City in 1976. The lectures were prepared with some assistance from Miss Rand, who attended all twelve of them and, after most, joined with me to answer questions from the audience. "Until or unless I write a comprehensive treatise on my philosophy," Miss Rand wrote that year in *The Ayn Rand Letter,* "Dr. Peikoff's course is the only *authorized* presentation of the entire theoretical structure of Objectivism, i.e., the only one that I know of my own knowledge to be fully accurate."

In 1984, eight years later and two years after her death, I began to revise the lectures for publication. I soon found that many of their formulations could be made more precise. I found arguments that I could now develop more cogently, examples that I could make more eloquent, and crucial new integrations that I only now understood. Above all, I found that the ideas required a more logical order of presentation. All these improvements changed the nature of the project. My task became not to edit, but to rewrite the lecture material.

Since some of Ayn Rand's most important ideas are expressed only briefly or not at all in her books, the absence of a reference note in my text does not imply that the point is my own. On the contrary, where no reference is given, the material in all likelihood is taken from the lengthy philosophic discussions that I had with Miss Rand across a period of decades. This is especially true of the material on metaphysics and epistemology, which were the primary subjects of our discussions, but it applies throughout.

Our discussions were not a collaboration: I asked questions; she answered them. In rewriting the lectures, moreover, I have not changed or added to any of Ayn Rand's ideas. My contribution is not to the substance of Objectivism, which is entirely Ayn Rand's achievement, but to the form of its presentation. The reader must, however, bear in mind that Ayn Rand has not seen the new wording or organization.

(For those who want to compare the lectures with the present book, cassettes of the former are still available for purchase from Second Renaissance Books, Box 4625, Oceanside, CA 92052.)

Because of my thirty years of study under her, and by her own statement, I am the person next to Ayn Rand who is the most qualified to write this book. Since she did not live to see it, however, she is not responsible for any misstatements of her views it may contain, nor can the book be properly described as "official Objectivist doctrine." "Objectivism" is the name of Ayn Rand's philosophy as presented in the material she herself wrote or endorsed.

To be objective, I identify the status of my work as follows: this book is the definitive statement of Ayn Rand's philosophy—as interpreted by her best student and chosen heir.

LEONARD PEIKOFF
December 1991

1

REALITY

Philosophy is not a bauble of the intellect, but a power from which no man can abstain. Anyone can *say* that he dispenses with a view of reality, knowledge, the good, but no one can implement this credo. The reason is that man, by his nature as a conceptual being, cannot function at all without some form of philosophy to serve as his guide.

Ayn Rand discusses the role of philosophy in her West Point lecture "Philosophy: Who Needs It." Without abstract ideas, she says,

> you would not be able to deal with concrete, particular, real-life problems. You would be in the position of a newborn infant, to whom every object is a unique, unprecedented phenomenon. The difference between his mental state and yours lies in the number of conceptual integrations your mind has performed.
>
> You have no choice about the necessity to integrate your observations, your experiences, your knowledge into abstract ideas, i.e., into principles.[1]

Your only choice, she continues, is whether your principles are true or false, rational or irrational, consistent or contradictory. The only way to know which they are is to integrate your principles.

> What integrates them? Philosophy. A philosophic system is an integrated view of existence. As a human being, you have no choice about the fact that you need a philosophy. Your only choice is whether you define your philosophy by a conscious, rational, disciplined process of thought and scrupulously logical deliberation—or let your subconscious accumulate a junk heap of unwarranted conclusions, false generalizations, undefined contradictions, undigested slogans, unidentified wishes, doubts and fears, thrown together by chance, but integrated by your subconscious into a kind of mongrel philosophy and fused into a single, solid weight: *self-doubt,* like a ball and chain in the place where your mind's wings should have grown.[2]

Philosophy, in Ayn Rand's view, is the fundamental force shaping every man and culture. It is the science that guides men's conceptual faculty, and thus every field of endeavor that counts on this faculty. The deepest issues of philosophy are the deepest root of men's thought (see chapter 4), their action (see chapter 12), their history (see the Epilogue)—and, therefore, of their triumphs, their disasters, their future.

Philosophy is a human need as real as the need of food. It is a need of the mind, without which man cannot obtain his food or anything else his life requires.

To satisfy this need, one must recognize that philosophy is a *system* of ideas. By its nature as an integrating science, it cannot be a grab bag of isolated issues. *All philosophic questions are interrelated.* One may not, therefore, raise any such questions at random, without the requisite context. If one tries the random approach, then questions (which one has no means of answering) simply proliferate in all directions.

Suppose, for example, that you read an article by Ayn Rand and glean from it only one general idea, with which, you decide, you agree: man should be selfish. How, you must soon ask, is this generality to be applied to concrete situations? What *is* selfishness? Does it mean doing whatever you feel like doing? What if your feelings are irrational? But who is to say what's rational or irrational? And who is Ayn Rand to say what a man should do, anyway? Maybe what's true for her isn't true for you, or what's true in theory isn't true in practice. What *is* truth? Can it vary from one person or realm to another? And, come to think of it, aren't we all bound together? Can anyone ever really achieve private goals in this world? If not, there's no point in being selfish. What kind of world *is* it? And if people followed Ayn Rand, wouldn't that lead to monopolies or cutthroat competition, as the socialists say? And how does anyone know the answers to all these (and many similar) questions? What *method* of knowledge should a man use? And how does one know *that?*

For a philosophic idea to function properly as a guide, one must know the full system to which it belongs. An idea plucked from the middle is of no value, cannot be validated, and will not work. One must know the idea's relationship to all the other ideas that give it context, definition, application, proof. One must know all this not as a theoretical end in itself, but for practical purposes; one must know it to be able to rely on an idea, to make rational use of it, and, ultimately, to live.

In order to approach philosophy systematically, one must begin with its basic branches. Philosophy, according to Objectivism, consists of five branches. The two basic ones are metaphysics and epistemology. Metaphysics is the branch of philosophy that studies the nature of the universe as a whole. (The Objectivist metaphysics is covered in the present chapter on "Reality.") Epistemology is the branch that studies the nature and means of human knowledge (chapters 2–5). These two branches make possible a view of the nature of man (chapter 6).

Flowing from the above are the three evaluative branches of philosophy. Ethics, the broadest of these, provides a code of values to guide human choices and actions (chapters 7–9). Politics studies the nature of a social system and defines the proper functions of government (chapters 10 and 11). Esthetics studies the nature of art and defines the standards by which an art work should be judged (chapter 12).

In presenting Objectivism, I shall cover the five branches in essential terms, developing each in hierarchical order, and offering the validation of each principle or theory when I first explain it.

The True, said Hegel, is the Whole. At the end of our discussion, to borrow these terms, you will see a unique Whole, the Whole which is Ayn Rand's philosophic achievement. You may then judge for yourself whether it is an important achievement—and whether it is True.

■　■　■　■

Every philosophy builds on its starting points. Where, then, does one start? What ideas qualify as primaries?

By the time men begin to philosophize, they are adults who have acquired a complex set of concepts. The first task of the philosopher is to separate the fundamentals from the rest. He must determine which concepts are at the base of human knowledge and which are farther up the structure— which are the irreducible principles of cognition and which are derivatives.

Objectivism begins by naming and validating its primaries. Ayn Rand does not select questions at random; she does not plunge in by caprice. She begins deliberately at the beginning—at what she can prove is the beginning, and the root of all the rest.

Existence, Consciousness, and Identity as the Basic Axioms

We begin as philosophers where we began as babies, at the only place there is to begin: by looking at the world. As philosophers, however, we know enough to state, as we look at anything: it *is*. This (I am pointing to a table) is. That (pointing to a person seated at it) is. These things (sweeping an arm to indicate the contents of the whole room) are. Something *exists*.

We start with the irreducible fact and concept of existence—that which is.

The first thing to say about that which is is simply: it is. As Parmenides in ancient Greece formulated the principle: what is, is. Or, in Ayn Rand's words: *existence exists*. ("Existence" here is a collective noun, denoting the sum of existents.) This axiom does not tell us anything about the nature of existents; it merely underscores the fact that they exist.[3]

This axiom must be the foundation of everything else. Before one can consider any other issue, before one can ask what things there are or what problems men face in learning about them, before one can discuss what one knows or how one knows it—first, there must *be* something, and one must grasp that there is. If not, there is nothing to consider or to know.

The concept of "existence" is the widest of all concepts. It subsumes everything—every entity, action, attribute, relationship (including every state of consciousness)—everything which is, was, or will be. The concept does not specify that a physical world exists.[4] As the first concept at the base of knowledge, it covers only what is known, implicitly if not explicitly, by the gamut of the human race, from the newborn baby or the lowest savage on through the greatest scientist and the most erudite sage. All of these know equally the fundamental fact that there *is* something, something as against nothing.

You the reader have now grasped the first axiom of philosophy. This act implies a second axiom: that you exist possessing *consciousness,* consciousness being the faculty of perceiving that which exists. Consciousness is not inherent in the fact of existence as such; a world without conscious organisms is possible. But consciousness *is* inherent in *your grasp* of existence. Inherent in saying *"There is something—* of which I am aware" is: "There is something—*of which I am aware."*

The fact of consciousness is also a fundamental starting point. Even if biologists or physicists were someday to give us a scientific analysis of the conditions of consciousness (in terms of physical structures or energy quanta or something now unknown), this would not alter the fact that consciousness is an axiom. Before one can raise any questions pertaining to knowledge, whether of content or of method (including the question of the conditions of consciousness), one must first *be* conscious of something and recognize that one is. All questions presuppose that one has a faculty of knowledge, i.e., the attribute of consciousness. One ignorant of this attribute must perforce be ignorant of the whole field of cognition (and of philosophy).

Consciousness, to repeat, is the faculty of perceiving that which exists. ("Perceiving" is used here in its widest sense, equivalent to "being aware of.") To be conscious is to be conscious of something.

Here is Ayn Rand's crucial passage in regard to the above:

> Existence exists—and the act of grasping that statement implies two corollary axioms: that something exists which one perceives and that one exists possessing consciousness, consciousness being the faculty of perceiving that which exists.
>
> If nothing exists, there can be no consciousness: a consciousness with nothing to be conscious of is a contradiction in terms. A consciousness conscious of nothing but itself is a contradiction in terms: before it could identify itself as consciousness, it had to be conscious of something. If that which you claim to perceive does not exist, what you possess is not consciousness.
>
> Whatever the degree of your knowledge, these two—existence and consciousness—are axioms you cannot escape, these two are the irreducible primaries implied in any action you undertake, in any part of your knowledge and in its sum, from the first ray of light you perceive at the start of your life to the widest erudition you might acquire at its end. Whether you know the shape of a pebble or the structure of a solar system, the axioms remain the same: that *it* exists and that you *know* it.[5]

A third and final basic axiom is implicit in the first two. It is the law of identity: to be is to be something, to have a nature, to possess *identity*. A thing is itself; or, in the traditional formula, A is A. The "identity" of an existent means that which it is, the sum of its attributes or characteristics.

> Whatever you choose to consider, be it an object, an attribute or an action, the law of identity remains the same [writes Ayn Rand]. A leaf cannot be a stone at the same time, it cannot be all red and all green at the same time, it cannot freeze and burn at the same time. A is A. Or, if you wish it stated in simpler language: You cannot have your cake and eat it, too.[6]

Ayn Rand offers a new formulation of this axiom: existence *is* identity.[7] She does not say "existence *has* identity"—which might suggest that identity is a feature separable from existence (as a coat of paint is separable from the house that has it). The point is that to be *is* to be something. Existence and identity are indivisible; either implies the other. If something *exists*, then *something* exists; and if there is a *something*, then there *is* a something. The fundamental fact cannot be broken in two.

Why, one might ask, use two concepts to identify one fact? This procedure is common in philosophy and in other fields as well. When men have several perspectives on a single fact, when they consider it from different aspects or in different contexts, it is often essential to form concepts that identify the various perspectives.

"Existence" differentiates a thing from nothing, from the absence of the thing. This is the primary identification, on which all others depend; it is the recognition in conceptual terms that the thing *is*. "Identity" indicates not that it *is*, but that *it* is. This differentiates one thing from another, which is a distinguishable step in cognition. The perspective here is not: it is (vs. it is not), but: it is this (vs. it is that). Thus the context and purpose of the two concepts differ, although the fact both concepts name is indivisible.

Like existence and consciousness, identity is also a fundamental starting point of knowledge. Before one can ask *what* any existent is, it must be something, and one must know this. If not, then there is nothing to investigate—or to exist.

Inherent in a man's grasp of any object is the recognition, in some form, that: there is something I am aware of. There is—existence; something—identity; I am aware of—consciousness. These three are the basic axiomatic concepts recognized by the philosophy of Objectivism.

An axiomatic concept, writes Ayn Rand, is

> the identification of a primary fact of reality, which cannot be analyzed, i.e., reduced to other facts or broken into component parts. It is implicit in all facts and in all knowledge. It is the fundamentally given and directly perceived or experienced, which requires no proof or explanation, but on which all proofs and explanations rest.[8]

Axiomatic concepts are not subject to the process of definition. Their referents can be specified only ostensively, by pointing to instances. Everything to be grasped about these facts is implicit in any act of adult cognition; indeed, it is implicit much earlier. "After the first discriminated sensation (or percept)," Miss Rand observes, "man's subsequent knowledge adds nothing to the basic facts designated by the terms 'existence,' 'identity,' 'consciousness.' . . ." Subsequent knowledge makes the explicit, conceptual identification of these facts possible. But the facts themselves—which are the data or constituents later to be integrated into the concepts— are present to and from the first such awareness. It is in this sense that a knowledge of axioms is "implicit" from the beginning. "It is this implicit knowledge," Miss Rand holds, "that permits [man's] consciousness to develop further."[9]

Being implicit from the beginning, existence, consciousness, and identity are outside the province of proof. Proof is the derivation of a conclusion from antecedent knowledge, and nothing is antecedent to axioms. Axioms are the starting points of cognition, on which all proofs depend.

One knows that the axioms are true not by inference of any kind, but by sense perception. When one perceives a tomato, for example, there is no evidence that it exists, beyond the fact that one perceives it; there is no evidence that it is something, beyond the fact that one perceives *it;* and there is no evidence that one is aware, beyond the fact that one *is* perceiving it. Axioms are *perceptual self-evidencies.* There is nothing to be said in their behalf except: look at reality.

What is true of tomatoes applies equally to oranges, buildings, people, music, and stars. What philosophy does is to give an abstract statement of such self-evident facts. Philosophy states these facts in universal form. Whatever exists, exists. Whatever exists is what it is. In whatever form one is aware, one is aware.

The above is the validation of the Objectivist axioms. "Validation" I take to be a broader term than "proof," one that subsumes any process of establishing an idea's relationship to reality, whether deductive reasoning, inductive reasoning, or perceptual self-evidence. In this sense, one can and must validate every item of knowledge, including axioms. The validation of axioms, however, is the simplest of all: sense perception.

The fact that axioms are available to perception does not

mean that all human beings accept or even grasp axioms in conscious, conceptual terms. Vast numbers of men, such as primitives, never progress beyond implicit knowledge of the axioms. Lacking explicit philosophic identification of this knowledge, they have no way to adhere to the axioms consistently and typically fall into some form of contradicting the self-evident, as in the various magical world views, which (implicitly) deny the law of identity. Such men stunt their minds by subjecting themselves to an undeclared epistemological civil war. The war pits their professed outlook on the world against the implicit knowledge on which they are actually counting in order to survive.

Even lower are the men of an advanced civilization who—thanks to the work of a genius such as Aristotle—know the explicit identification of axioms, then consciously reject them. A *declared* inner war—i.e., deliberate, systematic self-contradiction—is the essence of the intellectual life of such individuals. Examples include those philosophers of the past two centuries who reject the very idea of the self-evident as the base of knowledge, and who then repudiate all three of the basic axioms, attacking them as "arbitrary postulates," "linguistic conventions," or "Western prejudice."

The three axioms I have been discussing have a built-in protection against all attacks: they must be used and accepted by everyone, including those who attack them and those who attack the concept of the self-evident. Let me illustrate this point by considering a typical charge leveled by opponents of philosophic axioms.

"People *disagree* about axioms," we often hear. "What is self-evident to one may not be self-evident to another. How then can a man know that his axioms are objectively true? How can he ever be sure he is right?"

This argument starts by accepting the concept of "disagreement," which it uses to challenge the objectivity of any axioms, including existence, consciousness, and identity. The following condensed dialogue suggests one strategy by which to reveal the argument's contradictions. The strategy begins with A, the defender of axioms, purporting to reject outright the concept of "disagreement."

A. "Your objection to the self-evident has no validity.

There is no such thing as disagreement. People agree about everything."

B. "That's absurd. People disagree constantly, about all kinds of things."

A. "How can they? There's nothing to disagree about, no subject matter. After all, nothing exists."

B. "Nonsense. All kinds of things exist. You know that as well as I do."

A. "That's one. You must accept the existence axiom even to utter the term 'disagreement.' But, to continue, I still claim that disagreement is unreal. How can people disagree, since they are unconscious beings who are unable to hold ideas at all?"

B. "Of course people hold ideas. They *are* conscious beings—you know that."

A. "There's another axiom. But even so, why is disagreement about ideas a problem? Why should it suggest that one or more of the parties is mistaken? Perhaps all of the people who disagree about the very same point are equally, objectively right."

B. "That's impossible. If two ideas contradict each other, they can't both be right. Contradictions can't exist in reality. After all, things are what they are. A is A."

Existence, consciousness, identity are presupposed by every statement and by every concept, including that of "disagreement." (They are presupposed even by invalid concepts, such as "ghost" or "analytic" truth.) In the act of voicing his objection, therefore, the objector has conceded the case. In *any* act of challenging or denying the three axioms, a man reaffirms them, no matter what the particular content of his challenge. The axioms are invulnerable.

The opponents of these axioms pose as defenders of truth, but it is only a pose. Their attack on the self-evident amounts to the charge: "Your belief in an idea doesn't necessarily make it true; you must prove it, because facts are what they are independent of your beliefs." Every element of this charge relies on the very axioms that these people are questioning and supposedly setting aside. I quote Ayn Rand:

"You cannot *prove* that you exist or that you're conscious," they chatter, blanking out the fact that *proof* presupposes existence, consciousness and a complex chain of knowledge: the existence of something to know, of a consciousness able to know it, and of a knowledge that has learned to distinguish between such concepts as the proved and the unproved.

When a savage who has not learned to speak declares that existence must be proved, he is asking you to prove it by means of non-existence—when he declares that your consciousness must be proved, he is asking you to prove it by means of unconsciousness—he is asking you to step into a void outside of existence and consciousness to give him proof of both—he is asking you to become a zero gaining knowledge about a zero.

When he declares that an axiom is a matter of arbitrary choice and he doesn't choose to accept the axiom that he exists, he blanks out the fact that he has accepted it by uttering that sentence, that the only way to reject it is to shut one's mouth, expound no theories and die.

An axiom is a statement that identifies the base of knowledge and of any further statement pertaining to that knowledge, a statement necessarily contained in all others, whether any particular speaker chooses to identify it or not. An axiom is a proposition that defeats its opponents by the fact that they have to accept it and use it in the process of any attempt to deny it.[10]

The foregoing is not a proof that the axioms of existence, consciousness, and identity are true. It is a proof that they are *axioms,* that they are at the base of knowledge and thus inescapable. This proof itself, however, relies on the axioms. Even in showing that no opponent can escape them, Ayn Rand too has to make use of them. All argument presupposes these axioms, including the argument that all argument presupposes them.

If so, one might ask, how does one answer an opponent who says: "You've demonstrated that I must accept your axioms if I am to be consistent. But that demonstration rests on your axioms, which I don't choose to accept. Tell me why I should. Why can't I contradict myself?"

There is only one answer to this: stop the discussion. Axioms *are* self-evident; no argument can coerce a person who chooses to evade them. You can show a man that identity is inescapable, but only by first accepting the fact that A is A. You can show that existence is inescapable, but only by accepting and referring to existence. You can show that consciousness is inescapable, but only by accepting and using your consciousness. Relying on these three axioms, you can establish their position as the foundation of all knowledge. But you cannot convince another person of this or anything until he accepts the axioms himself, on the basis of his own perception of reality. If he denies them, it is a mistake to argue about or even discuss the issue with him.

No one can think or perceive for another man. If reality, without your help, does not convince a person of the self-evident, he has abdicated reason and cannot be dealt with any further.

Causality as a Corollary of Identity

So far we have been concerned, as adults, to identify the foundations of human cognition. In this context, the three axioms we have discussed are inescapable primaries: no conceptual knowledge can be gained apart from these principles. Chronologically, however, the three axioms are not learned by the developing child simultaneously. "Existence," Miss Rand suggests, is implicit from the start; it is given in the first sensation.[11] To grasp "identity" and (later) "consciousness," however, even in implicit form, the child must attain across a period of months a certain perspective on his mental contents. He must perform, in stages, various processes of differentiation and integration that are not given in the simple act of opening his eyes.

Before a child can distinguish *this* object from *that* one, and thus reach the implicit concept of "identity," he must first come to perceive that objects exist. This requires that he move beyond the chaos of disparate, fleeting sensations with which his conscious life begins; it requires that he integrate his sensations into the percepts of things or objects. (Such integration is discussed in chapter 2.) At this point, the child has reached, in implicit form, the concept of *"entity."*

The concept of "entity" is an axiomatic concept, which is presupposed by all subsequent human cognition, although it is not a basic axiom.[12] In particular, the grasp of "entity," in conjunction with the closely following grasp of "identity," makes possible the discovery of the next important principle of metaphysics, the one that is the main subject of the present section: the law of causality.

First, however, I must offer some clarification in regard to the concept of "entity." Since it is axiomatic, the referents of this concept can be specified only ostensively, by pointing to the things given to men in sense perception. In this case, one points to solid things with a perceivable shape, such as a rock, a person, or a table. By extension from this primary sense, "entity" may be used in various contexts to denote a vast array of existents, such as the solar system, General Motors, or the smallest subatomic particle. But all "entities" like these are reducible ultimately to combinations, components, or distinguishable aspects of "entities" in the primary sense.[13]

Entities constitute the content of the world men perceive; there is nothing else to observe. In the act of observing entities, of course, the child, like the adult, observes (some of) their attributes, actions, and relationships. In time, the child's consciousness can focus separately on such features, isolating them in thought for purposes of conceptual identification and specialized study. One byproduct of this process is philosophers' inventory of the so-called "categories" of being, such as qualities ("red" or "hard"), quantities ("five inches" or "six pounds"), relationships ("to the right of" or "father of"), actions ("walking" or "digesting"). The point here, however, is that none of these "categories" has metaphysical primacy; none has any independent existence; all represent merely aspects of entities.

There is no "red" or "hard" apart from the crayon or book or other thing that is red or hard. "Five inches" or "six pounds" presuppose the object that extends five inches or weighs six pounds. "To the right of" or "father of" have no reality apart from the things one of which is to the right of another or is the father of another. And—especially important in considering the law of cause and effect—there are no floating actions; there are only actions performed by entities. "Action" is the name for what entities do. "Walking" or "digesting" have no existence or possibility apart from the

creature with legs that walks or the body or organ with en-
zymes that does the digesting.

When a child has reached the stage of (implicitly) grasping "entity," "identity," and "action," he has the knowledge
required to reach (implicitly) the law of causality. To take this
step, he needs to observe an omnipresent fact: that an entity
of a certain kind acts in a certain way. The child shakes his
rattle and it makes a sound; he shakes his pillow and it does
not. He pushes a ball and it rolls along the floor; he pushes a
book and it sits there, unmoving. He lets a block out of his
hands and it falls; he lets a balloon go and it rises. The child
may wish the pillow to rattle, the book to roll, the block to
float, but he cannot make these events occur. Things, he soon
discovers, act in definite ways and only in these ways. This
represents the implicit knowledge of causality; it is the child's
form of grasping the relationship between the nature of an
entity and its mode of action.

The adult validation of the law of causality consists in
stating this relationship explicitly. The validation rests on two
points: the fact that action is action of an entity; and the law
of identity, A is A. Every entity has a nature; it is specific,
noncontradictory, limited; it has certain attributes and no others. Such an entity must act *in accordance with* its nature.

The only alternatives would be for an entity to act apart
from its nature or against it; both of these are impossible. A
thing cannot act apart from its nature, because existence *is*
identity; apart from its nature, a thing is nothing. A thing cannot act against its nature, i.e., in contradiction to its identity,
because A is A and contradictions are impossible. In any given
set of circumstances, therefore, there is only one action possible to an entity, the action expressive of its identity. This is
the action it will take, the action that is *caused* and necessitated by its nature.

Thus, under ordinary circumstances, if a child releases a
balloon filled with helium, only one outcome is possible: the
balloon will rise. If he releases a second balloon filled with
sand, the nature of the entity is different, and so is its action;
the only possible outcome now is that it will fall. If, under
the same circumstances, several actions were possible—e.g.,
a balloon could rise *or* fall (or start to emit music like a radio,
or turn into a pumpkin), everything else remaining the same—

such incompatible outcomes would have to derive from in-compatible (contradictory) aspects of the entity's nature. But there are no contradictory aspects. A is A.

Cause and effect, therefore, is a universal law of reality. Every action has a cause (the cause is the nature of the entity which acts); and the same cause leads to the same effect (the same entity, under the same circumstances, will perform the same action).

The above is not to be taken as a proof of the law of cause and effect. I have merely made explicit what is known implic-itly in the perceptual grasp of reality. Given the facts that action is action of entities, and that every entity has a nature—both of which facts are known simply by observation—it is self-evident that an entity must act in accordance with its na-ture. "The law of causality," Ayn Rand sums up, "is the law of identity applied to action. All actions are caused by entities. The nature of an action is caused and determined by the na-ture of the entities that act; a thing cannot act in contradiction to its nature."[14]

Here again, as in regard to axioms, implicit knowledge must not be confused with explicit. The explicit identification of causality (by the Greeks) was an enormous intellectual achievement; it represented the beginning of a scientific out-look on existence, as against the prescientific view of the world as a realm of miracles or of chance. (And here again the worst offenders philosophically are not the primitives who implicitly count on causality yet never discover it, but the modern sophisticates, such as David Hume, who count on it while explicitly rejecting it.)

Causality is best classified as a *corollary* of identity. A "corollary" is a self-evident implication of already established knowledge. A corollary of an axiom is not itself an axiom; it is not self-evident apart from the principle(s) at its root (an axiom, by contrast, does not depend on an antecedent con-text). Nor is a corollary a theorem; it does not permit or re-quire a process of proof; like an axiom, it *is* self-evident (once its context has been grasped). It is, in effect, a new angle on an established principle, which follows immediately once one grasps its meaning and the principle on which it depends.

Many of the most important truths in philosophy occupy this intermediate status. They are neither axioms nor theorems, but corollaries—most often, corollaries of axioms. In fact, the essence of metaphysics, according to Objectivism, is the step-by-step development of the corollaries of the existence axiom. The main purpose of this chapter is to unravel systematically the implications of "Existence exists."

Now let me reiterate that the causal link relates an entity and its action. The law of causality does not state that every *entity* has a cause. Some of the things commonly referred to as "entities" do not come into being or pass away, but are eternal—e.g., the universe as a whole. The concept of "cause" is inapplicable to the universe; by definition, there is nothing outside the totality to act as a cause. The universe simply *is;* it is an irreducible primary. An entity may be said to have a cause only if it is the kind of entity that is noneternal; and then what one actually explains causally is a process, the fact of its coming into being or another thing's passing away. Action is the crux of the law of cause and effect: it is action that is caused—by entities.

By the same token, the causal link does not relate two actions. Since the Renaissance, it has been common for philosophers to speak as though actions directly cause other actions, bypassing entities altogether. For example, the motion of one billiard ball striking a second is commonly said to be the cause of the motion of the second, the implication being that we can dispense with the balls; motions by themselves become the cause of other motions. This idea is senseless. Motions do not act, they *are* actions. It is entities which act—and cause. Speaking literally, it is not the motion of a billiard ball which produces effects; it is the billiard ball, the entity, which does so by a certain means. If one doubts this, one need merely substitute an egg or soap bubble with the same velocity for the billiard ball; the effects will be quite different.

The law of causality states that entities are the cause of actions—not that every entity, of whatever sort, has a cause, but that every action does; and not that the cause of action is action, but that the cause of action is entities.

Many commentators on Heisenberg's Uncertainty Principle claim that, because we cannot at the same time specify fully the position and momentum of subatomic particles, their action is not entirely predictable, and that the law of causality therefore breaks down. This is a non sequitur, a switch from epistemology to metaphysics, or from knowledge to reality. Even if it were true that owing to a lack of information we could never exactly predict a subatomic event—and this is highly debatable—it would not show that, *in reality,* the event was causeless. The law of causality is an abstract principle; it does not by itself enable us to predict specific occurrences; it does not provide us with a knowledge of particular causes or measurements. Our ignorance of certain measurements, however, does not affect their reality or the consequent operation of nature.

Causality, in the Objectivist viewpoint, is a fact independent of consciousness, whether God's or man's. Order, lawfulness, regularity do not derive from a cosmic consciousness (as is claimed by the religious "argument from design"). Nor is causality merely a subjective form of thought that happens to govern the human mind (as in the Kantian approach). On the contrary, causality—for Objectivism as for Aristotelianism—is a law inherent in being qua being. To be is to be something—and to be something is to act accordingly.

Natural law is not a feature superimposed by some agency on an otherwise "chaotic" world; there is no possibility of such chaos. Nor is there any possibility of a "chance" event, if "chance" means an exception to causality. Cause and effect is not a metaphysical afterthought. It is not a fact that is theoretically dispensable. It is part of the fabric of reality as such.

One may no more ask: who is responsible for natural law (which amounts to asking: who caused causality?) than one may ask: who created the universe? The answer to both questions is the same: existence exists.

Existence as Possessing Primacy over Consciousness

After a child has observed a number of causal sequences, and thereby come to view existence (implicitly) as an orderly, predictable realm, he has advanced enough to gain his first inkling of his own faculty of cognition. This occurs when he discovers causal sequences involving his own senses. For example, he discovers that when he closes his eyes the (visual) world disappears, and that it reappears when he opens them. This kind of experience is the child's first grasp of his own means of perception, and thus of the inner world as against the outer, or the subject of cognition as against the object. It is his implicit grasp of the last of the three basic axiomatic concepts, the concept of "consciousness."

From the outset, consciousness presents itself as something specific—as a faculty of perceiving an object, not of creating or changing it. For instance, a child may hate the food set in front of him and refuse even to look at it. But his inner state does not erase his dinner. Leaving aside physical action, the food is impervious; it is unaffected by a process of consciousness as such. It is unaffected by anyone's perception or nonperception, memory or fantasy, desire or fury—just as a book refuses to roll despite anyone's tantrums, or a pillow to rattle, or a block to float.

The basic fact implicit in such observations is that consciousness, like every other kind of entity, acts in a certain way and only in that way. In adult, philosophic terms, we refer to this fact as the "primacy of existence," a principle that is fundamental to the metaphysics of Objectivism.

Existence, this principle declares, comes first. Things are what they are independent of consciousness—of anyone's perceptions, images, ideas, feelings. Consciousness, by contrast, is a dependent. Its function is not to create or control existence, but to be a spectator: to look out, to perceive, to grasp that which is.

The opposite of this approach Ayn Rand calls the "primacy of consciousness." This is the principle that consciousness is the primary metaphysical factor. In this view, the function of consciousness is not perception, but creation of that which is. Existence, accordingly, is a dependent; the world is regarded as in some way a derivative of consciousness.

A simple example of the primacy-of-existence orientation would be a man running for his life from an erupting volcano. Such a man acknowledges a fact, the volcano—and the fact that it is what it is and does what it does independent of his feelings or any other state of his consciousness. At least in this instance, he grasps the difference between mental contents and external data, between perceiver and perceived, between subject and object. Implicitly if not explicitly, he knows that wishes are not horses and that ignoring an entity does not make it vanish. Contrast this approach with that of a savage who remains frozen under the same circumstances, eyes fixed sightless on the ground, mind chanting frantic prayers or magic incantations in the hope of wishing away the river of molten lava hurtling toward him. Such an individual has not reached the stage of making a firm distinction between consciousness and existence. Like many of our civilized contemporaries who are his brothers-in-spirit (and like the ostrich), he deals with threats not by identification and consequent action, but by blindness. The implicit premise underlying such behavior is: "If I don't want it or look at it, it won't be there; i.e., my consciousness controls existence."

The primacy of existence is not an independent principle. It is an elaboration, a further corollary, of the basic axioms. Existence precedes consciousness, because consciousness is consciousness of an object. Nor can consciousness create or suspend the laws governing its objects, because every entity is something and acts accordingly. Consciousness, therefore, is only a faculty of awareness. It is the power to grasp, to find out, to discover that which is. It is not a power to alter or control the nature of its objects.

The primacy-of-consciousness viewpoint ascribes precisely the latter power to consciousness. A thing is or does what consciousness ordains, it says; A does not have to be A if consciousness does not wish it to be so. This viewpoint represents the rejection of all the basic axioms; it is an attempt to have existence and eat it, too. To have it, because without existence there can be no consciousness. To eat it, because the theory wants existence to be malleable to someone's mental contents; i.e., it wants existence to shrug off the restrictions of identity in order to obey someone's desires; i.e., it wants existence to exist as nothing in particular. But existence *is* identity.

The above is to be taken not as a proof of the primacy of existence, but as an explication of a self-evidency implicit in the child's first grasp of consciousness. The ability to prove a theorem comes later. First one must establish the ideas that make possible such a process as proof, one of which is the primacy of existence. Proof presupposes the principle that facts are *not* "malleable." If they were, there would be no need to prove anything and no independent datum on which to base any proof.

Since knowledge is knowledge of reality, every metaphysical principle has epistemological implications. This is particularly obvious in the case of the primacy-of-existence principle, because it identifies the fundamental relationship between our cognitive faculty and existence. To clarify the principle further, I shall indicate here the kind of epistemology to which it leads.

If existence is independent of consciousness, then knowledge of existence can be gained only by extrospection. In other words, nothing is relevant to cognition of the world except data drawn from the world, i.e., sense data or conceptual integrations of such data. Introspection, of course, is necessary and proper as a means of grasping the contents or processes of consciousness; but it is not a means of external cognition. There can be no appeal to the knower's feelings as an avenue to truth; there can be no reliance on *any* mental contents alleged to have a source or validity independent of sense perception. Every step and method of cognition must proceed in accordance with facts—and every fact must be established, directly or indirectly, by observation. To follow this policy, according to Objectivism, is to follow *reason* (see chapter 5).

If a man accepts the primacy of consciousness, by contrast, he will be drawn to an opposite theory of knowledge. If consciousness controls existence, it is not necessary to confine oneself to studying the facts of existence. On the contrary, introspection becomes a means of external cognition; at critical points, one should bypass the world in the very quest to know it and instead look inward, searching out elements in one's mind that are detached from perception, such as "intuitions," "revelations," "innate ideas," "innate structures." In relying on such elements, the knower is not, he feels, cavalierly ignoring reality; he is merely going over the head of existence to its master, whether human or divine; he is seeking knowledge of fact directly from the source of facts, from the consciousness that creates them. This kind of metaphysics implicitly underlies every form of unreason.

The primacy-of-existence principle (including its epistemological implications) is one of Objectivism's most distinctive tenets. With rare exceptions, Western philosophy has accepted the opposite; it is dominated by attempts to construe existence as a subordinate realm. Three versions of the primacy of consciousness have been prevalent. They are distinguished by their answer to the question: upon *whose* consciousness is existence dependent?

Dominating philosophy from Plato to Hume was the *supernaturalistic* version. In this view, existence is a product of a cosmic consciousness, God. This idea is implicit in Plato's theory of Forms and became explicit with the Christian development from Plato. According to Christianity (and Judaism), God is an infinite consciousness who created existence, sustains it, makes it lawful, then periodically subjects it to decrees that flout the regular order, thereby producing "miracles." Epistemologically, this variant leads to mysticism: knowledge is said to rest on communications from the Supreme Mind to the human, whether in the form of revelations sent to select individuals or of ideas implanted, innately or otherwise, throughout the species.

The religious view of the world, though it has been abandoned by most philosophers, is still entrenched in the public mind. Witness the popular question "Who created the universe?"—which presupposes that the universe is not eternal, but has a source beyond itself, in some cosmic personality or will. It is useless to object that this question involves an infinite regress, even though it does (if a creator is required to explain existence, then a second creator is required to explain the first, and so on). Typically, the believer will reply: "One can't ask for an explanation of God. He is an inherently necessary being. After all, one must start somewhere." Such a person does not contest the need of an irreducible starting point, as long as it is a form of consciousness; what he finds unsatisfactory is the idea of existence as the starting point. Driven by the primacy of consciousness, a person of this mentality refuses to begin with the world, which we *know* to exist; he insists on jumping beyond the world to the unknowable, even though such a procedure explains nothing. The root of this mentality is not rational argument, but the influence of Christianity. In many respects, the West has not recovered from the Middle Ages.

In the eighteenth century, Immanuel Kant secularized the

religious viewpoint. According to his philosophy, the human mind—specifically, the cognitive structures common to all men, their innate forms of perception and conception—is what creates existence (which he called the "phenomenal" world). Thus God's will gives way to man's consciousness, which becomes the metaphysical factor underlying and ordering existence. Implicit in this theory is the *social* version of the primacy of consciousness, which became explicit with the Hegelian development from Kant and which has dominated philosophy for the past two centuries.

According to the social version, no one individual is potent enough to create a universe or abrogate the law of identity, but a *group*—mankind as a whole, a particular society, a nation, a state, a race, a sex, an economic class—can do the trick. In popular terms: one Frenchman alone can't bend reality to his desires, but fifty million of them are irresistible. Epistemologically, this variant leads to collective surveys—a kind of group introspection—as the means to truth; knowledge is said to rest on a consensus among thinkers, a consensus that results not from each individual's perception of external reality, but from subjective mental structures or contents that happen to be shared by the group's members.

Today, the social variant is at the height of its popularity. We hear on all sides that there are no objective facts, but only "human" truth, truth "for man"—and lately that even this is unattainable, since there is only national, racial, sexual, or homosexual truth. In this view, the group acquires the omnipotence once ascribed to God. Thus, to cite a political example, when the government enacts some policy (such as runaway spending) that must in logic have disastrous consequences (such as national bankruptcy), the policy's defenders typically deal with the problem by fudging all figures, then asking for "optimism" and faith. "If people believe in the policy," we hear, "if they want the system to work, then it will." The implicit premise is: "A group can override facts; men's mental contents can coerce reality."

A third version of the primacy of consciousness has appeared throughout history among skeptics and is well represented today: the *personal* version, as we may call it, according to which each man's own consciousness controls existence—for him. Protagoras in ancient Greece is the father of this variant. "Man," he said—meaning each man individually—"is the measure of all things; of things that are, that they are, and of things that are not, that they are not." In this view, each man's consciousness creates and inhabits its own private universe. Epistemologically, therefore, there are no standards or data of any kind to which a person must conform. There is only truth "for me" vs. truth "for you"—which truth is, for any individual, whatever he arbitrarily decrees it to be.

In regard to fundamentals, it makes no difference whether one construes existence as subservient to the consciousness of God, of men, or of oneself. All these represent the same essential metaphysics containing the same essential error. Objectivism rejects them all on the same ground: that existence *exists*.

If existence exists, then it has metaphysical primacy. It is not a derivative or "manifestation" or "appearance" of some true reality at its root, such as God or society or one's urges. It *is* reality. As such, its elements are uncreated and eternal, and its laws, immutable.

There were once Western philosophers who upheld the primacy of existence; notably, such ancient Greek giants as Parmenides and Aristotle. But even they were not consistent in this regard. (Aristotle, for example, describes his Prime Mover as a consciousness conscious only of itself, which serves as the cause of the world's motion.) There has never yet been a thinker who states the principle explicitly, then applies it methodically in every branch of philosophy, with no concession to any version of its antithesis. This is precisely what Ayn Rand does. Her philosophy is the primacy of existence come to full, systematic expression in Western thought for the first time.

The Metaphysically Given as Absolute

The Objectivist view of existence culminates in the principle that no alternative to a fact of reality is possible or imaginable. All such facts are necessary. In Ayn Rand's words, the metaphysically given is *absolute*.

By the "metaphysically given," Ayn Rand means any fact inherent in existence apart from human action (whether mental or physical)—as against "man-made facts," i.e., objects, institutions, practices, or rules of conduct that are of human origin. The solar system, for example, is metaphysically given; communication satellites are man-made. The law of gravity is metaphysically given; the laws against murder are man-made. The fact that man's life requires food is metaphysically given; the fact that some men, such as ascetics or anorectics, prefer to starve is man-made.

Let us focus now on the metaphysically given. As soon as one says about any such fact: *"It is"*—just that much—the whole Objectivist metaphysics is implicit. If the fact is, it is what it is (the law of identity). It is lawful, inherent in the identities of the relevant entities (the law of causality). It is independent of consciousness, of anyone's or everyone's beliefs and feelings (the primacy of existence). Such a fact *has to* be; no alternative to it is possible. If such a fact *is,* then, within the relevant circumstances, it is immutable, inescapable, *absolute.* "Absolute" in this context means necessitated by the nature of existence and, therefore, unchangeable by human (or any other) agency.

A fact is "necessary" if its nonexistence would involve a contradiction. To put the point positively: a fact that obtains "by necessity" is one that obtains "by identity." Given the nature of existence, this is the status of every (metaphysically given) fact. Nothing more is required to ground necessity.

Hume and Kant searched for a perceptual manifestation labeled "necessity," like a metaphysical glue sticking events together or holding facts in place; unable to find it, they proceeded to banish necessity from the world. Their search, however, was misbegotten. "Necessity" in the present sense is not a datum over and above existents; it is an identification of existents from a special perspective. "Necessary" names existents considered as governed by the law of identity. "To be," accordingly, *is* "to be necessary."

The above formula does not apply to man-made facts; the antonym of "necessary" is "chosen," chosen by man. Man-made facts, of course, also have identity; they too have causes; and once they exist, they exist, whether or not any particular man decides to recognize them. In their case, however, the ultimate cause, as we will see in the next chapter, is an act(s) of human choice; and even though the power of choice is an aspect of human identity, any choice by its nature could have been otherwise. No man-made fact, therefore, is necessary; none *had to* be.

In holding that the metaphysically given is absolute, Ayn Rand is not denying that man has the power of creativity, the power to adapt the materials of nature to his own requirements. A barren desert, for instance, may be the metaphysically given, but man has the power to change the circumstances responsible for its barrenness; he can decide to irrigate the desert and make it bloom. Such creativity is not the power to alter the metaphysically given (under the original circumstances, the desert necessarily remains barren); it is not the power to create entities out of a void or to make any entity act in contradiction to its nature. In Ayn Rand's words, creativity is the power

> to rearrange the combinations of natural elements. . . . "Creation" does not (and metaphysically cannot) mean the power to bring something into existence out of nothing. "Creation" means the power to bring into existence an arrangement (or combination or integration) of natural elements that had not existed before. . . . The best and briefest identification of man's power in regard to nature is Francis Bacon's "Nature, to be commanded, must be obeyed."

One can alter a natural condition only by enacting the requisite cause, the one demanded by the immutable laws of existence. Man's creativity, therefore, is not defiance of the absolutism of reality, but the opposite. In order to succeed, his actions must conform to the metaphysically given.[15]

The distinction between the metaphysically given and the man-made is crucial to every branch of philosophy and every area of human life. The two kinds of facts must be treated differently, each in accordance with its nature.

Metaphysically given facts *are* reality. As such, they are not subject to anyone's appraisal; they must be accepted *without evaluation*. Facts of reality must be greeted not by approval or condemnation, praise or blame, but by a silent nod of acquiescence, amounting to the affirmation: "They are, were, will be, and have to be."

> The metaphysically given [writes Ayn Rand] cannot be true or false, it simply *is*—and man determines the truth or falsehood of his judgments by whether they correspond to or contradict the facts of reality. The metaphysically given cannot be right or wrong—it is the standard of right or wrong, by which a (rational) man judges his goals, his values, his choices.[16]

Man-made facts, by contrast, being products of choice, must be evaluated. Since human choices can be rational or irrational, right or wrong, the man-made cannot be acquiesced in merely because it exists; it cannot be given the automatic affirmation demanded by a fact of reality. On the contrary, the man-made "must be judged," in Miss Rand's words, "then accepted or rejected and changed when necessary."[17]

To confuse these two kinds of facts is to court a series of disastrous errors. One kind of error consists in regarding the man-made as immutable and beyond challenge; the other, in regarding the metaphysically given as alterable.

The first is typified by the idea that "You can't fight city hall, or tradition, or the consensus of the times—that's reality." "Reality" is equated here with any decisions men make and cling to, whether right or wrong. "Realism," accordingly, becomes a synonym for mindless conformity. In this view, it is "unrealistic" to reject the supernatural if one's ancestors were religious—or to fight for capitalism if big government is the popular trend—or to reject racism when Hitler is in power—or to create representational art when the museums feature only smears—or to uphold principles when the schools turn out only pragmatists. This approach leads to the sanctioning of any status quo, however debased, and thus turns its advocates into pawns and accessories of evil. It makes sacrosanct any human conclusions, even those that contradict metaphysically given facts. The essence of this so-called "realism" is the evasion of reality.

The other kind of error consists in regarding the metaphysically given as alterable. This amounts not merely to evading reality, but to declaring war on it.

The attempt to alter the metaphysically given is described by Ayn Rand as the fallacy of "rewriting reality." Those who commit it regard metaphysically given facts as nonabsolute and, therefore, feel free to imagine an alternative to them. In effect, they regard the universe as being merely a first draft of reality, which anyone may decide at will to rewrite.

A common example is provided by those who condemn life because man is capable of failure, frustration, pain, and who yearn instead for a world in which man knows nothing but happiness. But if the possibility of failure exists, it *necessarily* exists (it is inherent in the facts that achieving a value requires a specific course of action, and that man is neither omniscient nor omnipotent in regard to such action). Anyone who holds the full context—who keeps in mind the *identity* of man and of all the other relevant entities—would be unable even to imagine an alternative to the facts as they are; the contradictions involved in such a projection would obliterate it. The rewriters, however, do not keep identity in mind. They specialize in out-of-context pining for a heaven that is the opposite of the metaphysically given.

A variant of this pining is the view that the fact of death makes life meaningless. But if living organisms *are* mortal, then (within the relevant circumstances) they are so necessarily, by the nature of the life process. To rebel against one's eventual death is, therefore, to rebel against life—and reality. It is also to ignore the fact that indestructible objects have no need of values or of meaning, which phenomena are possible *only* to mortal entities (see chapter 7).

Another example of rewriting reality, taken from epistemology, is provided by those skeptics who condemn human knowledge as invalid because it rests on sensory data, the implication being that knowledge should have depended on a "direct," nonsensory illumination. This amounts to the claim: "If I had created reality, I would have chosen a different cause for knowledge. Reality's model of cognition is unacceptable to me. I prefer my own rewritten version." But if knowledge does rest on sensory data, then it does so *necessarily,* and again no alternative can even be imagined, not if one keeps in mind the identity of all the relevant entities and processes (see chapter 2).

As with so many other errors, the historical root of the fallacy of rewriting reality lies in religion—specifically, in the idea that the universe was created by a supernatural Omnipotence, who could have created things differently and who can alter them if He chooses. A famous statement of this metaphysics was offered by the philosopher Leibnitz in the eighteenth century: "All is for the best in this best of all possible worlds." In Leibnitz's view, the universe is only one of many worlds; the others happen not to exist, because God in His goodness chose the present one as the best; but the others have always been *possible* and still are so today. This is the kind of metaphysics that tempts men to spend their time projecting and wishing for alternatives to reality. Christianity, indeed, invites such wishing, which it describes as the virtue of "hope" and the duty of "prayer."

By the nature of existence, however, such "hope" and "prayer" are futile. Leaving aside the man-made, *nothing is possible except what is actual.* The concept of "omnipotence," in other words, is logically incompatible with the law of identity; it is one or the other.

As with the doctrine of the primacy of consciousness, so with the idea of "possible universes": it has been taken over uncritically from religion by more secular thinkers, including even those who call themselves atheists and naturalists. The result is an entire profession, today's philosophers, who routinely degrade the actual, calling it a realm of mere "brute" or "contingent"—i.e., unintelligible and rewritable—facts. The lesson such philosophers teach their students is not to adhere to reality, but to brush it aside and fantasize alternatives.

Respect for reality does not guarantee success in every endeavor; the refusal to evade or rewrite facts does not make one infallible or omnipotent. But such respect is a necessary condition of successful action, and it does guarantee that, if one fails in some undertaking, he will not harbor a metaphysical grudge as a result; he will not blame existence for his failure. The thinker who accepts the absolutism of the metaphysically given recognizes that it is *his* responsibility to conform to the universe, not the other way around.

If a thinker rejects the absolutism of reality, however, his mental set is reversed: he expects existence to obey his wishes, and then he discovers that existence does not obey. This will lead him to the idea of a fundamental dichotomy: he will come to view *conflict with reality* as being the essence of human life. He will feel that clash or warfare between the self and the external world is not a senseless torture caused by an aberration, but the metaphysical rule. On one side of the clash, he will feel, are the desires and fantasies he seeks to elevate above existence; on the other, the "brute" facts inexplicably impervious to them.

The classic statement of this philosophy is given by Plato. In the *Timaeus,* discussing the formation of the physical world, Plato recounts the myth of the demiurge. Matter, we are told, was originally unformed and chaotic; a godlike soul enters and tries to shape the chaos into a realm of perfect beauty. The demiurge, however, fails; matter proves to be recalcitrant; it takes the imprint of beauty only so far and thereafter resists all efforts to perfect it. Hence, Plato concludes, matter is a principle of imperfection, inherently in conflict with the highest ideals of the spirit. In a perfect universe, matter *should* obey consciousness without reservation. Since it does not, the universe—not any man-made group or institution, but the physical universe itself—is flawed; it is a perpetual battleground of the noble vs. the actual.

What the *Timaeus* actually presents, in mythological form, is the conflict between existence and a mind that tries to rewrite it, but cannot. In effect, the myth's meaning is the self-declared failure of the primacy-of-consciousness viewpoint. The same failure is inherent in any version of Plato's creed. Whenever men expect reality to conform to their wish simply because it is their wish, they are doomed to metaphysical disappointment. This leads them to the dichotomy: my dream vs. the actual which thwarts it; or the inner vs. the outer; or value vs. fact; or the moral vs. the practical. The broadest name of the dichotomy is the "spiritual" realm vs. the "material" realm.

The theory of a mind-body conflict, which has corrupted every branch and issue of philosophy, does have its root in a real conflict, but of a special kind. Its root is a breach between some men's consciousness and existence. In this sense, the basis of the theory is not reality, but a human error: the error of turning away from reality, of refusing to accept the absolutism of the metaphysically given.

The man who follows and understands the opposite policy comes to the opposite conclusion: he dismisses out-of-hand the idea of a metaphysical dichotomy. A faculty of perception, he knows, cannot be an adversary of the world or the body; it has no weapons with which to wage any such war; it has no function *except* to perceive.

In due course, we will develop in detail the Objectivist position on the key aspects of the mind-body question. We will study the inner and the outer, value and fact, the moral and the practical, and several other such pairs, including reason and emotion, concepts and percepts, pure science and technology, love and sex. In every such case, Ayn Rand holds, the conventional viewpoint is wrong; man does not have to make impossible choices between the "spiritual" side of life and the "material." The relationship between the two sides, she holds, is not clash or warfare, but integration, unity, harmony.

The theory of mind-body harmony, like its Platonic antithesis, also has its root in a real correlate. *Its* root is the fundamental harmony and serenity that flows from accepting, as an absolute, the axiom that existence exists.

Idealism and Materialism as the Rejection of Basic Axioms

Now let us apply the principles we have been discussing to two outstanding falsehoods in the history of metaphysics: idealism and materialism.

The idealists—figures such as Plato, Plotinus, Augustine, Hegel—regard reality as a spiritual dimension transcending and controlling the world of nature, which latter is regarded as deficient, ephemeral, imperfect—in any event, as only partly real. Since "spiritual," in fact, has no meaning other than "pertaining to consciousness," the content of true reality in this view is invariably some function or form of consciousness (e.g., Plato's abstractions, Augustine's God, Hegel's Ideas). This approach amounts to the primacy of consciousness and thus, as Ayn Rand puts it, to the advocacy of consciousness *without* existence.

In regard to epistemology, Ayn Rand describes the idealists as mystics, "mystics of spirit." They are mystics because they hold that knowledge (of true reality) derives not from sense perception or from reasoning based on it, but from an otherworldly source, such as revelations or the equivalent.

The more sophisticated versions of idealism rest on technical analyses of the nature of percepts or concepts; these analyses will be considered in later chapters. The unsophisticated but popular version of idealism, which typically upholds a personalized other dimension, is religion. Essential to all versions of the creed, however—and to countless kindred movements—is the belief in the *supernatural.*

"Supernatural," etymologically, means that which is above or beyond nature. "Nature," in turn, denotes existence viewed from a certain perspective. Nature is existence regarded as a system of interconnected entities governed by law; it is the universe of entities acting and interacting in accordance with their identities. What then is a "super-nature"? It would have to be a form of existence beyond existence; a thing beyond entities; a something beyond identity.

The idea of the "supernatural" is an assault on everything man knows about reality. It is a contradiction of every essential of a rational metaphysics. It represents a rejection of the basic axioms of philosophy (or, in the case of primitive men, a failure to grasp them).

This can be illustrated by reference to any version of idealism. But let us confine the discussion here to the popular notion of God.

Is God the creator of the universe? Not if existence has primacy over consciousness.

Is God the designer of the universe? Not if A is A. The alternative to "design" is not "chance." It is causality.

Is God omnipotent? Nothing and no one can alter the metaphysically given.

Is God infinite? "Infinite" does not mean large; it means larger than *any* specific quantity, i.e., of *no* specific quantity. An infinite quantity would be a quantity without identity. But A is A. Every entity, accordingly, is finite; it is limited in the number of its qualities and in their extent; this applies to the universe as well. As Aristotle was the first to observe, the concept of "infinity" denotes merely a potentiality of indefinite addition or subdivision. For example, one can continually subdivide a line; but however many segments one has reached at a given point, there are only that many and no more. The *actual* is always finite.

Can God perform miracles? A "miracle" does not mean merely the unusual. If a woman gives birth to twins, that is unusual; if she were to give birth to elephants, that would be a miracle. A miracle is an action not possible to the entities involved by their nature; it would be a violation of identity.

Is God purely spiritual? "Spiritual" means pertaining to consciousness, and consciousness is a faculty of certain living organisms, their faculty of perceiving that which exists. A consciousness transcending nature would be a faculty transcending organism and object. So far from being all-knowing, such a thing would have neither means nor content of perception; it would be nonconscious.

Every argument commonly offered for the notion of God leads to a contradiction of the axiomatic concepts of philosophy. At every point, the notion clashes with the facts of reality and with the preconditions of thought. This is as true of the professional theologians' arguments and ideas as of the popular treatments.

The point is broader than religion. It is inherent in any advocacy of a transcendent dimension. Any attempt to defend or define the supernatural must necessarily collapse in fallacies. There is no logic that will lead one from the facts of this world to a realm contradicting them; there is no concept formed by observation of nature that will serve to characterize its antithesis. Inference from the natural can lead only to *more of the natural,* i.e., to limited, finite entities acting and interacting in accordance with their identities. Such entities do not fulfill the requirements of "God" or even of "poltergeist." As far as reason and logic are concerned, existence exists, and *only* existence exists.

If one is to postulate a supernatural realm, one must turn aside from reason, eschew proofs, dispense with definitions, and rely instead on faith. Such an approach shifts the discussion from metaphysics to epistemology. I will discuss the issue of faith in chapter 5.

For now, I will sum up by saying: Objectivism advocates reason as man's only means of knowledge, and, therefore, it does not accept God or any variant of the supernatural. We are *a-theist,* as well as a-devilist, a-demonist, a-gremlinist. We reject every "spiritual" dimension, force, Form, Idea, entity, power, or whatnot alleged to transcend existence. We reject idealism. To put the point positively: we accept reality, and that's all.

This does not mean that Objectivists are materialists.

Materialists—men such as Democritus, Hobbes, Marx, Skinner—champion nature but deny the reality or efficacy of consciousness. Consciousness, in this view, is either a myth or a useless byproduct of brain or other motions. In Objectivist terms, this amounts to the advocacy of existence without consciousness. It is the denial of man's faculty of cognition and therefore of all knowledge.

Ayn Rand describes materialists as "mystics of muscle"—"mystics" because, like idealists, they reject the faculty of reason. Man, they hold, is essentially a body without a mind. His conclusions, accordingly, reflect not the objective methodology of reason and logic, but the blind operation of physical factors, such as atomic dances in the cerebrum, glandular squirtings, S-R conditioning, or the tools of production moving in that weird, waltzlike contortion known as the dialectic process.

Despite their implicit mysticism, materialists typically declare that their viewpoint constitutes the only scientific or naturalistic approach to philosophy. The belief in consciousness, they explain, implies supernaturalism. This claim represents a capitulation to idealism. For centuries the idealists maintained that the soul is a divine fragment or mystic ingredient longing to escape the "prison of the flesh"; the idealists invented the false alternative of consciousness *versus* science. The materialists simply take over this false alternative, then promote the other side of it. This amounts to rejecting arbitrarily the possibility of a naturalistic view of consciousness.

The facts, however, belie any equation of consciousness with mysticism. Consciousness is an attribute of perceived entities here on earth. It is a faculty possessed under definite conditions by a certain group of living organisms. It is directly observable (by introspection). It has a specific nature, including specific physical organs, and acts accordingly, i.e., lawfully. It has a life-sustaining function: to perceive the facts of nature and thereby enable the organisms that possess it to act successfully. In all this, there is nothing unnatural or supernatural. There is no basis for the suggestion that consciousness is separable from matter, let alone opposed to it, no hint of immortality, no kinship to any alleged transcendent realm.

Like the faculty of vision (which is one of its aspects), and like the body, the faculty of awareness is wholly this-worldly. The soul, as Aristotle was the first (and so far one of the few) to understand, is *not* man's ticket to another reality; it is a development of and within nature. It is a biological datum open to observation, conceptualization, and scientific study.[18]

Materialists sometimes argue that consciousness is unnatural on the grounds that it cannot be perceived by extrospection, has no shape, color, or smell, and cannot be handled, weighed, or put in a test tube (all of which applies equally to the faculty of vision). One may just as well argue that the eyeball is unreal because it cannot be perceived by introspection, does not have the qualities of a process of awareness (such as intensity or scope of integration), and cannot theorize about itself, suffer neurotic problems, or fall in love. These two arguments are interchangeable. It makes no more sense arbitrarily to legislate features of matter as the standard of existents and then deny consciousness, than to do the reverse. The facts are that matter exists and so does consciousness, the faculty of perceiving it.

Materialists sometimes regard the concept of "consciousness" as unscientific on the grounds that it cannot be defined. This overlooks the fact that there cannot be an infinite regress of definitions. All definitions reduce ultimately to certain primary concepts, which can be specified only ostensively; axiomatic concepts necessarily belong to this category. The concept of "matter," by contrast, is not an axiomatic concept and does require a definition, which it does not yet have; it requires an analytical definition that will integrate the facts of energy, particle theory, and more. To provide such a definition is not, however, the task of philosophy, which makes no specialized study of matter, but of physics. As far as philosophic usage is concerned, "matter" denotes merely the objects of extrospection or, more precisely, that of which all such objects are made. In this usage, the concept of "matter," like that of "consciousness," can be specified only ostensively.

There is no valid reason to reject consciousness or to

struggle to reduce it to matter; not if such reduction means the attempt to define it out of existence. Even if, someday, consciousness were to be explained scientifically as a product of physical conditions, this would not alter any observed fact. It would not alter the fact that, given those conditions, the attributes and functions of consciousness are what they are. Nor would it alter the fact that in many respects these attributes and functions are unique; they are different from anything observed in unconscious entities. Nor would it alter the fact that one can discover the conditions of consciousness, as of anything else one seeks to know, only through the exercise of consciousness.

The monist insistence that, despite the observed facts, reality (or man) can have only *one* constituent, is groundless; it is an example of rewriting reality. The materialist equation of physics with science is equally groundless. Science is systematic knowledge gained by the use of reason based on observation. In using reason, however, one must study each specific subject matter by the methods and techniques suited to its nature. One cannot study history by the methods of chemistry, biology by the methods of economics, or psychology by the methods of physics. At the dawn of philosophy, the ancient Pythagoreans in an excess of enthusiasm attempted, senselessly, to equate mathematics with cognition and to construe the universe as "numbers." The modern behaviorists, with far less excuse, commit the same error in regard to physics.

"I want," the behaviorist says in effect, "to deal with entities I can weigh and measure just as the physicist does. If consciousness exists, my dream of making psychology a branch of physics is destroyed. Consciousness upsets my program, my goal, my ideal. Therefore, consciousness is unreal." In this statement, a desire is being used to wipe out a fact of reality. The primacy of consciousness is being used—to deny consciousness!

A philosophy that rejects the monism of idealism or materialism does not thereby become "dualist." This term is associated with a Platonic or Cartesian metaphysics; it suggests the belief in two realities, in the mind-body opposition, and in the soul's independence of the body—all of which Ayn Rand denies.

None of the standard terms applies to the Objectivist metaphysics. All the conventional positions are fundamentally flawed, and the ideal term—"existentialism"—has been preempted (by a school that advocates Das Nichts, i.e., *nonexistence*). In this situation, a new term is required, one which at least has the virtue of not calling up irrelevant associations.

The best name for the Objectivist position is "Objectivism."

2

SENSE PERCEPTION
AND VOLITION

Metaphysics, in the Objectivist viewpoint, is a highly delimited subject. In essence, it identifies only the fact of existence (along with the corollaries of this fact). The subject does not study particular existents or undertake to guide men in the achievement of a goal.

The case is different with regard to the other, much more complex branch at the base of philosophy: epistemology, which does study a particular subject matter, and does offer men practical guidance. Epistemology is the science that studies the nature and means of human knowledge.

Epistemology is based on the premise that man can acquire knowledge *only* if he performs certain definite processes. This premise means that a man cannot accept ideas at random and count them as knowledge merely because he feels like it. Why not?

The Objectivist answer has two parts. The first is that knowledge is knowledge of reality, and existence has primacy over consciousness. If the mind wishes to know existence, therefore, it must conform *to* existence. On the opposite metaphysics, Ayn Rand holds, epistemology would be neither necessary nor possible. If thought created reality, no science offering guidance to thought would be applicable; consciousness could assert whatever it wished, and reality would obey.

The second part of the answer pertains to the nature of *human* consciousness. Existence has primacy for animals, too, but they do not need cognitive guidance, because their knowledge is sensory or perceptual in nature. Human knowledge, however, though based on sensory perception, is conceptual in nature, and on the conceptual level consciousness displays a new feature: it is not automatic or infallible; it can err, distort, depart from reality (whether through ignorance or evasion). Man, therefore, unlike the animals, needs to discover a *method* of cognition. He needs to learn how to use his mind, how to distinguish truth from falsehood, how to validate the conclusions he reaches.

Epistemology is the science that tells a fallible, conceptual consciousness what rules to follow in order to gain knowledge of an independent reality. Without such a science, none of man's conclusions, on any subject, could be regarded as fully validated. There would be no answer to the question: *how do you know?*

Before one can study conceptual knowledge, however, one must cover two large topics: sense perception and volition.

Since concepts, according to Objectivism, are integrations of perceptual data, there can be no concepts apart from sense experience. There are no innate ideas, ideas in the mind at birth. Consciousness begins as a *tabula rasa* (a blank slate); all of its conceptual content is derived from the evidence of the senses. The sensory-perceptual level of consciousness, therefore—the base of cognition—must be studied first. We must establish the exact role of the senses in human knowledge and the validity of the information they provide. If the senses are not valid, if they are not instruments that provide a knowledge of reality, then neither are concepts, and the whole cognitive enterprise is aborted. If seeing is not believing, then thinking is worthless as well.

Since one precondition of epistemology is the fact that the conceptual level is not automatic, this fact, too, must be established at the outset. Before undertaking to offer cognitive guidance, a philosopher must define and establish man's power of volition. If man has no choice in regard to the use of his consciousness, then there can be no discussion of how he *should* use his mind; no norms would be applicable.

The topics of sense perception and volition constitute what we may call the anteroom of epistemology. In considering these topics, we are not studying conceptual knowledge. We are laying down the prerequisites of such a study (which begins in chapter 3).

The Senses as Necessarily Valid

The validity of the senses is an axiom. Like the fact of consciousness, the axiom is outside the province of proof because it is a precondition of any proof.

Proof consists in reducing an idea back to the data provided by the senses. These data themselves, the foundation of all subsequent knowledge, precede any process of inference. They are the primaries of cognition, the unchallengeable, the *self-evident*.

The validity of the senses is not an independent axiom; it is a corollary of the fact of consciousness. (As we have seen, it is only by grasping the action of his senses that a child is able to reach the implicit concept of consciousness.) If man is conscious of that which is, then his *means* of awareness are means of *awareness*, i.e., are valid. One cannot affirm consciousness while denying its primary form, which makes all the others possible. Just as any attack on consciousness negates itself, so does any attack on the senses. If the senses are not valid, neither are any concepts, including the ones used in the attack.

The purpose of philosophic discussion of the senses is not to derive their validity from any kind of antecedent knowledge, but to define their exact function in human cognition and thereby to sweep away the objections raised against them by a long line of philosophers. The purpose is not to argue *for* the testimony of our eyes and ears, but to remove the groundless doubts about these organs that have accumulated through the centuries.

Sensory experience is a form of awareness produced by physical entities (the external stimuli) acting on physical instrumentalities (the sense organs), which respond automati-

cally, as a link in a causally determined chain. Obeying inexorable natural laws, the organs transmit a message to the nervous system and the brain. Such organs have no power of
choice, no power to invent, distort, or deceive. They do not
respond to a zero, only to a something, something real, some
existential object which acts on them.[1]

The senses do not interpret their own reactions; they do
not identify the objects that impinge on them. They merely
respond to stimuli, thereby making us aware of the fact that
some kind of objects exist. We do not become aware of what
the objects are, but merely *that* they are. "The task of [man's]
senses," writes Ayn Rand, "is to give him the evidence of
existence, but the task of identifying it belongs to his reason,
his senses tell him only that something *is,* but *what* it is must
be learned by his mind."[2] It is only in regard to the "what"—
only on the conceptual level of consciousness—that the possibility of error arises. If a boy sees a jolly bearded man in a
red suit and infers that Santa Claus has come down from the
North Pole, his senses have made no error; it is his conclusion
that is mistaken.

A so-called sensory illusion, such as a stick in water appearing bent, is not a perceptual error. In Ayn Rand's view, it
is a testament to the reliability of the senses. The senses do
not censor their response; they do not react to a single attribute (such as shape) in a vacuum, as though it were unconnected to anything else; they cannot decide to ignore part of
the stimulus. Within the range of their capacity, the senses
give us evidence of everything physically operative, they respond to the *full context* of the facts—including, in the present instance, the fact that light travels through water at a
different rate than through air, which is what causes the stick
to appear bent. It is the task not of the senses but of the mind
to analyze the evidence and identify the causes at work (which
may require the discovery of complex scientific knowledge).
If a casual observer were to conclude that the stick actually
bends in water, such a snap judgment would be a failure on
the conceptual level, a failure of thought, not of perception.
To criticize the senses for it is tantamount to criticizing them
for their power, for their ability to give us evidence not of
isolated fragments, but of a total.

The function of the senses, Ayn Rand holds, is to sum up

a vast range of facts, *to condense a complex body of infor-mation*—which reaches our consciousness in the form of a relatively few sensations. We perceive a bunch of roses, for example, as red, cool, fragrant, and yielding to the touch. Such sensations are not causeless. They are produced by a complex body of physico-chemical facts, including the lengths of the light waves the roses reflect and absorb, the thermal conductivity of the petals, the chemical makeup of their molecules, and the type of bonding between them; these facts in turn reflect the underlying atomic structures, their electronic and nuclear features, and many other aspects. Our sensations do not, of course, identify any of these facts, but they do constitute our first form of grasping them and our first lead to their later scientific discovery. Science, indeed, is nothing more than the conceptual unravelling of sensory data; it has no other primary evidence from which to proceed.

If a "valid" sense perception means a perception the object of which is an existent, then not merely man's senses are valid. *All* sense perceptions are necessarily valid. If an individual of any species perceives at all, then, no matter what its organs or forms of perception, it perceives something that is. Conceptualization involves an interpretation that may not conform to reality, an organization of data that is not necessitated by physical fact; one can, therefore, "think about nothing," i.e., nothing real, such as a perpetual-motion machine or demonic possession or Santa Claus. But the senses sum up automatically what *is*.

Once a mind acquires a certain content of sensory material, it can, as in the case of dreams, contemplate its own content rather than external reality. This is not sense perception at all, but a process of turning inward, made possible by the fact that the individual, through perception, first acquired some sensory contents. Nor, as Aristotle observed, is there any difficulty in distinguishing dreams from perception. The concept of "dream" has meaning only because it denotes a contrast to wakeful awareness. If a man were actually unable to recognize the latter state, the word "dream" to him would be meaningless.

Our sensations are caused in part by objects in reality. They are also—an equally important point—caused in part by our organs of perception, which are responsible for the fact that we perceive objects in the form of sensations of color, sound, smell, and so forth. A being with radically different senses would presumably perceive reality in correspondingly different forms.

Ayn Rand observes, however, that a difference in sensory form among perceivers is precisely that: it is a difference in the *form* of perceiving the same objects, the same one reality. Such a difference does not pertain to cognitive content and does not indicate any disagreement among the parties. The senses of a man with normal vision, to take the standard example, do not contradict those of a color-blind man. When the former says about some object, "It is red," he must in reason mean by the statement: "It is an entity in reality of a specific nature such that, when it acts on *my* senses, I perceive it in the form of red color." That is true; that *is* what it is. Similarly, if the color-blind man says "It is gray," he has to mean: "It is an entity in reality of a specific nature such that, when it acts on *my* senses, I perceive it in the form of gray color." That also is true; that is what it is. Neither statement conflicts with the other. Both men are perceiving that which is and are doing so in a specific form.

Nor will these two men or any other perceiver with an intellect come to different conclusions about the nature of the object. In this respect, *differences in sensory form do not matter.* They have no consequences in regard to the content of cognition.

The role of the senses is to give us the start of the cognitive process: the first evidence of existence, including the first evidence of similarities and differences among concretes. On this basis, we organize our perceptual material—we abstract, classify, conceptualize. Thereafter, we operate on the conceptual level, making inductions, formulating theories, analyzing complexities, integrating ever greater ranges of data; we thereby discover step by step the underlying structures and laws of reality. This whole development depends on the sense organs providing an awareness of similarities and differences rich enough to enable a perceiver to reach the conceptual level. The development is not, however, affected by the *form* of such sensory awareness. As long as one grasps the requisite relationships in some form, the rest is the work of the mind, not of the senses. In such work, differences pertaining to the form of the initial data have no ultimate consequences.

That is why men with normal vision and men who are color-blind (or plain blind) do not end up with different theories of physics. The same would apply to a physicist from outer space, even if his sense organs were radically different from ours. Both species would be perceiving the same reality, and (leaving aside errors) would draw conclusions accordingly.

Species with different sense organs gain from perception different kinds (and/or amounts) of evidence. But assuming that a species has organs capable of the requisite range of discrimination and the mind to interpret what it perceives, such differences in sensory evidence are merely different starting points leading to the same ultimate conclusions. Imagine—to use a deliberately bizarre example of Miss Rand's—a species of thinking atoms; they have some kind of sensory apparatus but, given their size, no eyes or tactile organs and therefore no color or touch perception. Such creatures, let us say, perceive other atoms directly, as we do people; they perceive in some form we cannot imagine. For them, the fact that matter is atomic is not a theory reached by inference, but a self-evidency.

Such "atomic" perception, however, is in no way more valid than our own. Since these atoms function on a submicroscopic scale of awareness, they do not discover through their senses the kind of evidence that we take for granted. We have to infer atoms, but they have to infer macroscopic objects, such as a table or the Empire State Building, which are far too large for their receptive capacity to register. It requires a process of sophisticated theory-formation for them to find out that, in reality, the whirling atoms they perceive are bound into various combinations, making up objects too vast to be directly grasped. Although the starting points are very different, the cognitive upshot in both cases is the same, even though a genius among them is required to reach the conclusions obvious to the morons among us, and vice versa.

No type of sense perception can register everything. A is A—and any perceptual apparatus is limited. By virtue of being able directly to discriminate one aspect of reality, a consciousness cannot discriminate some other aspect that would require a different kind of sense organs. Whatever facts the senses do register, however, *are* facts. And these facts are what lead a mind eventually to the rest of its knowledge.

Sensory Qualities as Real

Now let us consider a further issue relating to sensory form and to the validity of the senses: the metaphysical status of sensory qualities themselves.

Since the objects we perceive have a nature independent of us, it must be possible to distinguish between form and object; between the aspects of the perceived world that derive from our form of perception (such as colors, sounds, smells) and the aspects that belong to metaphysical reality itself, apart from us. What then is the status of the formal aspects? If they are not "in the object," it is often asked, does it follow that they are merely "in the mind" and therefore are subjective and unreal? If so, many philosophers have concluded, the senses must be condemned as deceivers—because the world of colored, sounding, odoriferous objects they reveal is utterly unlike actual reality. This is the problem, a commonplace in introductory philosophy classes, of the so-called "two tables": the table of daily life, which is brown, rectangular, solid, and motionless; and the table of science, which, it is said, is largely empty space, inhabited by some colorless, racing particles and/or charges, rays, waves, or whatnot.

Ayn Rand's answer is: we *can* distinguish form from object, but this does *not* imply the subjectivity of form or the invalidity of the senses.

The task of identifying the nature of physical objects as they are apart from man's form of perception does not belong to philosophy, but to physics. There is no philosophic method of discovering the fundamental attributes of matter; there is only the scientist's method of specialized observation, experimentation, and inductive inference. Whatever such attributes turn out to be, however, they have no *philosophic* significance, neither in regard to metaphysics nor to epistemology. Let us see why, by supposing for a moment that physics one day reaches its culmination and attains omniscience about matter.

At that point, scientists know the ultimate ingredients of the universe, the irreducible building blocks that combine to make up physical objects apart from any relationship to man's form of awareness. What these ingredients are I do not pretend to know. For the sake of the argument, let us make the extravagant assumption that they are radically different from anything men know now; let us call them "puffs of meta-energy," a deliberately undefined term. At this stage of cognition, scientists have discovered that the material world as men perceive it, the world of three-dimensional objects possessing color, texture, size, and shape is not a primary, but merely an effect, an effect of various combinations of puffs acting on men's means of perception.

What would this sort of discovery prove philosophically? Ayn Rand holds that it would prove nothing.

If everything is made of meta-energy puffs, then so are human beings and their parts, including their sense organs, nervous system, and brain. The process of sense perception, by this account, would involve a certain relationship among the puffs: it would consist of an interaction between those that comprise external entities and those that comprise the perceptual apparatus and brain of human beings. The result of this interaction would be the material world as we perceive it, with all of its objects and their qualities, from men to mosquitoes to stars to feathers.

Even under the present hypothesis, such objects and qualities would not be products of consciousness. Their existence would be a *metaphysically given fact;* it would be a consequence of certain puff-interactions that is outside of man's power to create or destroy. The things we perceive, in this theory, would not be primaries, but they would nevertheless be unimpeachably *real*.

A thing may not be condemned as unreal on the grounds that it is "only an effect," which can be given a deeper explanation. One does not subvert the reality of something by explaining it. One does not make objects or qualities subjective by identifying the causes that underlie them. One does not detach the material world as we perceive it from reality when one shows that certain elements in reality produced it. On the contrary: if an existent is an effect of the puffs in certain combinations, by that very fact it must be real, a real product of the ingredients that make up reality. Man's consciousness did not create the ingredients, in the present hypothesis, or the necessity of their interaction, or the result: the solid, three-dimensional objects we perceive. If the elements of reality themselves combine inevitably to produce such objects, then these objects have an impregnable metaphysical foundation: by the nature of their genesis, they are inherent in and expressive of the essence of existence.

Such objects, moreover, would have to be discovered by anyone who wished to know the full nature of the universe. If somehow, like the fictitious atoms of our example, a man were able to grasp the puffs directly, he would still have to discover the fact that among their attributes is the potentiality, when appropriately combined, of generating a world of solid objects, with the qualities of color, texture, size, shape, and the rest. He who knew the puffs but not this potentiality would not know an aspect of reality that we already do know.

The dominant tradition among philosophers has defined only two possibilities in regard to sensory qualities: they are "in the object" or "in the mind." The former is taken to subsume qualities independent of man's means of perception; the latter is taken to mean "subjective and/or unreal." Ayn Rand regards this alternative as defective. A quality that derives from an interaction between external objects and man's perceptual apparatus belongs to neither category. Such a quality—e.g., color—is not a dream or hallucination; it is not "in the mind" apart from the object; it is man's *form* of grasping the object. Nor is the quality "in the object" apart from man; it is *man's* form of grasping the object. By definition, a form of perception cannot be forced into either category. Since it is the product of an interaction (in Plato's terms, of a "marriage") between two entities, object and apparatus, it cannot be identified exclusively with either. Such products introduce a third alternative: they are not object alone or perceiver alone, but object-as-perceived.

In a deeper sense, however, such products *are* "in the object." They are so, not as primaries independent of man's sense organs, but as the inexorable effects of primaries. Consciousness, to repeat, is a faculty of awareness; as such, it does not create its content *or even the sensory forms* in which it is aware of that content. Those forms in any instance are determined by the perceiver's physical endowment interacting with external entities in accordance with causal law. The source of sensory form is thus not consciousness, but existential fact independent of consciousness; i.e., the source is the metaphysical nature of reality itself. In this sense, *everything* we perceive, including those qualities that depend on man's physical organs, is "out there."[3]

Those who condemn the senses as deceptive on the grounds that sense qualities are merely effects on men are guilty of rewriting reality. Their viewpoint amounts to an ultimatum delivered to the universe: "I demand that the senses give me not effects, but irreducible primaries. That is how *I* would have created reality." As in all cases of this fallacy, such a demand ignores the fact that what is metaphysically given is an absolute. Perception is necessarily a process of interaction: there is no way to perceive an object that does not somehow impinge on one's body. Sense qualities, therefore, must be effects. To reject the senses for this reason is to reject them for existing—while yearning for a fantasy form of perception that in logic is not even thinkable.

Those who condemn the senses on the grounds that sense qualities "are different from" the primaries that cause them (the "two tables" notion) are guilty of the same fallacy. They, too, demand that the primaries be given to man "pure," i.e., in no sensory form. The view of perception that underlies this kind of demand is the "mirror theory." The mirror theory holds that consciousness acts, or should act, as a luminous mirror (or diaphanous substance), reproducing external entities faithfully in its own inner world, untainted by any contribution from its organs of perception. This represents an attempt to rewrite the nature of consciousness. Consciousness is not a mirror or a transparent stuff or any kind of ethereal medium. It cannot be explicated by analogy to such physical objects; as we have seen, the concept is axiomatic and the faculty *sui generis*. Consciousness is not a faculty of reproduction, but of perception. Its function is not to create and then study an inner world that duplicates the outer world. Its function is directly to look outward, to perceive that which exists—and to do so by a certain means.

As to the claim that the racing particles, puffs, or whatever that make up tables do not "look like" the peaceful brown things on which we eat in daily life, this is the literal reverse of the truth. "Looks" *means* "appears to our visual sense." The brown things are exactly what the puffs "look like." There are not "two tables." The brown things are a particular combination of the primary ingredients of reality; they are those ingredients as perceived by man.

We *can* know the content of reality "pure," apart from man's perceptual form; but we can do so only by abstracting away man's perceptual form—only by starting from sensory data, then performing a complex scientific process. To demand that the senses give us such "pure" content is to rewrite the function of the senses and the mind. It is to demand a blatant contradiction: a sensory image bearing no marks of its sensory character—or a *percept* of that which, by its nature, is the object only of a *concept*.

Although Ayn Rand's theory of perception has sometimes been called "naive realism," the term does not apply. Naive realism is an ancient form of the mirror theory; it claims that the senses do give us the content of reality "pure." The senses, naive realists hold, are valid *because* sensory qualities exist in objects independent of man's means of perception, which—in defiance of all evidence—are held to contribute nothing to our experiences.

The intention of naive realism, which is to uphold the unqualified validity of the senses, is correct. But the content of the theory, unable to deal with the issue of sensory form, fails to implement its intention and merely plays into the hands of the anti-senses cohorts.

Once again, the only accurate name for the Objectivist viewpoint is "Objectivism."

Consciousness as Possessing Identity

Implicit in the foregoing is a principle essential to the validation of the senses and, indeed, to all of epistemology. I mean Ayn Rand's crucial principle that consciousness has identity.[4]

Every existent is bound by the laws of identity and causality. This applies not only to the physical world, but also to consciousness. Consciousness—any consciousness, of any species—is what it is. It is limited, finite, lawful. It is a faculty with a nature, which includes specific instrumentalities that enable it to achieve awareness. It is a *something* that has to grasp its objects *somehow*.

The fact that consciousness has identity is self-evident; it is an instance of the law of identity. Objectivism, however, stands alone in accepting the fact's full meaning and implications. All the standard attacks on the senses—and wider: all the modern, Kant-inspired attacks on human cognition as such—begin with the opposite premise. They begin with the premise that consciousness *should not* have identity and conclude that, since it does, consciousness is invalid. (The naive realists accept the same premise, but hold that it poses no problem; consciousness, they say, *is* a characterless "mirror," i.e., a thing without any identity.)

In regard to the senses, the standard argument, long a staple of skeptics, has already been indicated: "A certain object looks red or sounds loud or feels solid, but that is partly because of the nature of human eyes, ears, or touch. Therefore, we are cut off from the external world. We do not perceive reality as it really is, but only reality as it appears to man." Here is the same argument as presented by Kantians, in regard to the conceptual faculty: "Certain abstract conclusions are incontestable to us, but that is partly because of the nature of the human mind. If we had a different sort of mind, with a different sort of conceptual apparatus, our idea of truth and reality would be different. Human knowledge, therefore, is only human; it is subjective; it does not apply to things in themselves." Here is the argument a third time, as applied to logic: "Even the most meticulous proof depends on our sense of what is logical, which must depend in part on the kind of mental constitution we have. The real truth on any question is, therefore, unknowable. To know it, we would have to contact reality directly, without relying on our own logical makeup. We would have to jump outside of our own nature, which is impossible."

We cannot escape the limitations of a human consciousness, the argument observes. We cannot escape our dependence on human senses, human concepts, human logic, the human brain. We cannot shed human identity. Therefore, the argument concludes, we cannot gain a knowledge of reality. In other words: our consciousness is something; it has specific means and forms of cognition; therefore, it is disqualified as a faculty of cognition.

This argument is not confined to human consciousness. It is an attack on *all* consciousness, human, animal, or otherwise. No matter how keen an animal's senses, the argument indicts them equally: since the animal cannot escape *its* organs of perception, it, too, must be imprisoned by them and cut off from reality. The same would apply to a Martian with unearthly senses; such a creature would never encounter things as they are, only things-as-processed-by-the-Martian-mechanism. Even God Himself—assuming He existed—would be cognitively impotent. Since He would grasp reality only through a divine means of awareness, He, too, could know only reality as it appeared to *His* consciousness. (I assume here that God would have to perceive reality by *some* means; if not, He would have no identity.)

What sort of consciousness *can* perceive reality, in the Kantian, anti-identity approach? The answer is: a consciousness not limited by any means of cognition; a consciousness which perceives no-how; a consciousness which is not of *this* kind as against that; a consciousness which is nothing in particular, i.e., which is nothing, i.e., which does not exist. This is the ideal of the Kantian argument and the standard it uses to measure cognitive validity: the standard is not human consciousness or even an invented consciousness claimed to be superior to man's, but a zero, a vacuum, a nullity—a non-anything.

In this view, identity—the essence of existence—invalidates consciousness, every kind of consciousness. Or: a means of knowledge makes knowledge impossible. As Ayn Rand observes in a critical formulation, this approach implies that "man is blind, because he has eyes—deaf, because he has ears—deluded, because he has a mind—and the things he perceives do not exist, *because* he perceives them."[5]

Ayn Rand's system rejects every aspect of this brazen attack on man, including all of its epistemological formulations and consequences.

Objectivists discard the locution "reality as it really is." The phrase is a redundancy; there is no "reality as it really isn't." The world men perceive is not merely "reality as it appears." There is no difference in this context between what appears and what is real. It is reality that appears to any consciousness—through the use of its means of cognition. To deny this is to succumb to the notion that grasping an object somehow, means not grasping it.

Nor do Objectivists speak of "things in themselves," which Kantians contrast to "things in relation to consciousness." The very terminology insinuates the notion that consciousness, by the mere fact of existing, is an agent of distortion.

For the same reason, Objectivists reject the key skeptic claim: that man perceives not reality, but only its effects on his cognitive faculty. Man perceives reality directly, not some kind of effects different from it. He perceives reality *by means of* its effects on his organs of perception. Nor can one reply that man's perception of reality, since it is mediated by the senses, is only "indirect." What then would "direct perception" denote? It would have to denote a grasp of reality attained without benefit of any means.

Ayn Rand rejects all these errors, because she rejects their root: she begins not by bewailing the nature of human consciousness, but by insisting on it. The fact that man's cognitive faculties have a nature does not invalidate them; it is what makes them possible. *Identity is not the disqualifier of consciousness, but its precondition.* This is the base from which epistemology must proceed; it is the principle by reference to which all standards of cognition must be defined.

Every process of knowledge involves two crucial elements: the object of cognition and the means of cognition—or; *What* do I know? and *How* do I know it?[6] The object (which is studied by the special sciences) is always some aspect of reality; there is nothing else to know. The means (which is studied by epistemology) pertains to the kind of consciousness and determines the form of cognition.

The start of a proper epistemology lies in recognizing that there can be no conflict between these elements.

Contrary to the skeptics of history, the fact of a means cannot be used to deny that the object of cognition is reality. Contrary to the mystics, the fact that the object is reality cannot be used to deny that we know it by a specific, human means.

The "how" cannot be used to negate the "what," or the

"what" the "how"—not if one understands that A is A and that consciousness is consciousness.

The Perceptual Level as the Given

So far, I have been considering sensory awareness as an adult phenomenon. Chronologically, however, there are two stages in man's development of such awareness: sensation and perception. This is a distinction with important philosophic implications.

The first stage of consciousness is that of sensation. A "sensation" is an irreducible state of awareness produced by the action of a stimulus on a sense organ. "Irreducible" here means: incapable of being analyzed into simpler conscious units. By its nature, a sensation lasts only as long as the stimulus. When light waves strike the retina, for instance, they produce a sensation of color; when the light is removed, the sensation disappears.

The most primitive conscious organisms appear to possess only the capacity of sensation. The conscious life of such organisms is the experience of isolated, fleeting data—fleeting, because the organisms are bombarded by a flux of stimuli. These creatures confront a kaleidoscopic succession of new worlds, each swept away by the next as the stimuli involved fade or change. Since such consciousnesses do not retain their mental contents, they can hardly detect relationships among them. To such mentalities, the universe is, in William James's apt description, a "blooming, buzzing confusion."

Human infants start their lives in this state and remain in it for perhaps a matter of months; but no one reading these words suffers such a state now. When you the reader look, say, at a table—not *think* of it, but merely turn your eyes toward it and *look*—you enjoy a different form of awareness from that of the infant. You do not encounter an isolated, ephemeral color patch or a play of fleeting sensations, but an enduring thing, an object, an *entity*. This is true even though the stimulus reaching your eyes is the very one that would reach an infant's.

The reason you see an entity is that you have experienced many kinds of sensations from similar objects in the past, and your brain has retained and *integrated* them: it has put them together to form an indivisible whole. As a result, a complex past mental content of yours is implicit and operative in your present visual awareness. In the act of looking at a table now, you are aware of its solidity—of the fact that, unlike brown water, it will bar your path if you try to walk through it; of its texture—unlike sandpaper, it will feel smooth to your fingertips; of many visual aspects outside the range of your glance, such as the underside of the top and the backs of the legs; of the heft you will feel if you lift the object; of the thud you will hear if you bang on it. All this sensory information (and much more) is tied to and cued by your present visual sensation. The result is your ability, when you look out, to see not merely a patch of brown, but a table.

Such an ability exemplifies the second stage of consciousness: the perceptual level. A "perception," in Ayn Rand's definition, "is a group of sensations automatically retained and integrated by the brain of a living organism, which gives it the ability to be aware, not of single stimuli, but of *entities*, of things."[7]

The important philosophic point of this discussion can be stated simply: "direct experience," according to Objectivism, means the *perceptual* level of consciousness.[8] As adults, as thinkers, and even as children beyond the infant stage, what we are given when we use our senses, leaving aside all conceptual knowledge, is the awareness of entities—nothing more, but nothing less.

We do not and cannot experience the world as infants do. Indeed, we have come to learn that an infant type of experience exists only because we have made a long series of scientific discoveries. Starting from perceptual fact, we formed a conceptual vocabulary. Then, step by step, we acquired substantial physical and psychological knowledge—knowledge of external stimuli; of our own sense organs, brain, and consciousness; and of the laws that govern the behavior of all these entities. Finally, we became able imaginatively to project our initial state and to conclude that the world must once have appeared to us as a chaos. That chaos, however, is not given to us as adults or philosophers. It is a sophisticated inference from what *is* given: the perceptual level.

The proper order of philosophy, therefore, is not the chronological order of our actual development.

Chronologically, the sensation stage comes first, then the perceptual, and then the conceptual. Epistemologically, however, *the perceptual stage comes first.* If one seeks to prove any item of human knowledge, on any subject, he must begin with the facts of perception. These facts constitute the base of cognition. They are the self-evident and the incontestable, by reference to which we validate all later knowledge, including the knowledge that, decades earlier, when we first emerged from the womb, we experienced a brief sensation stage.

There are philosophers (David Hume is the most famous) who deny the perceptual level. Such men give the sensation stage epistemological primacy, then seek to determine whether the fact of entities (and causality) can be established by inference from it. This is a dead end; from disintegrated sensations, nothing can be inferred. A consciousness that experienced only sensations would be like the mind of an infant; it could neither perceive objects nor form concepts (which is one reason Hume ended as a paralyzed skeptic). Hume's dead end, however, is self-imposed. Entities do not require inferential validation. The given *is* the perceptual level.

This last statement does not necessarily mean that the entities we perceive are metaphysical primaries; as we have seen, that is a question for science. It means that the grasp of entities is an *epistemological* primary, which is presupposed by all other knowledge, including the knowledge of any ultimate ingredients of matter that scientists may one day discover.

The integration of sensations into percepts, as I have indicated, is performed by the brain automatically. Philosophy, therefore, has no advice to offer in this regard. There can be no advice where man has no power to choose his course of behavior.

In regard to a more complex kind of integration, which we do not perform automatically, philosophy does have advice to offer—volumes of it. I mean the integration of percepts into concepts. This brings us to the threshold of the conceptual level of consciousness and to the second issue in the anteroom of epistemology: volition.

The Primary Choice as the Choice to Focus or Not

Man, according to Objectivism, is not moved by factors outside of his control. He is a volitional being, who functions *freely.* A course of thought or action is "free," if it is selected from two or more courses possible under the circumstances. In such a case, the difference is made by the individual's decision, which did not have to be what it is, i.e., which could have been otherwise.

To identify the exact locus of human freedom is a difficult task since it requires that one describe and distinguish complex states of consciousness. Once this has been done, however, the fact *that* man is free follows readily. Before we turn to validate free will, therefore, we must devote considerable space to defining its nature.

Let us begin with an overview of the Objectivist position. Consciousness is an active process, not a motionless medium, such as a mirror, which passively reflects reality.[9] To achieve and maintain awareness, a man's consciousness must perform a complex series of actions. The object of awareness, reality, simply exists; it impinges on a man's senses, but it does not do a man's cognitive work for him nor force itself on his mind. The man who waits for reality to write the truth inside his soul waits in vain.

The actions of consciousness required on the sensory-perceptual level are automatic. On the conceptual level, however, they are not automatic. This is the key to the locus of volition. Man's basic freedom of choice, according to Objectivism, is: to exercise his distinctively human cognitive machinery or not; i.e., to set his conceptual faculty in motion or not. In Ayn Rand's summarizing formula, the choice is: "to think or not to think."

> . . . to think is an act of choice. . . . Reason does not work automatically; thinking is not a mechanical process; the connections of logic are not made by instinct. The function of your stomach, lungs or heart is automatic; the function of your mind is not. In any hour and issue of your life, you are free to think or to evade that effort. But you are not free to escape from your nature, from the fact that *reason* is your means of survival—so that for *you,* who are

a human being, the question "to be or not to be" is the
question "to think or not to think."[10]

As long as a man is awake (and his brain intact), he is
conscious of reality in the sensory-perceptual form; this much
is given to him by nature. But consciousness in the form required by his survival is not given to man; it must be achieved
by a process of choice. Man's power of volition is the power
to seek such awareness of reality or to dispense with it. His
choice is to be conscious (in the human sense) or not.

Volition subsumes different kinds of choices. The primary
choice, according to Objectivism, the one that makes conceptual activity possible, is the choice to *focus* one's consciousness.

Let me introduce the concept of "focus" with a visual
analogy. A man cannot do much with his faculty of vision
until his eyes are in focus. Otherwise, his eyesight gives him
only a blur or haze, a kind of visual fog, in which he can
discriminate relatively little. Although the power of visual focus is not possessed by newborn infants, they acquire it very
early and soon automatize its use. As adults, therefore, our
eyes are automatically focussed; it takes a special effort for us
to unfocus them and dissolve the world into a blur.

A similar concept applies to the mind. In regard to
thought, as to vision, the same alternative exists: clear awareness or a state of blur, haze, fog, in which relatively little can
be discriminated. On the conceptual level, however, one must
choose between these alternatives. Intellectual clarity is not
given to man automatically.

"Focus" (in the conceptual realm) names a quality of
purposeful alertness in a man's mental state. "Focus" is the
state of a goal-directed mind committed to attaining full
awareness of reality.

As there are degrees of visual acuity, so there are *degrees
of awareness* on the conceptual level. At one extreme, there
is the active mind intent on understanding whatever it deals
with, the man prepared to summon every conscious resource
that will enable him to grasp the object of his concern. Such
an individual struggles to grasp *all* the facts he believes to be
relevant—as against being content with a splintered grasp, a
grasp of some facts while other data dimly sensed to be rele-

vant are left shrouded in mental fog, unscrutinized and un-identified. In addition, he struggles to grasp the facts *clearly,* with the greatest precision possible to him—as against being content with a vague impression, which loosely suggests but never congeals into a definite datum.

To achieve this kind of understanding, an individual can-not stare passively at whatever concretes, images, or words happen to strike his attention. He cannot abdicate his power to control his consciousness and ignore his own mental pro-cesses, on the premise that his brain or reality will do in his place whatever is necessary. On the contrary, he must commit himself to a course of self-conscious mental action—to the policy of mobilizing his faculty of thought. He must be pre-pared, when necessary, to conceptualize new data. This in-volves many processes, such as seeking out common denominators among observed concretes, formulating defini-tions, and integrating new material to one's past context of knowledge—all the while being guided by proper thinking methods (to the extent that one knows them). A mind on the premise of initiating such processes, when it apprehends the need for them, is a mind committed to full awareness. "Full awareness" does *not* mean omniscience. It means the aware-ness attainable by a man who seeks to understand some object by using to the full the evidence, the past knowledge, and the cognitive skills available to him at the time.

At the other extreme of the continuum is the man to whom everything beyond the sensory-perceptual level is a blur. An example would be a drunk who has not yet passed out. In this condition, the conceptual faculty has been effec-tively numbed (leaving aside some acquired vocabulary and knowledge that even he cannot escape). The mind of such an individual is not active or goal-directed. It is passive, drifting, dazed, oblivious to considerations like truth, clarity, context, or methodology; it merely experiences random stimuli, outer or inner, without self-awareness, continuity, or purpose. In the human sense of the term "conscious," this is a state of complete unconsciousness of reality. Drunkenness, of course, is merely a convenient illustration. The mental state of many people who have not taken a drop to drink is often indistin-guishable, in the respects here relevant, from the one just de-scribed.

Between the two extremes lies the spectrum of states of partial awareness, distinguished from one another by how conscientiously active the mind is: how much it seeks to grasp in a given situation, how clearly, and by what kinds of processes.

To "focus" one's mind means to raise one's degree of awareness. In essence, it consists of shaking off mental lethargy and deciding to use one's intelligence. The state of being "in focus"—in *full* focus—means the decision to use one's intelligence fully.

In situations where one's knowledge is already adequate, full awareness does not require any new conceptualization; it is attainable by a simple directing of attention. In such cases, one is in focus if he does not relinquish control of his consciousness: his mind remains self-aware and self-directed, and he is alert to the possibility that a process of cognition may be required at any time. For example, you may be walking down the street looking at passersby and shops, with no question preoccupying you. This qualifies as an instance of full focus if you are carrying out wide awake a mental purpose you have set yourself (even a simple one, such as observing the sights). It qualifies as focus if you know what your mind is doing and why, and if you are ready to begin a process of thought should some occurrence make it advisable. The alternative is to walk around in a daze, only partly awake, without setting any conscious purpose, and with little knowledge of or interest in the actions of your mind or the demands of reality.

Focus is not the same as thinking; it need not involve problem-solving or the drawing of new conclusions. Focus is the readiness to think and as such the precondition of thinking. Again a visual analogy may be helpful. Just as one must first focus his eyes, and then, if he chooses, he can turn his gaze to a cognitive task, such as observing methodically the items on a table nearby; so he must first focus his mind, and then, if he chooses, he can direct that focus to the performance of a conceptual-level task.

To change the analogy: the choice to focus, Miss Rand used to observe, is like throwing a switch; it may be compared to starting a car's motor by turning on the ignition. (Whether and where one drives are later issues.) This throwing of the switch consists of the exertion of one's mental capacity. This exertion is work and is experienced as such—not pain, but work, in the sense of basic mental *effort*. It is the effort required to reach and/or maintain full awareness. "Effort" means the expenditure of energy to achieve a purpose.

The exertion of such effort, according to Objectivism, never becomes automatic. The choice involved must be made anew in every situation and in regard to every subject a person deals with. The decision to focus on one occasion does not determine other occasions; in the next moment or issue, one's mind has the capacity to go out of focus, to relax its concentration, drop purpose, and lapse into a state of blur and drift. It retains this capacity no matter how long a person has practiced the policy of seeking full awareness. Focus never turns into a mental "reflex"; it must be willed continuously. This is inherent in calling it a matter of choice. The essence of a volitional consciousness is the fact that its operation always demands the same fundamental effort of initiation and then of maintenance across time.

The choice to focus, I have said, is man's primary choice. "Primary" here means: presupposed by all other choices and itself irreducible.

Until a man is in focus, his mental machinery is unable to function in the human sense—to think, judge, or evaluate. The choice to "throw the switch" is thus the root choice, on which all the others depend.

Nor can a primary choice be explained by anything more fundamental. By its nature, it is a first cause within a consciousness, not an effect produced by antecedent factors. It is not a product of parents or teachers, anatomy or conditioning, heredity or environment (see chapter 6). Nor can one explain the choice to focus by reference to a person's own mental contents, such as his ideas. The choice to activate the conceptual level of awareness must precede any ideas; until a person is conscious in the human sense, his mind cannot reach new conclusions or even apply previous ones to a current situation. There can be no intellectual factor which makes a man decide to become aware or which even partly explains such a decision: to grasp such a factor, he must already *be* aware.

For the same reason, there can be no motive or value-judgment which precedes consciousness and which induces a man to become conscious. The decision to perceive reality must precede value-judgments. Otherwise, values have no source in one's cognition of reality and thus become delusions. Values do not lead to consciousness; consciousness is what leads to values.

In short, it is invalid to ask: why did a man choose to focus? There is no such "why." There is only the fact that a man *chose:* he chose the effort of consciousness, or he chose non-effort and unconsciousness. In this regard, every man at every waking moment is a prime mover.

This is not to deny that a person's ideas can have effects, positive or negative, on his mental state. If an individual accepts a philosophy of reason, and if he characteristically chooses to be in focus, he will gradually gain knowledge, confidence, and a sense of intellectual control. This will make it easier for him to be in focus. After he practices the policy for a time, focussing will come to seem natural, his thought processes will gain in speed and efficiency, he will enjoy using his mind, and he will experience little temptation to drop the mental reins. On the other hand, if an individual accepts an anti-reason philosophy, and if he characteristically remains out of focus, he will increasingly feel blind, uncertain, and anxious. This will make the choice to focus harder. After a while, he will experience focus as an unnatural strain, his thought processes will become relatively tortured and unproductive, and he will be tempted more than ever to escape into a state of passive drift.

Both these patterns, however (and all the mixtures in between), are self-made. Human volition produced each condition, and the opposite choices remain possible. The first kind of man still has to throw the switch the next time, which takes an expenditure of effort. The second still has the capacity to focus, as long as he is sane. He has the capacity gradually (and painfully) to work his way out of his inner chaos and establish a better relationship to reality.

The most conscientious man, though he may have every inclination to use his mind, retains the power to decide not to think further. The most anti-effort mentality, despite all his fears and disinclinations, retains the power to renounce drift in favor of purpose.

So far we have discussed two basic choices: switching the mental machinery on or leaving it passive and stagnant. There is a third possibility, the aberration of *evasion*.

"Evasion," in Ayn Rand's words, is

> the act of blanking out, the willful suspension of one's consciousness, the refusal to think—not blindness, but the refusal to see; not ignorance, but the refusal to know. It is the act of unfocussing your mind and inducing an inner fog to escape the responsibility of judgment—on the unstated premise that a thing will not exist if only you refuse to identify it, that A will not be A so long as you do not pronounce the verdict "It *is*."[11]

The man who drifts in an out-of-focus state avoids mental purpose and effort. He *does not work to see,* to connect, to understand, a policy that pertains to all of his mental contents at the time. Evasion, by contrast, is an active process aimed at a specific content. The evader does expend effort; he purposefully directs his attention away from a given fact. He *works not to see* it; if he cannot banish it fully, he works not to let it become completely real to him. The drifter does not integrate his mental contents; the evader disintegrates them, by struggling to disconnect a given item from everything that would give it clarity or significance in his own mind. In the one case, the individual is immersed in fog by default; he chooses not to raise his level of awareness. In the other case, he expends energy to create a fog; he *lowers* his level of awareness.

Despite their differences, these two states of consciousness are closely related. If a drifter in a given situation apprehends (dimly or clearly) the need to initiate a thought process, yet refuses to do so, the refusal involves an evasion (he is evading the fact that thought is necessary). To be out of focus, therefore, does not as such imply that one has evaded; but to be out of focus in situations where one must make decisions or take action does imply it (it implies an evasion of one's need of consciousness in decision and action). Habitual evasion is thus what sustains a chronically out-of-focus state, and vice versa: the latter policy engenders a substantial anxiety, which makes the demands of life in reality seem threatening; so a series of evasions comes to seem tempting as an escape.

To an evader, a feeling of some kind is more important than truth. A man finds a certain fact or policy to be unpleasant, frightening, or guilt-provoking. Reality to the contrary notwithstanding, he does not *want* the fact to be real or the policy to be necessary; so he decides to blank out the offending datum. Or a certain idea or policy gives a man pleasure, reassurance, or relief, and he *wants* to believe in or practice it, even though he knows that reality is against him in the issue; so he decides to blank out what he knows. Both such men, in Ayn Rand's words, place an "I wish" above an "It is."[12] An example would be an individual who knows that his consumption of drugs is killing him, who wants to indulge but not to die, and who solves the problem by indulging blindly, simply evading the consequences.

Unlike the basic choice to be in or out of focus, the choice to evade a specific content is motivated, the motive being the particular feeling that the evader elevates above reality. But such a feeling is merely a precondition, not a cause or explanation; the choice to capitulate to it is irreducible. No matter what his emotions, a sane man retains the power to face facts. If an emotion is overwhelming, he retains the power to recognize this and to defer cognition until he can establish a calmer mood. Just as man has the capacity to place feelings above facts, so he has the capacity *not* to do so, to remain reality-oriented by an act of will, despite any temptation to the contrary. This, too, is an aspect of volition subsumed under the primary choice: to focus or not. The words "or not" cover both passive drift and active evasion.

The process of evasion, as we will see, is profoundly destructive. Epistemologically, it invalidates a mental process. Morally, it is the essence of evil. According to Objectivism, evasion is the vice that underlies all other vices. In the present era, it is leading to the collapse of the world.

Human Actions, Mental and Physical, as Both Caused and Free

The choice to focus or not is man's primary choice, but it is not his only choice. Man's waking life involves a continual selection among alternatives. Aside from involuntary responses, such as bodily reflexes, all human actions, mental and physical, are chosen by the actor. The man who is completely out of focus has abdicated his power of choice; he is capable of nothing but passive reaction to stimuli. To the extent that a man is in focus, however, the world with all its possibilities opens up to him. Such a man must choose what to do with his consciousness. He must decide to what goal, intellectual or existential, to direct it and by what means to achieve this goal.

Let me illustrate the wealth of human choices first in the mental realm. Assume that, having chosen to be in focus, you elect to solve some problem by engaging in a process of thought. (The same pattern of continual choice would apply to any deliberate mental process.)

To begin with, you must choose the problem. Reality does not force a decision on this matter. You may know that a certain question is essential to your life and values, but you can still decide not to wrestle with it now—or ever. Or several competing questions may all seem important, even intertwined; but none will instate itself as your purpose without your decision. *What* you think about depends on your choice.

Having selected a question, you must then decide (usually in stages) on the method of attacking it. You must decide the sub-questions you will ask and the cognitive acts you will perform to try to answer them. At the outset, for example, you may have a fleeting sense that certain relevant concretes have something in common. Will you concentrate on the similarities you dimly sense and struggle to draw the abstraction explicitly? Or do you decide that it is too much work, or that another angle of approach is more promising? If the latter, which one? and when will you come back to these concretes? and is it worthwhile to come back? The concretes themselves will not decide such matters; the choices are yours to make.

If you catch yourself using concepts that overlap confusingly or formulations that clash, will you stop to distinguish or reconcile them? The need for these processes will not compel you to perform them; you must choose what to do with your power of attention. If a trend of thought suggests vaguely an argument you once heard that seems relevant but does not come back immediately, will you grope to recall it? Since it does not come back automatically, you must work to bring it back—if you so choose. If you become stymied when thinking, what will you do next? Try another mode of attack? Retrace your steps in quest of an error? Turn to a new subject? Take a break and then try again? Give up?

The above merely indicates a pattern. An actual process of thought, even about a relatively simple subject, may involve hundreds of aspects, complexities, and subprocesses. There are countless possibilities confronting the thinker; so he cannot function at all except by repeated acts of choice. The basic choice is the choice to be in focus. This is the decision to put forth the effort necessary to grasp reality. But such a decision leaves one with innumerable options as to what in particular to grasp and how to do it. This is why the mental processes of different men, even if they start with the same information and ask the same question, can nevertheless be extremely different.

Thought is a volitional activity. The steps of its course are not forced on man by his nature or by external reality; they are chosen. Some choices are obviously better—more productive of cognitive success—than others. The point is that, whether right or wrong, the direction taken *is* a matter of choice, not of necessity.

The choices involved in performing a thought process are different in an important respect from the primary choice. These higher-level choices, as we may call them, are not irreducible. In their case it is legitimate to ask, in regard both to end and means: *why* did the individual choose as he did? what was the *cause* of his choice? Often, the cause involves several factors, including the individual's values and interests, his knowledge of a given subject, the new evidence available to him, and his knowledge of the proper methods of thinking.

The principle of causality does not apply to consciousness, however, in the same way that it applies to matter. In regard to matter, there is no issue of choice; to be caused is to be necessitated. In regard to the (higher-level) actions of a volitional consciousness, however, *"to be caused" does not mean "to be necessitated."*

An ancient philosophic dilemma claims that if man's actions, mental or physical, have no causes, then man is insane, a lunatic or freak who acts without reason. (This anticausal viewpoint is called "indeterminism.") But, the dilemma continues, if man's actions do have causes, then they are not free; they are necessitated by antecedent factors. (This is the determinist viewpoint.) Therefore, either man is insane or he is determined.

Objectivism regards this dilemma as a false alternative. Man's actions do have causes; he does choose a course of behavior for a reason—but this does not make the course determined or the choice unreal. It does not, because man himself decides what are to be the governing reasons. *Man chooses the causes that shape his actions.*

To say that a higher-level choice was caused is to say: there was a reason behind it, but other reasons were possible under the circumstances, and the individual himself made the selection among them.

The factors shaping a thought process, to stay with our example, do not work automatically. A man's previous knowledge, I have said, is one possible determinant. Such knowledge, however, does not apply itself automatically to every new topic he considers. If he relaxes his mental reins and waits passively for inspiration to strike him, his past conclusions, however potentially germane, will not necessarily thrust themselves into prominence. On the contrary, the man who thus turns inwardly sloppy may know a certain point perfectly well, yet end up with a conclusion that blatantly contradicts it. The contradiction eludes him because he is not paying full attention, he is not working to integrate all the relevant data, he is not ruled by a commitment to grasp the truth. As a result his own knowledge becomes ineffective, and his mental processes are moved instead by factors such as random feelings or associations.[13]

The same principle applies to the other factors shaping a man's thought. The new evidence available is a factor, *if* a man chooses to seek out that evidence. His knowledge of the proper methods of thinking is a factor, if he monitors his mental processes and tries to make use of such knowledge. His values and interests are a factor, if he is alert to grasp their application to a new situation. But if (as is possible) a person decides that all this is too much work, or if he dislikes some piece of evidence or some required method and starts to evade, then the above factors will not shape his mental activity. Instead, by his choice, they will be causally impotent.

A man's power of choice in a thought process is to maintain the tie between his mind and reality, or not to do so. This means: to concentrate on a question, on everything he knows to be relevant to it, and to keep this content clear and operative by a continuous, conscientious directing of his full attention—or to let some or all of the data lapse into fog, to let past knowledge fade, new evidence blur, methodological standards relax, and then drift to groundless conclusions at the mercy of random material fed by his subconscious.

If a man chooses the reality orientation, then the higher-level choices he makes will be shaped by causal factors relevant to a process of cognition. If he does not choose the reality orientation, then the flow of his mental contents will be shaped by a different kind of cause. In either case, there will be a reason that explains the steps of his mental course. But this does not imply determinism, because the essence of his freedom remains inviolable. That essence lies in the issue: what kind of reason moves a man? Has he chosen the reality orientation or its opposite? sustained full focus or self-made blindness?

Such is the choice, in each moment and issue, which controls all of one's subsequent choices and actions.

The same principle applies to the realm of physical action. Like mental processes, man's existential actions, too, have causes. Just as one cannot perform a thought process without a reason, so one cannot perform an action in reality without a reason. In general, the cause of action is what a man thinks, including both his value-judgments and his factual knowledge or beliefs. These ideas define the goals of a man's action and the means to them. (The relation between thought and feeling is discussed in chapter 5.)

Again, however, as in regard to processes of consciousness, cause and effect does not negate the reality of choice. Man's actions do reflect the content of his mind, but they do not flow from a specific content automatically or effortlessly. On the contrary, action involves continual choice, even after one has formed a full range of mental content, including a comprehensive set of value-judgments.

In regard to action, a man's choice—one he must make

in every issue—is: *to act in accordance with his values or not.*

To act in accordance with one's values (in the sense relevant here) is a complex responsibility. It requires that one know what he is doing and why. He has to assume the discipline of *purpose* and of a long-range course, selecting a goal and then pursuing it across time in the face of obstacles and/or distractions. It requires that one heed the *hierarchy,* the relative importance, of his values. This means: he keeps in mind the fact that some of his values are primary or immediately urgent, while others are subordinate or less imperative—and he determines the time and effort to be spent on a given pursuit accordingly. Thus he integrates the activity of the moment into the full context of his other goals, weighing alternative courses and selecting appropriately. And it requires that one choose the means to his ends conscientiously, making full use of the knowledge available to him. All this is involved in "acting in accordance with one's values." Yet all this is precisely what is not automatic.

A man can accept a set of values, yet betray them in action. He can actively evade the steps their achievement would require, or he can simply default on the responsibility involved. He can choose to live and act out of focus, to drop the discipline of purpose, ignore hierarchy, brush aside knowledge, and surrender to the spur of the moment. This kind of man lets himself drift through a day or a life pushed by random factors, such as sudden urges, unadmitted fears, or importunate social pressures. The twists of such a man's actions also have causes lying in his mental content. What moves him, however, is not the full context of his knowledge and values, but chance bits of content; the cause of his actions is a flow of disintegrated ideas and value-judgments that he allows to become decisive out of context, without identification or purpose. Like the mental drifter, the physical drifter, too, turns himself over to his subconscious, abdicating his power of conscious decision. The result is that he turns himself into the puppet of the determinists' theory, dangling on strings he does not know or control. But the fact remains that he *chose* this state.

In the realm of physical action, man's choice is twofold. First he must choose, through a process of thought (or nonthought), the ideas and values that will comprise his mind's content. Then he must choose to act on these ideas and values—to keep them operative as his guide amid all the vicissitudes of daily life. He must choose what to think, and then he must choose to practice what he preaches.

The similarity between the physical and mental realms is clear. In action as in thought, each step a man takes has a cause, which explains it. The indeterminist notion that freedom means a blind, senseless lurch—a so-called "Epicurean swerve"—is without justification. But this does not imply determinism. In regard to action, also, man is a sovereign entity, a self-mover. His inviolable freedom lies in the issue: what kind of cause moves him—long-range purpose or out-of-context promptings? Once again, what underlies such an alternative is a single root choice: to be conscious or not.

There is one further question to consider before we turn to the validation of volition. How does the law of causality apply to the primary choice itself? Since one cannot ask for the cause of a man's choice to focus, does it follow that, on this level, there is a conflict between freedom and causality?

Even in regard to the primary choice, Ayn Rand replies, the law of causality operates without breach. The form of its operation in this context, however, is in certain respects unique.

The law of causality affirms a necessary connection between entities and their actions. It does not, however, specify any particular kind of entity or of action. The law does not say that only mechanistic relationships can occur, the kind that apply when one billiard ball strikes another; this is one common form of causation, but it does not preempt the field. Similarly, the law does not say that only choices governed by ideas and values are possible; this, too, is merely a form of causation; it is common but not universal within the realm of consciousness. The law of causality does not inventory the universe; it does not tell us what kinds of entities or actions are possible. It tells us only that whatever entities there are, they act in accordance with their nature, and whatever actions there are, they are performed and determined by the entity which acts.

The law of causality by itself, therefore, does not affirm or deny the reality of an irreducible choice. It says only this much: if such a choice does exist, then it, too, as a form of action, is performed *and necessitated* by an entity of a specific nature.

The content of one's choice could always have gone in the opposite direction; the choice to focus could have been the choice not to focus, and vice versa. But the action itself, the fact of choosing as such, in one direction or the other, is unavoidable. Since man is an entity of a certain kind, since his brain and consciousness possess a certain identity, he *must* act in a certain way. He must continuously choose between focus and nonfocus. Given a certain kind of cause, in other words, a certain kind of effect *must* follow. This is not a violation of the law of causality, but an instance of it.

On the primary level, to sum up, man chooses to activate his consciousness or not; this is the first cause in a lengthy chain—and the inescapability of such choice expresses his essential nature. Then, on this basis, he forms the mental content and selects the reasons that will govern all his other choices. Nothing in the law of causality casts doubt on such a description.

If man does have free will, his actions are free *and* caused—even, properly understood, on the primary level itself.

Volition as Axiomatic

So far, I have been identifying the nature of man's power of choice, according to the Objectivist theory. But how is this theory validated? Can one prove that the choice to think is real, and not, as determinists would say, an illusion caused by our ignorance of the forces determining us? Can one prove that man's consciousness does not function automatically?

If man's consciousness *were* automatic, if it did react deterministically to outer or inner forces acting upon it, then, by definition, a man would have no choice in regard to his mental content; he would accept whatever he had to accept, whatever ideas the determining forces engendered in him. In such a case, one could not prescribe methods to guide a man's thought or ask him to justify his ideas; the subject of epistemology would be inapplicable. One cannot ask a person to alter or justify the mentally inescapable, any more than, in physical terms, one can ask him to alter or justify his patellar reflex. In regard to the involuntary, there is no alternative but to submit—to do what one must, whatever it is.

The concept of "volition" is one of the roots of the concept of "validation" (and of its subdivisions, such as "proof"). A validation of ideas is necessary and possible only because man's consciousness is volitional. This applies to any idea, including the advocacy of free will: to ask for its proof is to presuppose the reality of free will.

Once again, we have reached a principle at the foundation of human knowledge, a principle that antecedes all argument and proof. How, then, do we know that man has volition? It is a self-evident fact, available to any act of introspection.

You the reader can perceive every potentiality I have been discussing simply by observing your own consciousness. The extent of your knowledge or intelligence is not relevant here, because the issue is whether you use whatever knowledge and intelligence you do possess. At this moment, for example, you can decide to read attentively and struggle to understand, judge, apply the material—or you can let your attention wander and the words wash over you, half-getting some points, then coming to for a few sentences, then lapsing again into partial focus. If something you read makes you feel fearful or uneasy, you can decide to follow the point anyway and consider it on its merits—or you can brush it aside by an act of evasion, while mumbling some rationalization to still any pangs of guilt. At each moment, you are deciding to think or not to think. The fact that you regularly make these kinds of choices is directly accessible to you, as it is to any volitional consciousness.

The principle of volition is a philosophic axiom, with all the features this involves. It is a primary—a starting point of conceptual cognition and of the subject of epistemology; to direct one's consciousness, one must *be* free and one must know, at least implicitly, *that* one is. It is a fundamental: every item of conceptual knowledge requires some form of validation, the need of which rests on the fact of volition. It is self-evident. And it is inescapable. Even its enemies have to accept and use it in the process of any attempt to deny it. Let us see why.

When the determinist claims that man is determined, this applies to all man's ideas also, including his own advocacy of determinism. Given the factors operating on him, he believes, he had to become a determinist, just as his opponents had no alternative but to oppose him. How then can he know that his viewpoint is true? Are the factors that shape his brain infallible? Does he *automatically* follow reason and logic? Clearly not; if he did, error would be impossible to him.

The determinist's position amounts to the following. "My mind does not automatically conform to facts, yet I have no choice about its course. I have no way to choose reality to be my guide as against subjective feeling, social pressure, or the falsifications inherent in being only semiconscious. If and when I distort the evidence through sloppiness or laziness, or place popularity above logic, or evade out of fear, or hide my evasions from myself under layers of rationalizations and lies, *I have to do it,* even if I realize at the time how badly I am acting. Whatever the irrationalities that warp and invalidate my mind's conclusion on any issue, they are irresistible, like every event in my history, and could not have been otherwise." If such were the case, a man could not rely on his own judgment. He could claim nothing as objective knowledge, including the theory of determinism.

An infallible being, one that automatically grasps the truth—such as an animal (on its own level) or an angel, if such existed—can be devoid of volition, yet still acquire knowledge. Such a being does not need to perform a process of thought. But *man* (beyond the perceptual level) must think in order to know—he must think in a reality-oriented manner; and the commitment to do so is observably not inbuilt. If in addition it were not within man's power of choice, human consciousness would be deprived of its function; it would be incapable of cognition. This means: it would be detached from existence, i.e., it would not be conscious.

Volition, accordingly, is not an independent philosophic principle, but a corollary of the axiom of consciousness. Not every consciousness has the faculty of volition. Every fallible, conceptual consciousness, however, does have it.

If a determinist tried to assess his viewpoint as knowledge, he would have to say, in effect: "I *am* in control of my mind. I do have the power to *decide* to focus on reality. I do not merely submit spinelessly to whatever distortions happen to be decreed by some chain of forces stretching back to infinity. I am free, free to be objective, free to conclude—that I am not free."

Like any rejection of a philosophic axiom, determinism is self-refuting. Just as one must accept existence or consciousness in order to deny it, so one must accept volition in order to deny it. A philosophic axiom cannot be proved, because it is one of the bases of proof. But for the same reason it cannot be escaped, either. By its nature, it is impregnable.

▪   ▪   ▪   ▪

Most of the traditional opponents of determinism have regarded free will as mystical, as an attribute of an otherworldly soul that is antithetical to science and to man's this-worldly reason. The classic expression of this viewpoint is the disastrous Kantian slogan, "God, freedom, and immortality," which has had the effect of making "freedom" laughable by equating it with two bromides of supernaturalism. What reputable thinker cares to uphold volition if it is offered under the banner, "ghosts, choice, and the Pearly Gates"?

By identifying the locus of man's will as his conceptual faculty, Ayn Rand aborts such mysticism at the root. Will, in her view, is not something opposed or even added to reason. The faculty of reason *is* the faculty of volition. This theory makes it possible for the first time to validate the principle of volition objectively. It removes the principle once and for all from the clutches of religion.

After Ayn Rand, the fact of choice can no longer serve as ammunition for irrationalists. It becomes instead a testament to the power and the glory of man's mind.

Man's senses are valid. His mind is free. Now how should he use his mind?

At last we can leave the anteroom of epistemology and enter the great hall of its mansion.

3

CONCEPT-FORMATION

For man, sensory material is only the first step of knowledge, the basic source of information. Until he has conceptualized this information, man cannot do anything with it cognitively, nor can he act on it. Human knowledge and human action are *conceptual* phenomena.

Although concepts are built on percepts, they represent a profound development, a new scale of consciousness. An animal knows only a handful of concretes: the relatively few trees, ponds, men, and the like it observes in its lifetime. It has no power to go beyond its observations—to generalize, to identify natural laws, to hypothesize causal factors, or, therefore, to understand what it observes. A man, by contrast, may observe no more (or even less) than an animal, but he can come to know and understand facts that far outstrip his limited observations. He can know facts pertaining to *all* trees, *every* pond and drop of water, the universal *nature* of man. To man, as a result, the object of knowledge is not a narrow corner of a single planet, but the universe in all its immensity, from the remote past to the distant future, and from the most minuscule (unperceivable) particles of physics to the farthest (unperceivable) galaxies of astronomy.

A similar contrast applies in the realm of action. An animal acts automatically on its perceptual data; it has no power to project alternative courses of behavior or long-range consequences. Man chooses his values and actions by a process of thought, based ultimately on a philosophical view of existence; he needs the guidance of abstract principles both to select his goals and to achieve them. Because of its form of knowledge, an animal can do nothing but adapt itself to nature. Man (if he adheres to the metaphysically given) adapts nature to his own requirements.

A conceptual faculty, therefore, is a powerful attribute. It is an attribute that goes to the essence of a species, determining its method of cognition, of action, of survival. To understand man—and *any* human concern—one must understand concepts. One must discover what they are, how they are formed, and how they are used, and often misused, in the quest for knowledge.

This requires that we analyze in slow motion the inmost essence of the processes which make us human, the ones which, in daily life, we perform with lightninglike rapidity and take for granted as unproblematic. Happily, Ayn Rand has analyzed these processes systematically in *Introduction to Objectivist Epistemology*. I can, therefore, simplify the present discussion, covering only certain key aspects. I shall provide, in effect, an introduction to Miss Rand's *Introduction*. Those interested in a fuller presentation are referred to the book.

Differentiation and Integration as the Means to a Unit-Perspective

First, let us gain an overview of the nature of a conceptual consciousness. Following Miss Rand, let us begin by tracing the development in man's mind of the concept "existent."

"The (implicit) concept 'existent,' " she writes, "undergoes three stages of development in man's mind."[1] The first stage is a child's awareness of things or objects. This represents the (implicit) concept "entity." The second stage occurs when the child, although still on the perceptual level, distinguishes specific entities from one another; seeing the same object at different times, he now recognizes that it is the same one. This represents the implicit concept "identity."

These two stages have counterparts in the animal world. Animals have no concepts, not even implicit ones. But the higher animals can perceive entities and can learn to recognize particular objects among them. It is the third stage that constitutes the great cognitive divide.

Having grasped the identities of particular entities, human beings can go on to a new step. In Ayn Rand's words, they can grasp "relationships among these entities by grasping the similarities and differences of their identities."[2] A child can grasp that certain objects (e.g., two tables) resemble one another but differ from other objects (such as chairs or beds), and he can decide to consider the similar ones together, as a separate group. At this point, he no longer views the objects as animals do: merely as distinct existents, each different from the others. Now he also regards objects as related by their resemblances. To change the example: when you the reader direct your attention, say, to a person seated near you, you grasp not just entity, and not just *this* entity vs. that one over there, but: this *man,* i.e., this entity in relation to all the others like him and in contrast to the other kinds of entities you know. You grasp this entity as a member of a group of similar members.

The implicit concept represented by this stage of development is: *"unit."* "A unit," in Ayn Rand's definition, "is an existent regarded as a separate member of a group of two or more similar members."

"This is the key, the entrance to the conceptual level of man's consciousness. *The ability to regard entities as units is man's distinctive method of cognition,* which other living species are unable to follow."[3]

An animal cannot organize its perceptual field. It observes and reacts to objects in whatever order they happen to strike its consciousness. But man can break up the perceptual chaos by classifying concretes according to their resemblances. Even though people, cats, trees, and automobiles are jumbled together in reality, a man can say, in effect: "The similarities among people are so great and their differences from cats *et al.* are so striking that I am going to segregate the people mentally. I will continue to regard each person as a separate entity, but not as an unrelated entity. I will regard each as a member of a group of similars, i.e., as a unit."

The result is a new scale of cognitive ability. Given the unit-perspective, man can pursue knowledge purposefully. He can set aside percepts unrelated to a particular cognitive endeavor and concentrate on those that are relevant; he is able to specialize intellectually. In addition, since he treats the objects in the segregated group as units of a single concept, he can apply to all of them the knowledge he gains by studying only a comparative handful (assuming he forms his concepts correctly); he is capable of induction. And these invaluable capacities are only some of the consequences of the unit-perspective; its primary cognitive function is discussed at the end of this chapter.

When studying the unit-perspective, it is essential to grasp that in the world apart from man there are no units; there are only existents—separate, individual things with their properties and actions. To view things as units is to adopt a *human* perspective on things—which does not mean a "subjective" perspective.

> Note that the concept "unit" [writes Ayn Rand] involves an act of consciousness (a selective focus, a certain way of regarding things), but that it is *not* an arbitrary creation of consciousness: it is a method of identification or classification according to the attributes which a consciousness observes in reality. This method permits any number of classifications and cross-classifications: one may classify things according to their shape or color or weight or size or atomic structure; but the criterion of classification is not invented, it is perceived in reality. Thus the concept "unit" is a bridge between metaphysics and epistemology: units do not exist *qua* units, what exists are things, but *units are things viewed by a consciousness in certain existing relationships.*[4]

Without the implicit concept of "unit," man could not reach the conceptual method of knowledge. Without the same implicit concept, there is something else he could not do: he could not count, measure, identify quantitative relationships; he could not enter the field of mathematics. Thus the same (implicit) concept is the base and start of two fields: the conceptual and the mathematical. This points to an essential connection between the two fields. It suggests that concept-formation is in some way a mathematical process.

Before pursuing this lead, however, I want to give an orderly description of the conscious processes men must perform in order to be able to regard entities as units. I want to systematize the aspects of concept-formation to which we have already alluded.

Two main processes are involved, the two that are also essential to consciousness on the perceptual level: taking apart and putting together, or analysis and synthesis, or *differentiation* and *integration*.[5] "Differentiation" is the process of grasping differences, i.e., of distinguishing one or more objects of awareness from the others. "Integration" is the process of uniting elements into an inseparable whole.

In order to move from the stage of sensation to that of perception, we first have to discriminate certain sensory qualities, separate them out of the initial chaos. Then our brain integrates these qualities into entities, thereby enabling us to grasp, in one frame of consciousness, a complex body of data that was given to us at the outset as a series of discrete units across a span of time.

The same two processes occur in the movement from percepts to concepts. In this case, however, the processes differ in form and are not performed for us automatically by our brain.

We begin the formation of a concept by isolating a group of concretes. We do this on the basis of observed similarities that distinguish these concretes from the rest of our perceptual field. The similarities that make possible our first differentiations, let me repeat, are *observed;* they are available to our senses without the need of conceptual knowledge. At a higher stage of development, concepts are often necessary to identify similarities—e.g., between two philosophies or two political systems. But the early similarities are perceptually given, both to (certain) animals and to men.

The distinctively human element in the above is our ability to *abstract* such similarities from the differences in which they are embedded. An example is our ability to take out and consider separately the similar shape of a number of tables, setting aside their many differences in size, color, weight, and so on. "Abstraction" is the power of selective focus and treatment; it is the power to separate mentally and make cognitive use of an aspect of reality that cannot exist separately. This is a power animals do not possess. An animal perceives the whole object, including some similarities to other things and some differences from them; it may even, in certain instances, be capable of a rudimentary selective focus. But it cannot isolate or unite any group of concretes accordingly; it cannot *do* anything cognitively with the relationships it perceives. To its consciousness, the noting of similarities is a dead end. Man *can* do something: he makes such data the basis of a method of cognitive organization. The first step of the method is the mental isolation of a group of similars.

But an isolated perceptual group is not yet a concept. If we merely isolated, we could do little or nothing cognitively with the group, nor could we keep the group isolated. To achieve a cognitive result, we must proceed to integrate. "Integrating" percepts is the process of blending all the relevant ones (e.g., our percepts of tables) into an inseparable whole. Such a whole is a new entity, a mental entity (the concept "table"), which functions in our consciousness thereafter as a single, enduring unit. This entity stands for an unlimited number of concretes, including countless unobserved cases. It subsumes all instances belonging to the group, past, present, and future. Here is another parallel to mathematics.

> A concept [writes Ayn Rand] is like an arithmetical sequence of *specifically defined units,* going off in both directions, open at both ends and including *all* units of that particular kind. For instance, the concept "man" includes all men who live at present, who have ever lived or will ever live. An arithmetical sequence extends into infinity, without implying that infinity actually exists; such extension means only that whatever number of units does exist, it is to be included in the same sequence. The same principle applies to concepts: the concept "man" does not (and need not) specify what number of men will ultimately have existed—it specifies only the characteristics of man, and means that any number of entities possessing these characteristics is to be identified as "men."[6]

The tool that makes this kind of integration possible is language. A word is the only form in which man's mind is able to retain such a sum of concretes.

If a man, deprived of words, were to perform only the steps indicated so far, he would have before his mind a complex, unwieldy phenomenon: a number of similar objects and a resolve to treat them and everything like them together. This would not be a mental entity or a retainable mental state. Every time the man would want to use his concept, he would have to start afresh, recalling or projecting some relevant similars and performing over again the process of abstraction.

A word changes the situation dramatically. A word (aside from proper names) is a symbol that denotes a concept; it is a *concrete,* perceptually graspable symbol. Such a symbol transforms the sum of similars and the resolve to treat them together into a single (mental) concrete.

Only concretes exist. If a concept is to exist, therefore, it must exist in some way as a concrete. That is the function of language. "Language," writes Ayn Rand, "is a code of visual-auditory symbols that serves the . . . function of converting concepts into the mental equivalent of concretes."[7]

It is not true that words are necessary primarily for the sake of communication. Words are essential to the process of conceptualization and thus to all thought. They are as necessary in the privacy of a man's mind as in any public forum; they are as necessary on a desert island as in society. The word constitutes the completion of the integration stage; it is the form in which the concept exists. Using the soul-body terminology, we may say that the word is the body, and the conscious perspective involved, the soul—and that the two form a unity which cannot be sundered. A concept without a word is at best an ephemeral resolve; a word without a concept is noise. "Words transform concepts into (mental) entities," writes Miss Rand; *"definitions* provide them with *identity."*[8] (We will discuss definitions later.)

Now let us identify a problem in regard to concepts which has bedeviled philosophers from Greece to the present: what is the relationship of concepts to existents? To what precisely do concepts refer in reality?

There is no such problem in regard to percepts; a percept is a direct awareness of an existing entity. But a concept involves a process of abstraction, and there are no abstractions in reality. To what then does a concept actually refer? The best of the traditional answers, Aristotle's, is that a concept refers to what all the concretes in a given class possess in common. In this view, "manness" or "humanity," for instance, refers to the attribute(s) that is the same in every instance of the species. The problem is: what is this attribute and how does one discover it?

As far as perceptual awareness is concerned, there may be nothing the same in the concretes of a given concept. Individual men, for instance, vary, or can vary, in every respect one can name: height, weight, color, fingerprints, intelligence, and so on. We perceive many similarities among men, but nothing identical in all cases. Yet, when we reach the concept "man," we are treating men not as more or less similar, but in some way as identical: as equally, interchangeably, members of the group. This is inherent in creating a single unit to denote every member of the species. How is this possible? Exactly what and where is the "manness" that is alleged to inhere in us all?

In regard to any concept, what enables us to treat as the same a series of existents which, as far as we can *perceive,* have nothing the same about them?

In order to validate man's use of concepts, a philosopher must answer these questions. Otherwise, he leaves man's rational conclusions, on any subject, unrelated to reality and vulnerable to every form of attack, from mystics and skeptics alike. The mystics hold that the referents of concepts exist not in this world, but in a Platonic heaven; hence, they claim, revelation is superior to science. The skeptics hold that concepts have no objective basis in *any* world, but are arbitrary constructs—which makes all of human cognition arbitrary and subjective. The followers of these schools, who are legion, do not hesitate to voice their disdain for the process of thought. I mean the mentalities who hear a rational argument, then shrug in reply: "That's only abstractions; come down to earth"—or: "That's only semantics, only a matter of how people use words." The first of these bromides implies that abstractions are supernatural entities. The second implies that words, i.e., concepts, are a matter of social caprice. Both divorce concepts from concretes.

All along we have been using concepts to reach the truth. Now we must turn to the precondition of this use and face the fundamental problem of epistemology. We must ground concepts themselves in the nature of reality.

Concept-Formation as a Mathematical Process

Ayn Rand's solution to the problem lies in her discovery that there is an essential connection between concept-formation and mathematics. Since mathematics is the science of measurement, let us start by considering the nature and purpose of measurement.

"Measurement," writes Miss Rand, "is the identification of a relationship—a quantitative relationship established by means of a standard that serves as a unit."[9]

The process of measurement involves two concretes: the existent being measured and the existent that is the standard of measurement. Entities and their actions are measured by means of their attributes, such as length, weight, velocity. In every case, the primary standard is some easily perceivable concrete that functions as a unit. One measures length in units, say, of feet; weight in pounds; velocity in feet per second.

The unit must be appropriate to the attribute being measured; one cannot measure length in pounds or weight in seconds. An appropriate unit is an instance of the attribute being measured. A foot, for example, is itself a length; it is a specified amount of length. Thus it can serve as a unit to measure length. Directly or indirectly, the same principle applies to every type of measurement.

In the process of measurement, we identify the relationship of *any* instance of a certain attribute to a specific instance of it selected as the unit. The former may range across the entire spectrum of magnitude, from largest to smallest; the latter, the (primary) unit, must be within the range of human perception.

The epistemological purpose of measurement is best approached through an example. Consider the fact that the distance between the earth and the moon is 240,000 miles. No creature can perceive so vast a distance; to an animal, accordingly, it is unknowable and unfathomable. Yet man has no difficulty in grasping (and now even traversing) it. What makes this cognitive feat possible is the human method of establishing relationships to concretes we *can* directly perceive. We cannot perceive 240,000 miles, but that distance is expressed in miles, and a mile is reducible to a certain number of feet, and a foot is: *this* (I am pointing to a ruler). It works in the other direction also. A certain chemical reaction, a scientist reports, takes place in 4.6 milliseconds. A thousandth of a second is too small to be within the range of perceptual awareness. Yet by relating this time interval, as a fraction, to one that we can apprehend directly, we can grasp and deal with it as well. In both directions, Ayn Rand holds, and in regard to countless attributes, the

> purpose of measurement is to expand the range of man's consciousness, of his knowledge, beyond the perceptual level: beyond the direct power of his senses and the immediate concretes of any given moment. . . .
>
> The process of measurement is a process of integrating an unlimited scale of knowledge to man's limited perceptual experience—a process of making the universe knowable by bringing it within the range of man's consciousness, by establishing its relationship to man.[10]

Measurement is an anthropocentric process, because man is at its center. His scale of perception—the concretes *he* can directly grasp—is the base and the standard, to which everything else is related.

This brings us to Ayn Rand's momentous discovery: the connection between measurement and conceptualization. The two processes, she observes, have the same essential purpose and follow the same essential method.

In both cases, man identifies relationships among concretes. In both cases, he takes perceived concretes as the base, to which he relates everything else, including innumerable existents outside his ability to perceive. In both cases, the result is to bring the whole universe within the range of human knowledge. And now a further, crucial observation: in both cases, man relates concretes by the same method—by *quantitative* means. Both concept-formation and measurement involve the mind's discovery of a mathematical relationship among concretes.

Ayn Rand's seminal observation is that the similar concretes integrated by a concept differ from one another only quantitatively, only in the measurements of their characteristics. When we form a concept, therefore, *our mental process consists in retaining the characteristics, but omitting their measurements.*[11]

As a simple example, Miss Rand analyzes the process of forming the concept "length." A child observes that a match, a pencil, and a stick have a common attribute, length. The difference in this respect is only one of magnitude: the pencil is longer than the match and shorter than the stick. The three entities are the same in regard to the attribute, but differ in its measurement. What then does the child's mind have to do in order to integrate the three instances into a single mental unit? It retains the attribute while omitting the varying measurements.

> Or, more precisely [Miss Rand writes], if the process were identified in words, it would consist of the following: "Length must exist in *some* quantity, but may exist in *any* quantity. I shall identify as 'length' that attribute of any existent possessing it which can be quantitatively related to a unit of length, without specifying the quantity."[12]

This is the process—performed by the mind wordlessly—which enables the child not only to integrate the first instances of "length" that he observes, but also to identify future instances, such as the length of a pin, a room, a street. All such instances are *commensurable,* i.e., they can be related quantitatively to the same unit. They differ only in their specific measurements.

To omit measurements, Miss Rand stresses, does not mean to deny their existence. "It means that *measurements exist, but are not specified.* That measurements *must* exist is an essential part of the process. The principle is: the relevant measurements must exist in *some* quantity, but may exist in *any* quantity."[13]

Now let us work through another of Miss Rand's examples: the formation of the concept "table." Although this involves the same process, it is more complex to analyze, because the concept of an entity requires measurement-omission in regard to several attributes.

The child differentiates tables from other objects on the basis of a distinctive perceptual shape. All tables have a flat, level surface and support(s), and look, schematically, like this: π. In order to reach the concept, the child's mind must retain this characteristic, while omitting *"all* particular measurements, not only the measurements of the shape, but of all the other characteristics of tables (many of which he is not aware of at the time)."[14]

The concept "table" omits every measurement which, as an adult, one would have to specify in order to reproduce any particular table. The concept omits the geometric measurements of the shape of the surface—whether it is round, square, oblong, and so on. (One measures shapes, ultimately, by reducing them to the terms of linear measurement.) In addition, the concept omits the number of supports. It omits the measurements of the shape of the supports and of their position in relation to the surface (whether there is one cylindrical leg at the center, four rectilinear legs in the corners, etc.). It omits the measurements of size (within an appropriate range; e.g., tables can vary in height, but cannot be as tall as a skyscraper). It omits the measurements of weight, color, temperature, and the like.

The concept "table" integrates all tables, past, present, and future, regardless of these variations among them. How can it do so? When we form the concept, we retain all the above characteristics—there must be a surface of some shape, the legs must have some position in relation to the top, the object must have some height, weight, and so on; but the varying measurements of the characteristics are not specified. From *this* perspective tables are interchangeable, and one is able to form a mental unit that subsumes all of them.

Neither a child nor an adult knows all the characteristics of tables. For example, a child forming "table" may not yet have discovered the attribute of weight. Speaking literally, such a child cannot omit measurements of weight. His mind, however, is governed by a wordless policy applicable to all future knowledge. This policy, which represents the essence of the conceptual process, amounts to the following: "I know certain attributes of tables. Whatever other attributes I discover, the same process will apply: I will retain the attribute and omit its measurements." In this sense, in the form of an epistemological standing order, the concept may be said to retain *all* the characteristics of its referents and to omit *all* the measurements (these last within an appropriate range). This principle applies even in regard to characteristics unknown at a given stage of development.

The grasp of similarity, as we have seen, is essential to conceptualization. But what is similarity? In ordinary usage, objects are described as similar if they are partly the same, partly not; "similarity" denotes "partial identity, partial difference." In the context of concept-formation, the differences among similar concretes are apparent. The puzzle has been: what is the same? Ayn Rand's profound new answer is that the relationship among similars is mathematical. When two things are similar, what is the same is their characteristic(s); what differs is the magnitude or measurement of these. "[S]imilarity, in this context," she writes, "is the relationship between two or more existents which possess the same characteristic(s), but in different measure or degree."[15]

A man's grasp of similarity is actually his mind's grasp of a mathematical fact: the fact that certain concretes are commensurable—that they (or their attributes) are reducible to the same unit(s) of measurement. A man can relate such concretes to one another, bracketing them mentally into the same group, because his mind can relate each one quantitatively to the same standard; the only difference is the measurement of this relationship in the several instances. Given this perspective his mind, in order to proceed to form a new unit, need merely refrain from specifying the measurements.

Such is the essence of abstraction, according to Objectivism: men abstract attributes or characteristics *from their measurements.* The result is an outlook on existents that permits a new scale of integration.

The process of measurement-omission is performed for us by the nature of our mental faculty, whether anyone identifies it or not. To form a concept, one does not have to know that a form of measurement is involved; one does not have to measure existents or even know *how* to measure them. On the conscious level, one need merely observe similarities.[16]

Measurement as a conscious process presupposes a substantial conceptual development. It presupposes that one has already conceptualized separate attributes, knows how to count, and has defined suitable units and a method of relating objects to them in numerical terms. The measurement involved in forming concepts, however, which may be described as "implicit" measurement, does not require such knowledge.

When we (first) conceptualize, we focus on an attribute *perceptually,* not conceptually. Nor do we need a knowledge of numbers: for concept-formation, we need to discover commensurability, not specific quantitative data; the essence of the process is the omission of such data. To discover commensurability, we need to observe variations in degree or amount, such as longer/much longer/shorter/much shorter, and the same for hotter/colder, lighter/darker, rougher/smoother, and so on. Such variations are observed well before we know how to measure them explicitly or precisely. For example, we can *see* that some objects extend further or much further than others from a given point, before we know numbers or the concepts "length" or "foot." In the act of apprehending such a continuum of more-or-less, we are grasping the place within it of any particular length. We are thus grasping—in implicit, approximate form—that particular length's quantitative relationship to other instances of length. For this purpose, *any* perceived instance can serve as the standard. In other words, in the process of concept-formation, any perceived unit of the future concept can serve as the unit of measurement. (Any perceived length can serve as the base to which other lengths are implicitly related as more or less.)

Such is the means by which we are able to grasp, without the need of numbers or any other antecedent concepts, that all the relevant concretes are reducible to a common unit.

To learn how to express in numerical terms the implicit measurements involved in concept-formation is a later development, which is sometimes relatively simple and sometimes not. It was relatively simple, for example, once men had acquired a conceptual vocabulary, for them to demarcate "foot" or some equivalent as a unit of length and learn how to deploy a ruler. But an advanced science was required to discover a unit by which to measure colors (the wavelengths of light); or to discover a method of measuring the area of complex curvilinear figures (such a method is provided by integral calculus).

A form of measurement, in sum, makes concept-formation possible—and concepts in turn make numerical measurement possible. This interdependence reflects a fundamental fact about human cognition: the perspective essential to both processes—the quantitative reduction to a unit—is the same.

So far, we have been considering measurement primarily in regard to the integration of concretes. Measurement also plays a special role in the first step of concept-formation: the differentiation of a group from other things.

Such differentiation cannot be performed arbitrarily. For example, one can form a concept by distinguishing tables from chairs, but not by distinguishing tables from red objects. There is no basis on which to bring these two sets of concretes together before the mind, and no way to identify a relationship between them. The reason is that the relationships required for concept-formation are established quantitatively, by means of (implicit) measurements—and there is no unit of measurement common to table-shaped objects and red objects. The attributes of shape and color are *incommensurable.*

Miss Rand proceeds to develop the concept of the Conceptual Common Denominator (for short, the CCD). The CCD is "the characteristic(s) reducible to a unit of measurement, by means of which man differentiates two or more existents from other existents possessing it."[17] For example, one can differentiate tables from chairs or beds, because all these groups possess a commensurable characteristic, shape. This CCD, in turn, determines what feature must be chosen as the distinguishing characteristic of the concept "table": tables are distinguished by a specific *kind* of shape, which represents a specific category or set of geometric measurements within the characteristic of shape—as against beds, e.g., whose shapes are encompassed by a different set of measurements. (Once the appropriate category has been specified, one completes the process of forming "table" by omitting the measurements of the individual table shapes within that category.)

The above is merely a passing mention of a complex topic, but it indicates from a new aspect the mathematical basis of concept-formation. Measurement is essential to both parts of the process. We can differentiate groups only by reference to a commensurable characteristic(s); and we can integrate into a unit only concretes whose differences are differences in measurement. No aspect of the process is capricious. In both its parts, concept-formation depends on our mind's recognition of objective, mathematical relationships.

Ayn Rand's formal definition of "concept" condenses into a sentence every key idea discussed above. "A concept is a mental integration of two or more units possessing the same distinguishing characteristic(s), with their particular measurements omitted."[18]

In her treatise, Miss Rand covers all the main kinds of concepts, including concepts of motion, relationships, and materials. In each case, she explains how the principle of measurement-omission applies. Instead of pursuing this illustrative material, I want to turn to another question. Since the mind omits measurements whether a man knows it or not, one may ask, what is the practical purpose of the Objectivist theory of concepts?

In part, the answer is that philosophers have to know the mathematical aspects of concept-formation in order to define the rules to guide the conscious aspects of a thought process, the ones that *are* within men's deliberate, volitional control.

In deeper part, however, the answer is that the theory of measurement-omission is essential to the validation of conceptual knowledge and, therefore, to the validation of reason itself. In the long run, a scientific civilization cannot survive without such validation. So long as men remain ignorant of their basic mental process, they have no answer to the charge, leveled by mysticism and skepticism alike, that their mental content is some form of revelation or invention detached from reality. This kind of viewpoint can go into remission for a while, thanks to the remnants of a better past. Ultimately, however, if it is not burned out of men's souls completely by an explicit philosophic theory, it becomes the most virulent of cancers; it metastasizes to every branch of philosophy and every department of a culture, as is now evident throughout the world. Then the best among men become paralyzed by doubt; while the others turn into the mindless hordes that march in any irrationalist era looking for someone to rule them.

A proper theory of concepts is not sufficient to save the world. But it *is* necessary. The fact that concepts are valid tools of cognition whether we know it or not will not save us—not unless we *do* know it.

What the Objectivist theory of concepts accomplishes practically is the defense of man's mind on the level of fundamentals, along with the philosophic disarmament of its worst enemies. The key to this historic achievement lies in Ayn Rand's demonstration that concepts *are* based on and *do* refer to the facts of reality.

> Now [she writes] we can answer the question: To what precisely do we refer when we designate three persons as "men"? We refer to the fact that they are living beings who possess the *same* characteristic distinguishing them from all other living species: a rational faculty—though the specific measurements of their distinguishing characteristic *qua* men, as well as of all their other characteristics *qua* living beings, are different. (As living beings of a certain kind, they possess innumerable characteristics in common: the same shape, the same range of size, the same facial features, the same vital organs, the same fingerprints, etc., and all these characteristics differ only in their measurements.)[19]

A concept is not a product of arbitrary choice, whether personal or social; it has a basis in reality. But the basis is not a supernatural entity transcending concretes or a secret ingredient lurking within them. "Manness," to keep to the same example, is *men,* the real men who exist, past, present, and future; it is men viewed from a certain perspective.

A concept denotes facts—as processed by a human method. Nor does the method introduce any cognitive distortion. The concept does not omit or alter any characteristic of its referents. It includes every fact about them, including the fact that they are commensurable. It merely refrains from specifying the varying relations they sustain to a unit(s).

The answer to the "problem of universals" lies in Ayn Rand's discovery of the relationship between universals and mathematics. Specifically, the answer lies in the brilliant comparison she draws between concept-formation and algebra.

This is more than a mere comparison, as she shows, since the underlying method in both fields is the same.

> The basic principle of concept-formation (which states that the omitted measurements must exist in *some* quantity, but may exist in *any* quantity) is the equivalent of the basic principle of algebra, which states that algebraic symbols must be given *some* numerical value, but may be given *any* value. In this sense and respect, perceptual awareness is the arithmetic, but *conceptual awareness is the algebra of cognition.*
>
> The relationship of concepts to their constituent particulars is the same as the relationship of algebraic symbols to numbers. In the equation *2a = a + a,* any number may be substituted for the symbol *"a"* without affecting the truth of the equation. For instance: 2 × 5 = 5 + 5, or: 2 × 5,000,000 = 5,000,000 + 5,000,000. In the same manner, by the same psycho-epistemological method, a concept is used as an algebraic symbol that stands for *any* of the arithmetical sequence of units it subsumes.
>
> Let those who attempt to invalidate concepts by declaring that they cannot find "manness" in men, try to invalidate algebra by declaring that they cannot find *"a*-ness" in 5 or in 5,000,000.[20]

For centuries, rationalist philosophers have venerated mathematics as the model of cognition. What they have admired about the discipline is its deductive method. Objectivism, too, regards mathematics as an epistemological model, but for a different reason.

The mathematician is the exemplar of conceptual integration. He does professionally and in numerical terms what the rest of us do implicitly and have done since childhood, to the extent that we exercise our distinctive human capacity.

Mathematics *is* the substance of thought writ large, as the West has been told from Pythagoras to Bertrand Russell; it does provide a unique window into human nature. What the window reveals, however, is not the barren constructs of rationalistic tradition, but man's method of extrapolating from observed data to the total of the universe.

What the window of mathematics reveals is not the mechanics of deduction, but of *induction.* Such is Ayn Rand's unprecedented and pregnant identification in the field of epistemology.

Concepts of Consciousness as Involving Measurement-Omission

So far, we have discussed first-level concepts, as we may call them. A "first-level" concept, such as "table" or "man," is one formed directly from perceptual data. Starting from this base, concept-formation proceeds by a process of abstracting *from abstractions.* The result is (increasingly) higher-level concepts, which cannot be formed directly from perceptual data, but only from earlier concepts. For example, a child may integrate first-level concepts into wider ones, which identify more extensive knowledge, such as integrating "cat," "dog," "horse" into "animal" (and later, "animal," "plant," "man" into "living organism"). Or he may subdivide first-level concepts into narrower ones, which identify more precise differentiations, such as subdividing "man" according to profession, into "doctor," "policeman," "teacher" (and later "doctor" into "children's doctor," "dentist," "surgeon," etc.).

Higher-level concepts represent a relatively advanced state of knowledge. They represent knowledge available only to a mind that has already engaged in the requisite conceptualization. For instance, a child just emerging from the perceptual period cannot start conceptualizing by uniting his father, his dog, and a rosebush into the concept "organism." Only when the child has first conceptualized separately the various perceptually given entities is he capable of the more extensive acts of abstraction and integration that identify *their* common denominators. These latter are not available on the perceptual level, because only concretes exist: there are no such things as "organisms" to be seen—there are only men, dogs, roses. Similarly, a child cannot identify distinctions among men—he cannot grasp *types of men,* such as doctor or teacher—until he has first grasped and conceptualized man.[21]

The process of abstracting from abstractions continues on successively higher levels, each representing a greater (extensive or intensive) knowledge than the preceding level and presupposing a longer chain of earlier concepts. Concepts, therefore, differ from one another not only in their referents, but also in their *distance from the perceptual level.* The epistemological implications of this fact will be developed in the next chapter.

The subject of higher-level concepts, including the role of measurement-omission in such cases, is covered in chapter 3 of *Introduction to Objectivist Epistemology.* Since a proper theory must explain every kind of concept, I want to turn here to another kind: concepts of consciousness, such as "thought," "memory," and "love."

(In one sense, all concepts of consciousness are higher-level abstractions, since none can be formed without an abundance of earlier existential concepts. Given the latter, however, many concepts of consciousness may correctly be described as "first-level," since they are formed directly from one's observations of the mental state involved, with no previous concepts of consciousness being required.)

In general, concepts of consciousness are formed by the same method as existential concepts. The key to this realm lies in the fact that every process of consciousness involves two fundamental attributes, content and action.

"Content" here means the object of consciousness, that of which it is aware, whether by extrospection or introspection. Directly or indirectly, the object must be some aspect of existence; even states of consciousness can be grasped ultimately only in relation to the external world. "Action" here means the action of consciousness in regard to its content, such as thinking, remembering, imagining. Awareness, as we know, is not a passive condition, but a process of continuous activity.

The formation of the concept "thought" will illustrate the role of these two attributes in the present context.

Let us assume that a child has learned to speak and often performs the activity of thinking; now he is ready to conceptualize that activity. By what steps does he do it? (The same answer will apply whether a child learns the concept from others, as most people do, or reaches it on his own. In the former case, he must retrace the steps that others performed before him; otherwise the word "thought," to him, will be merely a memorized sound unrelated to his own knowledge or to clearly defined facts.)

As in the case of forming existential concepts, the child

begins by observing similarities and differences—similarities uniting several instances of thinking and differentiating them from his other mental activities. In the present context, observation means a process of introspection, i.e., of looking inward and directing one's cognitive focus to the facts of one's own consciousness.

The child, let us say, is given a problem in arithmetic at school; he tackles it by asking himself a series of questions, each answer leading to the next step, until he reaches the solution. So far, he is thinking, but not yet conceptualizing the activity. Then he goes home to play, but finds that his wagon is broken; again, he asks a series of questions, learning in experimental stages, say, as one strategy of repair suggests a better one. This kind of process recurs often. In each instance, although the content varies, there is a similarity he can note: a certain kind of purposeful pursuit of knowledge.

During the school assignment, the child may have felt dismay; during the wagon episode, excitement. In the first case, he may have produced little imagery; in the second, imagery may have been vivid and abundant. What the child needs to grasp, however, is that the similarity uniting the thinking processes differentiates them from these other mental activities, which may or may not accompany any given instance. At this point, the child has isolated several instances of thinking. These are the first units of his future concept.

Despite their similarities, the instances differ in various ways. What is required now, therefore, is an act of abstraction, i.e., of measurement-omission. In regard to a thought process, this involves two aspects.

One pertains to content. Thought is thought regardless of its content; the latter is a variable not specified in the concept. The concept "thought" thus omits all measurements that distinguish one content from another. (Content is a measurable attribute, because it is ultimately some aspect of the external world. As such, it is measurable by the methods applicable to physical existents.)

The second measurable attribute of thought is its *intensity*. "The intensity of a psychological process," writes Miss Rand, "is the automatically summed up result of many factors: of its scope, its clarity, its cognitive and motivational context, the degree of mental energy or effort required, etc."[22]

Thought processes, to continue the example, vary in the scope of the material they encompass, and (a related issue) in the length of the conceptual chain required to deal with such material, which indicates the amount a man had to know in order to perform a given process. Some thoughts deal with broad aspects of reality and involve complex abstractions from abstractions; other thoughts deal with fewer elements and employ concepts that are closer to the perceptual level. For instance, contrast thinking about the principles of concept-formation with thinking about the outfit you will wear to work tomorrow. The dimensions—the size, if you will—of the first process are vastly greater. The first, Ayn Rand says, is more intense than the second.

We are describing thought here in quantitative terms: we are speaking of more or less—of how many elements and how much one has to know. We are thus locating thought processes on a continuum of intensity and comparing them to one another by means of approximate measurement. As we know, this is all that is required for conceptualization; the latter does not involve the use of numbers.

There are other measurable aspects of the intensity of a thought process, such as the degree of effort a given thinker expends on it or the degree of clarity his thought attains—and different factors are involved in measuring the intensity of other kinds of mental processes. I have merely suggested the beginnings of an example. (A fuller discussion of concepts of consciousness can be found in chapter 4 of *Introduction to Objectivist Epistemology*.) But it is enough to indicate that the instances of a thought process vary in the measurements both of their content and of their intensity. Yet the concept "thought" subsumes *all* such instances. What makes such an integration possible? Our minds omit the measurements, retaining thereby only the characteristics of every unit, which are the same.

Here is Ayn Rand's formulation of the general principle in this realm:

> A concept pertaining to consciousness is a mental integration of two or more instances of a psychological process possessing the same distinguishing characteristics, with the particular contents and the measurements of the action's

intensity omitted—on the principle that these omitted measurements must exist in *some* quantity, but may exist in *any* quantity (i.e., a given psychological process must possess *some* content and *some* degree of intensity, but may possess *any* content or degree of the appropriate category).[23]

Some concepts of consciousness do not denote psychological processes. For example, there are concepts that denote *products* of psychological processes (such as "knowledge," "science," "concept"); one subcategory of them is concepts that denote *methods*, such as "logic." These kinds of concepts (which are touched on in Ayn Rand's treatise) are essential to human development—and to philosophy. Epistemology is concerned only with methodology; one of its basic tasks is to analyze the concept of "concept."

In addition to the above, Miss Rand observes, there is

the vast and complex category of concepts that represent integrations of existential concepts with concepts of consciousness, a category that includes most of the concepts pertaining to man's actions. Concepts of this category have no direct referents on the perceptual level of awareness (though they include perceptual components) and can neither be formed nor grasped without a long antecedent chain of concepts.[24]

For example, the concept "friendship" denotes a relationship between two people, one that involves a certain pattern of behavior flowing from a certain kind of mutual estimate. This concept cannot be formed or grasped merely by observing what the individuals do or how much time they spend together. It requires that their actions be integrated with several concepts of consciousness, such as "value," "interest," and "affection."

Since ethics, politics, and esthetics are all concerned with human actions insofar as they are directed by conscious choices and standards, concepts involving the above type of integration are especially prominent in philosophy. As we proceed, we will be analyzing them regularly.

Definition as the Final Step in Concept-Formation

The final step in concept-formation is definition. This step is essential to every concept except axiomatic concepts and concepts denoting sensations.

The perceptual level of consciousness is automatically related to reality; a sense perception is a direct awareness of a concrete existent. A concept, however, is an integration that rests on a process of abstraction. Such a mental state is not automatically related to concretes, as is evident from the many obvious cases of "floating abstractions." This is Ayn Rand's term for concepts detached from existents, concepts that a person takes over from other men without knowing what specific units the concepts denote. A floating abstraction is not an integration of factual data; it is a memorized linguistic custom representing in the person's mind a hash made of random concretes, habits, and feelings that blend imperceptibly into other hashes which are the content of other, similarly floating abstractions. The "concepts" of such a mind are not cognitive devices. They are parrotlike imitations of language backed in essence by patches of fog.

If a concept is to be a device of cognition, it must be tied to reality. It must denote units that one has methodically isolated from all others. This, in Ayn Rand's words, is the basic function of a definition: "to distinguish a concept from all other concepts and thus to keep its units differentiated from all other existents."[25]

In the early years, a child keeps his concepts tied to reality by the simple method of "ostensive" definition; he points to instances. He says: "By 'table,' I mean *this*." At a certain stage, however, this method ceases to work. The child acquires too many concepts, and increasingly they are higher-level abstractions, often involving concepts of consciousness. His abstract structure thus becomes so complex that the mere act of pointing will not differentiate the units of one concept from those of all others. This is the point at which formal definitions, which identify explicitly the nature of a concept's units, become necessary. (Axiomatic concepts and concepts denoting sensations can only be defined ostensively.)

A definition cannot list all the characteristics of the units; such a catalogue would be too large to retain. Instead, a definition identifies a concept's units by specifying their *essential* characteristics. The "essential" characteristic(s) is the fundamental characteristic(s) which makes the units the kind of existents they are and differentiates them from all other known existents. (This definition will become clear as we proceed.)

A proper definition is made of two parts, each of which follows from the nature of concept-formation. When we form a concept, we isolate its units by grasping a distinguishing characteristic. In the definition, this becomes what the medieval Aristotelians called the *differentia*. Further, we can differentiate only on the basis of a wider characteristic, the CCD, which is shared both by the concretes we are isolating and by the concretes from which we are isolating them. In the definition, this gives rise to the *genus*.

A definition in terms of genus and differentia is like a logical X ray of a concept. It condenses into a brief, retainable statement the essence of the concept-forming process: it tells us what distinguishes the units and from what they are being distinguished, i.e., within what wider group the distinction is being made. To give the standard example: if we conceptualize man by differentiating men from dogs, cats, and horses, then "animal" would be the genus—"rational," the differentia.

Since definitions are a step in the process of concept-formation, all their features reflect the nature of that process. Another such feature is the fact that definitions, like concepts, are *contextual*.

Conceptual knowledge is not acquired in a state of total ignorance or from the vantage point of omniscience. At any stage of development, from child to sage and from savage to scientist, man can make conceptual differentiations and integrations only on the basis of prior knowledge, the specific, limited knowledge available to him at that stage. Man's mind functions on the basis of a certain *context*. The context, states Miss Rand, "is the entire field of a mind's awareness or knowledge at any level of its cognitive development."[26]

This fact has profound implications for human knowledge in general (as we will see in chapter 4) and for definitions in particular. Definitions are contextual. Their purpose is to differentiate certain units from all other existents *in a given context of knowledge*. At an early stage, when one has made relatively few discriminations, a simple, obvious characteristic may achieve this purpose. Later, when one discovers new aspects of reality, that same characteristic may no longer serve to differentiate the units; the initial definition must then be revised. Our knowledge grows in stages, and we organize at each stage only the facts that are available.

To illustrate this point, Ayn Rand indicates the pattern by which the definition of "man" might develop as a child's cognitive context expands. The child's first (implicit) definition might amount to: "a thing that moves and makes sounds." If the child grasps only household objects and the people around him, this definition is valid: it does separate men from the other entities, such as tables and chairs, which the child knows. Then the child discovers cats and dogs. In this context, he must revise his definition, because it no longer separates the units from the entities he now knows. The first definition remains true as a description of men—men do still move and make sounds—but it can no longer serve as a definition of "man." Now the child might define "man" (implicitly) as "a living thing that walks on two legs and has no fur." This would be a valid definition within the new context. The same pattern applies to all the later stages of defining "man." It applies to most definitions as knowledge expands.[27]

When a definition is contextually revised, *the new definition does not contradict the old one.* The facts identified in the old definition remain facts; the knowledge earlier gained remains knowledge. What changes is that, as one's field of knowledge expands, these facts no longer serve to differentiate the units. The new definition does not invalidate the content of the old; it merely refines a distinction in accordance with the demands of a growing cognitive context.

Although the definition of "man" is dependent on context, we *can* determine an objective definition of "man," one that is universally valid. A universally valid definition—in this case, "rational animal"—is one that has been determined according to the widest context of human knowledge available to date. Miss Rand states the principle as applied to any concept: "An objective definition, valid for all men, is one that designates the *essential* distinguishing characteristic(s) and genus of the existents subsumed under a given concept—

according to all the relevant knowledge available at that stage of mankind's development."[28]

Although definitions are contextual, they are not arbitrary. The correct definition at any stage is determined by the facts of reality. Given any specific set of entities to be differentiated, it is the actual nature of the entities that determines the distinguishing characteristics. For example, once a child discovers dogs and cats, he cannot decide to retain his earlier definition. Since dogs and cats also move and make sounds, he must seek out new characteristics of men, ones that do differentiate them from such creatures. These characteristics are not a matter of caprice; they are determined by the facts about men, dogs, and cats, so far as one is able to observe and identify such facts. Definitions (like all truths) are thus "empirical" statements. They derive from certain kinds of observations—those that serve a specific (differentiating) function within the conceptualizing process.

Definitions are determined by the facts of reality—within the context of one's knowledge. Both aspects of this statement are crucial: reality *and* the context of knowledge; existence *and* consciousness.

A further rule of definition is necessary to clarify fully the concept of an "essential" characteristic: the rule of *fundamentality.*[29]

This rule applies when the units of a concept are observed to have more than one distinctive characteristic. The definition must then state the feature that most significantly distinguishes the units; it must state the fundamental. "Fundamental" here means the characteristic responsible for all the rest of the units' distinctive characteristics, or at least for a greater number of these than any other characteristic is. The definitional principle is: wherever possible, an essential characteristic must be a fundamental.

For example, one could not define "man" as an entity possessing a thumb, even if this feature were distinctive to man. If men had no thumbs but were otherwise the same as they are now, the species would still have to be conceptualized and defined; there would still be profound differences between man and other creatures. When one defines by fundamentals, however—e.g., when one defines "man" by reference to "rationality"—the definition identifies the root of the largest set of man's distinctive characteristics. It thus names that which most significantly sets man apart. It names that which "makes" man man, i.e., that which underlies and carries with it the greatest number of distinctively human characteristics.

The opposite of the principle of fundamentality is exemplified in certain kinds of psychotic thinking. One schizophrenic in New York City's Bellevue Hospital routinely equated sex, cigars, and Jesus Christ. He regarded all these existents, both in his thought and in his feelings about them, as interchangeable members of a single class, on the grounds that all had an attribute in common, "encirclement." In sex, he explained, the woman is encircled by the man; cigars are encircled by tax bands; Jesus is encircled by a halo. This individual, in effect, was trying to form a new concept, "encirclist." Such an attempt is a cognitive disaster, which can lead only to confusion, distortion, and falsehood. Imagine studying cigars and then applying one's conclusions to Jesus!

This mode of thought is calamitous because "being encircled" is *not* a fundamental; it is not causally significant; it does not lead to any consequences. It is a dead end. Groups erected on such a basis necessarily lead to cognitive stultification.

To define a valid concept in terms of nonfundamentals is to commit a similar error. Such a practice evades the actual basis of the concept, the root similarity uniting its instances, and substitutes instead an insignificant resemblance. This evasion converts a legitimate concept into the epistemological equivalent of "encirclist" and confounds the very purpose of conceptualization.

A definition in terms of fundamentals can be formulated only by reference to one's full knowledge of the units. In order to identify a fundamental distinguishing characteristic (and a fundamental integrating characteristic—the genus), one must take into account *all* the known facts in the case. One must bear in mind how the units differ from other things, how they resemble other things, and what causal relationships obtain within these two sets of attributes. Only on this basis can one establish that a certain characteristic is fundamental (within that context of knowledge).

Although a definition states only a few of the units' characteristics, therefore, it *implies* all the other characteristics one knows. It does so because this is the knowledge that determines and validates the definition. "As a legal preamble (referring here to *epistemological* law)," Ayn Rand notes, "every definition begins with the implicit proposition: 'After full consideration of all the known facts pertaining to this group of existents, the following has been demonstrated to be their essential, therefore defining, characteristic. . . .' "[30]

A definition is not an arbitrary selection of several of the units' features. On the contrary, a proper definition is a condensation, which implicitly includes *all* the known features. "A definition," writes Miss Rand, "is the condensation of a vast body of observations—and stands or falls with the truth or falsehood of these observations."[31]

Such condensation is indispensable if concepts are to achieve their cognitive purpose. The function of a definition, we have said, is to enable man to retain concepts (as against floating abstractions) in his mind. To retain a concept, however—to keep its units clearly distinguished—and then to use the concept in a cognitive process, one must be able to retain and make use of the wealth of data one has learned about the units. But one cannot hold data in mind in the form of an endless catalogue of unrelated items. What is required, therefore, is a deliberate cognitive processing of the units. What is required is a survey and analysis of similarities, differences, causal relationships, culminating in the selection of an *essential* characteristic, which serves to condense the total.

Such a characteristic, by virtue of its method of selection, is an invaluable tool of integration. It reduces a complex sum of features to a few relatively simple elements, expressed in the form of a brief, retainable statement.

A definition in terms of nonessentials achieves the opposite result. If one arbitrarily picks some distinguishing feature as definitional, then it does not proceed from any cognitive processing and does not carry with it the units' other features. Instead of condensing and enabling man to retain data, such a definition splinters and works to obliterate data. It fosters a grasp not of a concept's units, but merely of an isolated characteristic(s), one unconnected in the definer's mind to the other features of the units. If one were to define "man" by reference to his thumb, for example, the concept would become equivalent in one's mind to "some kind of thumb-haver"—while all man's other characteristics would be relegated to a limbo of the unprocessed, unrelated, and ultimately unretained. Such an approach works to detach a concept from its units; it turns a concept into a floating abstraction. The result is not to clarify a concept, but to invalidate it, along with any proposition that uses it.

The truth of a proposition depends not only on its relation to the facts of the case, but also on the truth of the definitions of its constituent concepts. If these concepts are detached from reality—whether through lack of any definition or through definition by nonessentials—then so are the propositions that employ them. A proposition can have no greater validity—no more of a relation to reality—than do the concepts that make it up. The precondition of the quest for truth, therefore, is the formulation of proper definitions. "The truth or falsehood of all of man's conclusions, inferences, thought, and knowledge," Miss Rand concludes, "rests on the truth or falsehood of his definitions."[32]

There is one sure sign that a man has failed to formulate proper definitions: his claim that a concept is interchangeable with its definition. This claim, widespread among modern philosophers, is a confession. It indicates that concepts, in such minds, do not stand for existents, but for random, floating characteristics.

A concept is *not* interchangeable with its definition—not even if the definition (thanks to the work of other men) happens to be correct.[33] "Man," for example, does not mean "animality" plus "rationality." It is not a shorthand tag substituting for two other words. It does not mean "anything whatever that has the characteristics of rationality and animality, no matter whether it has two legs or ten, requires oxygen or methane, is covered with skin or with fur." This approach to concepts is a brazen prescription for disintegration. It demands that one drop one's knowledge of everything about the units except the characteristics mentioned in the definition.

A concept designates existents, including *all their characteristics,* whether definitional or not. As an aid to the conceptualizing process, men select from the total content of the concept a few characteristics; they select the ones that best condense and differentiate that content at a given stage of human development. Such a selection in no way shrinks the concept's content; on the contrary, it presupposes the richness of the concept. It presupposes that the concept is an integration of units, including all their features.

If it is true that man walks on two legs, requires oxygen, and has no fur, then the concept "man" includes and refers to these facts also, even though they are not distinctive to man. Varying definitions of a concept in varying contexts are possible only because the concept means not its definition, but its units.

Just as a concept is not restricted to the defining characteristics, so it is not restricted to the *known* characteristics (a point mentioned earlier). A concept is an integration of units, which are what they are regardless of anyone's knowledge; it stands for *existents,* not for the changing content of consciousness. When we learn more about the units, we are learning about characteristics that the units possess by their nature; all such characteristics are included in the concept from the outset.

The term "man," for example, means not merely some isolated characteristics nor even all the human characteristics we already know; it means an entire (and as yet largely unwritten) library. "Man" means men, including everything true of them—every characteristic that belongs to such an entity in reality, whether discovered so far or not. This essential point Ayn Rand describes as the "open-end" nature of concepts:

> It is crucially important to grasp the fact that a concept is an "open-end" classification which includes the yet-to-be-discovered characteristics of a given group of existents. All of man's knowledge rests on that fact.
>
> The pattern is as follows: when a child grasps the concept "man," the knowledge represented by that concept in his mind consists of perceptual data, such as man's visual appearance, the sound of his voice, etc. When the child learns to differentiate between living entities and inanimate matter, he ascribes a new characteristic, "living," to the entity he designates as "man." When the child learns to differentiate among various types of consciousness, he includes a new characteristic in his concept of man, "ra-

tional''—and so on. The implicit principle guiding this process, is: "I know that there exists such an entity as man; I know many of his characteristics, but he has many others which I do not know and must discover." The same principle directs the study of every other kind of perceptually isolated and conceptualized existents. . . .

Since concepts represent a system of cognitive classification, a given concept serves (speaking metaphorically) as a file folder in which man's mind files his knowledge of the existents it subsumes. The content of such folders varies from individual to individual, according to the degree of his knowledge—it ranges from the primitive, generalized information in the mind of a child or an illiterate to the enormously detailed sum in the mind of a scientist—but it pertains to the same referents, to the same kind of existents, and is subsumed under the same concept. This filing system makes possible such activities as learning, education, research—the accumulation, transmission and expansion of knowledge.[34]

One important implication of the above is that a concept, once formed, does not change. The knowledge men have of the units may grow and the definition may change accordingly, but the concept, the mental integration, remains the same. Otherwise there would be no way to relate new knowledge of an entity to previous knowledge subsumed under an earlier-formed concept—because the concept would have changed; the file folder itself would be different. In addition, no two people's concept of the same entity would be the same if their knowledge varied, which would make communication impossible, and along with it education and the cognitive division of labor. All such activities presuppose the *stability* and *universality* of concepts. "Universality" here does not mean that two different languages necessarily use every concept of the other; it means that all men who do use a given concept are using the *same* one.

(Occasionally, a process of reclassification—a change in the filing system itself—is necessitated by advancing knowledge. Even in such a case, which is rare, a concept does not change, or vary from one man to another. The old concept is simply dropped outright and replaced by a new one.)

Let us sum up by extending Miss Rand's metaphor. The

file folder (the concept) is not the same as the label (the definition) that identifies and condenses the folder's contents. Nor is the folder restricted to its present contents. The folder exists so that we can separate out as a single unit, and then study and interrelate, *all* the data ever to pertain to a given subject. That is precisely what the concept enables us to do.

Concepts as Devices to Achieve Unit-Economy

I have indicated several ways in which concepts expand man's power of knowledge. The fundamental cognitive role of concepts, however, has not yet been discussed. Fundamentally, concepts are devices to achieve *unit-economy*. This idea can be grasped most easily by reference to an experiment with crows that is cited in *Introduction to Objectivist Epistemology*.[35]

The experiment was an attempt to discover the ability of birds to deal with numbers. When crows were gathered in a clearing in some woods, one man entered the clearing and walked on into the woods. As soon as he appeared, the crows hid in the treetops; they would not come out until the man returned and left the area. Then three men entered; again the crows hid. This time only two of the men left, and the crows did not come out; they knew that one still remained. But when five men came and then four left, the crows came out, apparently confident that the danger was now over. These birds, it seems, could discriminate and deal with only three units; beyond that, the units blurred or merged in their consciousness. The crow arithmetic, in effect, would be: 1, 2, 3, many.

This experiment illustrates a principle applicable to man's mind as well. Man too can deal with only a limited number of units. On the perceptual level, human beings are better than crows; we can distinguish and retain six or eight objects at a time, say—speaking *perceptually,* i.e., assuming we see or hear the objects but do not count them. But there is a limit for us, too. After a certain figure—when the objects approach a dozen, to say nothing of hundreds or thousands—we too are unable to keep track and collapse into the crow's indeterminate "many." Our mental screen, so to speak, is limited; it can contain at any one time only so many data.

Consciousness, any consciousness, is finite. A is A. Only a limited number of units can be discriminated from one another and held in the focus of awareness at a given time. Beyond this number, the content becomes an unretainable, indeterminate blur or spread, like this: ///////////////////////////

For a consciousness to extend its grasp beyond a mere handful of concretes, therefore—for it to be able to deal with an enormous totality, like all tables, or all men, or the universe as a whole—one capacity is indispensable. It must have the capacity to compress its content, i.e., to *economize the units* required to convey that content. This is the basic function of concepts. Their function, in Ayn Rand's words, is "to reduce a vast amount of information to a minimal number of units. . . ."[36]

A concept integrates and thus condenses a group of percepts into a single mental whole. It reduces an unlimited number of perceptual units to one new unit, which subsumes them all. It thereby expands profoundly the amount of material that a person can retain and deal with cognitively. Once the term "man" is defined and automatized in your consciousness, for example, the vast sum of its referents is available to you instantly; it is available in a single frame of awareness, without the need of your trying to visualize or describe and then somehow hold in mind all the individual men that are, have been, or will be. One mental unit has taken the place of an endless series, and you can proceed to discover an unlimited knowledge about the entity.

Philosophers often say that concepts are time savers. It is much more instructive to say that concepts are *space* savers.

A consciousness without concepts could not discover even the most elementary fact about man—say, that men have ten fingers. The problem is not merely that one cannot perceive every man, since they are spread across the earth and the centuries. Even if, in imagination, we were to endow a perceptual-level creature with unlimited transportation including time travel, information about all men would still transcend its mental capacity. The creature, let us say, perceives Tom, Dick, and Harry, grasps their hands in one frame of awareness. Then it turns to study Hugh, Victor, and Sally—and loses the first three. Like the crow, it cannot keep six entities discriminated in the focus of its awareness; the new units keep pushing the old ones out of mind; the mental content keeps evaporating. Even if the creature did somehow manage to survey every man, therefore, it still could not grasp any fact about all of them. It has no means of holding such a scale of information.

If the creature could articulate its plight (which would be a contradiction in terms), it would say: "If only my mind had room in one frame of consciousness for such a wealth of data; if only I could squeeze the countless units given successively in perception into a manageable compass; then I would be able to grasp a complex total, and not merely fleeting aspects of it." The translation of this plaint is: "If only I had concepts."

The remark that "A picture is worth a thousand words" has many valid applications. Ayn Rand's epistemology, however, offers us a different perspective. Her theory of concepts teaches, in effect, that "A word is worth a thousand pictures."

Conceptualization, she sums up, "is a *method* of expanding man's consciousness by reducing the number of its content's units—a systematic means to an unlimited integration of cognitive data."[37] Given the claims of today's so-called "drug culture," I cannot resist observing that it is the power of reason, of abstract thought, which in the literal sense expands consciousness—not mind-killing LSD or its like.

The principle of unit-economy is essential not only to the field of concepts, but also, as one might expect, to the field of mathematics.

Numbers have a function similar to that of concepts. When you the reader count a group of entities, each step of the count reduces the amount of material you need to hold in the focus of your consciousness. You grasp the total at each step in the form of a single mental unit: "one," then "two," then "three," and so on. Without counting, a quantity such as "ten" could be held in mind only in the form of ten units, like this: //////////—which you could hardly distinguish from ///////// or ///////////. This is another reason why our creature of a moment ago could not know that men have ten fingers; like the crow, it could grasp merely that the fingers are "many."

The same principle is evident in higher mathematics. An algebraic equation, for example, condenses pages of numerical calculations, reducing them to a single brief formula.

The principle of unit-economy has many further manifestations in the field of concept-formation. Proper definitions, I have said, are condensations, which enable us to retain in a single statement a complex set of the referents' features. Thus definitions, too, are unit reducers. The concept condenses its referents, reduces them to a single mental unit; the definition then condenses their known characteristics; it reduces these to a single statement. And such condensing continues as knowledge grows. A higher-level abstraction, for example, condenses concepts themselves. Thus "furniture" reduces to a single unit such first-level concepts as "chair," "table," and "bed." From start to finish, one cognitive need is evident: the mind's need to compress data into fewer units, so as to be able to deal with an ever-increasing scale of information.

The fact that concepts are devices to satisfy a need of the human mind does not mean that concepts are arbitrary. On the contrary, to achieve their cognitive purpose, concepts must be based on the facts of reality. They must be formed by reference to the mathematical relationships that actually obtain among concretes and defined in terms of objectively essential characteristics. Otherwise, one's power of thought meets its nemesis in such dead ends as "encirclist" or even worse.

Concepts do satisfy a need of man's mind, but they do so because they are not subjective inventions—because they do correspond to reality. Here again, as I remarked about definitions, two elements are critical: the mind *and* reality; consciousness *and* existence.

The principle of unit-economy—or the "crow-epistemology," as Ayn Rand called the principle informally—has many further applications. As one more illustration, consider the issue of literary style. Some styles are praised as economical; the writer communicates a complex content by means of relatively few words. Other writers are prolix, weighing our consciousness down with more units than the content requires. At the evil extreme of this continuum is the writer who deliberately flouts the crow-epistemology; he seeks to subvert the reader's consciousness by loading it methodically with more units than it can hold. For example, he gives you a seemingly endless sentence, with a jungle of qualifications, subordinate clauses, and parenthetical remarks erupting in the middle, all of which you must plow through and try to retain while you are still holding the subject of the main clause and waiting for the verb. After a few pages of such prose, the reader's mind simply closes, and the words turn into meaningless verbiage. That is the crow-epistemology asserting itself. When the number of units on his mental screen becomes excessive, then, like the crow, man becomes helpless.

Logically enough, the world master of the anti-economy style is, in regard to the content of his ideas, the world's greatest subverter of the conceptual faculty. For evidence of both points, consult the *Critique of Pure Reason*.

■   ■   ■   ■

Ayn Rand regarded her theory of concepts as proved, but not as completed. There are, she thought, important similarities between concepts and mathematics still to be identified; and there is much to be learned about man's mind by a proper study of man's brain and nervous system. In her last years, Miss Rand was interested in following up these ideas—in relating the field of conceptualization to two others: higher mathematics and neurology. Her ultimate goal was to integrate in one theory the branch of philosophy that studies man's cognitive faculty with the science that reveals its essential method and the science that studies its physical organs. Unfortunately, she did not live long enough to pursue this goal systematically. All she could do was to leave us some tantalizing but fragmentary leads indicating the direction in which epistemology should be developed in the future.[38]

Such leads are beyond our province here. What we must do is to apply the Objectivist theory of concepts, as Ayn Rand herself did, to the crucial questions of epistemology. We need to learn not only when (and when not) to form concepts, but above all, once they are formed, how to *use* concepts properly in the quest for knowledge.

4

OBJECTIVITY

According to Objectivism, epistemology is necessary for practical purposes, as a guide to man in the proper use of his conceptual faculty. We are ready to concretize this claim. We can now begin to identify the rules men must follow in their thinking if knowledge, rather than error or delusion, is their goal.

These rules can be condensed into one general principle: thinking, to be valid, must adhere to reality. Or, in the memorable words of the old *Dragnet* TV series, which can serve as the motto of all reality-oriented thought: "Just give us the facts, ma'am." But how does one reach "just the facts"? The answer lies in the concept of *objectivity;* it requires that one grasp the full philosophic meaning and implications of this concept.

When you grasp this concept, you will have an invaluable tool enabling you to assess and, if necessary, improve the quality of your own thinking. You will also understand why, out of all the possibilities, Ayn Rand chose to call her philosophy "Objectivism."

Concepts as Objective

The concept of "objective," which applies as a norm to all rational cognition, has its roots in the theory of concepts. "Objectivity" arises because concepts are formed by a specific process and, as a result, bear a specific kind of relationship to reality.

The conceptual faculty is an instrument that reduces units by omitting measurements. Or: concepts are a human method—of integrating perceptual data. Or: concepts are a device of our consciousness—to deal with existents. All these formulations point to a crucial fact. Concepts do not pertain to consciousness alone or to existence alone; they are products of a *specific kind of relationship* between the two. Abstractions are products of man's faculty of cognition and would not exist without it. But a faculty of cognition is concerned to grasp reality and must, therefore, adhere *to* reality.

On the one hand, there is a uniquely human contribution to the conceptual level of awareness, one that has no counterpart in the process of sense perception. In contrast to perception, conceptualization is not an automatic reaction to stimuli; it is not a passive gazing that awaits the infallible imprinting on the mind of some external entity. Concept-formation and use is precisely the realm that is not automatic or infallible, but volitional. In order to conceptualize, a man must expend effort; he must engage in the kind of mental work that no stimulus can necessitate. He must struggle to relate, connect, *process* an ever-growing range of data—and he must learn to do it correctly. Further: in such processing, the basic method he uses, measurement-omission, is dictated by the nature of *his* cognitive faculty, not by reality. The result is a human perspective on things, not a revelation of a special sort of entity or attribute intrinsic in the world apart from man. Take away the mechanism of human consciousness, and the realm of concepts, universals, abstractions is thereby erased. The concretes that exist, the objects of *perception*, would still remain—as concretes; but the perspective that regards them as units would be gone.

On the other hand, consciousness is the faculty of grasping that which is, and there *is* a metaphysical basis for concepts. There is something the same in reality about the units of a concept: their characteristics, which differ in various instances only in regard to their measurements. This is a fact about the concretes, not a creation of man. We can integrate perceptual entities into a mental unit only because these entities actually possess the same characteristics. We can treat existents as the same in a specified respect only because they *are* the same in that respect.

Concepts are condensations of data formed by a volitional process in accordance with a human method. The method is "human" because it expresses man's distinctive form of consciousness; it arises because of the nature and cognitive needs of man's mind. At the same time, the method (properly employed) conforms at each step to facts; otherwise it would be irrelevant to a *cognitive* need. Man, therefore, cannot project the products of this method outward, into reality apart from man—nor can he detach them from reality, either. Such products represent a special kind of union: they represent reality as processed by a volitional human consciousness. This is the status that Ayn Rand describes as *objective*. (A formal definition of the term is offered in the next section.)

The element of volition is crucial here. Percepts, too, are products of a relationship between existence and consciousness: they are a grasp of entities in a specific sensory form. But percepts are automatic; although they require a sequence of physiological steps, they involve no deliberate method of cognition and cannot depart from reality. Normative terms, therefore, such as "objective" and "nonobjective," are inapplicable to them.

If someone asks: where is a perceptual object, e.g., a man? it is accurate, even though we do perceive in a certain form, to answer: the object is out there, in the world. But if someone asks: where is a conceptual object, e.g., manness? Ayn Rand answers: such an object is neither "in the world" nor "in the eye of the beholder." Manness or any other "universal," she holds, *is* facts of the world, it is concretes—as reduced to a unit not by the eye, but by the mind of a conceptual being.

Now let us apply this discussion to another aspect of the theory of concepts: the status of essences (as the term is used in the context of the theory of definition).

On the one hand, according to Objectivism, essences are not attributes marked out by nature apart from man. "Essential" is not a metaphysical, but an epistemological term.[1] "Essential" designates characteristics that perform a certain function in connection with human conceptualization. The function is to differentiate and condense various bodies of data, and the characteristics that perform this function in one cognitive context may not do so in another. Since the category of "essence" arises because of a need of man's consciousness, the "essential" in each context has to reflect the state of human knowledge.

Since definitions *are* condensations of observed data, however, they are determined by such data; they are not arbitrary; they flow from the facts of the case. In this respect, as we have seen, definitions are "empirical" statements, and reality *is* the standard of what is essential.

Definitions are statements of factual data—as condensed by a human consciousness in accordance with the needs of a human method of cognition. Like concepts, therefore, essences are products of a volitional relationship between existence and consciousness; they too (properly formed) are *objective*.

In the traditional (Platonic and Aristotelian) viewpoint, every entity must have an essence or definition. This is not true in the Objectivist viewpoint. Since the designation of essentials arises only as an aid to the conceptualizing process, it is inapplicable apart from that process. Concretes that have not been integrated into a concept have no "essence"; in these cases, there is no need or possibility of a definition.

As Miss Rand points out, it is mandatory to conceptualize certain types of concretes, including:

(a) the perceptual concretes with which men deal daily, represented by the first level of abstractions; (b) new discoveries of science; (c) new man-made objects which differ in their essential characteristics from the previously known objects (e.g., "television"); (d) complex human relationships involving combinations of physical and psychological behavior (e.g., "marriage," "law," "justice").

These four categories represent existents with which men have to deal constantly, in many different contexts, from many different aspects, either in daily physical action or, more crucially, in mental action and further study. The mental weight of carrying these existents in one's head by means of perceptual images or lengthy verbal descriptions is such that no human mind could handle it. The need of condensation, of unit-reduction, is obvious in such cases.[2]

In other cases, Miss Rand points out, the opposite is true. It is impermissible to integrate certain concretes into a concept, because this would contradict, rather than satisfy, the requirements of cognition.

For example, there is no concept to designate "Beautiful blondes with blue eyes, 5'5" tall and 24 years old." Such entities or groupings are identified *descriptively* [by the use of several previously formed concepts, rather than by a single new one]. If such a special concept existed, it would lead to senseless duplication of cognitive effort (and to conceptual chaos): everything of significance discovered about that group would apply to all other young women as well. There would be no cognitive justification for such a concept—unless some *essential* characteristic were discovered, distinguishing such blondes from all other women and requiring special study, in which case a special concept would become necessary.

. . . Just as the requirements of cognition forbid the arbitrary subdivision of concepts, so they forbid the arbitrary integration of concepts into a wider concept by means of obliterating their *essential* differences. . . .[3]

An example of the latter error would be the attempt to subsume cigars, sex, and Jesus under the term "encirclist."

A third possibility is recognized by Ayn Rand. In certain cases "on the periphery of man's conceptual vocabulary," she holds, it is neither mandatory nor impermissible to form a concept, but *optional.*[4] For example, a language may be rich in close synonyms, which denote subtly different shades of meaning, such as "glad," "happy," "cheerful," "light-hearted," "joyful," "joyous." The requirements of cognition neither demand such synonyms nor prohibit them; as long as the basic, recurrent distinctions are separately conceptualized, lesser distinctions can be handled descriptively, if one chooses, by means of several concepts rather than a single one. Languages differ in such matters; most contain some words that cannot be translated into other tongues by a single word, but only by a phrase or even a paragraph. Such differences may have important literary implications—they determine the brevity and emotional eloquence with which one can communicate a given meaning; but they are cognitively and epistemologically insignificant.

This brings us to the Objectivist answer to the "borderline-case" problem.[5]

Where, philosophers are wont to ask, does one draw the line in grouping concretes that are neither essentially the same (as are a red table and a black one) nor essentially different (as are a table and a chair)? "Suppose"—a well-known professor of philosophy asked Miss Rand years ago—"someone invents a 'hanging table': an object with a flat, level surface designed to hold other objects, but which hangs from the ceiling by chains, rather than resting on legs on the floor. Is it 'really' a table or not? And how could anyone know?"

Precisely because the "hanger" is borderline, Miss Rand replied, one has several options. Since the entity does have some significant similarities to tables, one may choose to subsume it under that concept (which would require a contextual alteration in one's definition of "table"). Or: since the entity does have some significant differences from tables, one may form a new concept to designate it. Or: since the entity is not widespread and is of no importance in regard to further cognition, one may and probably would choose neither option. One need not designate it by any one concept, old or new, but may identify it instead by a descriptive phrase, which is exactly what the professor did in posing his question.

The borderline-case problem is no problem—not if one accepts an objective view of concepts and therefore of essences, with the classificatory options this makes possible.

Conceptual options, it must be noted, exist only within strictly defined limits. They exist only where the facts of reality can be organized by men in different ways *without this making any cognitive difference or leading to any contradiction*. In such cases, all the alternative modes of handling the facts are in accordance with reality. This situation provides no foothold for subjectivism to enter—any more than the simultaneous existence of English, French, and German does so.

Objectivity as Volitional Adherence to Reality by the Method of Logic

Different views of the nature of concepts lead to different views of the nature of cognition. They lead to different answers to the central question of epistemology: what is knowledge and how does man acquire it?

The objective approach to concepts leads to the view that, beyond the perceptual level, *knowledge is the grasp of an object through an active, reality-based process chosen by the subject.*

Concepts, like every other mode of cognition, must conform to the facts of reality. Human knowledge, therefore, is the *grasp,* not the creation, of an object. Beyond the perceptual level, however, such conformity can be attained only by a complex process of abstraction and integration. Since this process is not automatic, it is not automatically right, either. Man cannot, therefore, adopt a passive policy, one of waiting for truth to enter his mind. In the use of a concept, as in its formation, he must choose and act. He must initiate step-by-step cognitive functioning; he must be willing to expend the effort required by each step; and he must choose the steps carefully. They must constitute a *method* of cognition, a method that makes it possible for man's consciousness, when dealing with abstractions, to achieve by deliberate policy what is not guaranteed to it automatically: to remain in contact with the realm of reality.

The method of measurement-omission, being inherent in the conceptual faculty, is utilized by man whether he knows it or not. What we are seeking to identify here is a method to guide the conscious, volitional aspects of concept-formation and use.

Man does not need a method of cognition, mystics say, because on the most important matters he is incapable of error; if he turns his mind over to God, he is automatically right. Man is not automatically right, skeptics say, so his conclusions are untrustworthy and he cannot discover any method; in this view, man is incapable of truth. Man is not automatically right, Objectivism replies to both schools, and for this very reason he must define a method of cognition, a method that will guide his mental processes properly and thereby make a fallible being capable of truth.

For a volitional, conceptual consciousness, a method of knowing reality is both necessary *and* possible. To define such a method, Ayn Rand holds, is the purpose of epistemology.

The method must reflect two factors: the facts of external reality and the nature of man's consciousness. It must reflect the first, because consciousness is not a self-contained entity; it is the faculty of perceiving that which exists. The method must reflect the second factor, because consciousness has identity; the mind is not blank receptivity; it is a certain kind of integrating mechanism, and it must act accordingly.

Thus we reach Ayn Rand's view of objectivity, which is a derivative of her theory of concepts. Here, in my own words, is her definition. To be "objective" in one's conceptual activities is volitionally to adhere to reality by following certain rules of method, a method based on facts *and* appropriate to man's form of cognition.[6]

People often speak of "objective reality." In this usage, which is harmless, "objective" means "independent of consciousness." The actual purpose of the concept, however, is to be found not in metaphysics, but in epistemology. Strictly speaking, existents are not objective; they simply are. It is minds, and specifically conceptual processes, that are objective—or nonobjective.

The concept of "objectivity" is essential to a rational epistemology; it is a requirement of the proper development of human consciousness and, ultimately, of human survival. (The elements of objectivity in Aristotle's philosophy, even though incomplete and inconsistently formulated, enabled the West to achieve science and an industrial civilization.) A conceptual consciousness must focus on reality by a deliberate resolve, and it must discover and then choose to practice the method required to implement this resolve. Such is the fundamental state of mind that the concept of "objectivity" identifies and upholds—as against two deadly forms of error, deadly because each involves a breach between man's consciousness and reality. One error is: to seek a shortcut—to stare outward without engaging in thought, waiting for external entities (such as God) to do the necessary cognitive work and fill one with truth, a policy that reduces man to a state of mindlessness. The other error is: to give up—to turn inward and ignore reality. (These two errors are the essence of two nonobjective philosophies, which are discussed at the end of the chapter.)

Now we must proceed to the next question: if objectivity requires a method of cognition, what is it? The answer in a word is: *logic*. Logic is a volitional consciousness's method of conforming to reality. It is the method of reason.

Ayn Rand did not discover logic; Aristotle did. But Ayn Rand's definition covers the essence of the subject: "Logic is the art of *noncontradictory identification*."[7] The two key terms are "identification" and "noncontradictory."

Knowledge, we have said, is the "grasp" of an object. To grasp, we must now add, is to *identify,* i.e., to discover in some form the identity of that which exists. On the perceptual level, one learns only that an entity is, not what it is. Even so, perception is a form of apprehending identity: to perceive an entity is to perceive that it is *something*. The ability to define that identity in explicit terms is the next stage; this is the task of conceptual cognition, expressed in every question the mind can ask. Every type of question reduces to: "What is it?" For example, *"Why* did a certain event occur?" means: "What is the nature of the cause?" "How?" means "What is the process?" "Where?" means "What is the place?" Consciousness is a faculty of discovering identity.

This is so because existence has primacy; it sets the terms and consciousness obeys. To be is to have a nature; that is the law of existence—which defines thereby the function of consciousness: to discover the nature of that which is. Thus Ayn Rand's historic formulation, which brings together in six words the fundamental principle of being and its expression in the field of cognition: "Existence is Identity; Consciousness is Identification."[8]

By thus setting the task of consciousness, the law of identity acts as a bridge linking existence and consciousness, or metaphysics and epistemology. The law acts as a bridge in a second respect also. The law defines the basic rule of method required for a conceptual consciousness to achieve its task. In this regard, the law tells man: identifications must be *noncontradictory.*

There is, Aristotle observed, one fundamental kind of error possible to man, which invalidates any thought process committing it: the error of holding that a thing is A and non-A, that it *is* and *is not;* the error of holding a contradiction. A contradiction is a negation of identity and therefore of reality; to be A and non-A at the same time and in the same respect is to be nothing. "To arrive at a contradiction," writes Ayn Rand, "is to confess an error in one's thinking; to maintain a contradiction is to abdicate one's mind and to evict oneself from the realm of reality."[9]

Aristotle's law of contradiction states the above as a formal principle of thought: nothing can be A and non-A at the same time and in the same respect. This is not a different fact from the law of identity. It is a corollary of the latter, a restatement of it for the purpose of guiding human cognition.

The law of contradiction is the fundamental principle defining the method of reality-based thought, whatever its forms or complexities. (The study of these forms is the subject of the science of logic.) Whenever one moves by a volitional process from known data to a new cognition ostensibly based on these data, the ruling question must be: can the new cognition be integrated *without contradiction* into the sum of one's knowledge?[10]

A simple example from the field of deductive reasoning is the Socrates syllogism: "All men are mortal. Socrates is a man. Therefore, Socrates is mortal." The conclusion follows, because to deny it would be to contradict the premises; to deny Socrates' mortality would be tantamount to saying: "All men are mortal—and here's one who isn't." Although it is expressed in a variety of different applications, the same methodology—the avoidance of contradiction—is at the heart of every process of logic, whether deductive or inductive. In essence, logic is the method of observing facts (the premises), then consulting the law of contradiction, then drawing the conclusion that this law warrants. Logic, in other words, *is* "the art of noncontradictory identification."

It is important to note that the process must be grounded in observed fact. To derive a conclusion from arbitrary premises, which represent subjective whims, is not a process of logic. If I declare: "Apples are razors and oranges are blades; therefore, one can shave with fruit salad," this is not a process of cognition at all; it is merely an imitation of the form of logic while dropping its essence. If logic is to be the means of objectivity, a logical conclusion must be derived from reality; it must be warranted by antecedent *knowledge,* which itself may rest on earlier knowledge, and so on back, until one reaches the self-evident, the data of sense. This kind of chain and nothing less is what Objectivism requires as "proof" of an idea.

"Proof" is the process of establishing truth by reducing a proposition to axioms, i.e., ultimately, to sensory evidence. Such reduction is the only means man has of discovering the relationship between nonaxiomatic propositions and the facts of reality.

Many people regard logic not as a cognitive function, but as a social one; they regard it as a means of forcing other men to accept *their* arbitrary ideas. For oneself, according to this viewpoint, a farrago of unproved assertions would be satisfactory; logic, however, is necessary for polemics; it is necessary as a means of trapping opponents in internal inconsistencies and thereby of battering down one's enemy.

Objectivism rejects this approach. Proof is not a social ritual, nor is it an unworldly pursuit, a means of constructing rationalistic castles in the air. It is a personal, practical, selfish necessity of earthly cognition. Just as man would need concepts (including language) on a desert island, so he would need logic there, too. Otherwise, by the nature of human consciousness, he would be directionless and cognitively helpless.

If man knew everything about reality in a single insight, logic would be needless. If man reached conceptual truth as he does perceptual fact, in a succession of unconnected self-evidencies, logic would be needless. This, however, is not the nature of a conceptual being. We organize sense data in steps and in a definite order, building new integrations on earlier ones. It is for this reason that a method of moving from one step to the next is required. That is what logic provides.

The method of logic, therefore, does reflect the nature and needs of man's consciousness. It also reflects the other factor essential to a proper method: the facts of external reality. The principle which logic provides to guide man's mental steps *is* the fundamental law of reality.

This brings us to two large topics. One is necessary to clarify the idea of noncontradictory knowledge; the other, to clarify the concept of "proof." Both topics are indispensable if we are to grasp fully the nature of logic and thus of objectivity.

These two topics are context and hierarchy.

Knowledge as Contextual

Let me begin this topic on a familiar note, by recalling a well-known fallacy: quoting a person out of context. This means quoting some statement of his while ignoring other statements that constitute its background and determine its proper interpretation. By this device, one can make a person appear to advocate virtually any idea. Such quoting is fallacious, because men do not write or speak in a vacuum; they do not emit a stream of disconnected sentences, any one of which can stand independent of the rest. To communicate a viewpoint, a man must say many separate things, each relying on the others; the viewpoint is understood only when the listener grasps the *relationship* among the items and thus the total. To interpret any single remark, therefore, one needs to know: what else did the man say (or presuppose) that conditions his statement? What was the surrounding framework? What is the context?

The necessity of holding the context is not restricted to the use of quotations. Here is a different kind of example, involving the proper use of concepts.

Concepts are a relational form of knowledge. When we form a concept, we group objects on the basis of similarities, which we can detect only in relation to a background of contrasting entities. Two tables, perceived as separate objects, are simply different. To grasp their similarity, we must see them, say, in relation to chairs; then they emerge as similar, similar in shape as against the shape of chairs.

In other words, concepts are formed in a context—by relating concretes to a field of contrasting entities. This body of relationships, which constitutes the context of the concept, is what determines its meaning.[11]

Just as a quotation can be used out of context, so can a concept. The result is worse than a misleading sentence; it is a word dissociated from reality.

Here is a real-life example, taken from *A Theory of Justice,* the well-known book by Harvard philosopher John Rawls.[12] It is perfectly just, Rawls maintains, for society to sacrifice the men of intelligence and creative ability—to seize their products and redistribute them to the world's losers—because, he says, nobody worked to achieve his own gray matter; nobody *earned* his brain, which is a mere gift from nature.

This monstrous theory drops the context of the concept "earn." This concept was formed initially to distinguish between two groups of concretes. It was formed to identify men who, having been born with a healthy brain, choose in due course to use it and satisfy their desires by their own effort (they "earn" what they get), as against men who, though in many instances born with an equally healthy brain, stagnate mentally and then live as parasites on the effort of others. For *this* distinction, there is ample basis in reality; there is none for any alleged distinction between men who "work to achieve" their brain and men who do not. There is no such thing as "working to achieve one's brain." Who is working and by what means? If this sort of action were included in the concept "earning," it would not be a valid concept at all, but a fantasy. Rawls's illogic is evident. He takes a concept formed to organize a certain field of concretes, then drops the field and applies the term, as though it were a self-sufficient, non-relational entity, to a situation in which it has no application. The result is the destruction of the concept, its dissociation from reality.

Having given a minor and a major example (the use of quotations and of concepts), let me state in the widest terms the epistemological principle they illustrate. *Human knowledge on every level is relational.* It is an organization of elements, each relevant to and bearing on the others. Knowledge is *not* a juxtaposition of independent items; it is a unity. It is not a heap of self-sufficient atoms of consciousness, each of which can exist or be dealt with apart from the rest. On the contrary, knowledge at each stage is a total, a sum, a single whole.

The relational nature of knowledge derives from two roots, one pertaining to the nature of existence, the other, to the nature of consciousness.

Metaphysically, there is only one universe. This means that everything in reality is interconnected.[13] Every entity is related in some way to the others; each somehow affects and is affected by the others. Nothing is a completely isolated fact, without causes or effects; no aspect of the total can exist ultimately apart from the total. Knowledge, therefore, which seeks to grasp reality, must also be a total; its elements must be interconnected to form a unified whole reflecting the whole which is the universe.

Up to a point, a consciousness has no option in this regard. It cannot consistently disregard relationships among its contents because consciousness by its nature involves the discovery of relationships. This is true even on the preconceptual level. For instance, if one were exposed for life only to an undifferentiated expanse of blue sky, he would not perceive it; he would perceive nothing. But if an object of a different color were introduced, then he could differentiate and thus perceive. To achieve awareness, even on the perceptual level, a child must differentiate (and integrate); he must relate data.

On the perceptual level, this fact imposes no epistemological responsibility; the necessary relationships are given to us automatically. On the conceptual level, however, the fact that knowledge is relational does impose a responsibility; it becomes an issue that man must identify and then implement volitionally.

Leaving aside the primaries of cognition, which are self-evident, all knowledge depends on a certain relationship: it is based on a context of earlier information. "Context" means "the sum of cognitive elements conditioning an item of knowledge." This sum is what enables us to reach the new conclusion, to prove it, to interpret it, to apply it. This sum, in short, is what sets the item's relationship to reality and thus the item's meaning and proper use.

Hence an essential rule of contextual cognition: always hold the context. Or, to put the point negatively: context must never be dropped.[14] Out-of-context claims or proposals, like out-of-context quotations or concepts, are by their nature invalidated. Whenever one treats a conclusion as an atom unrelated to the rest of cognition, one thereby detaches the conclusion, along with the thought process involving it, from reality. If one drops context, one drops the means of distinguishing between truth and fantasy; anyone can then claim to prove anything, however absurd—just as, out of context, anyone can quote anybody to mean anything.

As an example, consider Neville Chamberlain's argument in favor of appeasing Hitler after the Munich conference of 1938. "Hitler," he said in effect, "demands Czechoslovakia. If we give in, his demand will be satisfied. The result will be peace in our time."

Mr. Chamberlain treated Hitler's demand as an isolated fact to be dealt with by an isolated response; to do this, he had to drop an immense amount of knowledge. He did not relate Hitler's demand to the knowledge already gained about the nature of Nazism; he did not ask for causes. He did not relate the demand to his knowledge of similar demands voiced by aggressor nations and even local bullies throughout history; he did not ask for principles. He did not relate his own policy to mankind's knowledge of the results of appeasement; despite ample indications, he did not ask whether his capitulation, besides satisfying Hitler, would also embolden him, increase his resources, hearten his allies, undermine his opponents, and thus achieve the opposite of its stated purpose. Chamberlain was not concerned with any aspect of a complex situation beyond the single point he chose to consider in isolation: that he would be removing Hitler's immediate frustration.

Deeper issues are involved in this example. Chamberlain was proposing a course of action while ignoring the field that defines the principles of proper action, ethics. He did not ask whether his course comported with the virtues of honor, courage, integrity—and, if not, what consequences this portended. He dropped the fact that foreign-policy decisions, like all human actions, fall within a wider context defined by moral philosophy (and by several other subjects as well). The prime minister wanted "peace at any price." The price included the evasion of political philosophy, history, psychology, ethics, and more. The result was war.

A context-dropper believes that he can understand and alter one element (such as Hitler's dissatisfaction of the moment) within a network of interrelated factors, while leaving everything else unseen and unaffected. In fact, however, a change in one element redounds throughout the network. Every proposal and every idea, therefore, must be judged in the light of the total picture, i.e., of the full context.

What is the *full* context of an idea? All knowledge is interrelated; every element of it is potentially relevant to the rest. The context one must hold, therefore, is not a mere fragment or subdivision of one's knowledge, however extensive, but: everything known at that stage of development, the *sum* of available knowledge. This is the only way to ensure that one's knowledge *is* a sum, i.e., a consistent whole. Such consistency is not a given, but an achievement, which requires a methodical, effort-demanding process.

How is a man to know whether he is contradicting himself at a given time? How is he to know whether some new proposal or idea, which may sound plausible, is consistent with what he already accepts? Since consciousness is finite and limited (the crow epistemology), his mind cannot compare old contents and new in a flash of synoptic insight; it cannot hold in a single frame of awareness all of his relevant former ideas and the new item being considered. There is only one alternative: a man must work to *integrate* a new idea. Since a conceptual consciousness is an integrating mechanism, it demands the integration of all its contents.[15]

One step at a time, a man must relate a new item to his previous ideas. To the extent of his knowledge, he must search for aspects, presuppositions, implications, applications of the new idea that bear on his previous views (in *any* field); and he must identify explicitly the logical relationships he discovers. If he finds a contradiction anywhere, he must eliminate it. Judging on the basis of the available evidence, he must either amend his former views or reject the new claim.

The above is subsumed by Ayn Rand under the formula: "logic is the art of noncontradictory identification." One is not using "logic" if one seeks consistency only among whatever ideas one happens to recall on the spur of the moment.

Blindness, i.e., ignoring all one's other views and thus not seeing one's contradictions, is not the means of being logical. Logic requires noncontradictory identification within the full context of one's knowledge, methodically surveyed; it requires an understanding of the fact that knowledge is a unity, not a realm of splintered propositions or disconnected subdivisions. Only if one keeps context can logic be the method of adhering to reality; only then can logic be the means of achieving *objectivity*.

Context-keeping is what Rawls and Chamberlain, in different ways, conspicuously did not try to do. But you the reader must do it, if knowledge is your goal—and, if the method is new to you, you should start now. Every new idea you read in these pages should represent the beginning, not the end, of a thought process; if the idea sounds reasonable, you should give it not merely a nod of approval, but hours of assiduous mental work. For example: suppose that, having accepted the altruist ethics, you then hear Ayn Rand's theory of egoism and find it appealing. You must then ask: "What arguments, if any, did I have for my previous view? Can I answer them? What arguments are offered for the Objectivist view? Do they stand up?" If you decide for egoism, you must then explicitly reject altruism, along with all the premises that led you to it and all the conclusions to which it leads, as far as you can pursue the trails. If you accepted altruism as the word of God, for instance, ask yourself: "What does my new ethics do to my view of the basis of ethics? What does it do to other ideas I have accepted as God's word—for example in regard to abortion, sex, evolution? What does all this imply for the belief in divine revelation or in God? Which philosophy has the better case—theism or atheism?" And, in the other direction: "How should I vote hereafter? What political system is consistent with an ethics of egoism? How does it relate to my present political views? Is it practicable?" And so on.

You cannot process all the relevant material in this case in a day or a week; a major reorganization of one's thought is a demanding task. Nor can you discover more connections than your present understanding of philosophy permits (if you miss some, they will emerge in due course, assuming you continue to practice the right methodology). But, within the limits of your time and knowledge, this is the *kind* of process you must perform—not only in regard to philosophical issues, but to any new conclusion, in any subject. Thought is identification and integration, the asking of "What?" and then "So what?"—"What is the new fact or claim?" and "What does it imply for the rest of my beliefs?"

The opposite of the policy of integration is exemplified by the *concrete-bound* mentality, to use Ayn Rand's term. This is the man who, as far as possible to a conceptual being, establishes no connections among his mental contents. To him, every issue is simply a new concrete, unrelated to what came before, to abstract principles, or to any context. On Monday, such a man may decide that taxes are too high; on Tuesday, that the government should provide more welfare services; on Wednesday, that inflation must be stopped—never thinking that these points are connected and that he is daily contradicting himself. (More government services, for example, mean higher taxes and/or inflation.) This kind of man is ripe for any demagogic proposal, however absurd, because to him the context that would reveal the absurdity is unreal.

A somewhat better case is the man who does integrate his mental contents, but only within an arbitrarily delimited square or compartment. An economist, for instance, may eagerly relate a new economic idea to other ideas within his field, but refuse to consider its implications for related fields (such as politics, ethics, history) or their implications for his own. "That's not my concern," such a man characteristically says about anything but his own specialty; "that's somebody else's domain." Ayn Rand calls this type of nonintegration *compartmentalization.*

Compartmentalization is an improper form of specialization. It consists not merely in specializing, but in regarding one's specialty as a dissociated fiefdom, unrelated to the rest of human knowledge. In fact, however, all knowledge is interconnected. To cut off a single field—any field—from the rest of cognition is to drop the vast context which makes that field possible and which anchors it to reality. The ultimate result, as with any failure of integration, is floating abstractions and self-contradiction. A simple example is the conservative economists who scornfully dismiss philosophy, then advocate the profit motive in economics and the Sermon on the Mount in church.

Integration, I have said, is something one must work to achieve. If a man merely coasts mentally, relying on his automatic functions, then his ideas, by default, will remain unconnected, floating, out-of-context. This is where philosophy should have come to mankind's rescue, by broadcasting to the world the method and the urgency of grasping cognitive relationships. Unfortunately, as we will soon see, philosophy has done the opposite: it has thrown its immense power on the side of disintegration.

Philosophy should not only have taught men the method of integration. It should itself be the outstanding practitioner of this method.

Since philosophy is the science that deals with the widest abstractions, it alone can act as the ultimate integrator of human knowledge.[16] Philosophy is preeminently the subject which can see the forest and, therefore, which can relate the special sciences to one another. It is philosophy which should arm the scientists with the right metaphysics and epistemology, and then preside over the total field of cognition, calling for a halt and a reappraisal whenever different areas begin to clash. For example, it should call a halt when physics starts to advocate causeless subatomic behavior while psychology is insisting on determinism (both of which doctrines happen to be false). This indeed is one crucial reason why man needs a philosophy: in order to ensure that knowledge *is* a unity rather than, as is now the case, a cacophony of warring specialties.

In today's chaos, every advance of knowledge is also a threat; it raises the possibility, even the likelihood, of some unforeseeable contradiction erupting somewhere. Hence the widespread bromide, which otherwise would be inexplicable, that the more you learn, the more confused you become and the less you know.

If you avail yourself of the power of a rational epistemology, you do not have to fear new data or new ideas. Every new item you integrate into the fabric of your knowledge will mean that much more fact on your side, that much more weight to your conclusions, that much more conviction to the total of your cognition. By this method, you will soon discover what, in logic, should have been the popular wisdom: that the more you learn, if you learn it properly, the more clear you become and the more you know.

Knowledge as Hierarchical

Let me introduce this topic by recalling my brief discussion of higher-level abstractions. I gave the example of a child moving from "cat," "dog," and "horse" to "animal," and then from "animal," "plant," and "man" to the even higher-level concept "organism." A first-level concept is one formed directly from perceptual data, without the need of prior conceptualization. Higher-level concepts, by contrast, represent a relatively advanced cognition. They cannot be formed directly from perceptual data, but presuppose earlier concepts.

The distinction between first- and higher-level concepts is most obvious when we reach the stage of integrating existential concepts with concepts of consciousness. Consider, for instance, a concept such as "culture" (as in "a nation's culture"). Unlike "cat" or "table," this term has no immediate perceptual referent; even if one keenly scrutinized all of men's activities, one would find no "culture" at which to gaze or point. "Culture" is an extremely high-level abstraction denoting the sum of a group's intellectual achievements. To reach such a concept, men had to integrate into a unit a number of earlier abstractions, such as "art," "science," "letters," and "manners." Each of these is itself an abstraction from abstractions, and one that unites perceptual with introspective elements. To reach "art," for instance, an individual must first conceptualize such products as painting, sculpture, and music—which involves differentiating certain kinds of physical objects and grasping in some terms that they embody a certain kind of conscious purpose. This in turn presupposes that the individual has already attained a substantial vocabulary of still more elementary concepts, including certain basic concepts of consciousness—all of it going back ultimately to direct observation of man and his perceptually graspable activities. An extensive conceptualization is required if one is to move from "man" to "painting," and more is required to reach "art," and still more to reach "culture."

Like every concept, "culture" is an integration of concretes—in this instance, of certain human products and actions. But the point is that, in this kind of case, the concept cannot be reached *directly* from its concretes. It presupposes that they have been conceptualized earlier, usually in several stages, on increasing levels of abstraction. A definite *order* of concept-formation is necessary. We begin with those abstractions that are closest to the perceptually given and move gradually away from them.

The same principle of order applies to every field of human knowledge, not merely to concept-formation. A child must observe that there are physical objects with certain properties before he can grasp the atomic theory of their structure and then, later, the permutations and combinations of subatomic particles. He must learn to count before he can understand arithmetic and then, on its basis, algebra and that which comes beyond it. He must learn to speak and combine words into sentences before he can identify types of sentences and of wording and then develop the rudiments of a literary style. And, in order to do any of the above, he must learn in implicit terms first, from sense perception, the basic axioms of existence, consciousness, and identity. Kindergarten must precede grade school, which must precede college.

The same principle applies not merely to a child learning established knowledge, but to every new discovery men make. This is why there were no Newtonian or Einsteinian theories in the ancient world, but only after a lengthy, gradual growth of knowledge. For instance, the sixteenth-century astronomer Tycho Brahe first made careful measurements in regard to the movements of the planets. This made it possible for Kepler to identify certain laws of planetary motion—which, along with other new knowledge (such as that gained by Galileo), made it possible for Newton to formulate universal laws of motion—which, in conjunction with many other discoveries, opened the road to nineteenth-century developments, and so on.

Human knowledge is not like a village of squat bungalows, with every room huddling down against the earth's surface. Rather, it is like a city of towering skyscrapers, with the uppermost story of each building resting on the lower ones, and they on the still lower, until one reaches the foundation, where the builder started. The foundation supports the whole structure by virtue of being in contact with solid ground.

If every concept and conclusion were accessible directly from observation, then knowledge would involve no principle of order; it would be an accumulation of primaries. In fact, however, cognitive items differ in a crucial respect: in their *distance from the perceptual level*. Certain items can be learned from simple sense experience. Others are not so easily available to man; they can be known only through a chain of increasingly complex cognitions, each level making possible the next one.

Knowledge, therefore, has a *hierarchical* structure. "Hierarchy," in general, as the Oxford English Dictionary reports, means "a body of persons or things ranked in grades, orders, or classes, one above another." A hierarchy of knowledge means a body of concepts and conclusions ranked in order of logical dependence, one upon another, according to each item's distance from the base of the structure. The base is the perceptual data with which cognition begins.

The concept of "hierarchy" in this sense is epistemological, not metaphysical. In reality, facts are simultaneous. The facts discovered by Einstein, for instance, do not come into existence later than the facts discovered by Newton; the facts themselves exist eternally. But an order of logical dependence among them exists from man's perspective, because man cannot come to know all facts with the same directness.

In some but not all cases, the hierarchy of human knowledge depends on the nature of man's senses—on the type of information they provide. To man, for example, the perception of macroscopic objects necessarily precedes the discovery of their atomic constituents. But to the mythical conscious particles that we fantasized in chapter 2, the hierarchy would be reversed. To them, the perception of atoms would be a primary, and the discovery of macroscopic objects would be a higher-level inference. In other kinds of cases, however, a particular hierarchical relationship seems to be inherent in conceptual cognition as such, no matter what the nature of a species' senses. For example: the grasp in some terms of the axioms of philosophy would presumably be a precondition of the cognitive development of any conceptual species, whatever its sensory apparatus.

Not all cases of hierarchical dependence, therefore, have the identical cause. But this does not alter the fact that all such cases do fall under the same principle. The principle is that knowledge follows a necessary order.

The principle of order does not preclude the existence of

cognitive *options*. For example: "organism" is a higher-level concept, which one can reach only after one has conceptualized in stages a variety of its instances. But there is no reason why one must reach it through "cat," "dog," "rosebush," rather than, say, through "horse," "bird," "orange tree." Similarly, one could not discover the law of gravitation without study and conceptualization of more elementary facts about motion; but nothing in epistemology requires that the culminating insight derive from the fall of an apple as against many other possibilities. A higher-level item *is* dependent on the grasp of a series of earlier items; but that series is not necessarily unique in content. Within the requisite overall structure, there may be many alternatives in detail.

The concept of "hierarchy" applies to learning-sequences only insofar as there is *no* option within them. It applies when a given cognitive step cannot be reached or understood without a certain kind of prerequisite.

Now let me relate the issues of context and hierarchy. A hierarchy is a type of context. The contextual view of knowledge states that cognition is relational. The hierarchical view identifies a particular kind of cognitive relationship: it states not only that every (nonaxiomatic) item has a context, but also that such context itself has an inner structure of logical dependence, rising gradually from a base of first-level items. The principle of context takes an overview; it looks at the sum of knowledge already acquired and says: it *is* a sum. The principle of hierarchy looks at the process by which a given item was learned and says: the simpler steps made the more complex ones possible.

This brings us to the practical significance of the present discussion. The epistemological responsibility imposed on man by the fact that knowledge is contextual is the need of integration. The responsibility imposed by the fact that knowledge is hierarchical is: the need of *reduction*.

If men had to move up the hierarchical structure by their own first-hand cognition; if they had to be clear about each step of knowledge before moving to the next; and if they had to retain in explicit terms the essence of the earlier material after going beyond it—then the fact of hierarchy would pose no problem. Under these conditions, an individual could not reach or use a higher-level item without knowing its tie to perceptual reality. The ideas of such a mind would never become floating abstractions; there would be no break in the chain connecting advanced concepts to the sensory data they ultimately subsume.

Men, however, can and often do try to move to higher levels of cognition without properly understanding the intermediate material. They do so through several causes, such as impatience, anti-effort, or simple error. The most common cause is intellectual dependence; many men are content to take over the concepts and conclusions *of other people* without understanding the steps that led to them. Such men attempt to function on the higher levels of a complex structure without having established the requisite base; their mental activity consists in building confusion on confusion, instead of knowledge on knowledge. In such minds, the chain relating higher-level content to perceptual reality is broken; these individuals' conceptual structure, or semblance of one, has no grounding; it is detached from facts and from cognition.

Context-keeping, as we know, is required if men's ideas are to be connected to reality. When the context is itself hierarchical, the successive levels of its structure are the connecting links. To keep the context in such a case is to identify and retain these links. This is where the process of reduction is necessary.

Reduction is the means of connecting an advanced knowledge to reality by traveling backward through the hierarchical structure involved, i.e., in the reverse order of that required to reach the knowledge. "Reduction" is the process of identifying in logical sequence the intermediate steps that relate a cognitive item to perceptual data. Since there are options in the detail of a learning process, one need not always retrace the steps one initially happened to take. What one must retrace is the essential logical structure.

Such retracing is a requirement of objectivity. Man's only direct contact with reality is the data of sense. These, therefore, are the *standard* of objectivity, to which all other cognitive material must be brought back.

As an example of reduction, let me take the concept "friend," mentioned in the last chapter, and identify some of the intermediate concepts linking it to perceptual reality. The method consists in asking repeatedly: what does one have to know in order to reach and understand a given step?

A baby or an animal can perceive two friends, can watch them talking, laughing, going out together, yet not reach the least idea of their "friendship." Something more than perceptual data is necessary in this case. What?

We must begin with a definition. A "friend" designates a person in a certain kind of human relationship, as against an acquaintance, a stranger, an enemy. In essence, the relationship involves mutual knowledge, esteem, and affection; as a result, the individuals take pleasure in each other's company, communicate with a high degree of intimacy, and display mutual benevolence, each sincerely wishing the other well. To identify so complex a relationship, one must have formed many earlier concepts, including "man," "knowledge," and "pleasure." Let us focus here on a central element, "esteem."

Again we ask: on what does this concept depend? "Esteem" designates a certain kind of favorable appraisal; one man "esteems" another when he recognizes in him qualities that he estimates as being of significant (moral) *value*. To grasp such a concept, therefore, one must first know many concepts that come earlier, including, above all, the concept "value." (One need not know the abstraction "value" as such. Some specification relevant to the concept "esteem," i.e., some identification of *moral* value, such as the concepts of "good" and "evil," would be sufficient here. But for simplicity we may neglect this point.)

The same root is presupposed by the concept "affection." "Affection" is an emotional response that derives from esteem, i.e., from the recognition of one's values in the character of another. If one had not yet reached the concept "value" in any terms, he might well feel something positive for another person, but he would be unable to identify the feeling as "affection."

Now we must ask: how does one reduce the concept "value"? "Value" is that which one acts to gain and/or keep (see chapter 7). What earlier concepts does *this* presuppose? Among other things, an individual must first learn that man pursues objects, i.e., he must grasp the concept "purpose"; and he must learn that man has the power to select his actions and purposes, i.e., he must grasp the concept "choice." Without these concepts, a child cannot form any normative abstractions, such as "good" and "evil," "desirable" and "undesirable," "value" and "disvalue." He cannot form or understand abstractions intended to guide his faculty of choice before grasping that he has such a faculty.

We have still not reached the perceptual level, but we are approaching it now. One *can* observe men pursuing objects—moving to a table in order to eat a meal, lying down on a bed in order to sleep, and so on—although one cannot conceptualize "purpose" until the elementary entities and actions involved (including certain processes of consciousness) have been conceptualized. And one can identify the act of choice introspectively, once one has processed enough existential data to have reached the stage of forming and distinguishing introspective concepts. The final steps backward, therefore, which I will not rehearse, do bring us eventually to first-level concepts, such as "table," "bed," "man." At this point, the reduction has been completed. It ends when we say: "And by this term—e.g., 'man'—I mean *this,*" as we directly point to the entity.

Here are the elements of the logical chain we have been identifying, this time in ascending order: *"Men* have to *choose* among *purposes* by means of their *values,* which fact generates certain kinds of mutual estimates and emotions, including *esteem* and *affection,* which make possible a certain kind of human relation, *friendship."*

What are the advantages of knowing such a chain? Part of the answer is self-protection. For example, if someone were to say to you: "Man is determined, 'choice' is a myth, no one can help what he does, so we should all have compassion for one another and be friendly"—your immediate reply, assuming the reduction is clear to you, would be: " 'Friendly?' How can *you* use that term?" The concept "friendship," you would point out, rests on the concept "choice." If determinism is true, then there can be no such higher-level abstractions as "moral value," "esteem," or "friendship."

Once you know the conceptual *roots* of "friendship," as Ayn Rand calls them—the chain of antecedent concepts linking it to perceptual reality—you know the rules of its proper use and you can recognize any egregious misuse. You can thus guard the clarity—the identity—of the concept in your own mind.

Or if a man tells you: "I disagree with your ideas, I object to your actions, I disapprove of your associates, but we're still friends, because I'm criticizing you for your own good and I like you just the same"—a claim that is all too common, especially among relatives—you would immediately reply: "If you reject everything important about me, how can you like me? For what attributes? What meaning does 'friendship' have once it is detached from the concept of 'values'?" Again, if you know the reduction, you can easily spot the error.

Errors of this kind are widespread. The fallacy involved was identified for the first time by Ayn Rand. She called it the fallacy of the "stolen concept."[17]

The fallacy consists in using a higher-level concept while denying or ignoring its hierarchical roots, i.e., one or more of the earlier concepts on which it logically depends. This is the intellectual equivalent of standing on the fortieth floor of a skyscraper while dynamiting the first thirty-nine. The higher-level concept—"friendship," in the above examples—is termed "stolen," because the individual involved has no logical right to use it. He is an epistemological parasite; he seizes, without understanding, a term created by other men who did observe the necessary hierarchical structure. The parallel to a parasite in matter, who seizes wealth created by others, is obvious.

The reason stolen concepts are so prevalent is that most people (and most philosophers) have no idea of the "roots" of a concept. In practice, they treat every concept as a primary, i.e., as a first-level abstraction; thus they tear the concept from any place in a hierarchy and thereby detach it from reality. Thereafter, its use is governed by caprice or unthinking habit, with no objective guidelines for the mind to follow. The result is confusion, contradiction, and the conversion of language into verbiage.

The antidote is the process of reduction. In regard to higher-level concepts, reduction completes the job of definition. The purpose of a definition is to keep a concept connected to a specific group of concretes. The definition of a higher-level concept, however, counts on the relevant lower-level concepts, which must themselves be connected to concretes; otherwise, the definition is useless. Reduction is what takes a person from the initial definition through the definitions of the next lower level and then of the next, until he reaches the direct perception of reality. This is the only means by which the initial definition can be made fully clear.

Before we leave the topic of conceptual reduction, let me point out that certain concepts—actually, pseudo-concepts—cannot be reduced to observational data. This is the proof that such concepts are invalid.

"Invalid concepts," writes Miss Rand, are "words that represent attempts to integrate errors, contradictions, or false propositions, such as concepts originating in mysticism [e.g., "ghost," "god," "gremlin"]—or words without specific definitions, without referents, which can mean anything to anyone, such as modern 'anti-concepts' [these are deliberately equivocal terms, such as "extremism," "McCarthyism," "isolationism"]." Any such term is detached from reality and "invalidates every proposition or process of thought in which it is used as a cognitive assertion."[18]

The test of an invalid concept is the fact that it cannot be reduced to the perceptual level. This means that nothing in reality gives rise to the concept. The test is not that the referent is unobservable. Science regularly refers to unobservables, such as atoms, genes, X rays. But one can identify the evidence supporting scientific concepts. One can define the sequence of steps by which men were led from observations to a series of conclusions, which were then integrated into new concepts to designate hitherto unknown entities. In regard to the language of religion, by contrast, this is precisely what cannot be done. The referents of "god," "angel," "devil" are not merely unobservable. The terms cannot be connected by any process to the perceptual level; they are nonreducible by their nature.

Reduction is necessary in regard to all higher-level content. It applies not only to concepts, but also to propositions.

Propositions too (if nonaxiomatic) must be brought back step by step to the perceptual level. They too are based on antecedent cognitions—on the chain of evidence that led to them—going back ultimately to direct observation. To a mind that does not grasp this chain, a higher-level proposition is arbitrary, noncontextual, nonobjective; it is detached from reality and from the requirements of human cognition. As I suggested earlier and can now explain more fully, this is why *proof* of an idea is necessary.

Proof is a form of reduction. The conclusion to be proved is a higher-level cognition, whose link to reality lies in the premises; these in turn eventually lead back to the perceptual level. Proof is thus a form of retracing the hierarchical steps of the learning process. (As with conceptual reduction, so with proof: the process identifies not the optional variants, but the essential links in the chain, the necessary logical structure relating a mental content to observational data.)

Proof is not a process of deriving a conclusion from arbitrary premises or even from arbitrarily selected true premises. Proof is the process of establishing a conclusion by identifying *the proper hierarchy of premises*. In proving a conclusion, one traces backward the order of logical dependence, terminating with the perceptually given. It is only because of this requirement that logic is the means of validating a conclusion *objectively*.

For example: if someone were to infer a given man's mortality from the fact that there is a huge funeral industry in every country, this would not be a proper proof. The funeral industry is a *consequence* of our knowledge of human mortality, not a precondition of such knowledge. The standard Socrates syllogism, by contrast, does validate its conclusion. It derives Socrates' mortality from a truly antecedent generalization (which in turn integrates countless observations of men and of other living organisms).

The above is also subsumed by Ayn Rand under her definition of "logic." *Logic requires a recognition of context and of hierarchy*. Logic is "the art of noncontradictory identification"—while observing the full context of knowledge, including its hierarchical structure. A logical conclusion is one which has been related without contradiction to the rest of a man's conclusions (the task of integration)—and which has been related step by step to perceptual data (the task of reduction). Between the two processes, man achieves a double check on his accuracy. Every conclusion must stand the test of his other knowledge *and* (through the necessary intermediate chain) the test of direct experience.

As with integration, so with reduction (both conceptual

and propositional): if the process is new to you, I suggest that you start now, but do it gradually, within the limits of your time and knowledge. It is probably best to start with concepts, which are the elements of propositions—particularly with fundamental concepts, whenever you sense that these are not clear to you. Then, as you see the need of it, you can bring into logical order other higher-level items.

Let me caution you to apply the method in essential terms only. Trying to work backward through every intermediate cognition involved would be excruciating and pointless. Instead, seek at first to reach an overview of the major connecting links, on the pattern of our treatment of "friend." Thereafter, should it prove necessary, you can fill in further nuances.

However you simplify the process, I regret to say, the task will not be an easy one. In a proper world, you would never have to engage in such a wholesale clarification of your knowledge. You would be performing the processes of reduction a step at a time as you were climbing the cognitive hierarchy; you would be taught the method of thought gradually from childhood, as you were developing. Then you would not have to face years of remedial work in order to undo years of conceptual chaos. Here again, as with the task of integration, you are the victims of a bad philosophy, which I shall soon name.

Let me conclude the discussion of hierarchy by explaining the principle of "Rand's Razor."[19]

A "razor" is a principle that slashes off a whole category of false and/or useless ideas. Rand's Razor is addressed to anyone who enters the field of philosophy. It states: *name your primaries.* Identify your starting points, including the concepts you take to be irreducible, and then establish that these *are* objective axioms. Put negatively: do not begin to philosophize in midstream. Do not begin with some derivative concept or issue, while ignoring its roots, however much such issue interests you. Philosophical knowledge, too, is hierarchical.

Today's philosophers not only evade this point, but reverse it, just as they reverse the principle that knowledge is contextual. In regard to context-keeping, they not only fail to integrate their theories; they crusade for *non*integration, insisting that every question they study is independent of the others, that philosophy consists of "piecemeal analyses," and that the cardinal sin is system-building. As an expression of this anti-contextual mentality, these same thinkers not only neglect the task of reduction; they brazenly invert the hierarchical order of knowledge.

As an example, I will quote from a recent skeptic, who asks: "How can I be sure that, every time I believe something, such as that there are rocks, I am not *deceived* into so believing by . . . a mad scientist who, by means of electrodes implanted in my brain, manipulates my beliefs?"[20] According to this approach, we cannot be sure that there are rocks; such a belief is regarded as a complex matter open to doubt and discussion. But what we can properly take as our starting point in considering the matter and explaining our doubt is: there are scientists, there are electrodes, men have brains, scientists can go mad, electrodes can affect brain function. All of this, it seems, is self-evident information, which anyone can invoke whenever he feels like it. How is it possible to know such sophisticated facts, yet *not* know that there are rocks? The author, who is a professor of philosophy, feels no need to raise such a question. He feels free to begin philosophizing at random, treating advanced knowledge as a primary and using it to undercut the direct evidence of men's eyes.

This individual does not merely use advanced knowledge while ignoring its roots; he uses the knowledge to destroy its own roots. And he does not merely misappropriate in this fashion a single term, but a complex body of conclusions. He is guilty not merely of one stolen concept, but of conceptual grand larceny. This is the kind of anti-hierarchical corruption that makes philosophies such as skepticism possible. It is this kind of philosophy that Rand's Razor slashes off at the root.

The rejection of hierarchy on so profound a scale amounts to the rejection of reason as such. It represents the attempt to enthrone naked whim as the ruler of cognition—which is not a mere error, but a form of willful irrationalism.

It is as futile to uphold true ideas while ignoring hierarchy as to uphold false ones. Contrary to today's conservatives, for example, it is not an axiom that man has the right to property. The right to property is a consequence of man's right to life; which right we can establish only if we know the nature and value of man's life; which conclusion presupposes, among other things, that objective value-judgments are possible; which presupposes that objective knowledge is possible; which depends on a certain relationship between man's mind and reality, i.e., between consciousness and existence. If a thinker does not know and count on this kind of structure, he can neither defend property rights nor define the concept nor apply it correctly. This is one of the reasons why today's conservatives are ineffectual.

It should now be clear why we began our study of Objectivism by identifying its axioms, and why we have been proceeding one step at a time to more advanced conclusions. Ayn Rand lives up to the demands of her Razor. Philosophy is hierarchical—and so, therefore, is Objectivism.

The opposite of Rand's Razor was stated eloquently years ago by a follower of General Semantics, whose name I have long forgotten. He said it to Miss Rand casually after some fruitless discussion, as though it were uncontroversial. Miss Rand had asked him where he started philosophically, and he replied: "I start where the last generation left off."

This is what no thinker can permit himself to do. He cannot take over unanalyzed and unreduced the context of his predecessors, including all of their contradictions, non sequiturs, and dead ends. This is the policy that has made progress in the humanities impossible; it is why philosophy for centuries has become ever more confused and problem-laden. When thinkers base their theories not on the facts of reality, but on the unscrutinized conclusions of their predecessors, the result is a uniquely repellent kind of intellectual structure—not a hierarchy of knowledge, but of increasingly contorted and insolvable errors.

This is where the advice offered by the philosopher in *Atlas Shrugged,* Hugh Akston, is eminently applicable: "Check your premises." If you propose to enter the field of philosophy, check your premises—see what they depend on, and what that depends on, all the way back to the base of the structure.

If your reduction is accurate, you will find that the base is the axiom with which we began: existence exists.

Intrinsicism and Subjectivism as the Two Forms of Rejecting Objectivity

Just as Ayn Rand's theory of concepts has implications for the rest of epistemology, so other theories of concepts have their own implications. Ayn Rand's theory leads her to define and demand objectivity in human cognition. Opposite theories lead to the opposite result. Intentionally or otherwise, they lead to the rejection of objectivity.

Historically, the three main theories of concepts are Platonic realism, Aristotelian realism, and nominalism.

Plato held that concepts refer to other-worldly universals—to nonmaterial Forms such as manness, tablehood, goodness, which, he believed, are independent of consciousness and of any concrete embodiments. This theory is known as "realism" because abstractions are viewed as external existents. They are viewed as features *intrinsic in reality,* apart from any relation to man or his mind. If a person is given a proper intellectual and moral preparation, Plato tells us, the memory of these entities, which men knew in a previous life, will gradually return. In the end, he thinks, the mind need merely remain motionless, passive, receptive, and the light of truth will automatically stream in, taking the form of a synoptic and ineffable intuition.

Aristotle's theory is more naturalistic than Plato's, but bears Plato's imprint. Every entity, says Aristotle, is a metaphysical compound made of two elements: form and matter, or structure and stuff. The first is the universalizing factor, the same in every instance of a group, which enables us to bring the instances together under a single concept. The second is the particularizing factor, unique to each instance, which makes each thing an unrepeatable concrete.

For Aristotle, universals are not other-worldly, but they are still phenomena *intrinsic* in reality. Universals, in this view, exist *in* particulars, as elements independent of man. Tablehood et al. are out there in the world as structural features of physical entities, structures independent of any process of consciousness. As to how one comes to know such features, Aristotle's answer, though more plausible than Plato's, comes down also to a passive receptivity or "intuition."

For him too the mind in the end must simply gaze outward and await the imprint of the appropriate externalities.

Aristotelian realism is a kind of commonsense Platonism. The theory is brilliant and even valid in many crucial ways. Its greatest virtue is its attempt to fight off both Plato and Protagoras; it is the only important attempt in history to defend a this-worldly but nonskeptic view of concepts. Despite its intention and its virtues, however, Aristotle's theory remains, in formal statement, a variant of Platonism and is thus vulnerable to similar objections.

Such a theory could not withstand the main opponent of realism in the theory of concepts, *nominalism,* which was developed largely by skeptic philosophers, from Protagoras to Hume to Dewey and Wittgenstein. Every existent, in this view, is unique; there is nothing the same uniting the members of a group; there is no metaphysical basis for classifications. There are, however, more-or-less-rough similarities linking particulars, so that it is often convenient to group various items under a single name. But no facts ever require a particular grouping; there is no objectively right or wrong way to form concepts. Men simply decide, for their own subjective purposes, to draw certain lines through the continuum of similarities offered by physical nature. We do not discover classes, as this idea is put; we create them.

According to the realist approach, *con*ception is to be construed on the model of *per*ception. In perception, there is a table out there, and we need merely expose ourselves to it, letting the entity imprint itself on our senses; the automatic result is a percept, which is infallible. So, it is said, for the next level of consciousness: in conception, there is a table-*hood* out there (whether in heaven or in physical tables); and again we need merely expose ourselves to it, letting the entity imprint itself on our minds; the automatic result will be an infallible concept. To which the nominalists retort: we have gazed diligently, but we cannot find these abstract entities or attributes; we can observe only unique particulars. Thus the traditional alternative: conceptualization as passive absorption of the external, or as a realm in which anything goes. The first side holds that universals are real ("out there"); the second, that they are nominal ("in here," in the sense of being arbitrary linguistic creations).

In the one view, concepts represent phenomena of existence apart from consciousness. In the other view, they represent phenomena of consciousness apart from existence. The first of these approaches, in any variant, Ayn Rand identifies as "intrinsicism"; the second, as "subjectivism."[21]

The intrinsicists, eager to ground human thought in the world of fact, project the products of man's conceptual activity outward, into reality apart from man. The subjectivists, rebelling against such projection, give up the quest for a grounding; man's conceptual products, they typically declare, being his chosen creations, his own perspective on things, are detached from reality. Neither school understands that such products, by their very nature, reflect both fact and choice, both existents and man's perspective on them, both reality *and* human consciousness.

The same false alternative dominates the traditional discussion of definitions.

The Platonic and Aristotelian realists regard essences as metaphysical. Certain characteristics, they say, are marked out immutably as "that which makes an entity itself"; this is a fact intrinsic in physical nature, independent of any need or state of human consciousness. Every entity, accordingly, must have an essence (and it must be fixed); so there is no option in regard to human classification, no room for contextual revision of definitions, and no answer, other than "intuition," to the problem of borderline cases.

To which nominalists reply: every aspect of an entity is a part of its nature. How then can we single out certain features as inherently more important than others? The "essential," they conclude, is made so by man, not by reality. Definitions, therefore, are subjective; they represent not fact or truth, but linguistic convention.

Here again the possibility of a third alternative—of essences as being man-made *and* reality-based, i.e., as being *objective*—has been ignored by both sides.

Now let us consider the broader epistemological implications of the standard theories.

The objective approach to concepts leads to the view that knowledge is the grasp of an object through an active, reality-based process chosen by the subject.

Intrinsicism leads to the view that knowledge is the grasp of an object through the passive absorption of revelations.

Subjectivism leads to the view that knowledge is the creation of an object through the active inner processes of the subject.

The intrinsicists (exemplified by Plato and Augustine) recognize that knowledge requires conformity to reality. But, they hold, there is no way to attain such conformity, on any level of awareness, except by passive exposure to external entities which, honestly attended to, impress themselves infallibly on one's awareness. It follows that no *method* of gaining conceptual knowledge is necessary, any more than a method is necessary on the perceptual level. Once one reaches the stage of perceiving entities, there is no special method of seeing a table and no possibility of seeing it incorrectly; one merely opens one's eyes and is struck by an incontestable datum. So it is, in this approach, with the "eye" of the mind. One cannot ask, in regard to abstract conclusions learned in such a fashion: "How do you know?" The ultimate reply is: "I just know." Or: "To those who understand, no explanation is necessary; to those who do not, none is possible."

Intrinsicists describe man's faculty of "just knowing" by many names, including "intuition," a "sixth sense," "extrasensory perception," "reminiscence," and "divine revelation." This last is the most suitable term, inasmuch as religion is the logical culmination of the intrinsicist theory.

Material entities do exist external to us and do act on us; but such action produces sense experience, not abstract ideas. What kind of external entity could create in us conceptual content? In the end, only a mind can be imagined in such a role, a mind that (somehow) already possesses the knowledge in question and chooses (somehow) to communicate it. This indeed was the historical development from Plato to Christianity. Plato's Forms, many of the ancients remarked, cannot be self-sufficient entities; abstractions can exist only as the content of an intellect. If abstractions are other-worldly phenomena, therefore, they must be construed as ideas in an other-worldly intellect, i.e., as thoughts in the mind of God, who periodically in his goodness reveals some of them to man. One churchman, Numenius, expresses the upshot in a perfect intrinsicist aphorism: "All knowledge is the kindling of the small light [man's mind] from the great light which illumines the world.''[22]

Intrinsicism begins by appearing to champion reality. It ends, however, by upholding the primacy of consciousness—of a supernatural consciousness.

Subjectivism, by contrast, is exemplified by Kant and John Dewey. It begins by advocating the primacy of consciousness—of human consciousness. (As the example of Kant indicates, subjectivism in the theory of concepts need not take the form of nominalism. In regard to most concepts, Kant claims to accept the Aristotelian approach. Officially, he regards only twelve concepts, the so-called categories, as subjective. But in his system these are the decisive concepts, which determine the status of all others; they are the concepts which, in conjunction with certain other innate mental structures, give rise to the whole empirical world.)[23]

The subjectivist rejects the mystic approach to epistemology; revelation, he recognizes, is not a valid means of knowledge. But, he continues, there is no other means of knowing an external object; it is revelation of some sort or nothing. Men must, therefore, give up the attempt to know reality; they must base their ideas on the content or structure of human consciousness apart from reality. The subject, in this view, does not grasp external facts; it creates facts out of its own resources. It *creates* its objects by its own inner processes. Such processes, by the nature of the theory, are arbitrary, i.e., not based on or derived from reality.

In the personal version of this doctrine, each individual creates his own private universe; in the social version, facts are the creation of a group. In every version, however, the standard of cognition is the same: knowledge is that which conforms to the subjective demands of the ruling consciousness, whether individual or collective.

The culmination of this approach is pragmatism. Pragmatism holds that the concept of "reality" is invalid; that the quest for absolutes is a perversion; and that truth is not correspondence to fact, but rather "that which works." "Works" here means "satisfies for the nonce the arbitrary desires of men."

The great achievement of Aristotle is that his epistemology did not develop in either the intrinsicist or the subjectivist direction. Whatever its Platonic aspects, his theory of concepts was close enough to reality to enable him to identify man's need of a cognitive method and thus to become the father of logic. As an advocate of this-worldly cognition, he spurned supernatural guidance; as an opponent of Sophism, he could not rest content with arbitrary feeling.

It is on Aristotle's epistemological discoveries, including his implicit recognition of context and hierarchy, that men have built ever since, to the extent that they *have* built cognitively, as against stagnating or regressing. Tragically, however, Aristotle's epistemology (in part, because of its contradictions, its own intrinsicist aspects) has seldom been a dominant historical factor. It has never had the monolithic, enduring influence enjoyed by intrinsicism (in the medieval era) and subjectivism (in the past two centuries). Neither of these two schools is equipped to grasp the need of logic.

The intrinsicist regards knowledge, in effect, as a series of thunderbolts from the beyond. In this view, each item (or set of items) is revealed to man as a separate, contextless deliverance. The subjectivist regards knowledge as a series of thunderbolts emanating from within human consciousness, whether personal or social. In this view, each item or set is invented as a separate, arbitrary caprice. Neither of these approaches can identify the cognitive necessity of integration, of reduction, of proof. Left to its own devices, neither feels the need of an "art of noncontradictory identification."

After Aristotle's discoveries, no school can afford to ignore logic. What the non-Aristotelians do, however, is not to use logic as a means of objectivity, but to take the field over, reinterpreting its nature in accordance with their own premises. The intrinsicists, who write off this world as unreal and unintelligible, detach logic from percepts. To these men, logic is a tool oriented to a higher reality; it is the means of making self-consistent the divine ideas (whether these are claimed to reach us through Scripture, innate endowment, or the Hegelian dialectic). The result is rationalism with its floating systems of thought, "floating" because unrelated to sensory evidence. The subjectivists, who reject supernaturalism and stress sensations or percepts, also detach logic from the world (they call it "logic without ontology"). To these men, logic is the means of achieving consistency among arbitrary semantic conventions. The result is modern empiricism with its linguistic castles in the air, and its conclusion that sensory data can perhaps be described, but not understood. In both approaches, logic is useless as a device of cognition, if "cognition" means a grasp of the facts of this world.

When men are deprived of their method of cognition, they have no means of validating their conclusions, no way to distinguish truth from error, fact from wish, reality from fantasy. The consequence is frustration and failure, the failure of their conclusions (including their moral conclusions) to serve as reliable guides to action. This is the cause that explains the popularity of the notion that an idea may be "good in theory, but not work in practice."

This notion is impossible to an Objectivist.[24] A theory is an identification of the facts of reality and/or of guidelines for human action. A good theory is a true theory, one that recognizes all the relevant facts, including the facts of human nature, and integrates them into a noncontradictory whole. Such a theory has to work in practice. If a man's course of action, thanks to his scrupulous use of logic, derives from a study of reality, then that course must be in harmony with reality. If so, what would prevent it from succeeding?

The theory-practice dichotomy is itself a theory; its source is a breach between concepts and percepts. Given such a breach, thought comes to be viewed as pertaining to one world (the world of Platonic Forms, or of Kantian "phenomena," or of linguistic constructs), while action is viewed as pertaining to an opposite world (the world of concretes, or of things-in-themselves, or of empirical data). In this set-up, one expects an idea to be schizophrenic. One expects it to be good in one world, but not in the other, good in theory, but not in practice.

The consequence is to offer mankind a monstrous choice. Practice theories that are impracticable, these theorists declare, or dismiss theory as a superfluity and even a threat. This means: remain loyal to concepts that clash with reality—or remain loyal to percepts by dispensing with concepts. The first is the intrinsicist choice; the second is the choice of the subjectivist.

If a thinker rejects the absolutism of the metaphysically given, I said in chapter 1, his attitude will lead him to a mind-body dichotomy. Having departed from reality as a matter of policy, he will come to regard conflict between the self and the world as the essence of human life. The theory-practice dichotomy is an eloquent example of this development and a key to its deeper understanding.

No one departs from reality on the perceptual level; one can do so only on the volitional, conceptual level. In a primitive society (and in regard to a specific problem at any time), this departure can occur by default or simple error, through men's ignorance of the proper methodology. In an advanced civilization, however, the only way such departure can be made to occur wholesale, with results disastrous for every problem and every branch of learning, is by means of a theory—a theory that subverts the conceptual level wholesale by detaching it from percepts. This is a disaster that only philosophers can create—or repair.

The primary source of the mind-body dichotomy and of all the suffering it has caused from Pythagoras to the present is a false view of the mind, i.e., of concepts. The solution is to return to the axioms of philosophy, existence and consciousness, and identify their actual relationship within a conceptual process.

Existence alone, says the intrinsicist, is the active factor in cognition; consciousness, in essence, contributes nothing; it is merely a receptacle, an emptiness waiting to be filled. Consciousness alone, says the subjectivist, is the operative factor in cognition; existence, being unreal or unknowable, is irrelevant. The one viewpoint seeks to efface consciousness, to deprive it of any nature in the name of an alleged fidelity to existence—and ends up regarding existence as a product of (a supernatural) consciousness. The ultimate practical result is the agony of the medievals' "age of faith." The other viewpoint seeks to efface existence in the name of the alleged power of consciousness, its power to create its own objects—and ends up regarding consciousness as cut off both from facts and from values, i.e., as impotent. The result is the agony of the modern skeptics' "age of anxiety."

The axioms of philosophy, however, cannot be sundered. There is no consciousness without existence and no knowledge of existence without consciousness. The advocate of objectivity grasps this fundamental fact. He recognizes that a volitional relationship between consciousness *and* existence is the essence of conceptual cognition. He alone, therefore, is able to uphold the primacy of existence, the efficacy of human consciousness, and the harmony of mind and body. The practical result of this kind of approach, though it was suggested briefly by the Renaissance, lies largely in the future.

I shall conclude by quoting from the final paragraphs of *Introduction to Objectivist Epistemology:*

> . . . the satisfaction of every need of a living organism requires an act of *processing* by that organism, be it the need of air, of food or of knowledge.
>
> No one would argue (at least, not yet) that since man's body has to *process* the food he eats, no objective rules of proper nutrition can ever be discovered—that "true nutrition" has to consist of absorbing some ineffable substance without the participation of a digestive system, but since man is incapable of "true feeding," nutrition is a subjective matter open to his whim, and it is merely a social convention that forbids him to eat poisonous mushrooms.
>
> No one would argue that since nature does not tell man automatically what to eat—as it does not tell him automatically how to form concepts—he should abandon the illusion that there is a right or wrong way of eating (or he should revert to the safety of the time when he did not have to "trust" objective evidence, but could rely on dietary laws prescribed by a supernatural power). . . .
>
> No one would argue that man eats bread rather than stones purely as a matter of "convenience."
>
> It is time to grant to man's consciousness the same cognitive respect one grants to his body—i.e., the same *objectivity.*[25]

▪   ▪   ▪   ▪

Ayn Rand is the first philosopher to identify the differences separating an intrinsicist, a subjectivist, and an objectivist approach to epistemology. She is the first to base a definition of "objectivity" on a proper theory of concepts. As a result, she is the first to define this essential cognitive norm fully and to specify the means by which men can adhere to it.

Ayn Rand is the first thinker to identify explicitly the fact that logic, *including the recognition of context and hierar-*

chy, is the method of achieving objectivity. This is the knowledge that is necessary to convert objectivity from elusive ideal to normal actuality. It is this knowledge that enables a man not only to base his conclusions on reality, but to do it consciously and methodically—to know *that* he is doing it and by what means—i.e., to be in control of the process of cognition.

If there are landmark discoveries in human thought, this is one of them.

The reason why Ayn Rand called her philosophy "Objectivism" should now be clear.

5

REASON

"Reason" is one of the central concepts in the philosophy of Ayn Rand. The whole of Objectivism amounts to the injunction: "Follow reason." But this formulation by itself offers little guidance, because "reason" is a complex higher-level concept. To grasp its meaning and implications, one must first grasp its hierarchical roots. These are what we have been studying at length.

"Reason," in Ayn Rand's definition, is "the faculty that identifies and integrates the material provided by man's senses."[1] Or, as we may now expand it: reason is the faculty that enables man to discover the nature of existents—by virtue of its power to condense sensory information in accordance with the requirements of an objective mode of cognition. Or: reason is the faculty that organizes perceptual units in conceptual terms by following the principles of logic. This formulation highlights the three elements essential to the faculty: its data, percepts; its form, concepts; its method, logic.

Is reason, so defined, a valid means of cognition? Does it bring man knowledge of reality? The question reduces to: are the senses valid? are concepts valid? is logic valid? To these questions, the answer has already been given.

Reason is the faculty which begins with facts (sensory data); which organizes these data in accordance with facts (the mathematical relationships among concretes); and which is guided at each step by rules that rest on the fundamental fact (the law of identity). The rules require that each cognition be reduced back *to* the facts one started with. In regard to reason's every element and aspect, from matter to form to method and from start to finish, one conclusion is inescapable: reason is the existence-oriented faculty.

"Why should I accept reason?" means: "Why should I accept reality?" The answer is that existence exists, and only existence exists. Man's choice is either to accept reason or to consign his consciousness and life to a void.

One cannot seek a proof that reason is reliable, because reason is the faculty of proof; one must accept and use reason in any attempt to prove anything. But, using reason, one *can* identify its relationship to the facts of reality and thereby validate the faculty. The past four chapters are the gist of the Objectivist validation.

To complete the case, we must now answer two further questions. Is reason man's *only* means of knowledge, or is there an alternative or supplement to it, such as emotion? And what is implied by "knowledge" in this context? Does reason, even if it is man's sole means of cognition, lead us merely to tentative insights and ephemeral hypotheses? Or does reason lead man to *certainty?*

In pursuing these questions, we will be developing several important epistemological corollaries of the Objectivist view of reason, as presented so far. These corollaries identify the difference between reason and emotion, between the logical and the arbitrary, and between human knowledge and omniscience.

Emotions as a Product of Ideas

Let us begin by defining the nature of emotions and their relationship to ideas. What is the connection between feeling and thinking?[2]

A feeling or emotion is a response to an object one perceives (or imagines), such as a man, an animal, an event. The object by itself, however, has no power to invoke a feeling in the observer. It can do so only if he supplies two *intellectual* elements, which are necessary conditions of any emotion.

First, the person must know in some terms what the object is. He must have some understanding or identification of it (whether true or false, specific or generalized, explicit or implicit). Otherwise, to him, the object is nothing; it is a mere cognitive blank, to which no one can respond.

Second, the person must evaluate the object. He must conclude that it is good or bad, desirable or undesirable, for his values or against them. Here too the mental content may take many forms; the value-judgments being applied may be explicit or implicit, rational or contradictory, sharply defined or vague, consciously known to the person or unidentified, even repressed. In whatever form the individual holds his values, however, he must estimate the object in accordance with them. Otherwise, the object—even if he knows what it is—is an evaluative blank to him. Such an object cannot trigger an emotional response; being regarded neither as a positive nor a negative, it is a matter of indifference.

Emotions are states of consciousness with bodily accompaniments and with spiritual—intellectual—causes. This last factor is the basis for distinguishing "emotion" from "sensation." A sensation is an experience transmitted by purely physical means; it is independent of a person's ideas. Touch a man with a red-hot poker, and he unavoidably feels certain sensations—heat, pressure, pain—regardless of whether he is a savage or a sophisticate, an Objectivist or a mystic. By contrast, love, desire, fear, anger, joy are not simply products of physical stimuli. They depend on the content of the mind.

To concretize the point, let us say that six men look at a screen on which a series of medical slides is projected; the slides contain cross sections of various bodily tissues. One man is a savage fresh from the jungle; to him, the procession of eerie shadows and colors—which is all he can make of it—suggests, say, something undreamed of and inexplicable, some ominous supernatural force; he feels a pang of dread. A second man is civilized but ignorant; he knows that the slides are something safe and scientific, but has no idea what they mean;

he yawns. A third man is a painter of the representational school; he too lacks medical knowledge but, focussing on a certain group of blobs, he thinks: "It reminds me of Kandinsky. How hideous!"—and feels a touch of revulsion. Then we bring St. Augustine to look at the screen; he understands only that this is a product of that blasphemous science of the pagans, and he feels anger, even outrage, in the presence of such "lust of the eyes." Then a physician comes in and feels a stab of sorrow; the screen reveals tissue taken from the body of his close friend and means, he understands, a fatal illness. Finally, an ivory-tower researcher looks at the screen. He has spent years looking for a certain type of growth to prove a complex anatomical theory, the culmination of his life's work; he sees the growth before him—and feels a surge of elation.

The same object has been perceived by members of the same species. Yet depending on their conceptual context—on their knowledge of what the object is and above all on their value-judgments—they feel superstitious dread or yawning indifference or esthetic revulsion or pious condemnation or painful depression or joyous exultation. What caused these emotional states? The slides? The physical object by itself? Clearly not. The cause is the slides *as identified and evaluated,* the slides as grasped and appraised by a *mind.*[3]

When, as a college teacher, I would reach the topic of emotions in class, my standard procedure was to open the desk, take out a stack of examination booklets, and, without any explanations, start distributing them. Consternation invariably broke loose, with cries such as "You never said we were having a test today!" and "It isn't fair!" Whereupon I would take back the booklets and ask: "How many can explain the emotion that just swept over you? Is it an inexplicable primary, a quirk of your glands, a message from God or the id?" The answer was obvious. The booklets, to most of them, meant failure on an exam, a lower grade in the course, a blot on their transcript, i.e., bad news. On this one example, even the dullest students grasped with alacrity that emotions do have causes and that their causes are the things men think. (The auditors in the room, who do not write exams, remained calm during this experiment. To them, the surprise involved no negative value-judgment.)

There are four steps in the generation of an emotion: perception (or imagination), identification, evaluation, response. Normally, only the first and last of these are conscious. The two intellectual steps, identification and evaluation, occur as a rule without the need of conscious awareness and with lightninglike rapidity.

Once a man has acquired a vocabulary of conceptual knowledge, he automatizes it, just as one automatizes the knowledge of spelling, typing, or any complex skill. Thereafter one does not need a process of learning in order to grasp that something is a booklet portending an examination; the application of the relevant concepts is immediate and unhesitating. Similarly, once a man has formed a series of value-judgments, he automatizes them. He does not need a process of appraisal in order to decide that he values a high grade on a test; the application of the relevant judgments is immediate. One's value-judgments, like one's past knowledge, are present in the subconscious—meaning by this term a store of the mental contents one has acquired by conscious means, but which are not in conscious awareness at a given time. Under the appropriate conditions, the mind applies such contents to a new object automatically and instantaneously, without the need of further conscious consideration. To many people, as a result, it seems as if men perceive and then feel, with no intervening factor. The truth is that a chain of ideas and value-judgments intervenes.[4]

I say "chain" because (after a child's early years) the intervening conclusions have a definite structure: value-judgments do not exist in a vacuum. Value-judgments are formed ultimately on the basis of a philosophic view of man and life—of oneself, of others, of the universe; such a view, therefore, conditions all one's emotions. If, for example, a man's basic mental set amounts to the idea that he is a helpless incompetent caught in an unknowable jungle, this will affect his value-judgments in every department of life. It will affect his character, his ambition, his work (if any), his preferences in friends, art, entertainment. By contrast, if a man holds that his mind is efficacious and the universe intelligible, he will form radically different values and, as a result, experience radically different wants, likes, and dislikes.

Most people hold their views of man and life only implicitly, not explicitly. But such views nevertheless are crucial:

they constitute the fundamental programming of a man's sub-conscious. As such, they shape all of his evaluative and affective life. (For further discussion of this point, see chapter 12.)

An emotion derives from a percept assessed within a context; the context is defined by a highly complex conceptual content. Most of this content at any time is not present in conscious awareness. But it is real and operative nonetheless.

What makes emotions incomprehensible to many people is the fact that their ideas are not only largely subconscious, but also inconsistent. Men have the ability to accept contradictions without knowing it. This leads to the appearance of a *conflict* between thought and feelings.

A man can hold ideas of which he is rarely or never aware and which clash with his professed beliefs. The former may be ideas which he has forgotten forming, or which he has accepted only by implication, without ever identifying the fact, or which he actively works not to know. If he then responds to an object in terms of such hidden mental contents, it will seem to him that his emotions are independent of his thinking and even at war with it. In fact, his emotions are still following from his conclusions, but he does not identify these latter correctly.

A young boy, for example, fills his subconscious across years with negative value-judgments in regard to his mother, who is cruel to him. He is not attentive to his mental processes, however, so that much of this content remains implicit and unidentified. As he grows up, he forgets his childhood experiences and the estimates they provoked. Besides, he has accepted the idea that it is evil to criticize one's parents; so he makes it a point to insist on his mother's virtues and to brush aside any criticisms (to repress them). Then one day, at a party or in a psychiatrist's office, he complains: "I admire my mother; my mind tells me there is every reason to love her. But my heart doesn't listen. I hate her. What's wrong with me?" What's wrong is that he does not know his mind, i.e., his actual, operative value-judgments.

Emotions are not inexplicable demons, though they become that if a man holds contradictions and does not identify his ideas explicitly. Even then, the cause of emotions remains the same. Strictly speaking, a "clash between thought and feeling" is a misnomer; every such clash is at root an ideational clash.

The reason this point has eluded philosophers is the mind-body dichotomy, which has dominated the West ever since Plato.

Reason, the dichotomy's advocates typically claim, deals with abstractions and is therefore "pure," "nonempirical," "nonmaterialistic"—while emotions are bodily and worldly. It follows that emotions are a factor independent of man's mind, that they are a nonrational and even an antirational element built into human nature. It follows further that man cannot live exclusively by the guidance of reason, since he must also contend with and express its antithesis.

Conflicts in men, Plato maintained—the conflicts so often observed between their professed beliefs and their feelings—are a result not of avoidable errors, but of metaphysical law. The universe is a realm of conflict (true reality vs. the world of particulars), and man, the microcosm, has to reflect this conflict. He, too, must be split into warring parts, with one element (the intellect) urging him upward to the eternal, and the other (passion) pulling him down into the muck of action and the physical.

Plato is the West's most influential advocate of the reason-emotion dichotomy. The issue, however, is wider than Platonism; as we saw in the last chapter, the cause is basically epistemological, not metaphysical. If, in any form, intrinsicist or subjectivist, a thinker detaches the mind from reality, i.e., detaches concepts from percepts, then he can hardly avoid a whole brood of artificial clashes—including a clash between the faculty that functions by means of concepts (reason) and the faculty that responds to percepts (emotions). And then he will bemoan the "frailty" of his thought in the face of his inexplicable feelings. Here again we see the ugly, distorted offspring of a fundamental philosophic error.

Ayn Rand sweeps this traditional perspective aside. She holds that man *can* live exclusively by reason. He can do it because emotions are consequences generated by his conclusions. And man's conclusions have this kind of generative power because they are not revelations or inventions detached from the arena of physical action. Concepts (including evaluations) are man's form of integrating percepts.

Reason as Man's Only Means of Knowledge

Now let us consider the epistemological implications of the above discussion.

Reason is a faculty of awareness; its function is to perceive that which exists by organizing observational data. And reason is a volitional faculty; it has the power to direct its own actions and check its conclusions, the power to maintain a certain relationship to the facts of reality. Emotion, by contrast, is a faculty not of perception, but of reaction to one's perceptions. This kind of faculty has no power of observation and no volition; it has *no means of independent access to reality,* no means to guide its own course, and no capacity to monitor its own relationship to facts.

Emotions are automatic consequences of a mind's past conclusions, however that mind has been used *or misused* in the process of reaching them. The ideas and value-judgments at the root of a feeling may be true or false; they may be the product of meticulous logic or of a slapdash mess; they may be upheld in explicit terms, or they may be subconscious and unidentified. In all these cases, positive and negative alike, the feeling follows obediently. It has no power to question its course or to check its roots against reality. Only man's volitional, existence-oriented faculty has such power.

Feelings or emotions are not part of the method of logic; they are not evidence for a conclusion. The fact that a man has a certain feeling means merely that, through some kind of process, he earlier reached a certain idea, which is now stored in his subconscious; this leaves completely open the question of the idea's relationship to reality. To identify this relationship, one needs a process of validating ideas, i.e., a process of reason.[5]

Although reason and emotion by their nature are in harmony, the appearance of conflict between them, as we have seen, is possible; the source of such appearance is a contradiction between a man's conscious and subconscious conclusions in regard to an evaluative issue. When this occurs, the conscious ideas may be correct and the subconscious ones mistaken. Or the reverse may be the case: a man may consciously uphold a mistaken idea while experiencing a feeling that clashes with it, one that derives from a true subconscious premise. In both kinds of case, however, the real clash is between the two ideas. And the only way to resolve the conflict, to *know* which side is correct, is to submit both ideas to the bar of reason.

Even if its intellectual root happens to be true, a feeling cannot know this fact; it cannot judge cognitive status. Only the mind can decide questions of truth.

In chapter 1, from a study of the primacy of existence, I concluded that feelings are no avenue to truth. Introspection, I said, is not a means of external cognition. Now, through a study of man's means of consciousness, this earlier discussion has been confirmed and completed. Metaphysics and epistemology unite. They unite in declaring that *"emotions are not tools of cognition."*[6]

Now we can answer the question: is reason man's *only* means of knowledge? The answer requires one to grasp that the only other means of knowledge ever proposed is feeling or emotion.

Some men who propose an alternative to reason are explicit emotionalists. Others, however, seeming to eschew reason *and* emotion, uphold the cognitive efficacy of a variety of candidates, such as intuition, revelation, dialectic inference, Aryan instinct, extrasensory perception, or drug-induced trances.

The elements of reason are objectively identifiable; abstractions such as "percept," "concept," and "logic" are reducible to the data of observation. But abstractions such as "intuition," "revelation," and the rest, precisely because they purport to name a faculty that transcends reason, cannot be given objective definition; there is no logical chain linking such abstractions to sensory data. As a result, there is no objective means by which to use or apply such terms. Technically, they are invalid concepts. Practically, a person who uses them has no recourse but to rely on his feelings.

How is a man to know that the voice he hears comes from God or a noetic trance or the blood of the master race, whereas the voice heard by his enemy, who claims an opposite message from the same source, is a delusion or a fake? The perennial answer is: the man simply knows. How? He *feels* it. How does he know that his enemy's claim is mistaken?

He *feels* it. How does he know that these feelings of his are reliable? He *feels* it.

When a person declares that reason is not man's only means of knowledge, he ends up, admittedly or not, counting on emotion as his means of knowledge. Emotion is the only function left to guide human consciousness once one sets aside the mind's sensory and conceptual activities.

The conclusion is clear: there is no alternative or supplement to reason as a means of knowledge. If one attempts to give emotions such a role, then he has ceased to engage in the activity of cognition. Instead, he is subverting the integrity of his mental processes and invalidating them—by introducing as their guide nonobjective elements. An unanalyzed emotion, an emotion whose intellectual roots one has not identified and validated by a process of reason, is merely a subjective event of one's consciousness. It may be compared to a floating abstraction, or to a higher-level proposition that one has not reduced to perceptual data. It is a mental state disconnected from reality, a state whose relation to fact one does not know.

Turning now to practical significance, the present discussion implies a crucial epistemological responsibility. If a man seeks to think rationally, he must grasp the distinction between reason and emotion. He must learn, then methodically observe, the difference between thought and feeling—between logic and desire—between percepts and concepts on the one hand, and hopes, wishes, hates, loves, fears on the other. By continuous self-monitoring, he must ensure that during any cognitive activity, feeling is set to the side—that it is not allowed to direct the course of the inquiry or affect its outcome. A rational inquiry is one directed not by emotion, but by thought, one that accepts as evidence not any species of passion, but only provable, objective fact.

The above is not an "anti-emotion" viewpoint. Emotions play an essential role in human life, and in this role they must be felt, nourished, respected. Without such a faculty, men could not achieve happiness or even survival; they would experience no desire, no love, no fear, no motivation, no response to values. The epistemological point, however, remains unaffected: the role of emotions, though essential, is not the discovery of reality. One casts no aspersion on eating or breathing if one denies that they are means of cognition. The same applies to feeling.

Objectivism is not against emotions, but *emotionalism*. Ayn Rand's concern is not to uphold stoicism or abet repression, but to identify a division of mental labor. There is nothing wrong with feeling that follows from an act of thought; this is the natural and proper human pattern. There is everything wrong with feeling that seeks to replace thought, by usurping its function.

If an individual experiences a clash between feeling and thought, he should not ignore his feelings. He should identify the ideas at their base (which may be a time-consuming process); then compare these ideas to his conscious conclusions, weighing the conflicts objectively; then amend his viewpoint accordingly, disavowing the ideas he judges to be false. What he should seek is not escape through repression, but full identification and then *rational* analysis of his ideas, culminating in a new, noncontradictory integration. The result will be the reestablishment in his consciousness of emotional harmony.

The above indicates the pattern of the proper relationship between reason and emotion in a man's life: reason first, emotion as a consequence. Reason is the fundamental faculty of human consciousness, the existence-oriented faculty. Emotion is a derivative, which must be treated as such. One must, therefore, begin any inquiry or undertaking with a focus on reality; i.e., one must begin with the commitment to obey reason, in every issue and at all costs. One proceeds to form conclusions, including value-judgments, accordingly (and to revise them when necessary). Then one experiences the emotions to which these conclusions lead. In this approach to life, reality and reason are given the primary position; they are regarded as one's guiding absolute, to which emotion must conform.

The alternative is the attempt to invert the relationship by making the sequence: emotion as a primary, reason and reality as derivatives. To such a person, an emotion, regardless of its source, is the guiding absolute, which takes precedence over thought and to which facts are expected to conform. This is the policy of placing an "I wish" above an "It is." The people who do it, Ayn Rand writes,

take their emotions as a cause, and their mind as a passive
effect. They make their emotions their tool for perceiving
reality. They hold their desires as an irreducible primary,
as a fact superseding all facts. An honest man does not
desire until he has identified the object of his desire. He
says: "It is, therefore I want it." They say: "I want it,
therefore it is."[7]

Epistemologically, this inversion means the rejection of
objectivity. Metaphysically, it means the primacy of consciousness and thus the rejection of reality. Psychologically,
it is what underlies the process of evasion. Ethically, therefore, it is the root of all evil.

Rationality in the present issue consists in forming one's
emotions on the basis of one's best, most scrupulously logical
perception of reality, and then in remembering that emotions
are consequences, which cannot be followed apart from reality. Irrationality consists in taking one's feelings, however
formed, as an absolute, then expecting reality to adjust to
them. Reality, however, will not adjust. A is A.

The Arbitrary as Neither True Nor False

Claims based on emotion are widespread today and are possible in any age. In the terminology of logic, such claims are
"arbitrary," i.e., devoid of evidence. What is the rational response to such ideas, whether they are asserted by others or
are a product of one's own fancy?

Granted that an arbitrary declaration does not qualify as
knowledge, might it nevertheless still be true? If so, should
one suspend judgment? Should one allow that it is unproved
but possible? Is one obliged to refute such an idea in order to
justify rejecting it? In short, what is the epistemological status
of the arbitrary, and how should claims of this kind be dealt
with by an exponent of reason?

Aside from offering practical guidance on a matter that is
urgent today, my deeper purpose here is to identify a corollary of the last chapter's discussion of logic. The corollary
illuminates from a new aspect the futility of any nonrational
approach to epistemology.

An arbitrary claim is one for which there is no evidence, either perceptual or conceptual. It is a brazen assertion, based neither on direct observation nor on any attempted logical inference therefrom. For example, a man tells you that the soul survives the death of the body; or that your fate will be determined by your birth on the cusp of Capricorn and Aquarius; or that he has a sixth sense which surpasses your five; or that a convention of gremlins is studying Hegel's *Logic* on the planet Venus. If you ask him "Why?" he offers no argument. "I can't prove any of these statements," he admits—"but you can't disprove them, either."

The answer to all such statements, according to Objectivism, is: an arbitrary claim is automatically invalidated. The rational response to such a claim is to dismiss it, without discussion, consideration, or argument.

An arbitrary statement has no relation to man's means of knowledge. Since the statement is detached from the realm of evidence, no process of logic can assess it. Since it is affirmed in a void, cut off from any context, no integration to the rest of man's knowledge is applicable; previous knowledge is irrelevant to it. Since it has no place in a hierarchy, no reduction is possible, and thus no observations are relevant. An arbitrary statement cannot be cognitively processed; by its nature, it is detached from any rational method or content of human consciousness. Such a statement is necessarily detached from reality as well. If an idea is cut loose from any means of cognition, there is no way of bringing it into relationship with reality.

An arbitrary claim is not merely an unwarranted effusion. By demanding one's consideration in defiance of all the requirements of reason, it becomes an affront to reason and to the science of epistemology. In the absence of evidence, there is no way to consider any idea, on any subject. There is no way to reach a cognitive verdict, favorable or otherwise, about a statement to which logic, knowledge, and reality are irrelevant. There is nothing the mind can do to or with such a phenomenon except sweep it aside.

An arbitrary idea must be given the exact treatment its nature demands. One must treat it as though nothing had been said. The reason is that, cognitively speaking, *nothing has been said.* One cannot allow into the realm of cognition something that repudiates every rule of that realm.

None of the concepts formed to describe human knowledge can be applied to the arbitrary; none of the classifications of epistemology can be usurped in its behalf. Since it has no relation to evidence, an arbitrary statement cannot be subsumed under concepts that identify different amounts of evidence; it cannot be described as "possible," "probable," or "certain." (These concepts are discussed in the next section.) Similarly, such a statement cannot be subsumed under concepts that identify different relations between an idea and reality. *An arbitrary statement is neither "true" nor "false."*

The concept of "truth" identifies a type of relationship between a proposition and the facts of reality. "Truth," in Ayn Rand's definition, is "the recognition of reality."[8] In essence, this is the traditional correspondence theory of truth: there is a reality independent of man, and there are certain conceptual products, propositions, formulated by human consciousness. When one of these products corresponds to reality, when it constitutes a recognition of fact, then it is true. Conversely, when the mental content does not thus correspond, when it constitutes not a recognition of reality but a contradiction of it, then it is false.

A relationship between conceptual content and reality is a relationship between man's consciousness and reality. There can be no "correspondence" or "recognition" without the mind that corresponds or recognizes. If a wind blows the sand on a desert island into configurations spelling out "A is A," this does not make the wind a superior metaphysician. The wind did not achieve any conformity to reality; it did not produce any truth, but merely shapes in the sand. Similarly, if a parrot is trained to squawk "2 + 2 = 4," this does not make it a mathematician. The parrot's consciousness did not attain thereby any contact with reality or any relation to it, positive or negative; the parrot did not recognize or contradict any fact; what it created was not truth or falsehood, but merely sounds. Sounds that are not the vehicle of conceptual awareness have no cognitive status.

An arbitrary claim emitted by a human mind is analogous to the shapes made by the wind or to the sounds of the parrot. Such a claim has no cognitive relationship to reality, positive or negative. The true is identified by reference to a body of evidence; it is pronounced "true" because it can be integrated without contradiction into a total context. The false is identified by the same means; it is pronounced "false" because it contradicts the evidence and/or some aspect of the wider context. The arbitrary, however, has no relation to evidence or context; neither term, therefore—"true" or "false"—can be applied to it.

Philosophically, the arbitrary is worse than the false. The false has a relation, albeit negative, to the facts of reality; it has reached the field of human cognition and invoked its methods, even though an error has been committed in the process. This is radically different from the capricious. The false does not destroy a man's ability to know; it does not nullify his grasp of objectivity; it leaves him the means of discovering and correcting his error. The arbitrary, however, if a man indulges in it, assaults his cognitive faculty; it wipes out or makes impossible in his mind the concept of rational cognition and thus entrenches his inner chaos for life.[9] As to the practical consequences of this difference, whom would you prefer to work for, talk to, or buy groceries from: a man who miscounts the people in his living room (an error), or who declares that the room is filled with demons (the arbitrary)?

Now let us note that some arbitrary claims (though by no means all) can be *transferred to a cognitive context* and converted thereby into true or false statements, which demonstrably correspond to or contradict established fact. It is not mere words that determine epistemological status, but their relation to evidence. A savage's memorized recital of an arithmetical sum, for example, would be like the parrot's; but the same utterance by a man who understands the reason behind it would constitute a truth. Or consider the claim that there is an infinite, omnipotent creator of the universe. If this claim is viewed as a product of faith or fantasy, apart from any relation to evidence, it has no cognitive standing. If one wishes, however, one can relate this claim to an established context, as I did in the opening chapter: one can demonstrate that the idea of God contradicts all the fundamentals of a rational philosophy. Thanks to such a process of integration, what was initially arbitrary attains cognitive status—in this instance, as a falsehood.

Even when it is possible, however, this kind of integration is never obligatory. To bring unwarranted claims into relation to human knowledge is not a requirement of cognition. Knowledge does not advance by a man's seizing on the arbitrary or letting it dictate the subject matter of his thought; no truth otherwise unknown can be uncovered thereby. What one can legitimately seek to achieve by such integration is not the proof or disproof of a claim, but merely the identification of the precise nature of an error, as in the God example—and even this much is of value only to those in whose mind it *is* an error (as against being the deliberately arbitrary).

No identification of error will affect the determined exponent of the arbitrary. If he hears his claim being related to counterevidence, he will act promptly to insulate it from logic. For example, he will answer objections as theologians have done through the centuries. "The meaning of 'God' is beyond the power of language to specify," they say. "God in this sense does not involve any contradiction of man's knowledge, as we would see clearly if only we could know Him—which we cannot, not in this life. Prove that *this* God does not exist."

This brings us back to the arbitrary qua arbitrary, i.e., to the kind of claim that cannot by its nature be related to any established fact or context. In order to concretize the Objectivist principle that such claims cannot be cognitively processed, I want to elaborate here on a venerable rule of logic: the rule that the onus of proof is on him who asserts the positive, and that one must not attempt to prove a negative.

The onus of proof rule states the following. If a person asserts that a certain entity exists (such as God, gremlins, a disembodied soul), he is required to adduce evidence supporting his claim. If he does so, one must either accept his conclusion, or disqualify his evidence by showing that he has misinterpreted certain data. But if he offers no supporting evidence, one must dismiss his claim *without argumentation,* because in this situation argument would be futile. It is impossible to "prove a negative," meaning by the term: prove the nonexistence of an entity *for* which there is no evidence.

The reason is the fact that existence exists, and *only* existence exists. A thing that exists is something; it is an entity in the world; as such, it has effects by which men can grasp and prove it—either directly, by perceptual means, or indirectly, by logical inference (e.g., the discovery of atoms). But a nonexistent is nothing; it is not a constituent of reality, and it has no effects. If gremlins, for instance, do not exist, then they are nothing and have no consequences. In such a case, to say: "Prove that there are no gremlins," is to say: "Point out the facts of reality that follow from the nonexistence of gremlins." But there are no such facts. Nothing follows from nothing.

All thought, argument, proof, refutation must start with that which exists. No inference can be drawn from a zero. If a person offers evidence for a positive, one can, if the claim is mistaken, identify his misinterpretations and in that sense refute him. But one cannot prove the corresponding negative by starting from a void.

For the sake of full clarity, I must add the following. One can infer from any truth the falsehood of its contradictories. For example, from "X was in New York during the Dallas shooting of Y" one can infer the falsehood of "X shot Y." Thus one *can* disprove a claim or "prove a negative" ("X is not guilty")—but only by demonstrating that the claim contradicts established knowledge; i.e., only by relating the claim to a positive cognitive context, when this is available. What one cannot do is prove a negative apart from such a relationship; what one cannot do is establish the falsehood of an arbitrary claim qua arbitrary. One establishes the false by reference to the true, not by reference to nothing.

Objectivism's refutation of theism, to take another example, is not a case of "proving a negative" in the sense vetoed by the onus-of-proof principle. Ayn Rand does not start with a zero and seek to discover evidence of God's nonexistence. She starts with reality, i.e., with (philosophically) known fact, then denies a claim that clashes with it. Nor, as I have made clear, does she expect any such refutation to be accepted by apostles of the arbitrary. These individuals will merely reformulate the claim so as to protect it from evidence, then insist again: "Prove that it is *not* so."

To this demand, there is only one valid response: "I refuse even to attempt such a task." An assertion outside the realm of cognition can impose no cognitive responsibility on a rational mind, neither of proof nor of disproof. The arbitrary is not open to either; it simply cannot be cognitively processed. The proper treatment of such an aberration is to refrain from sanctioning it by argument or discussion.

To dismiss a claim as "arbitrary" is not the equivalent of pleading ignorance or confessing indecision or suspending judgment. It is not the same as saying "I don't know" or "I haven't made up my mind" or "I have no opinion." These responses presuppose that an issue has a connection to human cognition; they presuppose that there is some evidence pertaining to the issue and, therefore, that it is legitimate to consider, even though one may be unable for various reasons to untangle it. For example, if the field is specialized, a given individual may not have the time to study the evidence, even though it is clear and abundant. Or the data may be so evenly balanced, or so fragmentary and ambiguous—for instance, in regard to judging a certain person's character—that one simply cannot decide what conclusion is warranted. In such cases, "I don't know" is an honest and appropriate statement.

If someone asks a man whether there are gremlins on Venus, however, there is no justification for the reply "I don't know." What doesn't he know? What evidence has he failed to study or been unable to clarify? What is the basis to believe that there *is* anything to learn on this subject? If the gremlin claim is arbitrary, there is no such basis. In this situation, the proper response is: "I *do* know. I know that any such claim is to be thrown out as inadmissible."

The reason that Objectivism rejects *agnosticism* should now be clear. This term applies not only to the question of God, but also to many other issues, such as ESP, reincarnation, demonic possession, astrology, the Arab claim of an international Zionist conspiracy, and the Marxist claim that the state will wither away. In regard to all such issues and claims, of which there are an unlimited number today, the agnostic is the man who says: "We can't prove that the claim is true. But we can't prove that it is false, either. So the only proper conclusion is: we don't know; no one knows; perhaps no one ever can know."

Agnosticism is not simply the pleading of ignorance. It is the enshrinement of ignorance. It is the philosophic viewpoint that demands such pleading—in regard to effusions that are disconnected from evidence. The viewpoint poses as being fair, balanced, impartial. As should now be obvious, however, it is rife with fallacies and with prejudice.

The agnostic treats arbitrary claims as matters properly open to consideration, discussion, evaluation. He allows that it is "possible" that these claims are "true," thereby applying cognitive descriptions to verbiage that is at war with cognition. He demands proof of a negative: it's up to you, he declares, to show that there are no demons, or that your sex life is *not* a result of your previous incarnation as a pharaoh of ancient Egypt.

The agnostic miscalculates. Typically, he believes that he has avoided taking any controversial position and is thus safe from attack. In fact, he is taking a profoundly irrational position. In struggling to elevate the arbitrary to a position of cognitive respect, he is attempting to equate the arbitrary with the logically supported. This is not merely an affirmation of ignorance; it is an *epistemological* egalitarianism intent on obliterating an essential distinction. Such an attitude is incomparably more destructive than any error committed by a man devoted to reason who takes definite stands on the basis of mistaken arguments.

A passion for the arbitrary does not derive from concern for logic. Its root is a feeling that has been given precedence over logic. In some agnostics, the feeling is cowardice, the simple fear that a stand on contentious issues will antagonize people. In other agnostics, the feeling is more convoluted. It is akin to glee, the malicious glee of subverting all ideas and thus of baiting the men who have the integrity required to hold convictions. This is the glee of the destroyer, the mindhater, the nihilist.

Of all the variants of emotionalism, nihilism is the ugliest. Don't let its exponents infect your mind or your methodology.

In considering any issue, never permit yourself one minute in the quicksands of a baseless "I don't know." Instead, establish first that the issue is related to the realm of evidence and thus deserves consideration. Then study the evidence, weighing the possibilities in accordance with the principles of logic. *Then make up your mind and take a stand.*

To pursue truth implies that one wants to find it. The

purpose and responsibility of a cognitive quest is to achieve the very thing the agnostic dreads most: cognition.

Let me conclude the present discussion by stating its broader significance. Logic *is* man's method of knowledge, and it cannot be defaulted on with impunity, as the emotionalists of all varieties seek to do. Any such default exacts a fearsome toll—epistemologically, the worst there is: it ejects the mental process in question from the realm of cognition.

One cannot get something for nothing—not in the field of material wealth, and not in the field of knowledge, either. One cannot reach truth, any more than knowledge, by accident. One can reach it only by a process of reason.

Certainty as Contextual

In turning to the question: does reason lead man to certainty? I must begin by reaffirming that human knowledge is limited. At every stage of conceptual development, a man has a specific cognitive context; he knows something, but not everything. Only on the basis of this delimited information can he gain new knowledge.

In the previous chapter, I stressed the importance of relating a new idea to the full context—of seeking to reduce the idea to the data of sense and to integrate it with the rest of one's conclusions. Now I want to develop a further point: once these logical requirements have been met, the idea has been *validated*. If a man evades relevant data; or if, defaulting on the process of logic, he jumps from the data to an unwarranted conclusion; then of course his conclusion does not qualify as knowledge. But if he does consider all the available evidence, and he does employ the method of logic in assessing it, then his interpretation must be regarded as valid.

Logical processing of an idea within a specific context of knowledge is necessary *and sufficient* to establish the idea's truth.

The point is that one cannot demand omniscience. One cannot ask: "How do I know that a given idea, even if it has been proved on the basis of all the knowledge men have gained so far, will not be overthrown one day by new information as yet undiscovered?" This plaint is tantamount to the declaration: "Human knowledge is limited; so we cannot trust any of our conclusions." And *this* amounts to taking the myth of an infinite God as the epistemological standard, by reference to which man's consciousness is condemned as impotent.

Consciousness has identity, and epistemology is based on the recognition of this fact. Epistemology investigates the question: what rules must be followed by a *human* consciousness if it is to perceive reality correctly? Nothing inherent in human consciousness, therefore, can be used to undermine it.

If a fact is inherent in human consciousness, then that fact is not an obstacle to cognition, but a precondition of it—and one which implies a corresponding epistemological obligation. For instance, man's primary contact with reality is sense perception (a fact)—and he must, therefore, ground his more advanced cognitions on this base (an obligation). Or: man integrates sensory material by a volitional, conceptual process—and he must, therefore, guide the process by adherence to logic. Or: man experiences his evaluations in the form of emotions, which are not perceptions, but reactions to them—and he must, therefore, separate such reactions from the cognitive activity of thought. None of these facts is a difficulty to be bewailed or somehow got around; each is a reality to be recognized and followed in the pursuit of knowledge. By its nature as an attribute of man's consciousness, each constitutes part of the context in which epistemological concepts arise. (I mean concepts such as "valid," "true," "certain," "absolute," etc.) In this approach to philosophy, there is no "problem" of the senses, of concepts, of emotions—or of man's nonomniscience.

Man is a being of limited knowledge—*and he must, therefore, identify the cognitive context of his conclusions*. In any situation where there is reason to suspect that a variety of factors is relevant to the truth, only some of which are presently known, he is obliged to acknowledge this fact. The implicit or explicit preamble to his conclusion must be: "On the basis of the available evidence, i.e., within the context of the factors so far discovered, the following is the proper conclusion to draw." Thereafter, the individual must continue to observe and identify; should new information warrant it, he must qualify his conclusion accordingly.

If a man follows this policy, he will find that his knowledge at one stage *is not contradicted* by later discoveries. He will find that the discoveries expand his understanding; that he learns more about the conditions on which his conclusions depend; that he moves from relatively generalized, primitive observations to increasingly detailed, sophisticated formulations. He will also find that the process is free of epistemological trauma. The advanced conclusions augment and enhance his earlier knowledge; they do not clash with or annul it.

I have already illustrated this fact in the discussion of contextual definitions. Here is another kind of example, drawn from the field of scientific induction. Some time ago, medical researchers learned to identify four types of blood: A, B, AB, and O. When blood was transfused from one individual to another, some of these blood types proved to be compatible while others were not (an undesirable reaction, hemolysis, occurred). For example, the blood of an A-type donor was compatible with that of an A-type recipient, but not with that of a B-type. Later, a new discovery was made: in certain cases, an undesirable reaction occurred even when blood of type A was given to an A-type recipient. Further investigation revealed another factor at work, the RH factor, which was found in the blood of some individuals but not others. The initial generalization (for short, "A bloods are compatible") was thus discovered to hold only under a circumstance that had earlier been unidentified. Given this knowledge, the generalization had to be qualified ("A bloods are compatible if their RH factors are matched").

The principle here is evident: since a later discovery rests hierarchically on earlier knowledge, it cannot contradict its own base. The qualified formulation in no way clashes with the initial proposition, viz.: "Within the context of the circumstances so far known, A bloods are compatible." This proposition represented real knowledge when it was first reached, and it still does so; in fact, like all properly formulated truths, this truth is immutable. Within the context initially specified, A bloods *are* and always will be compatible.

The appearance of a contradiction between new knowledge and old derives from a single source: context-dropping. If the researchers had decided to view their initial discovery as an *out-of-context* absolute; if they were to declare—in effect, as a matter of dogma: "A bloods will always be compatible, regardless of altered circumstances"; then of course the next factor discovered would plunge them into contradiction, and they would end up complaining that knowledge is impossible. But if a man reaches conclusions logically and grasps their contextual nature, intellectual progress poses no threat to him; it consists to a great extent in his identifying ever more fully the relationships, the connections among facts, that make the world a unity. Such a man is not dismayed to find that he always has more to learn. He is happy about it, because he recognizes that he is expanding and refining his knowledge, not subverting it.

Although the researchers cannot claim their discovery as an out-of-context absolute, they must treat it as a *contextual absolute* (i.e., as an immutable truth within the specified context).

The researchers must *know* that the initial generalization is valid—"know" as against guess, hope, or feel. It is only on this basis that they can progress to further discoveries. Since it is an established truth that A bloods are compatible under the circumstances so far encountered, the researchers are able to infer, when they observe a new reaction, the presence of a new factor. By contrast, when the anti-contextual mentality observes the new reaction, he stops dead. "My generalization was unreliable," he sighs, "science is a progression of exploded theories, everything is relative."

A man does not know everything, but he does know what he knows. The choice is not: to make unwarranted, dogmatic claims or to give up the cognitive quest in despair. Both these policies stem from the notion that omniscience is the standard. One side then pretends to have access to it somehow, while the other bewails our lack of such access. In reason, however, this kind of standard must be rejected. Conceptual knowledge rests on logic within a context, not on omniscience. If an idea has been logically proved, then it is valid and it is an absolute—*contextually*. This last term, indeed, does not introduce a factor distinct from logic and should not have to be stressed: to adduce evidence for a conclusion *is* to place it within a context and thereby to define precisely the conditions of its applicability.

Many people in our Kantian era think, mistakenly, that

absolutism is incompatible with a contextual approach to knowledge. These people define an "absolute" as a principle independent of any other fact or cognition; i.e., as something unaffected by anything else in reality or in human knowledge. Such a principle could come to be known only by revelation. An eloquent example of this approach was offered years ago by a famous relativist, who told his class that airplanes refute the law of gravitation. Gravitation, he explained, means that entities over a certain weight fall to the earth; but an airplane in flight does not. Someone objected that there are many interacting factors in reality, and that gravitation involves an object's falling only if the gravitational pull is not counteracted by an opposing force, as it is in the airplane's case. To which the professor replied: "Precisely. Gravitation is conditional; its operation depends on circumstances; so it is not an absolute." What then *would* qualify as an absolute? Only a fact that has no relationships to anything (like Hegel's supernatural Absolute). Such a fact would be knowable only "in itself," by mystic insight, without the "contamination" of any "external" context of evidence.

The modern definition of "absolute" represents the rejection of a rational metaphysics and epistemology. It is the inversion of a crucial truth: *relationships are not the enemy of absolutism; they are what make it possible.* We prove a conclusion on the basis of facts logically related to it and then integrate it into the sum of our knowledge. That process is what enables us to say: "Everything points to this conclusion; the total context demands it; within these conditions, it is unshakable." About an isolated revelation, by contrast, we could never be secure. Since we would know nothing that *makes* it so, we could count on nothing to *keep* it so, either.

Contextualism does not mean relativism. It means the opposite. The fact of context does not weaken human conclusions or make them vulnerable to overthrow. On the contrary, context is precisely what makes a (properly specified) conclusion invulnerable.

So far, I have considered only two mental states, knowledge and ignorance, and two corresponding verdicts to define an idea's status: "validated" or "unknown." Inherent in the mind's need of logic, however, is a third, intermediate status, which applies for a while to certain complex higher-level conclusions. In these cases, the validation of an idea is gradual; one accumulates evidence step by step, moving from ignorance to knowledge through a continuum of transitional states. The main divisions of this continuum (including its terminus) are identified by three concepts: "possible," "probable," and "certain."

The first range of the evidential continuum is covered by the concept "possible." A conclusion is "possible" if there is some, but not much, evidence in favor of it, and nothing known that contradicts it. This last condition is obviously required—a conclusion that contradicts known facts is false—but it is not sufficient to support a verdict of "possible." There are countless gratuitous claims in regard to which one cannot cite any contradictory fact, because they are inherently detached from facts; this does not confer on such claims any cognitive status. For an idea to qualify as "possible," there must be a certain amount of evidence that actually supports it. If there is no such evidence, the idea falls under a different concept: not "possible," but "arbitrary."

"Possible" (and its synonyms), like any legitimate term, denotes an objective concept; it does not offer emotionalists an epistemological blank check. To say "maybe" in a cognitive context is to make a definite claim—it is to assert an idea's positive relationship to the evidential continuum—and, like any other cognitive claim, this requires demonstration. Gremlins and their ilk may not be described as "possible."

"Evidence," according to the *Oxford English Dictionary,* is "testimony or facts tending to prove or disprove any conclusion." To determine whether a fact is "evidence," therefore, one must first define what proof of a given claim would consist of. Then one must demonstrate that the fact, although inconclusive, contributes to such proof, i.e., strengthens the claim logically and thus moves the matter closer to a cognitive resolution. If one has no idea what the proof of a conclusion would consist of—or if one holds that a proof of it is impossible—one has no means of deciding whether a given piece of information "tends to prove" it. If the terminus of a journey is undefined or unknowable, there is no way to judge whether one is moving toward it.

This is why there can be no such thing as "some evidence" in favor of an entity transcending nature and logic.

The term "evidence" in this context would be a stolen concept. Since nothing can ever qualify as a "proof" of such an entity, there is no way to identify any data as being a "part proof" of it, either. There is no way to validate such a notion as: "that which brings men closer to knowing the unknowable or proving the unprovable."

By contrast, to take a simple example, we do know in principle how to demonstrate a murderer's guilt; in this case the requirements of logical proof have been objectively defined. By reference to this standard, we can identify certain data as "evidentiary" while setting aside other information as irrelevant. Thus, schematically: if a man who hated the victim was present at the scene of his shooting, then, other things being equal, we can legitimately conclude: "Maybe he did it." To establish motive and opportunity does move the cognitive matter forward; since we know what would constitute a full case against a suspect, we are able to grasp that these points, while not conclusive, are at least part of what is needed. On the other hand, one cannot justify even a "maybe" by citing the facts that a given man had visited the victim a month earlier and disliked his taste in ties or murder mysteries. Such information has no tendency to establish guilt; it does not provide any part of a proper case against a suspect. (In some contexts, such information may warrant an investigation to determine whether evidence of the man's guilt can be found elsewhere.)

Now let us note that information about the capacities of a species is not evidence supporting a hypothesis about one of its members. From "Man is capable of murder" one cannot infer "Maybe Mr. X is the killer we are seeking." To validate the latter, one must have grounds to suspect that the human capacity in question was actually exercised by this individual. To change the example: it is possible for a human being to run the mile in less than four minutes, and it is possible for a living organism to reproduce after its kind. I cannot, however, go over to a crippled gentleman in his wheelchair and say: "Maybe you'll give birth to a son next week, when you finish running the mile to the hospital in 3.9 minutes—after all, you're living and human, and it is possible for such an entity to do these things."

"It is possible *for man* . . ." does not justify "It is possible *that this man . . ."* The latter claim depends on the individual involved and on the specific circumstances. It must, therefore, be supported by data that are equally specific.

Like all cognitive claims, possibilities are asserted within a context. Should it change, the verdict must change accordingly: the initial possibility may be weakened (even erased), or it may be strengthened. If favorable evidence continues to be discovered, at a certain point the claim stops being merely "possible." It becomes *probable.*

"Probable" indicates a higher range of the evidential continuum. A conclusion is "probable" if the burden of a substantial body of evidence, although still inconclusive, supports it. In this case, there are not merely "some" supporting data, but a relatively extensive amount, although these data have not yet reached the standard of proof. Because they have not, there are still objective grounds to remain in doubt about the final verdict.

To continue our example: if the investigation of the shooting reveals, say, only three suspects with motive and at least the appearance of opportunity; and one of these proves to have an ironclad alibi; and of the remaining two, one is familiar with firearms, answers police questions evasively, and has a criminal record—then, as this kind of data mounts up, the burden of a substantial body of evidence increasingly points to one individual, who thus becomes the likeliest suspect; although there are still grounds for doubt. These grounds, to repeat, are defined by reference to the standard of proof in this kind of case. Since we know what would constitute conclusive demonstration, we know that we have still not reached it. For instance, we have not yet established means, i.e., the suspect's access to the murder weapon.

Like possibilities, probabilities are asserted within a context and may be weakened or strengthened as it changes. If favorable evidence continues to be discovered, at some point the cognitive climax will be reached. The conclusion ceases to be a hypothesis and becomes knowledge. Such a conclusion is *certain.*

The concept of "certainty" designates knowledge from a particular perspective: it designates some complex items of knowledge considered in contrast to the transitional evidential states that precede them. (By extension, the term may be applied to all knowledge, perceptual and conceptual, to indicate that it is free of doubt.) A conclusion is "certain" when the evidence in its favor is conclusive; i.e., when it has been logically validated. At this stage, one has gone beyond "substantial" evidence. Rather, the total of the available evidence points in a single direction, and this evidence fulfills the standard of proof. In such a context, there is nothing to suggest even the possibility of another interpretation. There are, therefore, no longer any grounds for doubt.

To conclude our example: if further investigation reveals that the likeliest suspect was also, by the testimony of the gun seller, the purchaser of the murder weapon; that the killer must have been left-handed and so is this suspect; and that his fingerprints are on the gun; while the only other suspect has no known connection to the weapon, is right-handed, and has no idea how to use a gun—then, in this evidential context, a definite conclusion emerges. If one and only one individual has motive, opportunity, and means, he is the culprit. (I take this formulation of the standard of proof from Hercule Poirot.) At this point, our conclusion is certain. We have integrated all the available evidence and fulfilled the requirements of a complete case.

Certainty, like possibility and probability, is contextual. It is a verdict reached within a definite framework of evidence, and it stands or falls with the evidence. For example, a defense attorney could not save this suspect by brushing aside the context and uttering a string of arbitrary "maybe's," such as: "Maybe the gun seller lied . . . maybe the fingerprints are a frameup . . . maybe the criminal record is a mixup . . . maybe the suspect was really in Tibet and everyone who placed him at the murder scene was hypnotized." The question is: within the total evidential context, are there any objective data to support these hypotheses? If there are not, none is admissible in any discussion of cognitive assessment; none qualifies as "possible."

The above kind of context-dropping is the stock in trade of the anticertainty zealots. Let me give you an example closer to home. Once, when I was a college student, an instructor defending skepticism declared to the class: "You think I am Professor X. But how do you know I'm not an impostor, a consummate actor taking the professor's place?" Transpose this question to your own situation. How can you be certain when you attend a lecture that it is Y, a man you know well, who is speaking, rather than an impostor?

In this case, the standard of validation is the direct testimony of your eyes and ears, as identified conceptually and then integrated to whatever other knowledge of yours is relevant. Judged by this standard, the proper conclusion to draw is outside the realm of doubt. *All* the available information—everything you observe and everything you know—leads to your identification of the speaker: the occasion, his appearance, his tone of voice, his facial expressions, his posture and gestures, the content of his prepared remarks, the quality of his extemporaneous jokes, his knowledge of your name and face, and so on. If a skeptic were to say: "But man does have the ability to impersonate others; so isn't it at least possible that the speaker is an actor?" the reply would have to be: "That is a non sequitur. On what basis do you claim someone's exercise of this human ability here and now? Is there an iota of evidence to support such a hypothesis *in this context?*" Of course, there is not.

Contrast this with a situation in which doubt would be legitimate. From certain angles, say, the speaker looks rather strange, and his manner seems uncharacteristically stiff; occasionally he utters incongruous remarks. On this basis, you might well begin to wonder "Maybe he's sick," or "Maybe he's upset." It is still premature to hypothesize impersonation; but, to play out the example, suppose that, though a staunch Aristotelian, he suddenly endorses Kant as the greatest philosopher, and he does not recognize people he has known for years, and his hairline seems to be sagging a bit; then you would have grounds to raise further possibilities, such as "Maybe he's having a breakdown," or "Maybe it's an impostor." And then, for a happy epistemological ending to this story, suppose that the mask suddenly falls from his face and Boris Karloff stands revealed. Then you can say: "It *was* an impostor! I'm certain."

The same kind of analysis disposes of a related skeptic expedient, the "problem of error." The nature of this problem is best brought out by the following exchanges between a skeptic (S) and his opponent (O), who has just offered an argument to defend some viewpoint.

S: "Man is fallible. Even with the best of training and intentions, he is capable of error. So how can you be certain
you are not wrong?"

O: "Man's general capacity to err does not warrant a hypothesis of error in a particular case. And I have validated my
conclusion; I have demonstrated that in this case I am *right.*"

S: "But your validation itself might be fallacious. How do
you know it isn't?"

O: "Can you point to any sign of such fallacy, such as a
logical flaw in my argument, or a neglected fact, or an im-
properly defined term?"

Here the skeptic is stopped. In order to identify specific
fallacies, he would have to enter the field of knowledge; he
would have to concede that he is able to assess evidence and
thus distinguish truth from error. So the discussion has to end
with the skeptic simply sweeping aside the whole context and
declaring: "I can't specify your error, but maybe it's there. I
can't tell the difference between your argument and a perfectly valid one, but still, I'm not sure. Prove that this non-
detectable error does not exist."

Here again we see all the flaws inherent in the assertion
of the arbitrary.[10]

Certainty is a contextual assessment, and in countless situations the context permits no other. Despite the claims of
skeptics, doubt is not the human fate, with cognition being an
unattainable ideal. Doubt, rationally exercised, is a temporary, transitional state, which is applicable only to (some)
higher-level questions—and which itself expresses a cognitive
judgment: that the evidence one has is still inconclusive. As
such, doubt is made possible only by a vast context of knowledge in the doubter's mind. The doubter must know both facts
and logic; he must know the facts known so far—and also the
means by which in principle his doubt is eventually to be removed, i.e., what else is required to reach full proof.

Doubt that is not arbitrary or pathological is a self-limiting
condition, both in scope and in duration. It is not the norm
of the mind but, at most, a frequent stage on the road to the
norm, which, when reached, ends it.

Is man capable of certainty? Since man has a faculty of
knowledge and nonomniscience is no obstacle to its use, there
is only one rational answer: certainly.

Mysticism and Skepticism as Denials of Reason

Ayn Rand defines "knowledge" as "a mental grasp of a fact(s) of reality, reached either by perceptual observation or by a process of reason based on perceptual observation."[11] This definition, which the discussion so far has validated, can serve as a summary of the Objectivist epistemology. It also indicates our rejection of two widespread viewpoints. Contrary to skepticism, the definition affirms that man *can* "grasp reality." Contrary to mysticism, it affirms that such grasp is achieved only by observation and/or reason.

Mysticism is the theory that man has a means of knowledge other than sense perception or reason, such as revelation, faith, intuition, and the like. As we have seen, this theory reduces to emotionalism. It amounts to the view that men should rely for cognitive guidance not on the volitional faculty of thought, but on an *automatic* mental function, feeling.[12]

Philosophically, mysticism is an expression of intrinsicism; it is the only way to implement the latter. Intrinsicism defines no method of acquiring conceptual knowledge. Such knowledge, it holds, is gained automatically, by passive exposure to revelations of some sort, a process that results in one's "just knowing." This last is the mystical idea of cognition. In fact, however, since there are no revelations to absorb, the advocate of passivity ends up relying on the nonvolitional functions his consciousness does provide. That is, he becomes an emotionalist, coasting on his past conclusions and the automatic reactions they generate, while describing these latter as the voice of God.

In practice, the mystic's injunction to mankind amounts to the following: "It is not necessary to question or validate your ideas. Instead, take the content of your consciousness, however acquired, as a given, which qualifies as cognition simply because it is there." This is an appropriate and unavoidable policy for the lower animals, because their form of knowledge is perceptual. But it ignores completely the nature and requirements of the rational animal. The mystic characteristically exalts the spiritual and deprecates the physical. Yet he upholds, as the cognitive model for man to emulate, the unthinking automatism of a mindless brute.

Reason *is* man's spiritual endowment. When one rejects it, animality, or less, is all that remains.

Skepticism is an example of the "less." Skepticism is the theory that knowledge of reality is impossible to man by any means. This amounts to brushing reason aside as impotent— and more: it is a rejection of the axiom of consciousness. The skeptic upholds as the model for man to emulate not even an animal, but (as Aristotle was the first to remark) a vegetable.

Just as mysticism is allied with intrinsicism, so skepticism is allied with subjectivism. If one holds that mental activity consists in the creation, not the grasp, of an object, he will have to conclude that independent reality (assuming he accepts the concept at all) is unknowable.

If mysticism advocates the promiscuous acceptance of ideas, skepticism advocates their promiscuous doubt. The mystic "just knows" whatever he wants to believe; the skeptic "just doesn't know" whatever he wants not to believe. The operative term and guiding force here is "wants," i.e., feeling. *Both* viewpoints reduce to emotionalism; both represent the reliance on feeling as a cognitive guide. Both represent a denial of man's need of logic and an enshrinement of the arbitrary.

Both the mystic and the skeptic are exponents of faith in the technical sense of the term. "Faith" means acceptance on the basis of feeling rather than of evidence. The mystic has faith that there is a certainty which eludes the mind; the skeptic has faith that the mind's certainties are no certainty at all. And each clings to his faith with the tenacity of a religious zealot. Nor does either have any alternative in this regard. Both doctrines, if upheld at all, must be matters of faith; a proof of either would be fatal to it.

A process of proof commits a man to its presuppositions and implications. It thus commits him to an entire philosophic approach—to the validity of sense perception, the validity of reason, the need of objectivity, the method of logic, the processes of conceptual knowledge, the law of identity, the absolutism of reality. This approach is incompatible with the ideas of mystics and skeptics alike.

A God susceptible of proof would wither and starve the spirit of mysticism. Such an entity would be finite and limited; it would be one thing among others within the universe, a thing bound by identity and causality, capable of being integrated without contradiction into man's cognitive context, incompatible with miracles, revelations, and the other paraphernalia of unreason. Such an entity would not be an ineffable mystery transcending nature and science. It would be a part of nature to be studied by science, and it would be of no use whatever to a mystic. When Pascal cried: "Not the God of the philosophers, but the God of Abraham, Isaac, and Jacob!" he knew whereof he spoke.

The same applies to the skeptic's doubt. A doubt susceptible of objective validation would also have to be finite, contextual, and bound by the rules of evidence. Such a doubt would be one assessment among others within the universe of rational knowledge, not a supernatural anathema transcending that universe and annihilating it from without. A "scientific" doubt is of no more use to a skeptic than a "scientific" God is to a mystic. In both cases, the "science" contradicts the essence and purpose of the theory.

That essence and purpose is escape from reason—or, more exactly, escape from the *absolutism* of reason.

No one seeks to reject reason completely. What many men do seek, however, is not to be (in their words) "straitjacketed" by reason all the time, in every issue, twenty-four hours a day. It is to these men that mystics and skeptics alike offer a sanction and a loophole. "We all have the right," they say in effect, "to our own approach, our own subjective beliefs or doubts, as an occasional supplement to reason or breather from it. The rest of the time we will be perfectly rational." This means: "We want a deal, a middle of the road. We want to take *some* feelings as tools of cognition. We want a compromise between reason and emotionalism."

In reason, there can be no such compromise.

If one attempts to combine reason and emotionalism, the principle of reason cannot be his guide, the element that defines the terms of the compromise, because reason does not permit subjective feeling to have *any* voice in cognitive issues. Subjective feeling, therefore, which permits anyone anything he wants, must set the terms; it must be the element that decides the role and limits of reason. Thus the ruling principle of the epistemological middle-of-the-road'er is: "I will consult facts and obey the rules of evidence sometimes—when I feel like it."

This policy goes far beyond an occasional assertion of the arbitrary. It makes the use of logic itself a matter of caprice and thus elevates the arbitrary to the position of ruler of cognition. Such a policy is not a "compromise"; it cannot be described as "partial" emotionalism. It is the full-fledged, unadulterated variety. No emotionalist, however extreme, shuns every logical connection; none bypasses data acceptable to his feelings. What makes a man an emotionalist is the criterion by which he accepts an idea; to him, it is not the idea's logical support that counts, but its emotional congeniality. This is precisely the criterion that governs the so-called middle-of-the-road'er. Such a man may very well invoke the recital of evidence; but when he does, it is not an expression of the principle of objectivity. It is a sham, a social ritual without cognitive significance.

In regard to such a mentality, the skeptic claims are true: the emotionalist *is* cognitively impotent and cannot fully trust even his better ideas. He has no way to know which conclusions are better or worse, because he has jettisoned the human means of knowledge.

To deny the absolutism of reason is not a harmless indulgence, like having chocolates on a diet. It is more like taking arsenic three times a day as the essence of one's nutrition.

Mystics often say that, by enabling men to escape from the "prosaic" world of nature, they make life exciting. Skeptics often say that, by undermining all strong convictions, they make life safe. The facts belie these promises. In actuality, since both groups work to undercut man's mind, both lead to a single kind of result and always have done so. They lead to helplessness, terror, dictatorship, and starvation.

Whenever a man promises to lead you to a value, remind yourself of the fact that remaining in contact with reality is a requirement of achieving values. This will help you to resist the philosophic hustlers. It will tell you that the precondition of values is the use *and absolutism* of reason.

• • • •

There are many epistemological topics that I have not had space to cover in the foregoing discussions. Among the most important is the validation of scientific induction. On the polemical side, I have hardly touched on the dichotomy between rationalism and empiricism, with the many false alternatives it spreads, such as "logic vs. experience," "deduction vs. induction," "analytic truth vs. synthetic truth," "concepts vs. percepts," and so forth.[13] I plan to treat all this material in a more advanced work on Objectivist epistemology.

Happily, we do not need to know everything in order to know what we do know. And now we do know, in essential terms, the nature of reality and of our means of knowledge. That is, we know what is necessary in order to move from metaphysics and epistemology as such to the next topic in the philosophic hierarchy.

We have studied in detail a single attribute, the faculty of cognition. Now we must study the entity that possesses it: man.

6

MAN

There is no question more crucial to man than the question: what *is* man? What kind of being is he? What are his essential attributes?

Many thinkers and artists have sought to answer this question. They have looked at men and then offered a report on man's nature. Their reports have clashed through the ages. Aristotle defined man as the "rational animal." Plato and the medievals described other-worldly souls trapped in a bodily prison. Shakespeare dramatized man as an aspiring but foolish mortal, defeated by a "tragic flaw." Thomas Hobbes described a mechanistic brute. Kant saw man as a blind chunk of unreality, in hock to the unknowable. Hegel saw a half-real fragment of the state. Victor Hugo saw a passionate individualist undercut by an inimical universe. Friedrich Nietzsche saw a demoniacal individualist run by the will to power. John Dewey saw a piece of flux run by the expediency of the moment. Sigmund Freud spoke of an excrement-molding pervert itching to rape his mother.

Ayn Rand looked at men and saw the possibility of Howard Roark and John Galt.

A philosophical inquiry into man is not part of the special

sciences, such as psychology, history, or economics; it does not define detailed laws of human thought, feeling, or action. It is concerned only with fundamentals; hierarchically, a knowledge of such characteristics is a precondition of pursuing any specialized science. Ayn Rand refers to this inquiry as a study of man's *metaphysical* nature. The term is apt because, in some form, every fundamental of human nature involves the issue of man's relationship to reality.

In this inquiry, one is not concerned to discover what is right for man or wrong, desirable or undesirable, good or evil. A view of man is a step on the road to ethics, but the view itself does not include value-judgments. The concern here is a purely factual question: what *is* the essence of human nature?

Like the special sciences, value-judgments—ethical, political, and esthetic—presuppose an answer to this question. Until you decide in some terms *what you are,* you cannot know whether you should be selfish or just or free; whether you should admire George Washington or George III or George Bush; whether, for the unique satisfaction offered by art, you should turn to the statues of Praxiteles and Michelangelo or to the modern collages made of dirt and bus transfers. All such issues are derivatives. Their root is the nature of man.

A view of man, however, is not a primary; it rests on metaphysics and epistemology; it may be described as the center of a system of thought, the link between its abstract base and its practical culmination. This is why thinkers and artists have disagreed so often about man; they have approached the question from different fundamental premises.

Many aspects of the Objectivist view of man have already been covered; they are implicit or even explicit in the first five chapters of this book. I will be relying here, above all, on earlier conclusions about the relationship of consciousness to existence, about the nature of human consciousness (as conceptual and volitional), and about the relationship between reason and emotion.

According to Objectivism, however, a philosophic view of man is not exhausted by metaphysics and epistemology, nor does it at every point follow deductively from them; fresh observations are required. But they are observations made within the context of an established philosophic base. Given this context, the further conclusions to be drawn pose little difficulty.

Living Organisms as Goal-Directed and Conditional

If a fundamental difference is one which has enormous, pervasive manifestations, then the most fundamental difference among the entities we perceive is that between the animate and the inanimate. The starting point in the present inquiry, therefore, is the fact that man is a certain kind of living organism. What *is* an organism? More specifically, what is its essential, distinctive mode of action?

The actions of a living organism are self-generated and *goal-directed.* They are actions initiated by the organism for the sake of achieving an end.

Some entities act to gain or keep various objects; other entities do not. This difference is directly observable. An animal, for example, pursues food, water, shelter; a desk or a pebble pursues nothing. The latter kind of thing either remains inert or, when it moves, does so randomly, without any end of its own, simply by reaction to whatever external forces impinge upon it (such as human muscle power pushing the desk or a wind blowing the pebble).

Life is the opposite of the inert or the random. A plant, an animal, or a man is a complex, delicate, self-regulating integration of components. Each of its organs and processes has a function to perform in sustaining the total entity, and each works continuously, in harmony with the others, toward this end. Living action *is* goal-directed action; it consists in an entity's taking in raw material from the environment, then (through the activities of metabolism) in using the material for the sake of growth to maturity, self-maintenance, and self-repair. This last, though merely an aspect of the process, is an eloquent one. If we invade a desk (say, with a knife cut), nothing happens but the cut; but if we invade an animal's body with a cut (or a harmful germ), it instantly mobilizes its resources to fight off the attack, counteract any ill effects, heal its wounds. Inanimate matter pursues no goals; it is indifferent to consequences. A living entity is not indifferent. On the physical level, as Ayn Rand observes, "the functions of all living organisms, from the simplest to the most complex—from the nutritive function in the single cell of an amoeba to the blood circulation in the body of a man—are actions generated by the organism itself and directed to a single goal: the maintenance of the organism's *life.*"[1]

Most living entities have no power of choice. This kind of organism functions only as its nature requires, without any volition or even any awareness of its behavior (e.g., the actions of a plant or the internal bodily processes of an animal). But *what* its nature requires is that, within the limit of its capacities, it act to sustain itself. An organism without choice or awareness, like a plant, does act in response to external factors (e.g., climate or soil composition); but such an entity is not "merely" a responder. The reason is that what it does in response is to use external factors for its own end. Being a living creature, its response consists in initiating the kind of action that can preserve its life (e.g., a plant turning its leaves to reach the sunlight, stretching its roots toward damp soil at a distance, or growing around obstacles).

"Goal" is not synonymous with "purpose" (the latter term applies only to the goals of conscious beings, who are aware of and desire the objects they pursue). Objectivism does not endorse "teleology," if that means the theory that insentient entities can act purposefully, or that all organisms are moved by a conscious or subconscious striving. "Goal-directed" in this context, Ayn Rand explains, "designates the fact that the automatic functions of living organisms are actions whose nature is such that they *result* in the preservation of an organism's life."[2]

Living organisms initiate a consistent kind of action, which leads (within the limits of the possible) to a consistent outcome. This is the sense in which their action is "goal-directed."

Living organisms can (and must) act to pursue goals because an organism, unlike an inanimate object, faces the alternative of life or death.

"The existence of inanimate matter is unconditional," Ayn Rand writes in a crucial passage,

the existence of life is not: it depends on a specific course of action. Matter is indestructible, it changes its forms, but it cannot cease to exist. It is only a living organism that faces a constant alternative: the issue of life or death. Life is a process of self-sustaining and self-generated action. If an organism fails in that action, it dies; its chemical elements remain, but its life goes out of existence.[3]

Many inanimate objects—such as a house, a statue, even a planet—can be irretrievably destroyed. But these objects have no power to affect their fate one way or the other. They cannot engage in self-sustaining behavior, nor does their existence require such behavior (it requires only that they be left alone). In this sense, an inanimate object's existence *is* unconditional, a point ably explained by Dr. Harry Binswanger:

> The existence of inanimate objects is not conditional upon their actions: (1) inanimate objects are not capable of self-generated action, and (2) they will continue to exist as long as they are not acted upon by external forces. A living organism faces the constant alternative of life or death—not simply in that it can be annihilated by an external catastrophe (as, for instance, a stone can be pulverized by an advancing glacier)—but in that unless it can utilize the materials and energy in its environment to fuel the complex internal processes of self-maintenance, it will disintegrate.[4]

As Ayn Rand puts this point, life *is* motion, a definite course of motion; if the motion is defaulted on or fails, what ensues is the antithesis of life: stillness, which is the essence of death.[5] Death is the irreversible cessation of vital processes. Leaving aside the disintegration that follows it, death is a state that does not involve or require action. To achieve it, you need simply refrain from doing anything: lie down, do not move, do not eat, call a halt to the vital activities within your control (and, if you are in a hurry, to the pumping of your lungs and the beating of your heart); nothing else is required.

The fact of life—of conditional, goal-directed entities—has profound philosophic significance. It is a key to the nature of man and, as we will see in the next chapter, a necessary and sufficient condition of the existence of values. I must, therefore, stress the reality of the fact. For Objectivism, the distinction between the animate and the inanimate *is* fundamental.

Materialists today, dedicated to monism (and to rewriting reality), insist that every science be "reducible" to physics in a sense that denies both consciousness (see chapter 1) and life. In this view, living organisms are mere "appearance"; they are really nothing but a type of inanimate mechanism, like a highly complex robot or super-computer. This notion denies an entire field of observed data.

Whatever the ultimate explanation of biological phenomena—whether life derives from some as yet unknown (but nonmystical) element combining with matter as we now understand it, or from some special combination of known material ingredients—in either case, it will not alter the existence *or the identity* of a living organism; just as an explanation of consciousness, should such be forthcoming, would not alter *its* existence or identity. An explanation does not erase the reality it explains. No discovery in physics or biology can erase the difference between the living and the inanimate; no future knowledge can invalidate *this* knowledge.

A child unable to grasp so major a distinction as that between the living and the inanimate would be unable to progress very far in concept-formation; it would never reach the stage of science or philosophy. The notion of a sophisticated science retroactively undermining an observed distinction is absurd on its face. Since observations are the base of science, any such notion denies the hierarchical structure of cognition. It represents the fallacy of the stolen concept (or the stolen science).

Materialists are concept-stealers in another way, too. Robots and the like, to which these theorists seek to reduce life, are human inventions modeled on living organisms and designed to achieve human purposes. By their nature, therefore, such inventions presuppose the knowledge of life and the reality of purpose.

No matter what the study of optics discovers, it will never affect the distinction between red and green. The same applies to all observed facts, including the fact of life. No one will ever show that a man being shot and the bullet piercing his body are metaphysically interchangeable entities, since both are "merely collections of atoms in motion." One "collection" can *die;* the other cannot. In this profound sense, Ayn Rand is unanswerably right when she says that a living organism, but not matter as such, is destructible. The one can *become* inanimate; the other already *is.*

It is with this difference—I am tempted to say this "life-and-death" difference—that the study of human nature begins.

Reason as Man's Basic Means of Survival

Every living organism has a means of survival.

Plants survive by means of purely physical functions. They acquire the objects they seek, such as food, water, and sunlight, from the soil and air in which they grow, without the need of awareness. For every form of life above this level, however, consciousness is the basic means of survival.[6]

The lower conscious species (e.g., jellyfish or flatworms) appear to have only the faculty of sensation and act by responding to isolated, momentary stimuli; their guide to sustaining their life is the pleasure-pain mechanism built into their bodies. The higher animals are also guided by the pleasure-pain mechanism, but in their case it functions within the context of the faculty of perception. The higher animals grasp and deal with the world of entities (and are able to form automatic perceptual associations). The range of actions required for their survival is therefore wider. They have to learn a set of vital skills, such as hunting, storing food, hiding, or nest-building, which are impossible to the purely sensory species.

Man, too, experiences the sensations of pleasure and pain, but he is a conceptual being. The range of actions required for his survival is therefore the widest of all. His kind of consciousness makes possible and necessary a vast new repertoire of vital skills. Unlike sensations and percepts, however, concepts and their products are not automatic or infallible.

The lower conscious species may be said to survive by "instinct," if the term means an unchosen and unerring form of action (unerring within the limits of its range). Sensations and percepts are unchosen and unerring. An instinct, however—whether of self-preservation or anything else—is precisely what a conceptual being does not have. *Man cannot function or survive by the guidance of mere sensations or percepts.* A conceptual being cannot initiate action unless he knows the nature and purpose of his action. He cannot pursue a goal unless he identifies what his goal is and how to achieve it.[7]

No species can survive by regressing to the methods of more primitive organisms. An ape cannot survive by the method of a jellyfish, or a jellyfish by the method of an onion; the one cannot afford to dispense with its percepts, the other, with its sensations. For the same reason, a man cannot survive by the method of an ape.[8]

"A sensation of hunger," Ayn Rand observes,

> will tell [a man] that he needs food (if he has learned to identify it as "hunger"), but it will not tell him how to obtain his food and it will not tell him what food is good for him or poisonous. He cannot provide for his simplest physical needs without a process of thought. He needs a process of thought to discover how to plant and grow his food or how to make weapons for hunting. His percepts might lead him to a cave, if one is available—but to build the simplest shelter, he needs a process of thought.[9]

The nonhuman species, assuming they are fortunate, find ready-made in reality the simple objects their survival requires. In essence, given the primitive form of their consciousness, they adjust themselves to the given: they appropriate these simple objects from inanimate nature, or they use force against other organisms. Man, however, does not survive by adjusting himself to the given. He is not equipped to win in a contest of brute force against the animals—and the objects *his* life requires are not ready-made. Bread, shirts, apartments, hammers, matches, lightbulbs, and penicillin do not grow like weeds or wild berries, waiting for men to seize them. The goods we need, paraphrasing a line from *Atlas Shrugged,* are *not* here. They must be created by human action. They must be produced.

In order to produce, man must discover the types of materials available in nature, the potentialities they possess, the laws of their behavior, the techniques by which they can be reshaped into the sustenance of human survival. All this involves a special kind of knowledge—the kind that integrates past data with present observations in a form enabling its possessor to plan long-range and shape the course of his future.

The conclusion is evident. Epistemology tells us that reason is man's faculty of knowing reality. When conjoined with the observed fact that man is an organism who survives by means of his knowledge (and consequent action), the inference must be that reason is man's basic tool of survival.[10]

In the Objectivist view, the proposition that man is the rational animal does not mean that men always follow reason; many do not. Nor does it mean merely that man alone possesses the faculty of reason. It means that this faculty is a fundamental of human nature, because man is the organism who survives by its use.

A long-standing tradition, stretching from Plato to the present, deprecates the activities involved in human survival as mindless, perceptual-level, "materialistic"—while extolling reason as a "spiritual" organ concerned with "pure" contemplation. Before the Industrial Revolution, Ayn Rand has remarked, this version of the mind-body dichotomy, though thoroughly false, had a certain degree of plausibility. If one thinks—as did most of the ancients, the medievals, and the early moderns—that all the practical arts have long been discovered and that the process of keeping men alive consists primarily of physical labor, the labor of slaves or peasants repeating by rote the age-old motions of their ancestors, then the pursuit of rational knowledge does indeed appear to be nonpractical. It appears to be nothing but an unworldly self-indulgence of the aristocracy or the clergy.

The Industrial Revolution has blasted this perspective forever. It has demonstrated once and for all—on a scale spanning continents, centuries, and every detail of men's daily life—the tie between science and wealth, innovation and longevity, knowledge and power, concepts and survival.

What was always true though not obvious has become inescapable (except to those who wish to escape it). The mind is indispensable to human life. Abstractions are not a luxury, but a necessity. Thought is man's guide to action. *Reason is a practical attribute.*

The metaphysical fact about man that underlies these

truths is that man is *not* a battlefield of contending dimensions, spiritual and physical. He is, in Ayn Rand's words, "an indivisible entity, an integrated unit of two attributes: of matter and consciousness." Consciousness in his case takes the form of mind, i.e., a conceptual faculty; matter, of a certain kind of organic structure. Each of these attributes is indispensable to the other and to the total entity. The mind acquires knowledge and defines goals; the body translates these conclusions into action.[11]

In order to concretize this viewpoint fully, let us project an alternative to it. Let us, obeying the injunction of the centuries, try to choose between man's two attributes, embracing one while consistently rejecting its alleged antagonist.

Suppose a man decides to cast his lot with the mind or soul, while shunning matter and the body. What are his options? He might spend his time daydreaming—but no; the realm of physical action has been rejected; he cannot dream about what anyone could or should *do*. He might become a religious ascetic, but then he cannot give his attitude any worldly expression; he cannot even lacerate the flesh or utter a prayer to God (certain ancient sects forbade prayer in order to cleanse their religion of "materialistic" elements). He might become a hypocrite, as long as the theories he spins do not employ physical symbols (words) or make reference to physical objects. Or he might become a catatonic, out of contact with reality, immobile, waxy flexible; *that* he can be—as long as some low-grade "materialist" comes around to feed and bathe him.

On the other hand, if a man rejects the realm of the mind and casts his lot instead with matter and action, with mindless, physical action, what are his options? He might become a sleepwalker—but no; he cannot count on any previous knowledge or any subliminal awareness to guide his movements. He might become a Nazi killer or a plain brute—if, somehow, someone could tell him whom to kill and by what means. Or, again, he might become a psychotic, this time of the manic variety, out of contact with reality and flailing around grotesquely.

These patterns are as close as a man can come to "pure" thought or "pure" action. Pure thought is nonthought; it is devoid of reference to reality. Pure action is nonaction; it is purposeless movement. Both patterns, enacted consistently, mean suicide.

A being who is an integration of two attributes cannot function or survive by tearing them apart. "A body without a soul is a corpse," writes Ayn Rand, "a soul without a body is a ghost. . . ." Both corpse and ghost, she notes, are "symbols of death."[12]

The principle of mind-body integration—like its corollary, the fact that reason is a practical faculty—rests on observation; but the observation depends for its identification upon a proper philosophic context. In metaphysics, that context must include the primacy of existence; in epistemology, it must include the objective view of concepts. Any other philosophy will blind one to the empirical data. If one accepts the primacy of consciousness, he will expect desire to clash with external reality; if one accepts a nonobjective view of concepts, he will expect theory to clash with practice. On these premises, the universally observable fact about human nature—its metaphysical harmony—will be ignored, or brushed aside as misleading; while the most egregious falsehood will be accorded the status of a truism.

Let us conclude the present topic with some elementary history. Most people know about the backbreaking labor, the rampant superstition, the poverty, the sweeping plagues of that era of faith called the Dark and Middle Ages. Even in the seventeenth century, life expectancy in many Western European areas was still under twenty-five years. As late as the eighteenth century, nine out of ten working Americans were working full-time on the production and distribution of food.

Today, an enormously greater quantity and higher quality of food is made available by only one out of five working Americans, leaving 80 percent of the labor force free to create the previously unimaginable wealth of our era. Today, you can see the prosperity, the safety, the lifespan that America and the entire West enjoys, thanks to a cause that everyone has the means to know, but few choose to acknowledge.

You can also see how men elsewhere endure, suffer, and die in their youth. They die not only in war, but in peacetime, from starvation and disease. They die this way as the norm, the expected, the accepted—throughout the nonindustrialized, nonscientific, *nonrational* rest of the world.

Reason *is* man's tool of survival. From the simplest necessity to the highest abstraction, summarizes *The Fountainhead,* "from the wheel to the skyscraper, everything we are and everything we have comes from a single attribute of man—the function of his reasoning mind."[13]

Reason as an Attribute of the Individual

Reason is an attribute of the individual. There is no such thing as a collective mind or brain. Thought is a process that must be initiated and directed at each step by the choice of one man, the thinker. Only an individual qua individual can perceive, abstract, define, connect. Here again we are dealing with an empirical matter. The same observations which reveal that consciousness is an attribute of certain living organisms reveal that it belongs to separate organisms. And, in regard to man's consciousness, observation is what reveals that it is volitional.

The point is broader than consciousness. Entity, as we have seen, is the primary "category." Only entities can act— and to be an entity is to be an individual. A group of men is a derivative phenomenon; it is not an entity, but a collection of them, an aggregate of individuals. "All the functions of body and spirit," writes Ayn Rand, "are private. They cannot be shared or transferred." One cannot think for or through another person any more than one can breathe or digest food for him. Each man's brain, like his lungs and stomach, is his alone to use.[14]

Men can learn from other men, an ability that is invaluable in the struggle for survival. But learning is an active process; others do not implant their knowledge in a newcomer by surgery or sorcery. To learn from others is not to receive an unearned benefit; it is to understand their conclusions by grasping the reasons for them. This requires the independent exercise of the learner's own mind and constitutes an accomplishment on his part. Mindless recitation of truths reached by others is not cognition; and it is an obstacle, not an aid, to survival.

Men can build on what they learn from others; some men carry human knowledge further, and this too is an invaluable human ability. If an individual does reach a new conclusion, however, he does it as an individual and it is *his* breakthrough, not that of his predecessors. Their achievement was already completed; he is the one who added to it. What one receives from others, Ayn Rand observes, "is only the end product of their thinking. The moving force is the creative faculty which takes this product as material, uses it and originates the next step. This creative faculty cannot be given or received, shared or borrowed. It belongs to single, individual men."[15]

Different men may be familiar with different facts or fields which, when integrated, lead to greater knowledge than any of the men possessed alone. The integration, however, has to be performed by somebody. If many minds perform it (or any other cognitive step) at the same time, each is performing the same process, and each does it as an individual.

A conclusion can be the product of a discussion, of consultation, of "give and take." There is such a thing as an agreement to which many men contribute. An agreement, however, is not a primary. "An agreement reached by a group of men," writes Ayn Rand,

> to which separate men have contributed separate parts, is not a collective thought. It is the result of thought, the product, the secondary consequence. The primary act— the process of reason—the process of observing, considering, passing judgment—had to be performed by each man alone. . . .
>
> Men may share their *knowledge,* not their thinking. Knowledge is not thinking—it is the *result* of thinking, the product of the process of thought. The process of thought . . . cannot be performed collectively.[16]

All of the above applies not only to specific conclusions, but also to the learning of language. Language is not a "social creation," nor does its use make the mind a "social product." A language is a system of concepts, and concepts are a type of cognition. Every concept, like every conclusion, has to be formed by *someone,* then understood by others through a rational process, if it is to be of cognitive use to them. In the act of learning a language, if he is learning and not parroting, an individual is thinking; he is initiating the complex mental processes that make his ability to speak or write a personal attainment, not a social gift. Anything a man then goes on to discover while using the language is *his* achievement; it represents his creative faculty originating the next step of knowledge.

Just as others can make a man's cognitive task easier, so they can make it more difficult. They can enlighten a man with true ideas and proper guidance—or confuse him with falsehoods and dead ends. But just as the first circumstance does not turn the mind into a social product, neither does the second. The first does not *make* a man think. The second does not make him stop thinking.

As long as an individual is sane, he can choose to question and judge, or not to do so; if he judges, he has the capacity to reject what he hears from others. It does not take genius or even education to discover that other people, with their countless clashes, contradictions, and reversals, are not omniscient. In particular, a man can recognize the arbitrary, even if he does not know the truth. He can recognize that "Accept it because we say so" is no answer, even if he does not know the answer; and he can resolve to look for answers elsewhere and to keep on looking. A group can make a man miserable, at least for a while. It cannot make him anti-effort.

Because man is a volitional being, his cognitive faculty is free in relation to others. No matter what they think, do, teach, or evade, his mind remains his alone to use and direct. (I leave aside here cases such as a mind destroyed by physical torture, or a child paralyzed by irrationality before he reaches the age of thought.)

If other men *are* rational, an individual gains enormous benefits not only from their knowledge, but also from their actions. Men can achieve feats by specialization and joint effort that no man can achieve alone. This does not mean, however, that the thought involved in such feats is collective. In any joint undertaking, each man must do his own thinking to guide his own part of the work—if he is to contribute to the result anything other than mindless muscle power. And someone's thought must define the goal of the undertaking and integrate its components.

Since there is no collective thought, there is no collective creativity. "Joint effort" does not mean products that flow from nobody in particular or everybody in general. "No step was taken anywhere," writes Ayn Rand, "—no single nail was designed—by a group of men working in unison under the guidance of a majority vote." Every step forward "was the work, the creation and the achievement of some one individual man. Somebody had to think of it."[17]

The steps of human progress, Miss Rand continues, have not been a succession of equal, microscopic contributions. In every field, from philosophy to music to science to invention, there have been a few giants whose ideas were the great turning points—followed by many lesser men who elaborated some details of the giants' discoveries.

> The accomplishments of these modest men are not to be despised . . . [but] it is not out of their collected efforts that the basic, crucial, epoch-making achievements have come. . . .
> [T]he greater, the more primary, the more cardinal the achievement—the fewer men were responsible for it.[18]

We hear routinely about a "collective thought process." Let us try to concretize this notion. A member of some group, it would seem, has to suggest tentatively some half-formed idea, then withdraw it if the others do not take it up. If the thought, in the sense of the primary act, is actually to be "collective," no man can put forth or stand on any definite idea of his own; none can try to convince the others of *his* viewpoint or even reach such a selfish, individualistic mental product. Each must shrink from self-assertion and wait for the others to decide something—the others who are engaged in the same abstention, the same self-abnegation, the same empty, timorous waiting. The result is a committee meeting, such as the Board of Directors meeting of Taggart Transcontinental. That scene from *Atlas Shrugged* is not a caricature of collective thought, but a perfect example of it—except that what the scene dramatizes is not thought, but evasion.[19]

The notion of a "collective consciousness" is as arbitrary as that of a "supernatural consciousness." Both notions represent the primacy of consciousness. The older version of this metaphysics leads to the view that human consciousness is a fragment fed by a transcendent Mind, from which it is merely temporarily separated. The social version secularizes this conclusion; it views human consciousness as a fragment fed by a social Mind, from which it is not really, but only apparently separated (see Hegel, Marx, and Dewey). Neither of these views rests on any observed fact. Both are a priori deductions that flout the axioms of philosophy and fly in the face of facts.

Man is not a cell of some larger whole, supernatural or social. He is not a coral bush or even an ant, in the sense of an anatomically specialized organism that can survive only in a colony. A man can survive alone, on a desert island or a self-sustaining farm. Man's ability to survive is enhanced by his living in society—but only if it is a human society, which is governed by the power of reason; i.e., only if the individuals comprising it think and act as individuals, with everything this entails (see chapters 7 and 8).

The present discussion, let me repeat, is not concerned with value-judgments. The point here is not that men should be independent or individualistic. The point is that the collectivists from Plato to Dewey are wrong, wrong on the deepest level, wrong *metaphysically*. The fragment or cell about which they write does not exist. Only man exists, man the rational being. And a rational being's tool of survival *is*—not "should be," but "is"—an individual process, one that occurs only in a private mind and brain.

This brings us to a final conclusion about man. If reason is an attribute of the individual; and if the choice to think or not controls all of a man's other choices and their products, including the emotions he feels and the actions he takes; then the individual is *sovereign*. His own cognitive faculty determines not only his conclusions, but also his character and life. In this sense, man is self-created, self-directed, and self-responsible. Since he is responsible for what he thinks (or evades), he is responsible for all the psychological and existential consequences that follow therefrom. If we use the term "soul" to mean the essence of a person, which is his mind and its basic values, then, in Ayn Rand's crucial formulation: "[A]s man is a being of self-made wealth, so he is a being of self-made soul."[20]

The above does not imply that a man shapes his emotions directly, simply by the decision to focus or not. In this respect, emotions differ from thought and action: they are an automatic function. But a man does choose his emotions—ultimately. He does it by virtue of his ability to think, and if necessary to rethink an issue, rejecting an invalid idea at the root of some feeling and replacing it by a new conclusion.

Man controls the products of thought; he does it directly or indirectly; either way, however, he does it. The conclusion is that man—each man as an individual—is the master of his own destiny.

This conclusion does not mean that man is omnipotent or that he is immune to the actions of other men. It means that the individual chooses his own ends and the methods of attaining them (or chooses to default on this responsibility). It means that by his metaphysical nature man is not a pawn of forces beyond his control. He is not a product of conditioned reflexes or id instincts or the tools of production (thought determines action). He is not a puppet dancing on the strings of power lust, jealousy, anger, or any other "tragic flaw" (thought determines emotion). He is not a cipher ruled by fate or by any supernatural power (the arbitrary is inadmissible).

The theory of human impotence is invalid. Determinism in any variant is invalid.

Many people, unable to explain their emotions, do experience themselves as puppets moved by loves and hates that come they know not whence. The only cure for this condition would be their discovery of the actual cause of their emotions. The reason-emotion dichotomy, however, cuts off this possibility; by teaching that emotions are independent of thought, it makes permanent the feeling of metaphysical helplessness.

This false theory of emotion is essential to most variants of determinism; it is the most potent weapon determinists have in gaining converts. The two most popular variants of determinism, the heredity school and the environment school, may serve as illustrations here.

The first school treats emotions as a product of innate (genetic) structures. Everything essential to a man, it holds, including the character and feelings he will eventually develop, is a product of factors built into his body at birth. No one who understands the nature of emotions could entertain this theory for long. Such a person, rejecting materialism, would recognize the epistemological impossibility inherent in the approach. Innately set emotions, he would see, imply innate concepts and value-judgments, i.e., innate ideas.

Environmental determinism misunderstands emotions in a somewhat different way. According to most spokesmen of this school, society molds the individual through his experiences. A child, it is said, sees people, observes their actions and faces, hears their words, feels their caresses or blows; after years of such bombardment by perceptual data, he builds up certain habitual reactions, character traits, emotional patterns. What does this theory overlook? The fact that percepts do not invoke emotions; only percepts as interpreted and evaluated can do so, i.e., only percepts as conceptualized, conscientiously or otherwise, by a mind. And conceptualization is not a group function.

We are hammered today by the false alternative of "nature or nurture" as man's determiner. The first is taken to mean biology; the second, upbringing. The first theory suggests that the body by itself creates conceptual content in the individual's consciousness; the second, that parents or teachers do so. The first turns man into a helpless byproduct of matter; the second, of other people's minds. Both theories deny nature in the only applicable sense. Both deny the metaphysical nature of a rational being.

The mere advocacy of "free will" does not answer these deterministic views. If volition is held to be a superhuman faculty injected by God into man's earthly identity, as in the Christian tradition, then its possession does not make man efficacious or responsible. On the contrary, such a view makes volition irrelevant to man's life, to the formation of his desires, to the daily work of his mind. And then the road is open to a Kantian inference: will as a wholly supernatural (noumenal) feature, determinism and human helplessness as the truth on earth. The dead end of this road is the voluntarist conclusion that will is potent *because* reason isn't.

In this issue, too, Ayn Rand's viewpoint is revolutionary. Choice, she holds, is not a mystic factor superimposed on a deterministic creature. There is no dichotomy between will and nature or between will and reason. Reason *is* will, and therefore the power of choice is the power that rules man, in regard both to body (action) and soul. Man is not only free, he is the product of his freedom—which means: of his intellect.[21]

In Ayn Rand's theory, man is the opposite of the feeble creature imagined by religionists and behaviorists alike. He is not a palsied atom to be pitied or manipulated, but an autonomous entity to be respected and admired—on one condition: if he earns such respect by his choices. This applies to every man by his metaphysical nature. It applies to every individual with a rational faculty, whatever the degree of his intelligence.

Man qua man is a hero—if he makes himself into one.

■   ■   ■   ■

Man is an organism of a distinctive kind, living in a universe which has a definite nature. His life depends on a cognitive faculty which functions according to specific rules. This faculty belongs to man the individual.

What then should man *do?*

7

THE GOOD

Metaphysics and epistemology, like the natural sciences, are factual subjects. Their concern is to describe the universe and man's means of knowledge. Ethics or morality—I use the terms as synonyms here—is an evaluative subject. Its concern is not only to describe, but also to prescribe for man. Ethics is the branch of philosophy that, in Ayn Rand's words, provides "a code of values to guide man's choices and actions—the choices and actions that determine the purpose and the course of his life."[1]

According to Objectivism, such a code must deal with three basic, interrelated questions. For what end should a man live? By what fundamental principle should he act in order to achieve this end? Who should profit from his actions? The answers to these questions define the ultimate *value,* the primary *virtue,* and the particular *beneficiary* upheld by an ethical code and reveal thereby its essence.

The Objectivist position can be indicated in three words. The ultimate value is *life.* The primary virtue is *rationality.* The proper beneficiary is *oneself.*

Because of its evaluative nature, ethics has always posed a unique problem to philosophers, even to those who had no doubts about man's power to reason or to know the facts of reality. How, thinkers have wondered from the Greeks to the present, can value-judgments ever be proved? How can facts, any or all of them, lead logically to estimates, such as "good" or "evil," "right" or "wrong," "desirable" or "undesirable"? How can a knowledge of what *is* validate a conclusion stating what *ought* to be?

For centuries, since the atrophy of the religious approach to philosophy, the consensus among ethicists has been that these questions are unanswerable. Ethics, according to the received wisdom, is arbitrary; it is a field ruled by subjective feeling, dissociated from reality, reason, science. In this view, there is no disputing about value-judgments; there are no objective grounds on which to choose between production and theft, thought and evasion, Jesus and Judas, Jefferson and Hitler.

As its name suggests, Objectivism denies this denial of morality. Ayn Rand holds that facts—certain definite facts—do lead logically to values. What "ought to be" can be validated objectively. Ethics is a human necessity and a science, not a playground for mystics or skeptics.

The principles of morality are a product not of feeling, but of cognition.

Now let us see how to achieve cognition in this kind of field.

"Life" as the Essential Root of "Value"

The key to an understanding of ethics lies in its central concept, *"value."* Specifically, the key lies in the concept's existential basis and cognitive context.

This is the proper starting point of the field, which must precede the three issues I mentioned above. The first question to ask is not: what values should man accept? but rather: does man need to judge and select values at all? Is morality necessary or not, and if it is, why?[2]

To answer this question, one must know what the concept of "value" denotes. This is where Ayn Rand the ethicist begins. She does not treat morality—neither the field as such, nor any theory within it—as a primary. What facts of reality, she asks, give rise to the subject?

Like every concept, "value" is reached and defined on the basis of observation. One must isolate a group of similar concretes, then integrate them into a new mental unit. The crucial datum here is the fact of goal-directed action.

Ayn Rand defines "value" as "that which one acts to gain and/or keep."[3] "Value" denotes the object of an action: it is that which some entity's action is directed to acquiring or preserving.

As this account suggests, the concept of "value" implies specific preconditions. In Ayn Rand's words, " 'value' presupposes an answer to the question: of value to *whom* and for *what?* It presupposes an entity capable of acting to achieve a goal in the face of an alternative. Where no alternative exists, no goals and no values are possible."[4] This last point requires elaboration.

Goal-directed behavior is possible only because an entity's action, its pursuit of a certain end, can make a difference to the outcome. "Alternative" does not necessarily imply choice; it means that the entity is confronted by two possible results: either it acts successfully, gaining the object it seeks, or it does not (and thus fails to gain the object).

To put the point negatively: an object is outside the field of "value" if action in relation to it is inapplicable or necessarily ineffectual. If one is guaranteed to have a certain thing or not to have it, no matter what one's actions, then the thing is not an object one *acts* to gain and/or keep. For example, an alternative exists as to whether an animal gains food or whether a man gains a knowledge of the law of gravitation. Food and knowledge are not guaranteed to an entity no matter what it does; to be attained, each of these requires action, physical and/or mental. But no alternative exists in regard to the metaphysically given fact of gravitation itself, which is beyond anyone's power to affect. Accordingly, one cannot wonder: "Should I pursue this fact or flee from it?" The fact is not open to either course. In this kind of instance, there is no alternative and, therefore, no possibility of goal-setting. The fact as such can be neither "desirable" nor "undesirable"; it simply, inexorably, *is*. The metaphysically given, as we have seen in chapter 1, must be accepted without evaluation.

The concept of "value" presupposes an entity capable of generating action toward an object—an object that requires action if it is to be attained. These two presuppositions of "value"—the need of a valuer and of an alternative—are not independent factors. They are corollary aspects of a single condition.

The very observations that lead to the concept of "value" entail the next step in Ayn Rand's analysis. One does not observe desks or pebbles pursuing goals; one does observe men, animals, and plants doing so. *Living organisms* are the entities that make "value" possible. They are the entities capable of self-generated, goal-directed action—because they are the conditional entities, which face the alternative of life or death. They are thus the only kind of entities that can (and must) pursue values.

Ayn Rand describes the alternative of life or death as "fundamental." "Fundamental" means that upon which everything in a given context depends. "There is," she writes, "only one fundamental alternative in the universe: existence or non-existence—and it pertains to a single class of entities: to living organisms."[5] Let us expand on this important formulation.

The realm of existence is *the* metaphysical fundamental; it is that which every concrete and every issue presupposes. According to Objectivism, this fact has a critical application to the field of values. *The alternative of existence or nonexistence is the precondition of all values.* If an entity were not confronted by this alternative, it could not pursue goals, not of any kind.

The simplest way to clarify this point is to concretize Ayn Rand's example of the immortal robot. Such a robot, not facing the alternative of life or death, requires no action to sustain itself. It is "an entity which moves and acts, but which cannot be affected by anything . . . which cannot be damaged, injured or destroyed."[6] Imagine for a moment that this sort of entity were possible. What values could it act *for?* If the thing asked for suggestions, what goals could you recommend?

Could you tell it to enjoy a good meal? Since the robot

has no need of nutritive action, it has no mechanism of ingesting or digesting nutriment, no hunger pangs without food, no pleasure sensations from it. The subject of food and drink is outside its concern. What about advising it to go to the dentist so as to avoid the agony of a toothache? This robot does not have toothaches (or any need of teeth); since it cannot be damaged, it need not concern itself with "health" or "illness"; to it, such concepts are inapplicable. Could you urge the thing at least to come in out of the rain? The elements have no effect on an indestructible entity.

Once we remove the alternative of life or death, we remove the possibility of need satisfaction or need frustration, at least on the physical level, since "need" in this context denotes that which is required for survival. We thereby remove also the sensory incentives, the pleasure and pain sensations, which accompany need satisfaction or frustration in conscious creatures.

What about the psychological level? Can this entity, assuming it were to have a conceptual faculty, pursue goals that are not mediated by purely animalistic needs? Can abstract knowledge, say, be a value to it? What for? The robot has no use for knowledge as an aid in achieving its ends; so far, it has no ends. Is money a value? To buy what? So far, the robot has no use for material objects or services—neither a Rolls-Royce (it has no place to go) nor an army of menservants (it has no jobs to be done). Is a trip around the world a value—as relaxation, say, or rest? Rest from what? The thing does not engage in work.

Is having the love of friends a value to it? This begs the question. Friends are men who share the same values; in order to have a friend, one must first hold some values. What about the pursuit of happiness? Same answer; happiness is the emotion that proceeds from the achievement of one's values; it presupposes that one holds values. What about recommending the simplest hedonism: doing anything it feels like doing, merely because it feels like it, regardless of reasons? Same answer again; feelings presuppose value-judgments, which are precisely what our robot still lacks.

On both the physical and the psychological levels, this entity would be passive, unconcerned, uninterested. Since nothing makes any difference to it, it would be unable to initiate a step in any direction. Even though, in our hypothesis, many alternatives confront the robot (to learn science or not, to buy a car or not, etc.), none leads it to goal-directed action. There are no grounds for it to pursue one side of any alternative as against the other. There are no grounds, because the *fundamental* alternative—the value-generating alternative—does not apply in its case. There is no "to be or not to be."

To an indestructible entity, no object can be a value. Only an entity *capable of being destroyed and able to prevent it* has a need, an interest (if the entity is conscious), a reason to act. The reason is precisely: to prevent its destruction, i.e., to remain in the realm of reality. It is this ultimate goal that makes all other goals possible.

Goal-directed entities do not exist in order to pursue values. They pursue values in order to exist.

Only self-preservation can be an ultimate goal, which serves no end beyond itself. This follows from the unique nature of the goal. Philosophically speaking, the essence of self-preservation is: *accepting the realm of reality.*

Existence exists. The "realm of non-existence," if one wants to use such a term, is not a competitor to reality, as General Motors is to Ford, with some kind of advantages to be considered and weighed. The "realm of non-existence" is nothing; *it isn't*. Since only existence exists, *it* is the fundamental starting point in every branch of philosophy.

Metaphysically, one cannot go outside the realm of existence—e.g., by asking for its cause.

Epistemologically, one cannot employ the faculty of reason in such a quest—e.g., by asking for the "reason" why, in coming to conclusions, one should accept the realm of reality. This would be an attempt, futile on its face, to engage in reasoning while standing outside existence. The attempt is futile because reason cannot be neutral in this kind of issue, not even provisionally or momentarily; reason is the faculty of knowing that which is. A "reason" detached from reality, with no special allegiance to that which is, "impartial" and "unbiased" as between reality and unreality, would not be a cognitive faculty.

The same principle applies in regard to evaluation. Here, too, reality is the starting point, and one cannot engage in debates about why one should prefer it—to nothing. Nor can one ask for some more basic value the pursuit of which validates the decision to remain in reality. The commitment to remain in the realm of that which is is precisely what cannot be debated; because all debate (and all validation) takes place within that realm and rests on that commitment. About every concrete within the universe and about every human evaluation of these, one can in some context ask questions or demand proofs. In regard to the sum of reality as such, however, there is nothing to do but grasp: *it is*—and then, if the fundamental alternative confronts one, bow one's head in a silent "amen," amounting to the words: "This is where I shall fight to stay."

That, in effect, is what plants and animals (and rational men) do. It is why they act and what they act for. Such is the deepest reason why an indestructible robot has to be devoid of values.

Thus we reach the climax of Ayn Rand's argument. Only the alternative of life vs. death creates the context for value-oriented action, and it does so only if the entity's end is to preserve its life. By the very nature of "value," therefore, *any code of values must hold life as the ultimate value.* All of the Objectivist ethics and politics rests on this principle.

An ultimate value, Ayn Rand observes, is the end-in-itself "which sets the standard by which all lesser goals are evaluated. An organism's life is its *standard of value:* that which furthers its life is the *good,* that which threatens it is the *evil.*"

"Without an ultimate goal or end," she continues,

> there can be no lesser goals or means. . . . Metaphysically, *life* is the only phenomenon that is an end in itself: a value gained and kept by a constant process of action. Epistemologically, the concept of "value" is genetically dependent upon and derived from the antecedent concept of "life." To speak of "value" as apart from "life" is worse than a contradiction in terms [it would be a stolen concept].

Or, as she puts this last point in *Atlas Shrugged,* in her most important summarizing formulation: "It is only the concept of 'Life' that makes the concept of 'Value' possible."[7]

The distinctively Objectivist viewpoint here, let me repeat, is not that life is a precondition of other values—not that one must remain alive in order to act. This idea is a truism, not a philosophy.

Objectivism says that remaining alive is the *goal* of values and of all proper action.

Man's Life as the Standard of Moral Value

Now let us see how the principle of life as the standard of value applies to specific kinds of organisms—above all, to man.

Plants and animals initiate automatically the actions their life requires. Such entities may encounter adverse conditions beyond their capacity to cope with, such as drought, temperature extremes, or an absence of food. In addition, an animal's knowledge may prove inadequate (a large-scale example would be the lemmings that unwittingly swim out too far and perish). But whatever the conditions they encounter and whatever an animal's knowledge, there is no alternative in the functioning of these organisms: within the limits of their ability, they act necessarily to attain those objects that sustain their existence. They can be destroyed, but they cannot pursue their own destruction or even be neutral in regard to it. Implicitly, life is their inbuilt standard of value, which determines all their goals and actions.[8]

Man, however, is the living being with a volitional, conceptual consciousness. As such, leaving aside his internal bodily processes, he has no inbuilt goal or standard of value; he follows no *automatic* course of action. In particular, he does not automatically value or pursue self-preservation. The evidence of this fact is overwhelming; it includes not only deliberate suicides, but also people's frequent hostility to the most elementary life-sustaining practices. As examples, one may consider the Middle Ages, or the more mystical countries of the Near and Far East, or even the leaders of the modern West. For a human being, the desire to live and the knowledge of what life requires are an achievement, not a biological gift.

Like every entity, man has a nature; like the other organisms, he must follow a specific course of action if he is to survive. But man is not born knowing what that course is, nor does such knowledge well up in him effortlessly. He has to seek out the knowledge and then decide to act on it. Man, writes Ayn Rand, "has to hold his life as a value—by choice; he has to learn to sustain it—by choice; he has to discover the values it requires and practice his virtues—by choice."[9]

How is he to discover all this? *That* is the purpose of morality. "Morality," in Ayn Rand's definition, is "a code of values accepted by choice"[10]—and man needs it for one reason only: he needs it in order to survive. Moral laws, in this view, are principles that define how to nourish and sustain human life; they are no more than this and no less.

Morality is the instruction manual in regard to proper care and use that did *not* come with man. It is the science of human self-preservation.

Plants and animals pursue values, but not moral values; they have goals, but not ethics. Moral values are a subcategory of values, defined by two conditions. "Moral values" are *chosen* values of a *fundamental* nature. They are "fundamental" in the sense that they shape a man's character and life course. Other kinds of value, by contrast, are specialized—e.g., a man's estimates in regard to government or art, which constitute not his moral, but his political or esthetic values.

The last seven paragraphs offer a broad overview of a complex issue, which now requires detailed analysis. Until we understand step by step the exact purpose and role of morality in man's life, there is little point in our proceeding further in the field.

The first step here is the fact that man needs to act *long-range*.

"Long-range" means "allowing for or extending into the more distant future."[11] A man is long-range to the extent that he chooses his actions with reference to such a future. This kind of man sets goals that demand action across a significant time span; and, being concerned with such goals, he also weighs consequences, the future consequences of his present behavior. By contrast, a man is short-range if, indifferent to the future, he seeks merely the immediate satisfaction of an impulse, without thought for any other ends or results.

An animal has no need or capacity to be long-range, at least not in the human sense. An animal does not choose its goals—nature takes care of that; so it can act safely on any impulse. Within the limits of the possible, that impulse is programmed to be pro-life. But man cannot rely safely on random impulse. If he is to protect his life, he has to assess any potential action's relationship to it. He has to plan a course of behavior deliberately, committing himself to a long-range purpose, then integrating to it all of his goals, desires, and activities. Only in this way can the attainment of an ultimate purpose become an issue within his conscious control.

An action undertaken by a short-range mentality may lead accidentally to a beneficial result. If one swallows, buys, befriends, or votes for whatever or whomever one stumbles across on the spur of the moment, without reference to reasons, purposes, or effects, one may get away with it for a while; but only for a while. *Consistency,* in regard to any goal beyond the perceptual level or the routine, cannot be achieved by sense perception, subconscious habit, or luck. It can be achieved only by the aid of explicit values and knowledge.

No one could expect to reach the big sale uptown by pointing his car north, then steering at random, with no map, no plan, no knowledge of turning points or detours, no concern but the impulse of the moment. To reach a sale, however, is a modest quest. To preserve one's life is a more difficult task.

For any living organism, the course of action that survival demands is continuous, full-time, *all-embracing.* No action an organism takes is irrelevant to its existence. Every such action is either in accordance with what self-preservation requires or it is not; it is for the entity's life or against it. This is true even of so innocuous an action as a man's taking a nap. In one context (if he is tired after work, say, and needs to unwind), such an action may be beneficial; if he does it on the job, however, it may lead to unemployment; if he does it outdoors during a blizzard, he may never wake up. The principle involved in this simple example applies to every choice one makes; it applies to one's choices in regard to career, friends, investments, psychotherapist, entertainment. It applies whatever the form and scale of a choice's effects—which may be obvious or subtle, major or minor. The point is that every choice *has* effects which redound, directly or indirectly, on one's ability to survive.

Life *is* motion. If the motion is not self-preserving, then it is self-destroying.

Self-destroying action need not be immediately fatal. There is such a thing as drawn-out destruction, a state of affairs in which one is neither healthy nor dead, but in the process of moving from one condition to the other. Thus it is possible to deteriorate gradually for years, breathing all the while, but increasingly damaged. An obvious medical example, which has many counterparts that do not involve substance abuse, would be a long-term alcoholic or drug addict. In certain of these cases (though by no means all), the damage may be reversible—if one changes one's course in time, before the ultimate result becomes irrevocable. But none of this alters the fact that damage *is* damage; nor does it alter the fact that damage, untended, is progressive. Such a negative cannot be deliberately courted or even passively tolerated, not if self-preservation is one's goal.

The size and form of the damage are not relevant here. No threat to vitality—no undermining of one's capacity to deal successfully with the environment—can be countenanced if life is the standard of value. The reason is that no such threat can be inflicted *safely* on so complex and delicate an integration as a living organism. In a biological context, suffering "only a little damage" is comparable to taking "only a little cyanide" or playing "only an occasional game of Russian roulette." "Life" does not mean flirting with death and cannot be achieved by such means.

In regard to the issue of being long-range, there are differences among conscious species. A purely sensory organism knows nothing but the immediate moment. The higher animals, however, do and must project the future to some extent; they do it within the limits of their perceptual form of awareness. An animal's life, as Ayn Rand points out, "consists of a series of separate cycles, repeated over and over again, such as the cycle of breeding its young, or of storing food for the winter. . . . " Each of these cycles is undertaken afresh, as a separate unit, without connection in the animal's awareness to the cycles of its past or future. An animal cannot grasp or deal with the total of its lifespan and does not need to do so.[12]

In this respect, too, Ayn Rand observes, man is unique. *"Man's* life is a continuous whole: for good or evil, every day, year and decade of his life holds the sum of all the days behind him."[13] Man can and must know not merely tomorrow's requirements or this season's, but every identifiable factor that affects his survival. He can assess not merely the proximate, but also the remote consequences of his choices. It is not enough for him to consider the chance of a toothache next week; he also needs to know whether he is courting bankruptcy next month, an anxiety attack next year, an invasion of human predators in the next decade, or a nuclear holocaust in the next generation.

With the advent of the human species, the need to project the future reaches its climax. The temporal scale of man's concern must be not any isolated day or cycle, but his entire lifespan. Just as man's knowledge must be integrated into an all-encompassing sum, so must his actions. "If he is to succeed at the task of survival . . . ," Ayn Rand concludes, "man has to choose his course, his goals, his values in the context and terms of a lifetime."[14]

Here, then, is the problem. Man must be long-range. He must know the survival significance of every action he takes. And he must know it in relation to the timespan of an entire human life. The problem is: what can make such a cognitive feat possible?

The answer is: the same kind of consciousness that makes it necessary.

Man can retain and deal with so vast a quantity of data only by the method of unit-reduction. He can gain knowledge of decades still ahead of him only by means of the faculty that integrates perceived concretes to an unlimited number of unperceived but similar ones, past, present, and future. He can achieve the long-range outlook he needs only by the use of concepts.

If man is to sustain and protect his life, he must *conceptualize* the requirements of human survival.

This means that he must confront the array of human choices and actions, in all its bewildering complexity, and achieve unit-economy. He must ask: what are the fundamental choices, the ones which shape all the others? And what abstractions integrate all the instances of such choices from the aspect of their relationship to self-preservation? In other words, what generalizations identify—in condensed, retainable form—the effect on man's life of different kinds of choices?

An adult determines whether a previously unperceived

object is a man, an animal, or an automobile by applying to the new experience his earlier formed concepts. The man who has conceptualized the requirements of survival decides by a similar epistemological method whether or not in any particular case to tell a lie—or to work for his keep—or to compromise his convictions—or to give to charity—or to fight an advancing dictatorship. He decides not by feeling or by polls and not by trying to assess each new situation without context, as though he were an infant, but by the application of his earlier formed moral concepts.

The common name of this latter form of cognition (which extends far beyond moral issues) is *"principle."* A "principle" is a general truth on which other truths depend. Every science and every field of thought involves the discovery and application of principles. Leaving aside certain special cases, a principle may be described as a fundamental reached by induction. Such knowledge is necessary to a conceptual consciousness for the same reason that induction and the grasp of fundamentals are necessary.[15]

A moral principle, accordingly, is not something sui generis. Properly speaking, it is a type of scientific principle, identifying the relationship to man's survival of the various basic human choices. A man who acts "on moral principle" in this sense is neither a martyr, a zealot, nor a prig; he is a person guided by man's distinctive faculty of cognition. For a rational being, principled action is the only effective kind of action. To be principled is the only way to achieve a long-range goal.

In the Objectivist view, moral principles are not luxuries reserved for "higher" souls or duties owed to the supernatural. They are a practical, earthly necessity to anyone concerned with self-preservation.

The only alternative to action governed by moral principle is action expressing short-range impulse. But for man, as we know, the short-range, viewed long-range, is self-destructive. This is the practical point missed by pragmatism, which tells people to judge each choice not by reference to abstract theory, but only by its results after it has been tried; which insists that today's results need not recur tomorrow; and which urges that each situation be approached "experimentally," "on its own terms." Such a philosophy amounts to the declaration: drop your mind, discard your capacity for thought, decide each case *perceptually*. This is precisely what man cannot do; not for long.

The Objectivist morality, I have said, defines a *code* of values. By "code" here Ayn Rand means an integrated, hierarchically structured, noncontradictory system of principles, which enables a man to choose, plan, and act long-range. Man needs such a code, as should now be clear, not merely because he has free will, but because he is a living organism, who must learn to use his free will correctly. He needs a moral code because his life requires a specific course of action and, being a conceptual entity, he cannot follow this course except by the guidance of concepts.

What then is the standard of *moral* value? A valid code of morality, Ayn Rand concludes, a code based on reason and proper to man, must hold *man's life* as its standard of value. "All that which is proper to the life of a rational being is the good; all that which destroys it is the evil."[16]

Let me repeat that the standard, inherent in the whole argument, is *man's* life. "Man's life" or "man's survival qua man" means, in Ayn Rand's definition, "the terms, methods, conditions and goals required for the survival of a rational being through the whole of his lifespan—in all those aspects of existence which are open to his choice."[17] To state the point another way, "man's life" means life in accordance with the *principles* of human survival.

The Objectivist standard of morality is not a momentary or a merely physical survival; it is the long-range survival of man—mind and body. The standard is not "staying alive by any means," because, once we speak in long-range terms, there is only one means of sustaining human life. As Ayn Rand puts it, the standard is not "survival at any price, since there's only one price that pays for man's survival: reason."[18]

"Man's life" is not a separate or "higher" ideal arbitrarily added to "life." It is merely the standard of life applied to man. Life, for any living creature, means life *as* that creature, life in accordance with its specific means of survival. There is no dichotomy between existence and identity. *To be,* for a man, is to be *a man*.

Any standard of morality other than Objectivism's can have only one ultimate result. "Since life requires a specific course of action," Ayn Rand observes, "any other course will destroy it."[19] To support her point, we have more than the evidence of theory. We also have the sobering spectacle of all the countries and centuries that tried some version of "non-life" as their standard.

They got what they asked for.

Rationality as the Primary Virtue

What *are* the principles of human survival? What objects must man hold as values if he is to preserve his life, and what virtues must he practice in order to achieve them?

The faculty of reason is man's basic tool of survival. The primary choice is to exercise this faculty or not. If life is the standard, therefore, the basic moral principle is obvious. It tells us the proper evaluation of reason.

According to Ayn Rand, there are three basic values "which, together, are the means to and the realization of one's ultimate value. . . . "

> To live, man must hold three things as the supreme and ruling values of his life: Reason—Purpose—Self-esteem. Reason, as his only tool of knowledge—Purpose, as his choice of the happiness which that tool must proceed to achieve—Self-esteem, as his inviolate certainty that his mind is competent to think and his person is worthy of happiness, which means: is worthy of living. These three values imply and require all of man's virtues . . . [20]

The last two of these I will defer until the next chapter. The greatest of them, however, which makes the others possible, is the first. Epistemology tells us that reason is *valid;* it is man's means of knowledge. Ethics draws the practical conclusion: if one chooses to live, one must hold reason as a *value.*

To value reason is the opposite not only of rejecting it, but also of accepting it dutifully. In regard to the mind, the Objectivist is not disinterested or grudging. He does not say: "I myself would rather be irrational, but, since A is A, I agree not to hold contradictions." On the contrary, grasping the vital role of consciousness, he awards reason the fundamental place in his *personal* value structure. He is the man who cherishes his means of survival, who recoils from the prospect of subverting it, who is uplifted by the spectacle of dry objectivity. "[T]he noblest act you have ever performed," said Ayn Rand, "is the act of your mind in the process of grasping that two and two make four."[21] She did not intend the statement as hyperbole.

The magnificent fire in Ayn Rand's ethics—her inspiring affirmations of man the hero, creative work, selfish joy, individual liberty—all of it is a derivative. The root is the primary moral estimate of Objectivism, its estimate of reason.

Every moral value entails a lifelong course of virtue. "Virtue," in the Objectivist definition, is "the action by which one gains and keeps [a value]."[22] The action in this instance—the virtue that develops, preserves, and applies the faculty of reason, thereby making possible every other human value—is rationality.

"Rationality," according to Ayn Rand, is "the recognition and acceptance of reason as one's only source of knowledge, one's only judge of values and one's only guide to action."[23] This means the application of reason to every aspect of one's life and concerns. It means choosing and validating one's opinions, one's decisions, one's work, one's love, in accordance with the normal requirements of a cognitive process, the requirements of logic, objectivity, integration. Put negatively, the virtue means never placing any consideration above one's perception of reality. This includes never attempting to get away with a contradiction, a mystic fantasy, or an indulgence in context-dropping.

Rationality means the acceptance of reason as a principle of human survival and *as an absolute*.

Animals exercise their faculty of consciousness automatically; man does not. "For an animal," writes Ayn Rand, "the question of survival is primarily physical; for man, primarily epistemological."[24] Rationality, accordingly, is the *primary* obligation of man; all the others are derivatives of it. If man needs to choose his actions by reference to principles, this virtue names the root principle. Indeed, it underlies the very need of moral principles. To act on principle is itself an expression of rationality; it is a form of being governed by one's conceptual faculty.

By the same token, there is only one primary vice, which is the root of all other human evils: irrationality. This is the deliberate suspension of consciousness, the refusal to see, to think, to know—either as a general policy, because one regards awareness as too demanding, or in regard to some specific point, because the facts conflict with one's feelings. Vice, in the Objectivist view, is not a rewarding policy; it is unconsciousness—willful, self-induced unconsciousness, while one continues to move around and function. To a conscious organism no course of behavior can be more dangerous.

The above is a generalized overview. Now let me consider certain aspects of rationality in greater detail.

To begin with, one cannot follow reason unless one exercises it. Rationality demands continual mental activity, a regular, daily process of functioning on the conceptual level of consciousness. This involves much more than merely forming enough concepts to be able to speak or read a book. In Ayn Rand's description, it involves

> an actively sustained process of identifying one's impressions in conceptual terms, of integrating every event and every observation into a conceptual context, of grasping relationships, differences, similarities in one's perceptual material and of abstracting them into new concepts, of drawing inferences, of making deductions, of reaching conclusions, of asking new questions and discovering new answers and expanding one's knowledge into an ever-growing sum.[25]

A man does not qualify as rational if he walks around in a daze but once in a while, when someone mentions a fact, he wakes up long enough to say "I'll accept that," then relapses again. Rationality requires the systematic *use* of one's intelligence.

Ayn Rand's novels abound in instructive examples of this aspect of virtue. Consider, for instance, Howard Roark's encounter with the Dean at the beginning of *The Fountainhead*. The Dean tells him that men must always revere tradition. Roark regards this viewpoint as senseless, but he does not ignore it. Roark is not a psychologist, nor does the field interest him much; but he does deal with men, he knows that there are many like the Dean, and he is on the premise of *understanding what he deals with*. So he identifies the meaning of the event in the terms available to him. There is something here opposite to the way I function, he thinks, some form of behavior I do not grasp—"the principle behind the Dean," he calls it—and he files this observation in his subconscious with the implicit order to himself: be on the lookout for any data relevant to this problem. Thereafter, when such information becomes available (new examples or aspects in new contexts), he recognizes and integrates it. In the end, by a process whose steps the reader has seen, Roark reaches the concept of the "second-hander"—and of the opposite kind of man, whom he represents. At that point, he grasps what the issue is on which his own fate and that of the world depend.

Whatever the heroes in Ayn Rand's novels deal with, including work, romance, art, people, politics, and philosophy, they seek to understand it, by connecting the new to what they already know and by discovering what they do not yet know. They are men and women who like and practice the process of cognition. This is why they are usually efficacious and happy individuals, who achieve their values. Their commitment to thought leads them to a sustained growth in knowledge, which maximizes the possibility of successful action.

In citing the Roark example, I do not mean to suggest that rationality has to involve the discovery of new ideas. The exercise of reason applies within the sphere of each man's knowledge, concerns, and ability. The point is not that one must become a genius or even an intellectual. Contrary to a widespread fallacy, reason is a faculty of human beings, not of "supermen."[26] The moral point here is always to grow mentally, to increase one's knowledge and expand the power of one's consciousness to the extent one can, whatever one's profession or the degree of one's intelligence. Mental growth is possible on some scale to every person with an intact brain.

It requires the expenditure of effort, however, the effort of initiating and maintaining a state of full consciousness. Effort does not mean pain or duty, but it does mean struggle, because conceptual knowledge is a volitional attainment that involves the risk of error and the need of continual, scrupulous mental work. The men of virtue are the men who choose to practice and welcome this kind of struggle on principle, as a lifelong commitment.

Their opposites are the anti-effort mentalities, who seek to coast through life, hoping that knowledge and values will somehow materialize without labor or cost whenever one wishes for them. This attitude represents the subversion of virtue at the root; it is resentment of the fact that virtue is necessary. The best symbol here is the Garden of Eden before the Fall, which the Judeo-Christian tradition regards as paradise. Such a projection elevates mental stagnation to the status of ideal. No long-range action is required of Adam and Eve, no work, no plan, no focus; they need merely lie around, munch fruit, and follow orders.

The mental practice that underlies the anti-effort attitude is the act of *evasion,* of blanking out some fact of reality which one dislikes. This act constitutes the essence of irrationality and, therefore, of evil. Evasion is the Objectivist equivalent of a mortal sin. It is the only such sin that we recognize, because it is what makes possible every other form of moral corruption.[27]

No one seeks to evade the total of reality. Evaders believe that the practice is safe because they feel they can localize it. Ultimately, however, they cannot.

The reason is that everything in reality is interconnected. In logic, therefore, to sustain an evasion on any single point, one would be forced gradually to expand and to keep expanding the scope of one's blindness. For example, suppose that you decide to evade only in regard to the issue of God's existence, which you want to accept without evidence; in regard to everything else, you say, you will follow reason. What, in pattern, will happen to your mental processes thereafter? Can you remain rational in dealing with the rest of metaphysics, including such topics as the eternity of the universe, the absolutism of Identity, and the impossibility of miracles? Any of these topics, squarely faced, threatens to expose and upset your evasion. What about your thinking in regard to epistemology, including your view of the arbitrary and the issue of faith versus reason? What about ethics and God's supposed moral commandments? What about God's reputed political views—e.g., on pornography, prayer in the schools, abortion? What about the clash between Genesis and the theory of evolution? If you tried consistently to protect only your single starting evasion, turning aside methodically from everything that might threaten it, directly or indirectly, that single evasion would lead you step by step to one ultimate result: total nonperception.

The above is the negative expression of a principle discussed in chapter 4: man's need of integration. Just as every idea has a relationship to one's other ideas, and none can be accepted until it is seen to be an element of a single cognitive whole; so every fact has a relationship to other facts, and none can be evaded without tearing apart and destroying that kind of whole.

In actuality, our discussion of a methodically consistent evader is merely a pedagogical device. An evader is not concerned with consistency; he does not seek to protect his evasion by identifying conscientiously the implications of new cognitive material; if that were his policy, he would not be evading. The evader's method is not to follow his evasion logically, wherever it leads, but to ignore logical relationships. His method is to deal with ideas and facts piecemeal, accepting or rejecting disconnected bits of content at random, by reference to feeling.

The evader does want the "safety" of localizing his evasions, and he practices the only method there is of achieving such localization: *not knowing* his evasions' implications. This means that he discards the principle of integration.

By its nature, evasion is a form of nonintegration. It is the most lethal form: the willful *dis*integration of mental contents. A man in this condition no longer has the means to determine consistency or contradiction, truth or falsehood. In his consciousness, *all* conceptual content is reduced to the capricious, the baseless, the arbitrary; no conclusion qualifies as knowledge in a mind that rejects the requirements of cognition. Thus the real evader, like the hypothetical one I mentioned first, reaches only one end and one kind of "safety": all-encompassing blindness. This is the explanation of Ayn Rand's statement that "a concession to the irrational invalidates one's consciousness. . . ."[28]

The mind can no more tolerate "a little irrationality" than

the body can tolerate "a little malignancy." Both evils, once introduced, start to consume any healthier elements.

Every virtue, according to Objectivism, has two aspects, one intellectual, the other existential. Since man is a unity made of mind and body, every virtue has an application in both realms; each involves a certain process of consciousness and, as its expression in reality, a certain course of physical action.

The existential side of rationality is the policy of acting in accordance with one's rational conclusions. There is no point in using one's mind if the knowledge one gains thereby is not one's guide in action.

This aspect of rationality subsumes several obligations.[29] It requires that one choose not only his abstract values but also his specific goals by a process of rational thought—as against choosing some goal by an act of whim while dropping the full context of one's knowledge and of one's other goals. It requires that one know what his motives are—as against drifting through a day or a life, pushed one knows not where by unidentified impulse. It requires that one choose the means to his ends by reference to explicitly defined principles, both moral and scientific—as against trying to build a bridge, a newscast, a marriage, or world peace by the aid of concrete-bound habit, undigested slogans, or "the seat of one's pants." And it requires that one then enact the means, accepting the law of causality in full—as against seeking effects without causes or causes without effects. This last issue needs elaboration.

To seek effects without causes means to desire a certain object, perhaps a perfectly legitimate one, but take no action to gain it. The individual in such a case relies on the fact that he wants or prays for the effect. If one asks him: "But how will it ever be achieved?" his answer, often merely implicit, is an evasion: "Somehow."[30]

If a man wants a certain effect, it is his responsibility to discover and enact the necessary cause. If he wants a fulfilling love affair, for instance, he cannot sit in his lonely apartment pining for a soulmate "somehow" to materialize. He must define what specifically he seeks in a woman and then start looking actively for her. Or if a woman wants a career as a writer, she cannot forever put off writing while waiting for inspiration "somehow" to strike. She must find the means to create her inspiration and then pick up a pen. The same principle applies to the desire for wealth, happiness, freedom, or any other value. It is not enough to say: "X is a good thing, I want it." Since neither God nor society can perform a miracle, the policy of Christian "hope" is the opposite of virtue. Like every living thing, including in their own way the lilies of the field, a human being, if he is to gain his ends, must toil and spin.

A particularly irrational variant of the above vice is the attempt to *reverse* cause and effect. In this case, the individual wishes for an unearned effect, but only as a senseless means to an end. He hopes that the effect, somehow, will provide him with the cause which he refused to enact or achieve. As examples, Ayn Rand cites people who want "unearned love, as if love, the effect, could give [them] personal value, the cause"—or who want "unearned admiration, as if admiration, the effect, could give [them] virtue, the cause"—or who want "unearned wealth, as if wealth, the effect, could give [them] ability, the cause."[31] In all such cases, the individual does not actually want the ostensible object of his quest, such as love or money. He wants the *meaning* of the object; he wants the pretense that he has achieved its cause, while evading the fact that he hasn't and that he never intends to achieve it.

The converse error is to seek causes without effects. This means: taking a certain action while evading and expecting to escape its consequences. We have already mentioned alcoholics and drug addicts who shut their eyes to the self-destructiveness of their behavior. The same phenomenon exists in many other forms. An example is the people who regularly want more favors from the government or more bureaus, while ignoring the escalation of controls this involves and the political denouement it forebodes. Many of these people do not want dictatorship, any more than an alcoholic wants the d.t.'s, and they have the ability to know the effect of their actions; yet they demand every step that leads to the omnipotent state while blanking out the future. The motto of all such people is: "I can get away with it!" But A is A, and they can't, not long-range.

The policy of evading causality—whether one wishes somehow to gain or to escape an effect—is a form of placing an "I wish" above an "It is." In this respect, it is like all the other variants of irrationality. As we saw in chapter 5, the only alternative to the acceptance of reason is emotionalism. This brings me to the topic of virtue and emotion.

In epistemology, we concluded that emotions are not tools of cognition. The corollary in ethics is that they are not guides to action.

Ayn Rand defines "whim" as "a desire experienced by a person who does not know and does not care to discover its cause."[32] Such a person does not wish to introspect or to analyze. He does not seek to identify the premises that underlie his desire or to determine whether these premises conform to reality. He simply wants a certain item. He wants it *because* he wants it. This is what Ayn Rand calls "whim-worship."

Whim-worship is to ethics what mysticism is to epistemology. The two practices are invalid for the same reason and lead to the same destructive results.

The proper approach in this issue is not reason versus emotion, but reason first and then emotion. This approach, as we have seen, leads to the harmony of reason and emotion, which is the normal state of a rational man. His feelings, accordingly, are the opposite of whims; they are consequences of rational, explicitly identified value-judgments. A man with this kind of psychology and self-knowledge does not repress his desires. He is eager to feel and to give his feelings full reality in the hours and choices of his life. To him, such a policy is a form of expressing in action the judgment of his mind.

The desires of a rational man are stronger than those of a whim-worshiper. The reason is that the rational man experiences his values in undiluted form. Since he has identified and integrated his mental contents, every aspect of them contributes to his certainty; nothing in his premises or psychology tames the fire of his passion. If a man wants to eat his cake and have it, too, he is necessarily torn, unsure of his direction, self-doubtful; the very contradiction mutes the intensity with which he can desire either side of it. But if a man wants something with the unbreached dedication of a person who knows his own mind and knows that his desire is in full accordance with reality, then he *wants* it.

In ethics as in epistemology, there is no dichotomy between reason and emotion. Once again, the truth is: think, and you shall feel.

I must add that anyone, for perfectly innocent reasons, may in some issue experience a clash between emotions and ideas. The rational course then is to defer action on the issue until the clash has been resolved. First, one should discover where one's error lies and correct it; then one can act—assuming time permits such deliberation. If it doesn't, if some emergency requires an immediate decision, then the person in conflict has to act without full self-knowledge. In such a case, he must be guided by his mind, i.e., by his best conscious judgment of what is consonant with reality, even if his emotions protest. When the crisis is over, he can inquire into the source of his emotional dissent and reestablish mental harmony.

This completes our first discussion of virtue. The decline of the West, someone once observed, can be symbolized by the fact that the term "virtue"—which comes from "vir," Latin for "man"—has been turned upside down across the centuries. It has evolved from meaning "manliness" in a man to meaning "chastity" in a woman. Objectivism restores the term's original sense. We mean by "virtue" the kind of action appropriate to a human being.

The action is rationality.

The Individual as the Proper Beneficiary of His Own Moral Action

Now let us turn to the last of the three basic ethical questions, the question of the proper beneficiary. The answer involves a distinction between the standard of ethics and the purpose of ethics.

An ethical standard, writes Ayn Rand, means

> an abstract principle that serves as a measurement or gauge to guide a man's choices in the achievement of a concrete, specific purpose. "That which is required for the survival of man *qua* man" is an abstract principle that applies to every individual man. The task of applying this principle to a concrete, specific purpose—the purpose of living a life

proper to a rational being—belongs to every individual man, and the life he has to live is his own.[33]

Each individual must choose his values and actions by the standard of man's life—in order to achieve the purpose of maintaining and enjoying his own life. Thus Objectivism advocates *egoism*—the pursuit of self-interest—the policy of selfishness.

The concept of "egoism" identifies merely one aspect of an ethical code.[34] It tells us not what acts a man should take, but who should profit from them. Egoism states that each man's primary moral obligation is to achieve his own welfare, well-being, or self-interest (these terms are synonyms here). It states that each man should be "concerned with his own interests"; he should be "selfish" in the sense of being the beneficiary of his own moral actions. Taken by itself, this principle offers no practical guidance. It does not specify values or virtues; it does not define "interests" or "self-interest"—neither in terms of "life," "power," "pleasure," nor of anything else. It simply states: whatever man's proper self-interest consists of, that is what each individual should seek to achieve.

The alternative is the view that man's primary moral obligation is to serve some entity other than himself, such as God or society, at the price of subordinating or denying his own welfare. In this view, the essence of morality is unselfishness, which involves some form of self-sacrifice.

Though I have often implied the Objectivist position on the present question, it is only at this point that I am able to address the issue explicitly. The reason is that egoism, like every other principle, requires a process of validation—and until now, the context needed to prove (and properly interpret) egoism had not been established.

In the Objectivist view, the validation of egoism consists in showing that it is a *corollary* of man's life as the moral standard.[35]

"Only the alternative of life vs. death," I said earlier, "creates the context for value-oriented action. . . ." And "only self-preservation," I said, "can be an ultimate goal. . . ." Now I need merely add the emphasis required to bring out the full meaning of these formulations. The alternative with which reality confronts a living organism is its *own* life or death. The goal is *self*-preservation.

Leaving aside reproduction, to which every organism owes its existence, this is the goal of all automatic biological processes and actions. When a plant turns its leaves to reach the sunlight, when an animal digests food or regulates its internal temperature or turns at a sudden sound to discover the source, the organism is pursuing the values *its* survival demands. As a living entity, each necessarily acts for its own sake; each is the beneficiary of its own actions.

Plants and animals may not, however, be described as "egoistic"; the term "self-sustaining" covers the facts of their kind of behavior. Concepts such as "egoistic," along with its synonyms and antonyms (such as "selfish," "altruistic," "self-less"), are *moral* terms. These terms apply only to an entity with the power of choice; they designate a mode of functioning that has been adopted in the face of an alternative. Plants and animals do not have to decide who is to be the beneficiary of their actions. Man does have to decide it.

In the case of man, self-sustaining behavior is not preprogrammed. Even though man's bodily processes are guided automatically by the value of life, we saw earlier, he must decide as a conscious entity to accept life as his moral standard. A similar point applies in the present issue. Even though man's bodily processes aim automatically at *self*-preservation, he must decide as a conscious entity to accept this end as his moral purpose. Because his consciousness is volitional, man must *choose* to accept the essence of life. He must choose to make self-sustenance into a fundamental rule of his voluntary behavior. The man who makes this choice is an "egoist."

"Egoistic," in the Objectivist view, means self-sustaining by an act of choice and as a matter of principle.

The wider principle demanding such egoism is the fact that survival requires an all-encompassing course of action. A man's life cannot be preserved, not in the long-range sense, if he views the task as a sideline serving some other kind of goal. If an action of his is not *for* his life, then, as we have seen, it is against his life—it is self-inflicted damage, which, uncorrected, is progressive. This principle applies without restriction, to every aspect of a man's actions; it is particularly obvious, however, when the aspect is not some complex means or lesser ends, but the ruling goal of a man's existence. To accept anything other than one's own life in *this* kind of issue—to incorporate into one's ultimate purpose any variant or tinge of self-denial—is to declare war on life at the root.

Life requires that man gain values, not lose them. It requires assertive action, achievement, success, not abnegation, renunciation, surrender. It requires self-tending—in other words, the exact opposite of sacrifice.

A "sacrifice" is the surrender of a value, such as money, career, loved ones, freedom, for the sake of a lesser value or of a nonvalue (if one acquires an equal or a greater value from a transaction, then it is an even trade or a gain, not a sacrifice). A rational man, however, chooses his values and their hierarchical ranking not by whim, but by a process of cognition. To tell such a man to surrender his values is to tell him: surrender your judgment, contradict your knowledge, sacrifice your *mind*. But this is something a man dare not sacrifice.[36]

The process of thought requires a man to follow the evidence wherever it leads, without fear or favor, regardless of any effects such action may have on the consciousness of others. He must follow the evidence whether others agree with his conclusions or not, whether their disagreement is honest or not, whether his conclusions accord with their wishes or not, whether his conclusions make them happy or not. Since thought is an attribute of the individual, each man must be *sovereign* in regard to the function and product of his own brain. This is impossible if morality demands that a man "place others above self."

There is no dichotomy between epistemology and ethics—which means, in this issue, between the process of cognition and its beneficiary. A man cannot offer unswerving allegiance to logic, if he holds that his moral duty is to surrender his conclusions in order to satisfy unchosen obligations to others. He cannot guide his faculty of awareness by the dictates of his own independent judgment, if he believes that he is rightfully a mere means to the ends of others and that his mind, therefore, is *their* property. He cannot combine in the same consciousness the status of cognitive sovereign with that of moral serf.

If a man's brain, like an industrialist's factory, is not his to profit from, then it is not his to control. The result in both cases is that the entity viewed as the proper beneficiary—others or society—moves to take over the prerogatives of ownership. In regard to a factory, this takeover is called "socialism" and leads to the destruction of the factory. In regard to a brain, it is called "faith in the leader" and leads to the cessation of thought.

The need to be "concerned with one's own interests" applies in every realm of endeavor, including, above all, the realm of the intellect. There can be no interest greater to a rational being than the interest in his tool of survival—which can function only as *his* tool of survival. Just as the basic value, man's life, requires the ethics of egoism, so does the primary virtue. Rationality requires that a man be able righteously to say: my mind is my means of achieving *my* goals in accordance with *my* judgment of fact and of value. "[T]he most *selfish* of all things," as Ayn Rand puts the point, "is the independent mind that recognizes no authority higher than its own and no value higher than its judgment of truth."[37]

We are often told that the pursuit of truth is selfless since a personal interest acts as an agent of distortion. The premise underlying this claim is that man's goals are necessarily irrational and, therefore, that he faces an agonizing dilemma: to uphold either truth *or* his interests, reason and reality *or* his values. If a man's goals are not irrational, however, they demand of him a recognition of facts. In such a case, the discovery of truth is an eminently selfish policy, because it is an indispensable means to attaining one's ends. It is not selfless to know what one is doing and why.

If a man's personal interest is the passion to live and succeed *in* reality, that motive is the incentive to the most rigorous objectivity he can practice—on the premise that ignorance is not bliss. By contrast, if one had no personal interest in knowing facts, or if he viewed facts as the enemy of his values, what would prompt him to undertake the challenge of cognition? The truth is the reverse of the conventional notion. Selflessness is not the precondition of objectivity, but its obstacle. In actuality, the selfless is the mindless.

Whether one studies the nature of life, of value, of virtue, or of cognition, the conclusion is the same. To be, for a rational being, *is* to be selfish—by an act of choice.

The Objectivist view of the nature of selfishness is implicit in the validation of the principle. The principle arises within the context of the requirements of man's survival. These, therefore, determine the principle's proper interpretation.

Ayn Rand upholds *rational self-interest.* This means the ethics of selfishness, with man's life as the standard of value defining "self-interest," and rationality as the primary virtue defining the method of achieving it. Within the Objectivist framework, indeed, the term "rational self-interest" is a redundancy, albeit a necessary one today. We do not recognize any "self-interest" for man outside the context and absolute of reason.

In the Objectivist interpretation, the principle of egoism subsumes all the values and virtues already discussed (along with all those still to be discussed). Egoism requires noncontradictory goals, long-range thought, principled action, and the full acceptance of causality. The selfish man, in short, is no other than the rational man—because he recognizes that any default on rationality is harmful to his well-being. The contrapositive of this point is that *ir*rationality is *un*selfishness.

Unfortunately, for a reason I shall soon indicate, egoism has been advocated through the centuries mainly by subjectivists. The result is several corrupt versions of egoism, which most people now regard as the self-evident meaning of the concept. So I must keep stressing the fact that Objectivism upholds objectivity and therefore rejects all these versions. We reject the idea that egoism permits the evasion of principles. We reject the equation of egoism with irresponsibility, context-dropping, or whim-worship. We reject the notion that selfishness means "doing whatever you feel like doing." The fact that you feel like taking some action does not necessarily make it an action compatible with your "interests," in the legitimate sense of that term. There are countless examples of people who desire and pursue self-destructive courses of behavior.

One such course consists of a person sacrificing others to himself.

Since egoism is a principle of human survival, it applies to all human beings. *Every* man, according to Objectivism, should live by his own mind and for his own sake; every man should pursue the values and practice the virtues that man's life requires. Since man survives by thought and production, every man should live and work as an independent, creative being, acquiring goods and services from others only by means of trade, when both parties agree that the trade is profitable. A proper discussion of all these points will occupy us during subsequent chapters.

At this stage, I want merely to dissociate Ayn Rand's approach from the subjectivist idea of dealing with others. Egoism, in the Objectivist interpretation, does *not* mean the policy of violating the rights, moral or political, of others in order to satisfy one's own needs or desires. It does not mean the policy of a brute, a con man, or a beggar. It does not mean the policy of turning other men, whether by clubs or tears, into one's servants. Any such policy, as we will see in due course, is destructive not only to the victim, but also to the perpetrator. It is condemned as immoral, therefore, by the very principle of selfishness.

The best formulation of the Objectivist view in this issue is the oath taken by John Galt, the hero of *Atlas Shrugged*. "I swear—by my life and my love of it—that I will never live for the sake of another man, nor ask another man to live for mine." The principle embodied in this oath is that human sacrifice is evil no matter who its beneficiary is, whether you sacrifice yourself to others or others to yourself. Man—every man—is an end in himself.[38]

If a person rejects this principle, it makes little difference which of its negations he adopts—whether he says "Sacrifice yourself to others" (the ethics of altruism) or "Sacrifice others to yourself" (the subjectivist version of egoism). In either case, he holds that human existence requires martyrs; that some men are mere means to the ends of others; that somebody's throat must be cut. The only question then is: your life for their sake or theirs for yours? This question does not represent a dispute about a moral principle. It is nothing but a haggling over victims by two camps who share the same principle.

Objectivism does not share it. We hold that man's life is incompatible with sacrifice—with sacrifice as such, *of* anybody *to* anybody. We reject both the above theories on the same ground. As Ayn Rand states the point in *The Fountain-*

head, the rational man rejects masochism and sadism, submission and domination, the making of sacrifices and the collecting of them. What he upholds and creates is a self-sufficient ego.[39]

People often ask if there are not conflicts of interest among men—e.g., in regard to work or romantic love—which require someone's sacrifice. Objectivism answers that there are no conflicts of interest among *rational* men, who live by production and trade, who accept the responsibility of earning any value they desire, and who refuse to make or accept sacrifices. There is a "conflict of interest," if one wants to call it that, between a banker and a bank robber; but not among men who do not allow robbery or any equivalent into their view of their interests. The same applies to all values, including romantic love. (This latter example is discussed in *Atlas Shrugged.)*[40]

Now, having removed the worst obstacle to understanding egoism (its equation with the vicious act of sacrifice), let us consider the relation of self to others afresh. Let us consider this subject as one would approach it in a proper culture, where lengthy polemics against vice would be unnecessary.

The essential fact to grasp here is that social existence is an asset to man in the struggle for survival.

If we leave aside dictatorships, which are much less safe to their inhabitants than a desert island, the advantages of life in society are obvious. "The two great values to be gained from social existence," writes Miss Rand, "are: knowledge and trade."[41] Men can transmit from one generation to the next a vast store of knowledge, far more than any individual could gain by himself in a single lifetime. And if men practice the division of labor, an individual can achieve a degree of skill and a material return on his effort far greater than he could attain if he lived in solitude.

Egoism, accordingly, does not mean that a man should isolate himself from others or remain indifferent to them. On the contrary, a proper view of egoism requires that a man identify the role of others in his own life and then evaluate them appropriately.

Certain men—those who think, live independently, and produce—are a value to one another. They are a value by the standard of man's life and of each individual's own self-interest. By the same standard, the opposite kinds of men—the evaders, the parasites, the criminals—are the opposite of a value. If one lives or deals with other men at all, their *moral character* is relevant to one's own survival and can be an issue of enormous significance to it, for good or for evil. To concretize this principle further, one need merely project the effects on one's well-being that would flow from living in a society made up of goose-stepping Nazis—or of the American Founding Fathers—or of mindless Babbitts out of *Main Street*—or of men such as John Galt and Francisco D'Anconia in the Atlantis of *Atlas Shrugged*.

The above principle introduces a broad new context for the pursuit of value. It points us to the realm of *personal* relationships. When men evaluate the moral character of others, as we saw in chapter 4, they respond emotionally, feeling esteem and affection for those individuals whose values they share. The result is the phenomena of admiration, friendship, love (and, unfortunately, of their negatives as well). Friendship and love are a crucial aspect of an egoist's life, not merely because most people happen to want personal relationships, but because it is rational to want such, if the value standards involved are legitimate.

The attainment of such relationships, as of any other value, requires a proper course of thought and action. It requires that a person define and validate the specific values of character (and their hierarchy) that he regards as important to him personally. It requires that he recognize these values when he encounters them, i.e., that he learn to identify objectively the traits possessed by others (and by himself). And it requires that he seek from others, assuming they want it too, the form and degree of intimacy—of sharing his thoughts, his feelings, his life—which are appropriate given the degree of their mutual value-affinity. The result, if one can find the requisite individuals, will be an ascending scale of new pleasures added to one's life, ranging from the pleasure of a promising acquaintance to the rapture of romantic love.

By their very nature, all such responses to others are selfish. They are selfish because they rest ultimately on self-preservation—on the value to one's *own* life of other men who share one's values. They are selfish because they demand self-esteem—the confidence to rely on one's own conclusions and seek out one's own values in the person of another. They are selfish because they *are* pleasures, and deeply personal ones at that.[42]

We are often told that love (like the pursuit of truth) is selfless. A "selfless love" would be one unrelated to the lover's own life, judgment, or happiness; such a thing defies the very nature of love. "A 'selfless,' 'disinterested' love," writes Ayn Rand, "is a contradiction in terms: it means that one is indifferent to that which one values." Here again the truth is the opposite of the conventional idea. The egoist is not a man incapable of love; he is the *only* man capable of it. "To say 'I love you,' " as Howard Roark observes, "one must know first how to say the 'I.' "[43]

According to the subjectivist viewpoint, an egoist is an individual who is indifferent or hostile to everyone but himself. This view is irrelevant to Objectivism. The Objectivist does not say: "I value only myself." He says: "If you are a certain kind of person, you become thereby a value to me, in the furtherance of my own life and happiness." It is the invoking of this purpose, not the absence of loving, that constitutes egoism in the present matter.

The same purpose determines the nature and extent of the help one may properly give to others who are in trouble.[44] (This is a marginal moral issue. If suffering were the metaphysical norm, if the essence of human life consisted in rescuing victims from fires, floods, diseases, bankruptcy, or starvation, it would mean that man is not equipped to survive.)

Any action one takes to help another person, Ayn Rand holds, must be chosen within the full context of one's own goals and values. One must determine the time, the effort, the money that it is appropriate to spend, given the position of the recipient in one's evaluative hierarchy, and then act accordingly. To give a person less than he deserves, judging by one's own hierarchy, is to betray one's values. To give him more is to divert resources to a recipient who is unworthy of them by one's own definition, and thus again to sacrifice one's values.

It follows that a man must certainly act to help a person in trouble whom he loves, even to the point of risking his own life in case of danger. This is not a sacrifice if he loves the individual—say, his wife—because what happens to her makes a life-and-death difference to him personally and self-ishly. If it does not make such a difference to him, then what-ever the name of his feeling, it is not "love." By the same reasoning, a man must certainly not help others promiscu-ously. He must not help men who defy his values, or who declare war on him, or of whom he has no knowledge what-ever. If a man is to qualify as self-sustaining and self-respecting, he must not help, let alone love, his enemy, or even his neighbor—not until he discovers who the neighbor is and whether the person deserves to be helped.[45]

As to helping a stranger in an emergency, this is moral under certain conditions. A man may help such a person if the concept "emergency" is properly delimited;[46] if no sacrifice is involved on the helper's part; if the recipient is not the cause of his own suffering, i.e., the helper is supporting not vices but values, even though it is only the potential value of a fellow human being about whom nothing evil is known; and, above all, if the helper remembers the moral status of his action. Extending help to others in such a context is an act of generosity, not an obligation. Nor is it an act that one may cherish as one's claim to virtue. Virtue, for Objectivism, con-sists in creating values, not in giving them away.

You may and should help another man, or befriend him, or love him, if in the full context *you*—your values, your judg-ment, your life—are upheld thereby and protected. The prin-ciple of your action must be selfish. You may never properly accept the role of selfless servant to others or the status of sacrificial animal. (Further aspects of the Objectivist view of love are discussed in chapters 8 and 9.)

We often hear it said with a cynical shrug that all men are selfish. This claim is doubly wrong, as fact and as estimate. It is wrong as fact, because men can sacrifice their own interests; nowadays, they do it regularly, as the state of the world at-tests. It is wrong as estimate, because the cynicism implies that selfishness is evil.

Selfishness, as Objectivism interprets the concept, is not an innate weakness, but a rare strength. It is the achievement of remaining true to one's own life and one's own mind. This is not something to be taken for granted or cursed. It is something that must be learned, taught, nurtured, praised, enshrined.

The Objectivist interpretation does not represent an attenuated or "unselfish" type of egoism. We advocate plain egoism, the kind that actually achieves the selfish goal of sustaining one's own existence. Man's life as the moral standard is not a "higher" addition to life. Similarly, rational egoism is not a "higher" version of egoism.

The policy I have been discussing is properly called "selfishness." Further, if one accepts an objective approach to cognition, Ayn Rand's ethics is the only one fully entitled to that term of honor.

Those who reject the principle of selfishness will find in the history of ethics two main alternatives. One is the primordial and medieval theory that man should sacrifice himself to the supernatural. The second is the theory that man should sacrifice himself for the sake of other men. The second is known as "altruism," which is not a synonym for kindness, generosity, or good will, but the doctrine that man should place others above self as the fundamental rule of life.

I shall not attempt in this book to identify the contradictions and evils of these two theories. Ayn Rand has covered this ground too well—in theory, in practice, in history, and from every aspect I can think of. If her works have not already convinced you that the morality of self-sacrifice is the morality of death, nothing I can add will do so, either.

I shall confine myself here to one polemical observation. The advocates of self-sacrifice, in either version, have never demanded consistency. They have not asked men to sacrifice their goods, pleasures, goals, values, and ideas as a matter of principle. Even the saints had to eschew such a course, which would be tantamount to instant suicide. The moralists of selflessness expect a man to go on functioning, working, achieving—else he would have no values to give up. They expect him to exercise his mind for his own sake and survival, and then to deny his judgment as the spirit moves them. They expect him to be ruled by whim, the whim of the relevant authority or beneficiary, whenever it injects itself into the process and demands to be paid off.

These moralists expect you to live your life on a part-time basis only, while trying to get away on the side with sundry acts of self-immolation, just as drug addicts pursue some regular nourishment while trying to get away with their periodic fixes.

Neither of these contradictions, however, is practicable. Man's life does require adherence to principle. Nor is the above a distortion of the theory of self-sacrifice. It is what that theory actually means. Short of suicide, this is all that can be denoted in reality by the notion of a living entity practicing "anti-egoism."

The content of "the good" should now be clear. The good, in Ayn Rand's view, is man the individual sustaining life by reason, *his* life, with everything such a goal requires and implies.

Values as Objective

Since integration is crucial to the process of understanding, let us now connect the ethical knowledge we have been gaining to its roots in the Objectivist metaphysics and epistemology.

In general terms, the connection is evident. A morality of rational self-interest obviously presupposes a philosophic commitment to reason. But let us be more specific. Let us identify the role in this context of Ayn Rand's theory of concepts, which is the essence of her view of reason. More than anything else, this is the theory that makes the Objectivist ethics possible.

For Objectivism, values, like concepts, are not intrinsic or subjective, but objective.[47]

Just as concepts do not represent intrinsic features of reality, but presuppose a mind that performs a certain process of integration, so values are not intrinsic features of reality. Value requires a valuer—and moral value, therefore, presupposes a certain kind of estimate made by man; it presupposes an *act of evaluation*. Such an act, as we know, is possible only because man faces a fundamental alternative. It is possible only if man chooses to pursue a certain goal, which then serves as his standard of value. The good, accordingly, is not good in itself. Objects and actions are good *to* man and *for* the sake of reaching a specific goal.

But if values are not intrinsic attributes, neither are they arbitrary decrees. The realm of facts is what creates the need to choose a certain goal. This need arises because man lives in reality, because he *is* confronted by a fundamental alternative, and because the requirements of his survival, which he does not know or obey automatically, are set by reality (including his own nature). The particular evaluations a man should make, therefore—both in regard to ultimate purpose and to the means that foster it—do not have their source in anyone's baseless feeling; they are discovered by a process of rational cognition, the steps of which have already been indicated.

Moral value does not pertain to reality alone or to consciousness alone. It arises because a certain kind of living organism—a volitional, conceptual organism—sustains a certain relationship to an external world. Both these factors—man *and* the world, or human consciousness and reality—are essential in this context. The good, accordingly, is neither intrinsic nor subjective, but objective.

Here is Ayn Rand's statement of the point:

> The *objective* theory holds that the good is neither an attribute of "things in themselves" nor of man's emotional states, but *an evaluation* of the facts of reality by man's consciousness according to a rational standard of value. (Rational, in this context, means: derived from the facts of reality and validated by a process of reason.) The objective theory holds that *the good is an aspect of reality in relation to man*—and that it must be discovered, not invented, by man.[48]

An evaluation presupposes the capacity to think; it is a type of abstraction, i.e., a product of the process of concept-formation and use. This is why one's theory of concepts determines one's theory of values. It is why, in the objective approach, the description italicized by Ayn Rand above applies both to concepts and to values.

Concepts are aspects of reality in relation to man. That is: concepts designate facts—perceived objects with their similarities and differences—as condensed by human consciousness, in accordance with a rational method (logic). Similarly, the good is an aspect of reality in relation to man. That is: the good designates facts—the requirements of survival—as identified conceptually, and then evaluated by human consciousness in accordance with a rational standard of value (life).

Moral knowledge, therefore, follows the basic pattern of all conceptual knowledge. If one wishes to discover moral truth, he cannot rely either on passive perception of the external or on mental events divorced from the external. Instead, he must actively process perceptual data. He must integrate and then evaluate the relevant data using the method of logic. The method enables him to evaluate noncapriciously by leading him to grasp the function of a moral standard in human life. The result is the identification and validation of *objective* value-judgments.

The term "objective," let me stress here, does not apply to all values, but only to values chosen by man. The automatic values that govern internal bodily functions or the behavior of plants and animals are not the product of a conceptual process. Such values, therefore, are outside the terminology of "objective," "intrinsic," or "subjective." In this regard, automatic values are like sense data. Sense data are neither "objective" nor "nonobjective." They are the base that makes possible man's later cognitive development; they thereby make possible all the standards, including "objectivity," which are eventually defined in order to guide human choices. Similarly, automatic biological processes and the sensations that accompany them are the base that makes possible man's later evaluative development.

Because her philosophy regards objectivity as essential to conceptualization, Ayn Rand rejected from the outset any nonrational view of ethics. Ethics deals with concepts, which, in her system, are forms of integration occurring within a cognitive hierarchy that is based on sense perception. This is the underlying theory that guided her in seeking out the proper, step-by-step reduction of "value." The result of such reduction was her discovery of a new code of morality.

Conventional moralists hold that ethics flows from arbitrary acts of consciousness, whether divine or human, social or personal. Such ethical codes express the primacy-of-consciousness metaphysics. Objectivism, because it upholds an objective theory of value, is the first ethics in history to express consistently the primacy of existence.

Existence, we say—the metaphysically given facts of reality, including the identity of man—is what demands of human beings a certain course of behavior. This is the only approach to ethics that does not culminate in disaster. Only a code based on the demands of reality can enable man to act in harmony with reality.

The "demands" of reality, however, are not commandments, duties, or "categorical imperatives." Reality does not issue orders, such as "You must live" or "You must think" or "You must be selfish." The objective approach involves a relationship between existence *and* consciousness; the latter has to make a contribution here, in the form of a specific choice. Existence, therefore, does demand of man a certain course, it does include the fact that he must act in a certain way—*if;* if, that is, he chooses a certain goal.

"Reality confronts man with a great many 'musts,' " writes Miss Rand,

> but all of them are conditional; the formula of realistic necessity is: "You must, if—" and the "if" stands for man's choice: "—if you want to achieve a certain goal." You must eat, if you want to survive. You must work, if you want to eat. You must think, if you want to work. You must look at reality, if you want to think—if you want to know what to do—if you want to know what goals to choose—if you want to know how to achieve them.[49]

We have discussed the acceptance of cause and effect as an aspect of the virtue of rationality. Now let us take a wider view. The field of ethics itself, including all moral virtues and values, is necessitated by the law of causality. Morality is no more than a means to an end; it defines the causes we must enact if we are to attain a certain effect. Thus Ayn Rand's statement that the principle replacing duty in the Objectivist ethics is causality, in the form of the memorable Spanish proverb "God said: Take what you want and pay for it."[50]

If life is what you want, you must pay for *it,* by accepting and practicing a code of rational behavior. Morality, too, is a must—*if;* it is the price of the choice to live. That choice itself, therefore, is not a moral choice; it precedes morality; it is the decision of consciousness that underlies the need of morality.[51]

Ayn Rand's approach to morality is unique. As the whole history of philosophy demonstrates, it is an approach that is unimaginable to the advocates of a nonobjective view of concepts.

The intrinsicist school holds that values, like universals or essences, are features of reality independent of consciousness (and of life). The good, accordingly, is divorced from goals, consequences, and beneficiaries. The good is not good *to* anybody or *for* anything; it is good in itself. One can come to know such an object only by the standard intrinsicist means: mystic insight. Thereafter, one "just knows" good and evil; one knows them automatically and infallibly, without benefit of any cognitive method.

Although it purports to discover values in external reality, intrinsicism actually cuts the tie between values and reality. By divorcing value from purpose and beneficiary, the theory makes value-judgments pointless and arbitrary. Why then should men concern themselves with ethical issues? The most common intrinsicist answer is: God (or some equivalent, like Kant's noumenal self) has issued commandments, and it is man's duty to obey them.

"Duty" is not a synonym for "virtue." "Duty," Ayn Rand writes, means "the moral necessity to perform certain actions for no reason other than obedience to some higher authority, without regard to any personal goal, motive, desire or interest."[52] Such an approach means the severing of ethics both from reason and from values. When a man acts to achieve his values, said Kant, he is amoral; he is outside the field of ethics. To deserve moral credit, in this view, a man must do his duty without reference to any personal goal or to any future effects on his own life and happiness. He must do his duty as an act of pure selflessness, simply because it is his duty. Kant calls this "acting *from* duty."

By its nature, a duty ethics defaults on the task of ethics. Since it detaches virtues from values, it offers man no guidance in the job of living. The crucial problems of human existence, the daily decisions men must make in regard to goals such as work, love, friendship, freedom, happiness—all this, for the intrinsicist, is beside the point. Ethics, he believes, defines man's obligations to the supernatural; it transcends what the vulgar call "real life."

Real life, however, remains a fact. It continues to demand a specific course of action—of rational, selfish action—which the duty advocates not only ignore but seek to countermand. The result is a moral code that is worse than useless, a code that dooms man to an unendurable dichotomy: virtue versus pleasure, one's character versus one's welfare, the moral versus the practical, ethics versus survival. It would be difficult to imagine a greater assault than this on man's life, or a greater negation of morality.

Although most people pay lip service to the duty approach, they know enough to resent it. Hence the bad name which "the good" now has—the odor of boredom, pain, and senselessness that permeates the subject of morality in the public mind.[53]

The subjectivist school, to which we may now turn, holds that values, like concepts and definitions, are creations of consciousness independent of reality. In this view, values *are* related to the goals of men or other acting entities. But no such goal, it is added, can be rational, none can have a basis in the realm of fact. The good, accordingly, is divorced from reason; it is whatever the arbitrary desires of consciousness decree it to be. Hence there is no such thing as moral knowledge; there is merely subjective preference.

Subjectivists of the social variety, despite their rejection of intrinsicism, also tend to advocate a duty approach to morality. Since a human group of some kind is the creator of reality, they believe, its members' arbitrary wishes are the standard of right and wrong, to which the individual must conform. The group thus assumes the prerogatives of the divine moral legislator of the intrinsicists, and self-sacrifice for society becomes the essence of virtue, replacing self-sacrifice for God. This approach, though offered to us as modern, is merely a secularized version of the ethics of religion. To secularize an error is still to commit it.

Subjectivism of the personal variety leads to a more distinctive (though equally false) ethics: the irrationalist or whim-worshiping version of egoism, typified by the stand of the Sophists in the ancient world and of most Nietzscheans in the modern. In this view, the consciousness of each individual is the creator of its own reality. Each man, therefore, must be guided by his own arbitrary feelings; he must act to gratify *his* desires, whatever they happen to be and whatever the effects on other men (who are assumed to be acting in the same fashion). It follows that every man is a threat to every other; the essence of human life is a clash of senseless passions, and one's only hope is to cheat, crush, or enslave the rest of mankind before they do it to him. This is the theory that makes "selfishness" in the public mind a synonym for "evil." It is a theory that divorces "selfishness" from every intellectual requirement of man's life. In this approach, "selfishness" becomes the frantic shriek: "The good is whatever I feel is good for me, murder not excluded."

In reason and reality, such an attitude is the opposite of what self-interest requires. But this does not deter a subjectivist. He jettisons reason and reality from the outset.

Despite all their differences, intrinsicists and subjectivists agree on fundamentals. This is true in ethics as in epistemology. Ethical principles, both schools agree, are rationally indefensible; there is no logical relationship between the facts of this world and value-judgments; morality requires a message from the beyond. One school then claims to have received such a message, while the other, rejecting this claim, throws out the whole field as noncognitive.

Neither approach grasps man's need of morality, neither can be practiced without pitting man *against* reality—and both are eager to insist that no third alternative is possible.

When they hear about the Objectivist ethics, philosophy professors from both groups ask, as though by reflex, the same question. "If the choice to live precedes morality," they say, "what is the status of someone who chooses *not* to live? Isn't the choice of suicide as legitimate as any other, so long as one acts on it? And if so, doesn't that mean that for Rand, too, as for Hume or Nietzsche, ethics, being the consequence of an arbitrary decision, is itself arbitrary?"

In answer to this, I want to mention first that suicide *is* sometimes justified, according to Objectivism. Suicide is justified when man's life, owing to circumstances outside of a person's control, is no longer possible; an example might be a person with a painful terminal illness, or a prisoner in a concentration camp who sees no chance of escape. In cases such as these, suicide is not necessarily a philosophic rejection of life or of reality. On the contrary, it may very well be their tragic reaffirmation. Self-destruction in such contexts may amount to the tortured cry: "Man's life means so much to me that I will not settle for anything less. I will not accept a living death as a substitute."

The professors I just quoted, however, have an entirely different case in mind. They seek to prove that values are arbitrary by citing a person who would commit suicide, not because of any tragic cause, but as a primary and an end-in-itself. The answer to this one is: no.

A primary choice does not mean an "arbitrary," "whimsical," or "groundless" choice. There *are* grounds for a (certain) primary choice, and those grounds are reality—all of it. The choice to live, as we have seen, is the choice to accept the realm of reality. This choice is not only *not* arbitrary. It is the precondition of criticizing the arbitrary; it is the base of reason.

A man who would throw away his life without cause, who would reject the universe on principle and embrace a zero for its own sake—such a man, according to Objectivism, would belong on the lowest rung of hell. His action would indicate so profound a hatred—of himself, of values, of reality—that he would have to be condemned by any *human* being as a monster. The moment he would announce his decision seriously he would be disqualified as an object of intellectual debate. One cannot argue with or about a walking corpse, who has just consigned himself to the void—the void of the nonconscious, the nonethical, the non-anything.

Ethics *is* conditional, i.e., values are not intrinsic. But values are not subjective, either. Values are objective.

■   ■   ■   ■

Because of the influence of religion, the code of sacrifice has always dominated the field of morality, as far back as historical evidence goes. A handful of Western thinkers did reject this code. The two with the best and fullest ethical systems were Aristotle and Spinoza, each of whom sought in his own way to uphold the value of life, the virtue of rationality, and the principle of egoism. But even these rare dissenters were influenced, both in method and content, by Platonic and by subjectivist elements.

Although men in the West, roused by such dissent, did occasionally rebel against the moral creed of the religionists, there was no solid intellectual base to support their rebellion. As a result, it was always partial, compromised, and short-lived. The fresh new start petered out each time, defeated by its own unwitting deficiencies, contradictions, and moral concessions.

Ayn Rand is the first moralist to say no to the dogma of self-sacrifice—to say it righteously, consistently, and with full philosophic *objectivity*. She is thus the first to identify in completely rational terms what that dogma is doing to the human race and what the alternative to it is.

This marks a historic turning point. It is the moral liberation of man, his rescue from the torture chamber of the humanitarians. It means the possibility, after all the centuries of wreckage and carnage, of man's life on earth, his life in the pure sense of the term—uncontradicted, unblemished, unbreached.

So far, this kind of world is only a possibility. The reality, perhaps, lies far in the future. But at least it *is* possible, and now we know it.

8

VIRTUE

"Rationality" is a broad abstraction. Now we must learn more fully how to apply it to the concrete choices of human life. We must study the derivative virtues (and values) recognized by the Objectivist ethics.

Since these virtues are expressions of rationality, they are logically interconnected, both in theory and in practice. None can be validated in isolation, apart from the others; nor can a man practice any one of them consistently while defaulting on the others. In defining a series of virtues, Ayn Rand is abstracting, separating out for purposes of specialized study elements of a single whole. What she seeks to clarify by this means, however, is the whole. The Objectivist ethics upholds not disconnected rules, but an integrated way of life, every aspect of which entails all the others.

The essence of this way of life, as we know, involves a certain relationship between man's consciousness and reality. In a primacy-of-consciousness philosophy, virtue consists of allegiance to the ruling consciousness, such as God or society. In Ayn Rand's philosophy, virtue consists of allegiance to *existence;* it consists of a man's recognizing facts and then acting accordingly. The virtues are differentiated from one another according to the particular metaphysically given facts they identify.

In *Atlas Shrugged,* Ayn Rand defines six major derivatives of the virtue of rationality. That is the account I am following.[1] Miss Rand did not regard this list as necessarily exhaustive or the order of its items as logically mandatory. Her concern was not to cover every application of virtue, but to identify the essentials of rationality in the most important areas and aspects of human life. This is the minimum moral knowledge needed by a man if he seeks to follow reason consistently, as a matter of principle, in his daily choices and actions.

The six derivative virtues are independence, integrity, honesty, justice, productiveness, and pride. After we have discussed them, we will consider a widespread vice, which represents the destruction of all of them. The vice is the initiation of physical force against other men.

Independence as a Primary Orientation to Reality, Not to Other Men

The virtue of independence, in Ayn Rand's definition, is "one's acceptance of the responsibility of forming one's own judgments and of living by the work of one's own mind. . . ."[2]

The classic statement of this virtue appears in *The Fountainhead,* when Roark contrasts the creator with the second-hander:

> Nothing is given to man on earth. Everything he needs has to be produced. And here man faces his basic alternative: he can survive in only one of two ways—by the independent work of his own mind or as a parasite fed by the minds of others. The creator originates. The parasite borrows. The creator faces nature alone. The parasite faces nature through an intermediary.
>
> The creator's concern is the conquest of nature. The parasite's concern is the conquest of men.
>
> The creator lives for his work. He needs no other men. His primary goal is within himself. The parasite lives second-hand. He needs others. Others become his prime motive.

> The basic need of the creator is independence. The
> reasoning mind . . . demands total independence in func-
> tion and in motive. To a creator, all relations with men
> are secondary.
>
> The basic need of the second-hander is to secure his
> ties with men in order to be fed. He places relations first.[3]

If a man lived on a desert island, a policy of dependence
would be impossible to him. He would have to think, act,
produce on his own or suffer the consequences. He would
have to focus on reality or perish.

The same principle applies when one lives in society. The
presence of other men does not change the nature of man or
the requirements of his life. Others can properly offer one
many values; they cannot, however, become one's means of
survival or basic frame of reference. They cannot be treated
as a substitute for reason or reality—not with impunity.

The independent man, Roark says, "does not function
through [others]. He is not concerned with them in any primary matter. Not in his aim, not in his motive, not in his
thinking, not in his desires, not in the source of his energy."[4]
The independent man who lives in society learns from others
and may choose to work jointly with them, but the essence
of his learning and his work is the process of thought, which
he has to perform alone. He needs others with whom to trade,
but the trade is merely an exchange of creations, and his primary concern is the act of creating; his concern is his own
work. He may love another person and even decide that he
does not care to live without his beloved; but he chooses his
love as a complement to his work, and he chooses by his own
rational standards, for the sake of his own happiness. He may
enjoy receiving approval from others, but others are not the
source of his self-esteem; he esteems himself, then enjoys receiving approval only when he independently approves of the
approvers. This kind of man gains many values from mankind
and offers many values in return; but mankind is not his motor, his sustainer, or his purpose.

Ayn Rand describes such an individual as the man of "self-
sufficient ego."[5] The primary in his consciousness—that which
comes first in any issue—is not other men, but reality as perceived by his mind. In fundamental terms, such a man does

not need others; he acts among them just as he would without them. In principle, he is as alone in society as on a desert island.

The opposite policy consists in dropping one's mind and accepting as one's guide a different primary: people. This type of person is not moved by a concern for logic or truth; he is oriented basically not to reality, but to other men—to what they believe, what they feel, what he can wheedle out of or pump into them, what he can do to, with, or for them. The man who acquires his beliefs by accepting the consensus of his "significant others"; the man who gains his sense of self-worth from prestige, i.e., from reputation in the mind of others, regardless of their standard of judgment; the man who gets ahead not through work, but through pull; the social worker whose function is not to create, but to redistribute the wealth created by others; the criminal or dictator who lives by initiating force against others—these are some of the "second-handers" described in *The Fountainhead*.[6] They are men who live through or within others, men to whom solitude, in principle, means death.

A parasite, biologically, is a creature that lives on or in an organism of another species. The second-hander, however, is unique. He has no counterpart in the world of biology. He is a parasite on his own species.

The relationship between the virtue of independence and the fundamentals of metaphysics, epistemology, and ethics is readily apparent.

Whether explicitly or otherwise, the independent man grasps the distinction between the metaphysical and the man-made. Conformity to the metaphysically given, he understands, is essential to successful action; the man-made may be accepted only if and when it achieves or flows from such conformity. This kind of individual fulfills the basic requirement of human survival: he knows how—by reference to what absolute—to form his ideas and choose his actions.

To the second-hander, by contrast, the man-made—whether rational or irrational, true or false, good or evil—becomes the equivalent of reality. This kind of individual, having detached himself from the realm of existence, has no standard by which to judge others; he has no way to know whose ideas to follow, whose behavior to copy, whose favor to curry. Such a person reduces himself to helplessness, the fundamental helplessness of having left his life to the mercy of blind chance. The result is most people's desperate need for an authority, religious or secular, who will take over their lives, make their value-judgments, and tell them what to do. The independent man will refuse any such role, but the worst second-hander of all, the power-luster, is eager to accept it. Thereafter, he destroys everyone, including himself.

The independent man accepts the primacy of existence. In some terms, he understands that A is A no matter what men's desires or beliefs. The dependent switches to the primacy of consciousness. He devotes himself not to the task of identifying that which is, but to imitating, appeasing, serving, or forcing the consciousnesses on whom he depends. As to reality, he believes—insofar as he considers the issue at all—that he can safely leave the realm to others to deal with. "Nothing," he feels, "is more powerful than my neighbors, my tribe, my colleagues, my armies, or my leader."

The independent man understands in some terms that reason is man's means of knowledge; as a result, he accepts the responsibility of practicing the virtue of rationality. The parasite cannot justify his own default, but he does not *want* to do the necessary work; he does not want to exert the effort that an independent, creative existence would require. He wants the "freedom," when he feels like it, to coast mentally or evade. Such a person is not always a passive type. He may struggle, act, even make a certain kind of long-range plan and figure out the means of implementing it (e.g., he may spend years planning how to rob a bank or enslave a nation). But none of this qualifies as "effort" in the moral sense or as rationality. Within the framework of the parasite's life, struggle does not represent a commitment to focussing on reality or to being guided by his conceptual faculty. On the contrary, his struggle is an attempt to escape from reality and from the need to conceptualize. There is no such thing as a parasitism based on fact or defended by an appeal to principle. There is only a brazen double standard: "He will work and I will get away with my desire to cash in on the results."

Mental activity motivated by whim and streaked with evasion is not a form of reason, but of its opposite; just as inferences drawn from arbitrary premises and riddled with contradictions are the opposite of logic. Neither reason nor logic can be defined in terms of context-dropping.

The ego or self, Ayn Rand holds, is the mind. The independent man, therefore, is the only genuine egoist. The second-hander—whether he seeks to exploit others and/or to serve them—is an opposite breed. In placing people above reality, he renounces his ego. Whatever his goal or intended beneficiary, such a man is a literal altruist; he "places others above self" in the deepest sense and pays the price. The price is the fact that the selfless is the mindless.

If man's survival depends on the proper functioning of his consciousness, then Ayn Rand's ethics is not arbitrary. Her code of egoism-as-independence defines the one form of human life in which, as a matter of principle, man is able to be conscious.

Like every virtue, independence involves both an intellectual and an existential component.

Intellectually, independence, to repeat Miss Rand's words, is "one's acceptance of the responsibility of forming one's own judgments." It is one's recognition of the fact that the mind is an attribute of the individual and that no person can think *for* another. An intellectually independent man processes perceptual material by the use of his own rational faculty. In dealing with any question, whether of fact or value, end or means, philosophy or science, he follows the method of objectivity. A second-hander, by contrast, is a parasite of cognition, who accepts the ideas of others on faith. He is the man who says: "I don't care whether others have reasons for their conclusions or not. If an idea is good enough for my neighbors (or my grandfather, my subjects, my pope, my president), it's good enough for me."

The term "independent thought" is a redundancy. Either a man is struggling to identify facts, to integrate, to understand—this is at once a state of thought and of independence. Or he accepts the conclusions of other men without regard to facts, logic, understanding. This is a state of dependence and of nonthought. Even if the conclusions thus accepted happen to be true, they are of no cognitive value to the parasite. In his consciousness, those conclusions are not truth, but the arbitrary.

Just as egoism does not mean retreating to a desert island,

so independence does not mean rediscovering on one's own the sum of human cognition. The ability to profit from the thinking of others is the time-saver that makes human progress possible. One should, therefore, learn as much as he can from others. The moral point is that he actually be learning, i.e., engaged in a process of cognition, not of parroting.

Virtue does not require that one's mental contents be original. What it requires is a certain method of dealing with one's mental contents, whoever initially conceived them. The moral issue is not: who was first? but: is one a man of reason or of faith?

A rational man does not treat independence as the validation of an idea. He does not say, as certain subjectivists do: "I myself accept this idea; therefore, it must be true." On the contrary, he is independent precisely in order to be objective. He says: "This idea is true in reason; therefore, I accept it."[7]

Similarly, independence is not the assertion of one's own *feelings,* regardless of the reasons behind them. Independence is not the vice of whim-worship; it is a trait applicable not to emotion, but to the function of the mind. If a person accepts ideas because he has looked at reality first-hand, then he is an independent man regardless of his feelings, no matter how similar they are to those of other men. By the same token, if he has turned his soul over to society to program, then he is a dependent, no matter how unique any of his feelings happen to be.

The man who takes pride in the "independence" of his feelings is usually dominated by one feeling in particular: hostility. His notion of being independent in the realm of ideas is to affront people by rejecting whatever they believe simply because they believe it. By definition, such a person is unconcerned with logic or reality; his ideas are shaped entirely by other men—in reverse. This kind of mentality, which poses as being courageous, represents an especially ugly form of dependence.

Since intellectual independence is a product of the choice to think, it is an attainment open to everyone. As we have seen, a man can be cognitively helped or hampered by his environment. But he cannot be turned into a thinker or a robot without his own consent (leaving aside cases such as the infliction of physical torture or damage). A thinker, therefore, deserves moral credit, regardless of his parents, his teachers, his society; and a robot, moral blame.

Now let us consider the existential side of the virtue of independence.

Thought is not an end in itself, but a means to action. If life is the standard, man must think in order to gain knowledge, then use his knowledge to guide him in creating the material values his life requires. This means: he must be a self-supporting entity; he must finance his activities by his own productive effort; he must work for a living. (Even a wealthy heir or lottery winner is morally obliged to work, as we will see in due course.)

Since man is an integration of two attributes, mind and body, every virtue reflects this integration. None can be practiced spiritually but not materially, or vice versa. The dependent in the spiritual realm, since he does not think, creates no wealth. He becomes thereby a dependent in matter. The dependent in the material realm makes the actions of others his means of survival. He becomes thereby the kind of person who "places relations first," i.e., he becomes a dependent in spirit.

If a man is to be first-handed, he must begin by reaching independent conclusions. Then he must accept the responsibility of implementing his conclusions in practice, i.e., he must pay his own way. He must be self-reliant in the mental world *and* in the physical world.

In a division-of-labor society, no one produces by himself all the goods and services that his life requires. What he does produce is an economic value he can offer to others in exchange for the things he wants; he produces the value-equivalent of the goods and services he seeks. A man who deals with others by this method is the opposite of a dependent. He relies on his own power of creativity in order to survive. He counts on the value of his work being recognized by rational men, not on getting favors from any person or clique. He is not restricted to dealing with a clique; potentially, the whole world is his customer. Nor does he benefit from a policy of conformity. In a free country, intellectual independence and material wealth tend to be concomitant; the more a producer exercises his own best judgment regardless of the momentary notions or passions of the crowd, the more economically successful he becomes (see chapter 11).

It is often said that no one is independent because we all rely on others; e.g., on the grocer who supplies us with bread. This claim evades an obvious question: do you pay your grocer, or do you offer him only a sob story (or a stickup)? The term "dependence" in its pejorative sense cannot be stretched to subsume both these policies. Those who find this distinction difficult to grasp and who prattle about the "interdependence" of our "complex" society may seek further clarification from any grocer.

Individuals who trade their own creations are not parasites. The dependents among men in this issue are the noncreators. Some of them do not care to perform any kind of work, but plead for unearned support from others; in the terminology of *Atlas Shrugged,* these are the moochers. Others turn criminal and seize the unearned; these are the looters. Others peddle various forms of mysticism (e.g., astrology), which, though noncriminal, contribute nothing to the maintenance of human life or actively undermine it. Others—by far the largest subcategory—are the Peter Keatings, who hold a legitimate job but drift through it out of focus, exercising no judgment, reaching no conclusions, merely imitating the motions of those around them.

All of these types are "fed by the minds of others" in the literal sense of "fed." All want the effects of reason without the need of exercising the faculty. All seek not to practice virtue or abolish it but, in Ayn Rand's eloquent phrase, to be "hitchhikers of virtue."[8] None has any answer to the question: by what right do you choose such a course?

"Existential independence," according to the Objectivist ethics, means supporting oneself in a rational field of endeavor by using a first-handed approach. This last means performing one's work with an active mind, on the premise of understanding the job and finding ever better ways to do it, turning out standard products more efficiently or discovering superior ones. Every job, from ditch digging to philosophy, begs for these kinds of innovation. What innovation requires, however, is a worker in focus, ready to throw aside routine, ask questions, challenge tradition, and, if necessary, suffer opposition, when the drones around him see that their lethargy is being disturbed. This type of worker, on any scale of endeavor, is the creator of wealth, through whose effort all the noncreators live. He is the individual who fulfills the second half of Ayn Rand's definition of "independence." He "lives by the work of his own mind."

The role of independence in human life is writ large, for all to see, in the lives of the great creators. Not all independent men are great creators; but all great creators by definition are independent men, at least to the extent of their creativity. These are the men whose achievements—from logic, geometry, and science to anesthesia, concertos, power looms, and rockets—have lifted mankind out of raw nature and into a human mode of existence.

Whoever takes a great step forward leaves a chasm behind. In the best of societies, he has to wait patiently, alone, for other men to catch up; and most societies to date have hardly been the best. Hence the fate suffered so often by geniuses, inventors, and innovators—not only hatred, ridicule, persecution, martyrdom, but the necessity to spend one's life and precious hours fighting against their root: against mental passivity, slothful ignorance, willful deafness, enshrined falsehood. "But the men of unborrowed vision went ahead," said Roark. "They fought, they suffered and they paid. But they won."[9]

No further argument for the virtue of independence should be necessary; not if man's life is the standard of value.

Integrity as Loyalty to Rational Principles

"Integrity" is loyalty in action to one's convictions and values.[10]

As its name suggests, this virtue is one's recognition of the fact that man is an integrated being, a unity made of matter and consciousness. As such, he may, in Ayn Rand's words, "permit no breach between body and mind, between action and thought, between his life and his convictions. . . ."[11]

Few men flout their *perceptual* knowledge. Aside from the lowest cases—such as those who are high on LSD or on the Reverend Jim Jones—a man does not walk into the path of a speeding truck "because I feel like it" or "because the leader expects it." The consequences of such action are too clear. On the conceptual level, however, the consequences of flouting one's knowledge are not thus inescapable. On the contrary, as we saw in chapter 2, to keep one's value-judgments operative amid the vicissitudes of life is a volitional task. It requires that one act in focus, holding the full context of one's knowledge and retaining the perspective of long-range purpose. Context of this kind can be held and long-range purpose achieved, philosophy tells us, only if man functions by the guidance of *principles*.

To avoid any breach between action and thought, a man must learn the proper principles, then follow them methodically, despite any unwarranted pleas or demands from any source, inner or outer. Integrity isolates this aspect of the moral life; it is the virtue of acting as an absolute on (rational) principle. It is the principle of being principled.

A person may experience a desire or fear that tempts him to contradict his own considered value-judgments. Or, through plain inertia, he may be reluctant to initiate the actions entailed by his views. Or—this is by far the most common case—other men may disagree with him and demand that he follow their ideas, not his own. In all these cases, integrity remains the same; it is the policy of practicing what one preaches, regardless of emotional or social pressure. It is the policy of not allowing any consideration whatever to overwhelm the conclusions of one's mind, neither one's own feelings nor those of others.

It is not a breach of integrity, but a moral obligation, to change one's views if one finds that some idea he holds is wrong. It *is* a breach of integrity to know that one is right and then proceed (usually with the help of some rationalization) to defy the right in practice. To do this, a person must willfully brush aside his knowledge; he must blind himself to what he already sees and pretend that he does not think what he knows he does. This is what Ayn Rand calls "faking one's consciousness."[12]

The man of integrity recognizes that he knows what he knows, that what is right is right, and that this knowledge may not properly be evaded when the time comes to act. It may not be evaded for the sake of achieving "spontaneity," "security," "social harmony," or any other end. The alternative is to reject morality, dispense with cognition, and suspend one's conceptual faculty. On such a person, the conceptual faculty wreaks its own revenge, as we will see shortly.

In regard to consciousness, integrity requires that a man *have* convictions. If an individual evades the responsibility of considering ideas, if he is moved not by his intellect but by his feelings, his neighbors, his prescribed routine, then there can be no question of his acting in accordance with his ideas. By defaulting on the task of thought, such a man makes every virtue impossible to himself.

But holding explicit ideas is not enough. Like independence, integrity is a derivative of rationality and precludes any form of emotionalism. It does not mean loyalty to arbitrary notions, however strongly one feels they are true. Adolf Hitler acting faithfully to carry out his hatred of the Jews is not an example of virtue. Integrity means loyalty not to a whim or delusion, but to one's knowledge, to the conclusions one can prove logically. Like every other virtue, therefore, integrity presupposes a mind that seeks knowledge, a mind that accepts and follows reason.[13]

Turning now to action, any individual, however rational, may experience temptation at times. He may be tempted to take a wrong action by an out-of-context emotion. This is in no way immoral, so long as the individual does not act on the emotion, but looks at reality and summons the full context to consciousness, thereby reclaiming his knowledge of the action's harmful consequences. When a rational man thus reasserts the facts, the temptation vanishes (assuming he holds no subconscious contradictions on the issue). In purely physical cases, the pattern is obvious to everyone. A person may be eager to eat a succulent pie; but not if he discovers that the juice is poison. For Objectivism, moral evil is the spiritual equivalent of poison. There is no element of soul or body urging men to succumb to such a thing; there is no inbuilt attraction to falsehood, brainlessness, or suicide.

The challenge of a man's life is not to struggle against immoral passions, but to see the facts of reality clearly, in full focus. Once a man has done this in a given situation, there is no further difficulty in regard to him acting on what he sees.

When integrity is recognized to be a matter of self-preservation, its practice comes to seem irresistible. Thus Ayn Rand's eloquent reply, when she was praised for her courage in fighting the Establishment. "I am not brave enough to be a coward," she said. "I see the consequences too clearly."

If one's moral principles are irrational, however, he will reach the opposite conclusion; he will regard integrity as chimerical, a point illustrated throughout the centuries by religious philosophers. In their view, a person may know full well what is the right and the good; but he will nevertheless be seduced by the evil. He will be seduced not just occasionally, owing to some temporary error, but ceaselessly and inescapably, by virtue of the "lower" elements in his nature, which is "only human." The classic formulation here is the lament of Paul: "I do not understand what I am doing. . . . I can will, but I cannot do what is right. I do not do the good things that I want to do, I do the wrong things that I do not want to do. . . . What a wretched man I am!"

If one demands of man obedience to duty, the rejection of pleasure, the practice of sacrifice, then of course men will be assaulted by temptation, the temptation—inherent not in any "lower" nature but in the vital requirements of a rational being—to seek values, to pursue happiness, to achieve their own welfare. If people believe that such concerns are vices, then the practice of integrity is not only impossible to them, but a threat; to the extent that they enact *their* preachments, their survival is imperilled. Hence the mystics' unfailing claim that, because of "practical" or "earthly" or "bodily" considerations, moral perfection is unattainable. So it is, if "perfection" is defined by intrinsicist dogmas. To irrational principles, one cannot be loyal. Ideas that are not derived from reality cannot be consistently practiced in reality.

In dealing with other men, as with his own emotions, the man of integrity is an absolutist. In cases of disagreement or conflict, he is willing to listen to others, certain others, and—up to a point—to modify his behavior in order to gain their cooperation; but he is not willing to bargain about morality. Being an "extremist," he rejects today's most popular attack on integrity: the creed urging as the essence of virtue the practice of *compromise*.

A "compromise" is "an adjustment of conflicting claims by mutual concessions."[14] In reason, the validity of such a procedure depends on the kind of concession a man is making.

If a man makes concessions in regard to concretes within the framework of rational moral principles that both parties accept, then his action may be entirely proper; but not if he compromises moral principles themselves. As an example of the first case, Ayn Rand cites two traders, who agree that the buyer of an article is obliged to pay the seller, but who disagree about a given article's monetary worth; they resolve the conflict by finding an intermediate price satisfactory to both. As against: a man dealing with a burglar, who expects to seize goods without payment; the "adjustment" then consisting in the man agreeing—without duress, as his idea of a moral resolution—to give the burglar free of charge only part of the goods he came to steal. This would be compromise in regard to principle, and, as Miss Rand observes, it would mean "a total surrender—the recognition of [the burglar's] *right* to one's property." Once a man makes this kind of concession, he leaves himself helpless: he surrenders not only some of his property, but also the *principle* of ownership. The burglar thereby gains the upper hand in the relationship and the power to determine its future. He gains the inestimable advantage of being sanctioned as virtuous. What he concedes in the compromise is merely a concrete (some of the loot) for a while. It is only "for a while," because there is no longer any way to stop him when he comes back tomorrow for more loot.[15]

An obvious similarity exists between this case and that of a country able to defend itself which decides nevertheless to "negotiate" with an aggressor, agreeing to some of the latter's arbitrary demands in the name of being "flexible" and preserving "peace." Such a country thereby invites more demands, to be answered by more "flexibility"; it is doomed from the start (assuming it does not change its policy). By conceding the propriety of "some" aggression, it has dropped the *principle* of self-defense and of its own sovereignty; which leaves it without moral grounds to object to the next depredation. (The alternative to such capitulation is not necessarily war; on the contrary, a free nation's strength, moral and military, is the greatest deterrent to war.)

Now suppose, to change the example completely, that a

man wants to be neither a Roark nor a Keating, but a "middle-of-the-road'er" in regard to the virtue of independence. He will look at reality first-hand, he decides, except when an issue is highly controversial, in which case he will conform to society. Such an individual has subordinated thought to safety, the safety of not affronting others, however irrational their beliefs happen to be. This man may very well exercise his judgment on many occasions (as does Keating himself), but he does it only by the permission of others. Despite his intention, therefore, he has become an "extremist." Like a slave, though by his own choice, his guiding *principle* is obedience. A slave is allowed by his masters to think on his own some of the time.

In the very act of a man endorsing a compromise between clashing ways of life, the essence of one, independence, has been thrown out; while its opposite has become the ruling absolute. This is part of the reason why such a man grows increasingly mindless with the passage of time.

As a last example, consider a judge on the bench who, eager to be reappointed, agrees to rig his verdicts "once in a while" at the behest of his political bosses, in cases where they have an urgent interest in the outcome. Such a man has dropped the principle of justice. Justice cannot countenance a single act of injustice. What sets the terms of this judge's compromise, therefore, and directs his verdicts is the principle of favoritism, which permits whatever the bosses authorize, including many verdicts that are not tainted, when this is palatable to them. In such a court, fairness is possible, but only by accident. The essence of the system is the replacement of fairness by pull.

In chapter 5, we saw that the attempt to reach a compromise between reason and emotionalism means the rejection of reason and the enshrinement of emotionalism. The same argument applies, as in logic it must, to every moral compromise (whether or not it involves capitulation to others). One accepts a rational principle either as an absolute or not at all.

There is no "no-man's land" between contradictory principles, no "middle of the road" that is untouched by either or shaped equally by both. Even the most short-range mentality cannot escape the influence of principles; as a conceptual being, he cannot act without the guidance of some fundamental integrations, whether explicit or implicit. And just as, in economics, bad money drives out good; so, in morality, bad principles drive out good. If a man tries to combine a rational principle with its antithesis, he thereby eliminates the former as his guide and adopts the latter. This is the mechanism by which the conceptual faculty avenges itself on the unprincipled man.

If, like Faust, you try to make a deal with the devil, then you lose to him completely. "In any compromise between food and poison," Ayn Rand writes, "it is only death that can win. In any compromise between good and evil, it is only evil that can profit."[16]

The reason for this is not that evil is more powerful than good. On the contrary, the reason is that evil is powerless and, therefore, can exist only as a parasite on the good.

The good is the rational; it is that which conforms to the facts of reality and thereby fosters man's life. Such a principle must be upheld as an absolute and practiced without contradiction; it acquires no advantages from its antithesis. "The rational (the good) has nothing to gain from the irrational (the evil)," observes Ayn Rand, "except a share of its failures and crimes. . . ."[17] To continue our examples: a property owner does not need the help of a burglar who is trying to loot him. Nor does a free country need the attacks of an aggressor. Nor does Roark need the approval or cooperation of Keating. Nor does the administration of justice benefit from subversion by corrupt bosses. (Nor does a judge gain any value, not in the long-range sense, by becoming a pawn of such bosses.) By its very nature, the good can only lose by trafficking with the evil.

The evil is in exactly the opposite position. The evil is the irrational; it is that which clashes with the facts of reality and thereby threatens man's life. Such a principle cannot be upheld as an absolute or practiced without contradiction, not if one wishes to avoid immediate destruction. Evil has to count on some element of good; it can exist only as an exception to virtue, on which it is relying. "The irrational," observes Miss Rand, "has everything to gain from the rational: a share of its achievements and values."[18] A producer does not need a burglar, but a burglar does need the producer on whom he preys. And so do bandit nations need freer countries—which they seek not to annihilate, but to rule and loot. Nor does a Keating type want to throttle every act of independent judgment; the most primitive collectivist tribe knows in some terms that somebody has to think to some extent, or they all will starve. Nor does a political boss seek to reverse every proper verdict; on the contrary, the boss mentality counts on the appearance of justice, so that men will respect the courts, so that then, when the boss wishes it, he can intervene behind the scenes and cash in on that respect.

Evil is not consistent and does not want to be consistent. What it wants is to inject itself into the life-sustaining process sometimes—short-range, out-of-context, at whim. To achieve this end, it needs only a single concession by the good: a concession of the principle involved, a concession that evil *is* proper "sometimes." Such a compromise is evil's charter of liberty. Thereafter the irrational is free to set the terms and spread by further whim, until the good—and man—is destroyed.

The power of the good is enormous, but depends on its consistency. That is why the good has to be an issue of "all or nothing," "black or white," and why evil has to be partial, occasional, "gray." Observe that a "liar" in common parlance is not a man who always, conscientiously, tells falsehoods; there is no such creature; for the term to apply to a person, a few whoppers on his part is enough. Just as a "hypocrite" is not a man who scrupulously betrays every idea he holds. Just as a "burglar" is not a man who steals every item of property he sees. Just as a person is a "killer" if he respects human life 99.9 per cent of the time and hires himself out to the Mafia as an executioner only now and then.

To be evil "only sometimes" *is* to be evil. To be good is to be good *all* of the time, i.e., as a matter of consistent, unbreached principle.

The above is the full reason why Objectivism condemns as vicious today's cult of compromise. These cultists would achieve the same end result more honestly by being explicit immoralists, who tell men openly to reject the good and practice the evil. Evil is delighted to compromise—for it, such a deal is total victory, the only kind of victory it can ever achieve: the victory of plundering, subverting, and ultimately destroying the good.

Politically, the source of today's cult of compromise is the mixed economy (see chapter 11). Intellectually, the direct source is the skeptics of philosophy. If a man asks "Who am I to know?" he can hardly be loyal to the knowledge he denies having. Nor can a pragmatist be loyal to his mind, claiming as he does that "truth" is a name for whatever satisfies men's desires. Nor can an agnostic, who boasts that his mind remains "open" no matter what the state of the evidence. Nor can a relativist, who declares that there are no absolutes. All such individuals, whatever their pose, dispense with convictions as a matter of conviction and are, therefore, malleable. In their view, loyalty to principle—whether the principle be self-interest, independence, justice, or any other—is dogmatism; it is "rigidity" and disruption of the social fabric.

Since skeptics stand *for* nothing in theory, they can stand *by* nothing in practice.

Behind the skeptics in this issue, making them possible, are the religionists, with their centuries-long monopoly on morality. During the Renaissance, supernatural absolutes were rejected as a failure, but no giant arose to define a rational alternative. The intellectuals had only one recourse: to drop all absolutes and repudiate the very idea of principled action. The result was the substitution of "modernism" for medievalism. It was the exchange of one antilife viewpoint for another.

The alternative of intrinsicism vs. subjectivism always leads to tragedy. In the present case, its casualty is the virtue of integrity, i.e., the virtue of loyalty to the conceptual faculty.

This is precisely the outcome to be expected from two false theories of concepts.

Honesty as the Rejection of Unreality

"Honesty" is the refusal to fake reality, i.e., to pretend that facts are other than they are.[19] Pretense, as we know, is metaphysically impotent. It can neither erase an existent nor create one.

The virtue of honesty requires that one face the truth on every issue one deals with: the truth, the whole truth, and nothing but the truth (anything less would permit faking). This is a corollary of the virtue of rationality, which requires a state of full focus. If rationality, as we may say, is the commitment to reality, then honesty is its obverse: it is the rejection of unreality. The exponent of the first acknowledges that existence exists; of the second, that *only* existence exists.

The man who traffics in unreality, seeking to make it his ally, thereby makes reality his enemy. All facts are interconnected. Thus the first step of faking, like a man's first act of evasion, leads to the next; neither practice can be contained. Ultimately, the dishonest individual comes into conflict not merely with an isolated datum, but with the realm of existence as such. His policy commits him to the invention of a competitor to existence, a growing world of unreality, like a supernatural dimension that clashes at every point with the actual world. The latter, therefore, becomes his nemesis. It becomes a time bomb waiting to explode in his face.

The man who fakes reality believes that he or others can profit thereby. The honest man does not believe it. He does not seek to obtain any value by means of deception, whether of himself or of others. In Ayn Rand's words, he recognizes "that the unreal is unreal and can have no value, that neither love nor fame nor cash is a value if obtained by fraud. . . . "[20]

Value is objective. It is an evaluation made by reference to a standard (man's life) that is itself derived from reality. Value is thus a *form of truth;* it is a type of identification, which, to be warranted, must correspond to reality. The satisfaction of a desire, accordingly, is not necessarily a value; it may be a disvalue. The correct assessment follows from the relation between the desire and man's life, i.e., between the desire and reality. A desire that conflicts with the realm of reality, like a proposition that conflicts with fact, is invalid. The one is no more a part of "the good" than the other is a part of "the true."

The man who seeks to obtain a value through faking is confronted by one fundamental obstacle: that which exists, i.e., the particular facts he is struggling to erase or rewrite. In the nature of the case, his policy creates a dichotomy between fact and desire; implicitly, it raises "value" above that which exists and thus represents a breach with reality. This is why dishonesty cannot be a means of attaining values. It is also why, as with any form of emotionalism and any breach of the good, the policy of dishonesty has a single end result (barring a basic change in character, and restitution where appropriate): the spread of evil throughout the perpetrator's own mind and life.

Since man lives in reality, he must conform to reality—such is the argument for honesty. Any other course is incompatible with the requirements of survival. It is incompatible both with cognition and with evaluation.

In regard to consciousness, honesty consists in taking the process of cognition seriously.[21] This requires that one reject any form of intellectual pretense, whether in relation to method, motive, or content.

In method, intellectual honesty means developing an active mind—as Ayn Rand puts it, "knowing what one does know, constantly expanding one's knowledge, and *never* evading or failing to correct a contradiction."[22] The man who defaults on this responsibility, who is satisfied with a policy of nonintegration, whether in the form of mental stagnation or outright evasion, is engaged in a pretense. No matter what his beliefs, he is not pursuing knowledge, but faking its pursuit.

In regard to motive, intellectual honesty means seeking knowledge because one needs it to act properly. Such a person intends to practice any idea he accepts as true.[23] The alternative is the pretense of a hypocrite, who fakes an interest in ideas as a form of role-playing, usually for the purpose of impressing others.

In regard to content, as a result, the intellectually honest man refuses to fake in his own mind any specific item—any fact, field, or value. If one is guided by reason and motivated by the need of action, he does not lie to himself. He has no use for rationalizations, mystic inventions, or any other version of rewriting reality. He does not fake science by pretending that feelings prove truth, or self-esteem by pretending that approval from others proves value. He does not fake morality by feigning anyone's "right" to receive the unearned or anyone's "duty" to give it. He is not a mediocrity eaten by envy who feigns greatness, or a genius hungry for popularity who feigns mediocrity. The honest man may commit many errors, but he does not indulge in illusions, including the illusion that life requires illusions. He does not pretend *anything*.

Intellectual honesty is more profound an issue than not telling lies to one's neighbors. It means becoming a priest of truth in every aspect of one's mind, life, and soul.

Turning now to honesty in action, I want to cover the topic (and concretize the opening discussion of honesty) by working through a standard example. It is the kind raised by the ancient Sophists and still grappled with by textbooks on ethics. Why, these sources ask, should a man not execute a well-planned swindle—sell stock in a fake gold mine, say— then, ill-gotten cash in hand, take off for parts unknown, free to enjoy all the advantages of money without the need to work? Well, why not?

Let us begin by concretizing the dishonesty this behavior would involve. The con man in our example has to lie about the location of the mine (to avoid detection, he places it, let us suppose, in a distant country). He has to lie about such things as the number of workers, the scale of operations, the quality of the mine's output. His "proof" that the mine has been properly registered and the ore properly assayed is a lie (does he fabricate documents from real agencies or fabricate the agencies?). So is his "proof" that the foreign government involved is favorable to the enterprise. His crowning lie, of course, pertains to the killing that his investors can expect to make, judging by current market conditions and the best economic forecasts.

There is more. If asked, he would likely have to lie about the identity of his partners or his other investors; lie about his background and qualifications (does he use confederates to vouch for him and lie to them also, being afraid fully to trust them?); lie to his banker when he deposits the victims' huge checks; lie to his friends before he disappears, so that he cannot be traced—and then, having started his new life, lie to any new acquaintances about where he used to live, what he used to do, how he got his money (or lie to conceal the fact that he does have money).

Each of the con man's lies clashes with one or more facts and, therefore, creates a risk of his detection and exposure by anyone with access to the facts. Anyone who knows something—about mining, or the distribution of gold ore, or the science of geology, or the country claimed as the site, or the policies of its government, or the agencies of assay, or economic forecasting; or about con men in general, or about this one in particular, about his associates, haunts, accent, spending habits, or MO—becomes a threat, to be dealt with by further lies; lies designed to cash in on one person's special ignorance, contradictory lies to stay clear of another person's special knowledge. In the end, if we suppose that the loot runs out and the liar has not been caught, the very premises that led him to carry out the scheme—successfully, as he thinks—will most likely prompt him to embark on another one, involving a new pack of lies.

The above are details, all of which may be inapplicable in a particular case. Theoretical discussion cannot tell us which falsehoods an individual will spread, how many, how skillfully he will do it, or how rapidly the lies will escalate. Philosophy can tell us only this much: reality is a unity; to depart from it at a single point, therefore, is to depart from it in principle and thus to play with a lighted fuse. The bomb may not go off. The liar may blank out the power of his nemesis: that which is, and may get away with any given scheme; he may win the battle. But if such are the battles he is fighting, he has to lose the war.

The first thing he loses in the process of turning irrational is his independence. The man who wages war against reality is (by definition) defying all the rules of proper epistemology. Like the man who evades in private, without social purpose, he thus subverts at the root the cognitive power of his consciousness. The con man, however, usually makes no pretense of counting on cognition in order to prosper; he counts on his ability to manipulate others. *People* become to him more real than the fragments of reality he still recognizes. People become his means of survival, but in a form worse than that of the typical second-hander.

The liar is a parasite not on people as such, but on people who are deludable—people qua ignorant, blind, gullible. What such people believe and expect—what they expect falsely, thanks to him—this is the power he must deal with and pander to. The liar thinks he has turned others into his puppets, but his course makes him their pawn. It makes him a dependent of the lowest kind: a dependent not merely on the consciousness of others, which is bad enough, but on their unconsciousness. Such a man, in Ayn Rand's words, is a fool—"a fool whose source of values is the fools he succeeds in fooling. . . ."[24]

A similar analysis applies to every moral virtue and value. Is the liar a man of integrity? His method of action consists in eschewing moral principles and trying to get away with the fraud of the moment. Is he productive? His policy is to live not by his own creative work, but by bilking others of the fruits of theirs. Is he just? His goal is to obtain the unearned. Is he self-confident? Not if the term means confidence in one's ability to deal with reality. Is he happy? Not if happiness presupposes moral character (see chapter 9). Can he be proud? Only in a depraved sense: proud of his ability to delude others, to break the laws of human life, to cheat on reality and escape the consequences—which, however, he does not succeed in doing.

Virtue, as Socrates held, *is* one; to cheat on any of its aspects is to cheat on all. The dishonest man is not only dishonest; in Ayn Rand's view, he betrays every moral requirement of human life and thereby systematically courts failure, pain, destruction. This is true by the nature of dishonesty, by the nature of the principle it involves—even if, like Gyges in Plato's myth, the liar is never found out and amasses a fortune. It is true because the fundamental avenger of his life of lies is not the victims or the police, but that which one cannot escape: reality itself.[25]

Conventional moralists regard honesty as a trade-off. An object attained by fraud, they say, may be a real value to the defrauder, but he should weigh this value (e.g., a million-dollar payoff) against the disvalues attendant on fraud (retaliation by others, loss of reputation, etc.), and then decide which action in a particular case will probably yield the greater balance of good over evil. This kind of calculus rests on a nonobjective approach to evaluation; it assumes that the million dollars is a value either in itself (intrinsically) or because the con man wants it (subjectively). Such an approach ignores the role in evaluation of the facts of reality; it ignores man's life and the rules it requires.

These moralists advise the impossible. They want one to weigh the long-range consequences of competing actions without reference to any objective ethical standard or *principle*. In practice, this theory amounts to pragmatism, i.e., emotionalism. Whatever one chooses by such means is wrong—and harmful.

Objectivism rejects the "trade-off" viewpoint. Just as no statement can be declared a truth out of context, so no object—neither an A at school, a lover's caress, a piece of cake, nor a million dollars—can be declared a value out of context. In evaluating an object or course of action, one must first define its relationship to the moral principles required by man's life. If, holding the full context, one sees that it conforms to these principles, one may then proceed as necessary to weigh pros and cons. But if it violates rational principle—*if, in any form, it involves a denial of reason and reality*—that ends the matter. There is then no trade-off to consider, no calculus to perform, no value to gain; there is only destruction. Would anyone debate cutting off his head in order to acquire for himself a million dollars? Would he weigh the "gain" against the loss? Or would he say: "Nothing can be a 'gain' to me if its condition is that kind of loss"? The same applies to subverting one's mind.

Jesus' question "What shall it profit a man if he gain the whole world and lose his own soul?" is admirably exact. The man who "loses his soul" is, in virtue of such a condition, outside the concept of "profit." Of course, Jesus' question is not valid if read to imply a dichotomy between the world and the soul. It is instructive only if taken in one meaning: that the integrity of man's consciousness, its principled harmony with existence, is the precondition of man's benefitting from any of the splendor the world holds out to him.

This point applies to all human behavior, not only to the issue of honesty. *Just as, in epistemology, irrational mental processes detach a conclusion from the realm of cognition; so, in ethics, irrational action detaches a goal from the realm of evaluation.* Whenever an object, spiritual or material, is sought or obtained by behavior in conflict with moral principle—whether the behavior involves fraud, improper compromise, the initiation of force, or any other evil—the means employed, by their very nature, clash with reality and thereby deprive the object in that context of any evaluative standing.

Once the guidance of principle is dropped, there is no rational method of evaluating an object.

We are often told that someone's "noble ideal" can be attained only by evil actions, which we are then urged to perform ("the end justifies the means"). Objectivism rejects this license to immorality. The end does *not* justify the means. The truth is the exact opposite: an immoral means invalidates the end. The full statement of Ayn Rand's view is that the end-in-itself, man's life, determines the fundamental means of human action (the proper principles); and these in turn delimit the concretes one can validly pursue in a given context. The ultimate value sets the virtues, which then guide men in the assessment of any particular object proposed as a goal. This is the only approach that escapes the impossible dilemma of means vs. ends, or virtue vs. value. The escape consists in recognizing that virtues are not their own reward or a species of self-torture, but a selfish necessity in the process of achieving values.

Conventional moralists usually regard honesty as a form of altruism. They regard it as the selfless renunciation of all the values one could have obtained by preying on the naiveté of one's fellows. Objectivism discards any such notion. In both its forms—honesty with oneself and to one's fellows—the present virtue, like every other, is an expression of egoism. Every virtue defines an aspect of the same complex achievement, the one on which man's survival depends: the achievement of remaining true to that which exists.

We can now deal summarily with the issue of "white lies." The ethical status of a lie is not affected by the identity of its intended beneficiary. A lie that undertakes to protect other men from the facts represents the same antireality principle as the con-man variety; it is just as immoral and just as impractical. A man does no service to his fellows by becoming their accomplice in blindness. Nor does he gain any moral credit thereby; an improper practice is not improved by attaching to it an altruistic justification. If anything, the latter merely compounds the evil. It removes the liar a step further from reality.

Is honesty then an absolute?

Just as particular objects must be evaluated in relation to moral principles, so moral principles themselves must be defined in relation to the facts that make them necessary. Moral principles are guides to life-sustaining action that apply within a certain framework of conditions. Like all scientific generalizations, therefore, moral principles are absolutes within their conditions. They are absolutes—*contextually*.

For example, a man is obliged to be self-supporting. But this does not make it wrong for a college student, even one well out of his teens, to be supported by his parents—assuming that their help involves no self-sacrifice and that the student actually studies. In such a case, the student is not defaulting on independence, but preparing himself to meet its demands. Virtues presuppose the processes of human growth and education; they cannot be invoked out of context, as dogmas in a void. Another example here pertains to the virtue of integrity. A man is obliged to practice what he preaches— when he has the political freedom to do it. But he has no obligation to preach or practice any idea that would invite the attention, say, of the Gestapo or the IRS.

The same approach applies to the interpretation of honesty. The principle of honesty, in the Objectivist view, is not a divine commandment or a categorical imperative. It does not state that lying is wrong "in itself" and thus under all circumstances, even when a kidnapper asks where one's child is sleeping (the Kantians do interpret honesty in this way). But one may not infer that honesty is therefore "situational," and that every lie must be judged "on its own merits," without reference to principle. This kind of alternative, which we hear everywhere, is false. It is another case of intrinsicism vs. subjectivism preempting the philosophical field.

Lying is absolutely wrong—under certain conditions. It is wrong when a man does it in the attempt to obtain a value. But, to take a different kind of case, lying to protect one's values from criminals is not wrong. If and when a man's honesty becomes a weapon that kidnappers or other wielders of force can use to harm him, then the normal context is reversed; his virtue would then become a means serving the ends of evil. In such a case, the victim has not only the right but also the obligation to lie and to do it proudly. The man who tells a lie in this context is not endorsing any antireality principle. On the contrary, he is now the representative of the good and the true; the kidnapper is the one at war with reality (with the requirements of man's life). Morally, the con man and the lying child-protector are opposites. The difference is the same as that between murder and self-defense.

There are men other than criminals or dictators to whom it is moral to lie. For example, lying is necessary and proper in certain cases to protect one's privacy from snoopers. An analysis covering such detail belongs, however, in a treatise on ethics.

In discussing integrity, I said that to be good is to be good "all of the time." I can be more precise now. To be good is to obey moral principles faithfully, without a moment's exception, *within the relevant context*—which one must, therefore, know and keep in mind. Virtue does not consist in obeying concrete-bound rules ("Do not lie, do not kill, do not accept help from others, make money, honor your parents, etc."). No such rules can be defended or consistently practiced; so people throw up their hands and flout all rules.

The proper approach is to recognize that virtues are broad abstractions, which one must apply to concrete situations by a process of thought. In the process, one must observe all the rules of correct epistemology, including definition by essentials and context-keeping.

This is the only way there is to know what is moral—or to be honest.

Justice as Rationality in the Evaluation of Men

"Justice" is the virtue of judging men's character and conduct objectively and of acting accordingly, granting to each man that which he deserves.[26]

In order to achieve one's goals in any field, one must choose among alternatives—which requires that one know the things around one and judge them rationally. This applies even to the humblest undertakings, such as picking out today's wardrobe, furnishing the spare room, or selecting a spot for a picnic. It applies to one's dealings with men, also.

The necessity of knowledge and judgment is especially important in regard to men because the differences among them are more consequential than those among shirts, sofas, or parks. Men are beings of self-made soul; they have the faculty of volition, with everything this implies. The wrong shirt can ruin your appearance; the wrong man can kill you.

The science that defines a criterion for evaluating volitional beings is morality. To be able to deal properly with men, therefore, it is essential that one determine their relationship to the laws of morality. It is essential that one pronounce moral judgment.[27]

Since morality is concerned with a man's fundamental values, moral judgment enables one to know the essence that actuates him; it identifies the principles shaping his character and conduct. In the Objectivist approach, such judgment penetrates to the root principle, the one covering a man's primary use of his faculty of volition. Moral judgment distinguishes the men who choose to recognize reality from the men who choose to evade it. Such knowledge is necessary on practical grounds, in order to plan one's actions and protect one's interests. If a man is good by the Objectivist standard, if he is rational, honest, productive, then, other things being equal, one can expect to gain values in dealing with him. If a man is evil, however, if he is irrational, dishonest, parasitical, one can expect from such dealing not value, but loss.

The policy of pronouncing moral judgment is like a policy of human prospecting while wearing a bulletproof vest. It is a process of methodically seeking out and cherishing the virtuous traits one needs in others, such as effort, courage, idealism, while being alert to the opposites of these traits and to their destructive potential. By contrast, the man who adopts a policy of moral neutrality, refraining equally from praise or blame, does not wipe out the moral facts thereby. What he accomplishes instead is to blind himself to the role of morality in man's life, subvert his own character, and lose the ability to deal with other men on the basis of objective principle. The result, among other things, is to consign his human relationships to the realm of chance—and to do even worse: willfully to deprive the good among men of his sanction and support, while becoming an ally of the evil. He becomes an ally in the sense of leaving that evil uncensured and unopposed, free to continue its course of destruction.

The refusal to judge, like any kind of agnosticism, is itself the taking of a stand, in this case a profoundly immoral stand:

> When your impartial attitude declares, in effect, that nei-
> ther the good nor the evil may expect anything from you—
> whom do you betray and whom do you encourage? [asks
> Ayn Rand]
>
> . . . so long as men have to make choices, there is no
> escape from moral values; so long as moral values are at
> stake, no moral neutrality is possible. To abstain from con-
> demning a torturer, is to become an accessory to the tor-
> ture and murder of his victims.

"Only the good," Ayn Rand writes elsewhere, "can lose by a
default of justice and only the evil can profit. . . ."[28]

Justice does more than guard a man in his direct dealings
with others. Whether one personally deals with another man
or not, his virtuous traits are a value to one, if not directly,
then indirectly or at least potentially. The principle of justice,
therefore, protects one's survival more broadly. Justice works
to sustain all the men who think and who support human
existence, while chastening and counteracting their antipodes. The principle of injustice achieves the opposite result.
In one form or another, it works to sustain the destroyers
among men, while undermining the thinkers and producers.

In essence, justice is the policy of preserving those who
preserve life. It is allegiance to those who have sworn allegiance to life. It is, therefore, a virtue fundamental to the morality of life.

The Objectivist position is the opposite of the injunction
"Judge not that ye be not judged." Our policy, in Ayn Rand's
words, is: "Judge, and be prepared to be judged."[29] If man's
life is one's standard, one must identify the moral status of
every person, issue, and event within the field of his concerns; then, within the limits of his power, he must guide his
actions accordingly, dealing with and/or sanctioning only men
who are virtuous (in mixed cases, sanctioning only the virtuous element within a man), while shunning and condemning
men who are vicious. This is the mandate of the virtue of
justice.

(Moral judgment is not the only form of evaluating men.
Moral values are fundamental values; on their basis, many specialized kinds of value are defined, including intellectual value,
esthetic value, and economic value. Such values, too, must be

judged objectively, and their creators or possessors treated appropriately. The virtue of justice thus has many applications that do not involve moral appraisal as such. But the precondition of all such derivative evaluations is moral evaluation, which latter also indicates the pattern of a just process in any of its forms. I am, therefore, restricting myself to justice qua moral judgment, i.e., to justice in its basic form.)

Intellectually, justice consists in the use of reason to reach one's moral estimates. This is a demanding responsibility; it involves not unthinking condemnation or approval, but a process of cognition, the same process in essence that one employs in regard to inanimate objects.[30] In judging an individual's character and conduct, the just man follows the same epistemological principles as a scientist; he is ruled by the same single-minded concern: to discover the truth. This requires of him two steps: first he must identify the facts of a given case; then he must evaluate them by reference to objective moral principles.

In every process of justice, one must begin as a juror struggling to grasp the facts. Is the accused a murderer, the juror must ask, or is he the victim of an error or frame-up? Similarly, does your friend, as someone has suggested, malign you behind your back, or is the charge mistaken or itself malicious? Did your child's teacher punish him for no reason, as your child claims, or was there a reason? Of the employees of yours competing for a promotion, which one is the most reliable, honest, productive? In short, what *are* a man's attributes or actions? To be just, such is the question one must work to answer first, taking into account all the available evidence. Injustice in this connection would be any indulgence in emotionalism, any form of being influenced in one's factual conclusions by something other than fact (by prejudice, say, or favoritism). The blindfolded statue symbolizing justice is not blind to the facts of reality. What the blindfold shuts out is any feeling detached from facts, whether the feeling be desire or fear, pity or hope, hatred or love. What it shuts out is the subjective and the arbitrary, leaving the individual free to engage in a purely rational process of cognition.

The time one should devote to inquiry of this kind depends on the context. In general, in life as in law, a person is to be regarded as innocent of wrongdoing until proven guilty.

If one wants only to buy a quart of milk, therefore, no special assessment of the grocer is indicated; absent information that he is trafficking in illicit or tainted goods, one may legitimately assume that the man is reputable. As the relationship involved becomes more significant, however—if one is a juror in court, say, or wants to invite a person to become one's business partner or the companion of one's child—then, obviously, special study and assessment do become necessary.

Moral judgment does not include psychologizing.[31] The facts that one seeks in order to reach a moral assessment are those within a man's conscious control: his convictions, his statements, his actions. These facts are ascertainable by any rational observer. A moral judge does *not* seek out subconscious premises, motives, or problems—which may not even be known by the person, and which can be diagnosed only by a qualified psychologist or psychiatrist. Leaving aside psychotics, men are responsible beings, who must be treated as such; they are not helpless products of psychopathology, to be excused or condemned on the grounds of hidden demons. Some men are healthy; they have no demons. Even a neurotic, however, retains his sovereignty; despite his anxieties and defenses, he retains the ability to perceive reality and to control his actions. His psychological problems, accordingly, are his concern, not other people's—unless he allows his problems to materialize in the form of overt irrationality, in which case it is the overt behavior that others must observe and judge.

What one needs to know in order to appraise a man morally is not: what did his mother say or do when he was three? The proper question is: what does *he* say and do now?

When the facts of a case have been determined, the next step of justice is to evaluate them by reference to *objective* moral principles. This step is a further expression of the primacy-of-existence orientation, which dictated the fact-gathering stage, and it is essential to the virtue of justice. There is no more sense or morality in a judge identifying the facts, then reaching his verdict by arbitrary feeling, than there would be in a physician collecting medical data, then borrowing his diagnosis from the local witch doctor.

One form of evaluative subjectivism is to judge others while upholding no explicit moral principles, either because one has never bothered to consider the subject or because one repudiates all moral absolutes. A judge of this sort praises or condemns as a matter of whim; he thus discards both justice and practicality. His verdict is detached from the actual nature and deserts of the individual who is being judged; as a result, it is useless as a guide to action.

The same injustice occurs if one does apply explicit principles, but they are themselves nonobjective. Suppose, for example, you determine by painstaking investigation that your friend *is* guilty of maligning you, and you then overlook it. Suppose you even praise him for it, declaring: "A person should love those who despitefully use and persecute him. It is good if others wound my vanity; it teaches humility." This kind of moral judgment discards the virtue of justice. Your evaluative criterion here is detached from the facts that make moral judgments necessary; your principle contradicts the requirements of man's life. The result is an act of injustice—and its consequences. Your embrace of your hypocritical friend, for instance, does not change his behavior or protect you from him. Instead, it serves to rationalize and reward his corruption while imperiling your own future interests. If you define good and evil in irrational terms, then treat men accordingly, your policy leads only to destruction.

When judging men, one must bear in mind that there can be no universal estimate. Since the moral is the volitional, there is no rule to the effect that all men are good, evil, *or mixed.*[32] This last condition is by far the commonest, thanks to the ideas now dominant. But that does not justify extrapolation to the species. It does not justify universal denunciation ("All men are morally black")—or its mealy-mouthed offshoot: universal middle-of-the-road'ism ("All men are gray"), with its twin corollaries: all-embracing whitewash ("There's some good in the worst of us") and all-embracing sneer ("There's some bad in the best of us").

Immoral bromides cannot replace moral judgment. They do not remove one's responsibility to differentiate good men from evil. Nor do they relieve one of the painful necessity of distinguishing within the mixed or gray soul its constituent elements of black and white (of vice and virtue): gray, after all, is nothing but a mixture of these two elements. I say "painful" because it is simple, if one's principles are rational, to identify the heroes and monsters among men. The gray cases, however, typically present one with arduous cognitive problems. Which element, one must try to determine, rules which aspect of a mixed person's character? Which element, if either, is more basic? How stable is their current pattern of coexistence? And, assuming that a relationship with the person is necessary and proper, how can one arrange to deal with the white side while not being vulnerable to the depredations of the black? In practical life, such questions are vital, and no snap judgment can answer them. Only a dispassionate, meticulous process of justice can do it.

There is no greater obstacle to such a process than the theory of altruism. First, altruism inverts moral judgment, teaching people to admire self-sacrifice and to belittle self-preservation as amoral or worse. Then, since the theory cannot be practiced consistently, it leads people to hate the very fact of moral judgment. Moral estimates, such people explain, are cruel; a good man is really not good, but lucky, while an evil man or group is really not evil ("He couldn't help it!" "They don't mean it!"). At the same time, since morality cannot be avoided and since consistent altruism is impossible, the theory prompts people, when they do judge, to condemn everybody indiscriminately. All these policies—moral inversion, moral neutrality, and sweeping condemnation—defy the virtue of justice. All work to promote the evil at the expense of the good. It is no hindrance to the concentration camp guard and no solace to his victim, if one defines torture as virtue; or if one averts one's gaze; or if one criticizes both men alike as "gray," insisting that there must be some virtue in the whip-wielding fiend and some vice in the body writhing at his feet.

A rational morality sweeps all this corruption aside. Justice, it holds, like all virtues, is an absolute, an aspect of the proper relationship between one's consciousness and existence. Justice is fidelity to reality in the field of human assessment, both in regard to facts and to values. Or, as Judge Narragansett in *Atlas Shrugged* puts it, "Justice is the act of acknowledging that which exists." Injustice, by contrast, like all vices, is a form of evading reality; it consists in faking the character not of nature, but of men.[33]

This brings us to justice in the realm of action, which consists in "granting to each man that which he deserves."

To "deserve," states the Oxford English Dictionary, is to

"become worthy of recompense (i.e., reward or punishment), according to the good or ill of character or conduct." A reward is a value given to a man in payment for his virtue or achievement; it is a positive such as praise, friendship, a sum of money, or a special prerogative. A punishment is a disvalue inflicted in payment for vice or fault; it is a negative such as condemnation, the withholding of friendship or even outright ostracism, or the loss of money or prerogative, including (in criminal cases) the loss of freedom or of life itself. The recompense appropriate in content and scale to a particular case must be determined contextually, by reference to the nature and merits of the case. The principle, however, is the same in all cases: justice in action consists in requiting the positive (the good) in men with a positive and the negative with a negative. This is the truth behind the rule "An eye for an eye" (although that formulation addresses only justice to the evil). It is the truth symbolized by the scale in the hands of the statue of justice, the scale whose trays balance equal weights. One weight represents cause, the other, effect; one, a man's behavior, the other, payment appropriate to it.

The validation of this aspect of justice is the facts of reality. It is reality that gives rise to the need of morality; it is therefore a metaphysically given fact that virtue, properly defined, is the policy that leads to value, pleasure, the positive, while vice is crowned by loss, pain, the negative. Since this is not a fact men can alter, their only choice is to accept it as a principle of their own actions—or to ignore or try to reverse it, and suffer the consequences. Whether brought about by failure to consider the issue or by evasion, these latter alternatives mean ultimately: to inflict deprivations on the men who are good, while conferring values—approval, support, trade, wealth—on their antipodes. Such a policy places man-made rules in contempt of reality. It turns virtue into a liability and evil into an asset, thereby subverting moral action at the root and making man's life impossible.

The "retributivists" in the history of philosophy declare that a man must be recompensed for his actions independent of their consequences; he must be recompensed as an absolute simply because he *deserves* a certain treatment. The Utilitarians (who control the criminal justice system) reply that there are no absolutes and that the decision to reward or punish must be based not on deserts but on probable consequences. Here again we see the false alternative of intrinsicism vs. subjectivism. "Desert" *is* essential to justice; but it is a moral concept, and morality is a means to an end. All virtues, accordingly, justice included, must be validated by reference to consequences. But consequences—the long-range consequences of an action for human life—can be predicted only by means of principles, and principles can perform this function only if accepted as absolutes. Desert, therefore, as the one school insists, is an absolute—but only because, as the other school says, the test of virtue is its results. Here as elsewhere it is senseless to introduce a dichotomy between principle and life, or between morality and practicality.

Turning now to the question: what rewards and punishments *do* men deserve to receive from one another? the answer is: precisely what each man's rational self-interest requires that he give. Men deserve from you, first, that you reach objective moral estimates of them; then, that you take these estimates seriously, using them as guides to your action, including the emotional responses you offer to others and the human relationships you agree to undertake. In this regard, there is an important form of action that I have not yet elaborated.

Since morality is man's motive power, there is no spiritual reward one can offer as consequential as one's *moral sanction*—and no spiritual deprivation as harsh as withholding it.

The first of these comes first. The conventional view is that justice consists primarily in punishing the wicked. This view stems from the idea that evil is metaphysically powerful, while virtue is merely "impractical idealism." In the Objectivist philosophy, however, vice is the attribute to be scorned as impractical. For us, therefore, the order of priority is reversed.

Justice consists first not in condemning, but in admiring—and then in expressing one's admiration explicitly and in fighting for those one admires. It consists first in acknowledging the good: intellectually, in reaching an objective moral verdict; then existentially, in defending the good—speaking out, making one's verdict known, championing publicly the men who are rational (one also praises them to their face, if there is a context to indicate that this would be a value to the person rather than an intrusion). Evil must be combatted, but then it is to be brushed aside. What counts in life are the men who support life. They are the men who struggle unremittingly, often heroically, to achieve values. They are the Atlases whom mankind needs desperately, and who in turn desperately need the recognition—specifically, the moral recognition—to which they are entitled. They need to feel, while carrying the world on their shoulders, that they are living in a human society and that the burden is worth carrying. Otherwise, like the protagonists of Ayn Rand's novel, they too, properly, will shrug.

It is important to tell Kant that he has rejected reality and is wrong; it is more important that Aristotle find someone who understands that he has recognized reality and is right. It is important to condemn the school that abuses a child's mind; it is more important to praise the teacher or the mother who despite such schools manages to bring up a child as a rational being. It is important to vote today's politicians out of office; but they will merely be replaced by equivalents unless we cherish and install an opposite kind of leadership. It is important, if property rights are to be preserved, that a robber be caught; it is more important to the same goal that the great industrialists *not* be vilified as "robber barons," but, somewhere, hear the words "Thank you."

In all such instances, *Atlas Shrugged* is the model to follow. The book is a historic act of justice, because it is an act of homage. It is a bestowal on the world's thinkers and creators of the recognition, the gratitude, the moral sanction, which they have rarely received but abundantly earned.

In regard to the evil one encounters, the corollary act of justice is the refusal to sanction it.

This is why, insofar as one has a choice, one must boycott evil men (and nations). Dealing with them not only benefits them materially, while exposing oneself to their machinations. It also implies that one regards them as safe, civilized, reputable, an implication that amounts to extending to the evil one's moral approval and one's encouragement for the future.

To refuse to sanction evil does not necessarily involve accosting its representatives, if no purpose is served thereby.[34]

Justice does not require that a man volunteer unsolicited denunciations to random individuals. There is, however, one situation in which a man must speak out: when his own convictions are attacked in his presence and his silence would imply his endorsement of the attack. Even in such a case (e.g., at a party), there is no need to make a speech to a person uninterested in the issue or closed to reason. A firm "I do not agree" is sufficient, both morally and practically.

The above presupposes that the dissenter is not in the power of the irrational, as he would be in a dictatorship, say, or in the class of a professor who solicits his opinion, then grades him down for disagreement (which does not happen as often as some students think, but does happen sometimes). In such situations, a dissenter has no obligation to speak out no matter what anyone may infer from his silence. Justice cannot require that a man sacrifice himself to someone else's evil.

So far, we have been considering justice as it would apply to any human relationship, however impersonal—if one were merely a cultural observer, for example, or a juror in court. Now let us consider the virtue in a positive and personal context. What does justice consist of when one man seeks a value from another?

Justice in this context is adherence to the *trader principle*.[35]

Every act of justice is in a sense an act of trade. This is inherent in the fact that justice is a form of rationality, a response to something in reality and not a caprice. Rewards and punishments are not undeserved gifts or penalties; they are payments. They are what one gives to a man in *exchange* for what one gets. In any value-seeking relationship, accordingly, whether the value sought be material or spiritual, the exponent of justice is the man who gives in return for what he receives and who expects to receive in return for what he gives. He is the man who neither seeks something for nothing nor grants something for nothing.

The trader principle states that, if a man seeks something from another, he must gain title to it, i.e., come to deserve it, by offering the appropriate payment. The two men, accordingly, must be traders, exchanging value for value by mutual consent to mutual benefit. "A trader," writes Ayn Rand, "is a man who earns what he gets and does not give or take the undeserved."[36]

The trader principle presupposes the foundations of the Objectivist ethics. It rests on the role of reason in human survival and on the principle of egoism. Since the individual's mind is the basic creator of values and since man is not a sacrificial animal, the individual has a right to demand payment for his values. Nor does any man or group have a right to override this right. Leaving aside the claims of children on their parents, no person by the mere fact of his existence or needs has a claim on the assets of others. To "deserve" a positive, material or spiritual, is not a primary condition; it is an effect, to be achieved by enacting its cause. The cause is a certain course of thought and action, a course in which one creates and/or offers values. (One "deserves" a negative by virtue of defaulting on some responsibility of thought or action.) If we use the term "earn" to name the process of enacting the cause—of coming to merit a certain recompense by engaging in the requisite behavior—we can say that, in a rational philosophy, there is no "unearned desert." *A man deserves from others that and only that which he earns.* Such is the approach to human relationships derived from the Objectivist base and expressed in the trader principle.

Since there is no value without virtue, there is, in Ayn Rand's words, "no escape from justice." "Nothing," she explains, "can be unearned and unpaid for in the universe, neither in matter nor in spirit—and if the guilty do not pay, then the innocent have to pay it."[37]

That the innocent should pay is the demand of those who reject the trader principle. Such people claim that values are the product of God or society, to which power, they add, the individual owes unconditional service. In this view, certain men, such as the needy, become "deserving" in a new, invalid definition of the term. They "deserve" to receive values simply because they lack and wish for them—as a recompense for no action, as a payment for no achievement, in exchange for nothing. In this approach, the "deserved" is turned into a caprice; the concept is thus vitiated and the virtue of justice swept aside. It is replaced by what is called "social justice," which policy consists in expropriating the creators in order to reward the noncreators.

In the material realm, the trader principle, like the virtue of independence, prohibits both looting and mooching. It requires that one pay others for the goods or services one seeks from them.

The same principle applies in the spiritual realm, to responses such as admiration, friendship, love. Here too a man must deserve what he seeks from others. And here too he can deserve it only by earning it, only by creating the values of character that make his relationship with others a trade. "Love," writes Ayn Rand, "is the expression of one's values, the greatest reward you can earn for the moral qualities you have achieved in your character and person, the emotional price paid by one man for the joy he receives from the virtues of another."[38]

In the Objectivist approach, there can be no looters or moochers of the spirit, either. One may not attempt to gain a positive response by making threats or by exhibiting need, by practicing blackmail or by pleading for emotional alms, by inflicting pain on another individual or by holding out one's own pain as a claim. Both the giver and the receiver of a positive response must function as independent equals, with no evasion or victims, each person adhering to reality, each profiting from the relationship. Love as a response to a person's value is an acknowledgment of facts. As such, it has a moral meaning for both parties and imposes a double responsibility: the lover must be rational—and so must be the beloved; he or she must be the kind of self-made soul who has earned such a love.

Contrast this approach with the one upheld in the Sermon on the Mount. We should, Jesus tells us, love our neighbors regardless of desert, apart from their character and even because of their vices. This is love not as payment for joy, but as self-sacrifice; not as recompense to the good, but as a blank check to the evil; not as an act of loyalty to existence, but as the deliberate rejection of man's life. Those who claim to want this Christian response—to want causeless love, love "for themselves" as against their thoughts, actions, character, or works—are staging a fraud. They demand that love be divorced from values, then struggle to reverse cause and effect, pretending that love, the effect, can create in them personal worth, the cause. But causeless love would be meaningless; it would represent no acknowledgment of virtue.

Just as a man's character traits must be given a deserved response, so must a change in his traits. If a good man turns bad, one acknowledges reality by reversing one's former estimate of him. The same applies if a bad man turns good. Just as love must be earned, so must condemnation—and *forgiveness*.

Forgiveness in moral issues is earned, if the guilty party makes restitution to his victim, assuming this is applicable; and then demonstrates objectively, through word and deed, that he understands the roots of his moral breach, has reformed his character, and will not commit such wrong again. Forgiveness is unearned, if the guilty party wants the victim simply to forget (evade) the breach and forgive without cause—or if he offers as cause nothing but protestations of atonement, which the victim is expected to accept on faith. In regard to minor moral lapses, it is not difficult for a man to demonstrate the necessary understanding and reform. If the vice is sizable, however, such demonstration is no easy matter; in many cases, it is impossible. When a man commits an evil like a major robbery or deception, to say nothing of worse crimes, it is difficult even to know what evidence would be required to convince others of his reform. This problem is one of the many penalties of vice, and it is the responsibility not of the good, but of the evil to solve it; assuming, what is seldom if ever the case, that moral reform is what the evil man is seeking.

Forgiveness, which is legitimate when earned, must be distinguished from mercy. If justice is the policy of identifying a man's deserts and acting accordingly, mercy is the policy of identifying them, then *not* acting accordingly: lessening the appropriate punishment in a negative case or failing to impose any punishment. Mercy substitutes for justice a dose of the undeserved and does so in the name of pity; the pity is not for the innocent among men or the good, but for the perpetrators of evil. The innocent man (or the truly reformed wrongdoer) asks for justice, not mercy. He *wants* what is coming to him.

The practical consequences of mercy are eloquently clear in today's courtrooms, the ones where criminals are righteously set free not owing to any doubt about their actions or to any objective mitigating circumstances, but as an act of compassion for "helpless products of society." The man who gains by such an act is the criminal. The men who lose are his victims: both the individual he preyed on or his survivors, who conclude bitterly that there is no justice; and the future victims, whom the criminal, unpunished and undeterred, is now free to go after.

We often hear that "requiting evil with good" works to melt the heart of the wicked. There is no evidence to support this claim. To requite evil with good does not mean to strengthen the white element of a morally gray man by an act of deserved kindness directed to his better nature. The policy consists in rewarding the black qua black. The essence of the black, however, is the attempt to cheat and sneak, the attempt to evade moral principles and get away with it—which is precisely what mercy or unearned forgiveness or causeless love (or unlimited smiling diplomacy) permits and encourages. No evildoer can be "melted" so long as his victims compete with one another in offering him their favors, their sanction, and their other cheek.

Like all religions, Christianity is incompatible ultimately with every virtue. It seems to take special pride, however, in its principled exhortation to injustice, particularly in the spiritual realm. If men are to have any chance for a future, it is this aspect of the Christian ethics above all others—this demand, at once brazen and mawkish, for unearned love, unearned approval, unearned forgiveness—that the West must reject, in favor of a solemn commitment to its moral antithesis: the trader principle.

I have saved for the end of the present discussion a theory that urges the complete repudiation of justice: egalitarianism, which is a Kantian version of Christianity.[39] "Egalitarianism" in this context does not mean that men should be equal before the law. Nor does it mean that men should be granted "equal treatment" in the sense of principled treatment, as against the injustices that flow from a double standard. It means that "equality" supersedes justice.

In this view, the most heroic creator on earth, the most abysmal villain, and every person in between should share equally in every value, from love to prestige to money to important jobs to college degrees to newspaper coverage to political power, regardless of what any individual deserves or earns or has or has not done—regardless of his character, his achievements, his ability, his talent, his flaws, his vices, his virtues. For centuries, altruists had implied as much, but even the Communists were too civilized to admit it. Their final heirs, headquartered at Harvard, have no such reservations.

Since it is obviously impossible to live by such a philosophy, since men could not survive for the space of a year if the rewards of virtue were methodically siphoned in this way into the lap of the undeserving, the egalitarian proposal can have only one purpose and result: destruction. The purpose is not to benefit the evil, but to smash the good. This is the particular form of injustice that John Galt has in mind when he refers in his climactic speech to "the collapse to full depravity, the Black Mass of the worship of death, the dedication of your consciousness to the destruction of existence."[40]

Egalitarianism is the act of kicking the scale from the hands of the statue of justice while stripping off its blindfold, leaving men to be ruled not by ordinary prejudice, which would be bad enough, but by the most virulent kind: the prejudice that Ayn Rand identifies as "hatred of the good for being the good."

In her essay "The Age of Envy,"[41] Ayn Rand discusses many examples of this attitude, which has been rampant in our culture, including the hatred of intelligence, of beauty, of ability, of virtue, of technology, of happiness. It is a hatred pursued by those who feel it not as a means to an end, but as a metaphysical rage, for its own sake.

If you who befriend the virtue of justice study this essay, you will understand more fully why you must pronounce moral judgment, in whatever forum is open to you. If you do not make yourself heard, there is a professorial brigade that will, a brigade that is eager to take over and pronounce its benediction on the annihilation of mankind.

Productiveness as the Adjustment of Nature to Man

"Productiveness" is the process of creating material values, whether goods or services. Such creation is a necessity of human survival in any age, whether the values take the form of bearskins, clubs, a pot full of meat, and paintings on the walls of caves; or of skyscrapers, ballet, brain surgery, and a gourmet meal aboard a computerized spaceship; or of the unimaginable luxuries and splendors yet to come.

The other living species, as we have seen, survive by consuming ready-made values. (I am leaving aside such primitive forms of productive action as the nest-building of birds or the hills and tunnels of the ants.) From bearskins on up, however, the values required by man's survival must be conceived and then created. For a conceptual being, the only alternative to creativity is parasitism.

The other species survive in essence by adjusting themselves to their background, assuming they have the good fortune to find in nature the things they need. Man survives by adjusting his background to himself. Since he reshapes the given, he does not have to count on good fortune or even on the absence of disaster. "If a drought strikes them," Ayn Rand observes, "animals perish—man builds irrigation canals; if a flood strikes them, animals perish—man builds dams; if a carnivorous pack attacks them, animals perish—man writes the Constitution of the United States."[42]

Just as there cannot be too much rationality, so there cannot be too much of any of its derivatives, including productiveness. Just as there is no limit to man's need of knowledge and therefore of thought, so there is no limit to man's need of wealth and therefore of creative work. Intellectually, every discovery contributes to human life by enhancing men's grasp of reality. Existentially, every material achievement contributes to human life by making it increasingly secure, prolonged, and/or pleasurable. There can be no such thing as a man who transcends the need of progress, whether intellectual or material. There is no human life that is "safe enough," "long enough," "knowledgeable enough," "affluent enough," or "enjoyable enough"—not if man's life is the *standard* of value. (Nor, despite the Malthusian claims of the ecologists, is there any possibility of man exhausting natural resources.

Leaving aside the rest of the universe, the earth alone, as one economist[43] has observed, is nothing but a giant ball made of such resources, waiting to be reached and exploited by human ingenuity.)

The practical benefits of productiveness are too obvious to be debated. What I want to focus on is an aspect of productiveness that has been ignored or denied by previous philosophies: its *spiritual* meaning and necessity.[44]

Productive work, writes Ayn Rand, "is the process by which man's consciousness controls his existence, a constant process of acquiring knowledge and shaping matter to fit one's purpose, of translating an idea into physical form, of remaking the earth in the image of one's values. . . ."[45] As this statement makes clear, productiveness, like every virtue, involves two integrated components: consciousness and existence; or thought and action; or knowledge and its material implementation. Neither of these components is dispensable to any productive man or activity.

Knowledge, as Francis Bacon stated, is power. It is an instrument enabling man to support his life. It is a product of consciousness to be applied to reality: to be followed, embodied, used. This is why productiveness is defined as the creation of *material* values. The discovery of knowledge is the first step. But the purpose of the knowledge is to make possible an existential value, such as a new type of machine, a new method of transportation, or a new method of living.

Contrary to the classic philosophical tradition, knowledge is not something to be gained or enjoyed for its own sake. It is not a fulfillment to be pursued with "disinterest" or because it is "pure," i.e., divorced from matter and action. It is a commodity that satisfies a definite practical interest, the interest in survival.

In a division-of-labor society, a man may properly specialize in cognition. But as long as the knowledge he acquires remains unembodied, it is not yet a productive achievement (nor does it work yet to support man's life). If the scientist or scholar is to qualify as productive, he must proceed in due course to the next step. He must give his discoveries some form of existence in physical reality and not merely in his consciousness—usually, by writing treatises or delivering lectures.

A scientist may not care himself to carry the process of embodiment further. Life in the ivory tower, however, is not a license to disdain "the practical world." In particular, it is not a license to turn a discovery over promiscuously to all comers, regardless of its harmful potential and of their character and purpose. This is tantamount to abetting the worst elements of mankind in their work of destruction. For details, one may read the story of Project X in *Atlas Shrugged*.

A treatise or lecture, however brilliant, is not an end in itself. The mind-body integration required by productiveness is not complete until the knowledge is turned into some form of material wealth. In this step, too, specialization is typically involved. The most important performers of *this* crucial feat are the inventors, the engineers, the industrialists.

There is no dichotomy between "pure" science and "gadgets." Science is related to technology as theory is to practice; as metaphysics and epistemology are to ethics and politics; as philosophy is to life; or as mind is to body. In all these cases, the first apart from the second is purposeless; the second apart from the first is impossible.

The converse of "knowledge is power" is the principle that wealth is thought. I refer here not only to the thought of scientists, but to that of every man, whatever his job or ability, who is involved in creative work.

Every form of material asset beyond an animal's level, beyond wild fruit or raw meat eaten in a dank cave, is made possible by man's cognitive faculty: by intelligence, imagination, ingenuity. Whoever creates anything of value out of natural resources has to rely on his mind; he needs a context of conceptual knowledge and a specific idea to guide his action. This kind of intellectual content is necessary to make a Stone Age club, let alone the tools and weapons of the Iron Age. The issue becomes obvious, however, when we consider the achievements enjoyed by the West today, the wealth that, in quantity and inventive genius, surpasses not only the meager products but also the most extravagant fantasies of all previous ages combined.

The direct source of today's wealth was the Industrial Revolution. That was the great turning point when men moved within the space of a few generations from subsistence to plenty. Its cause—which has had no counterpart in the "underdeveloped" world—was two earlier developments: the Renaissance, the philosophic revolution in favor of this world; and the political revolution of the seventeenth and eighteenth centuries, the discovery of man's rights. The cause was reason and freedom, which made possible knowledge and action, i.e., modern science and the modern entrepreneur. The effect was the sudden outpouring of abundance—which most people nowadays take for granted and, thanks to bad philosophy, ascribe to "biological drives," natural resources, or physical labor. All of these, however, had existed from time immemorial. Only one "drive" was new and only that power, therefore, qualifies as the fundamental creator of wealth: liberated human thought.

The fields of art and science are recognized to be realms open to great achievement; their representatives are venerated as men of stature. They are venerated because people do *not* regard such men as producers, but as selfless seekers after purely spiritual ends. Inventors, engineers, industrialists, by contrast, the men whom common parlance terms "producers," have been ignored in virtue of this status, or have been condemned as "selfish materialists."

In the Objectivist view, productive ability *as such* deserves the highest accolades. Commercial or technological ability, like any other form of life-sustaining efficacy, is not an amoral "know how" or "can do." Nor is it merely a "practical" asset. It is a profound *moral* value.[46]

Productive ability is a value by the standard of man's life— and because, like all values, a course of virtue is required in order to gain and keep it. An individual is not born with the knowledge, the skills, or the imaginative ideas that give rise to greatness or even competence in any creative field. He must acquire, then use, all these assets by a volitional process. At each step this process requires effort, purpose, and the commitment to reality. It requires all the attributes inherent in the development and use of the rational faculty, including conscientious focus, independent judgment, the concern with long-range goals, and the courage to remain true in action to one's knowledge.

The ability to create material values is not a primary. It must itself be created. Its source is man's noblest qualities.

Some jobs offer a greater intellectual challenge than others and allow for greater achievement. But every job above plain physical labor requires for its effective performance a significant element of personal worth within the worker. A worthless person—the type who meanders semi-awake through a prescribed routine, indifferent to what he is doing and passively compliant with the rules of his tribe—is productively useless. Such a type, so far from being able to sustain his life, cannot even sort the mail or collect the garbage, as any victim of today's unions can attest.

In every human field—in business as in art, in industry as in science, in manufacturing as in philosophy—the physical demands of the work are relatively minimal. A few jobs in an industrial society are still open to brute strength or endurance; what is paramount in every other case is the mental activity a job requires. "Whether it's a symphony or a coal mine," Ayn Rand writes, "all work is an act of creating and comes from the same source: from an inviolate capacity to see through one's own eyes. . . . "[47] That is why a businessman, fully as much as an artist, is an exponent of human spirituality. (I speak of the essence of these fields in a rational context, not of the kind of practitioners who abound in them today.) The preeminence of the mental, however, does not mean detachment from the physical. That is why an artist, fully as much as a businessman, is and has to be up to his neck in matter. Art, like any legitimate field, has a life-sustaining purpose. Its creation demands objective, reality-oriented thought, then the embodiment of that thought in a physical medium. If the creator of a product claims to transcend all this, if he asserts proudly that he is cut off from life, objectivity, reality (and, therefore, from any reputable means of self-support), then his line of work is not art, but a species of con game. That is why a coal-mine operator who turns out some coal, or even a sweeper at the mine who stays in focus, is productively *and spiritually* miles above the composer who discovers from the universities, then docilely concocts, the kind of noise that has been authorized for the nonce as "avant-garde."

No rational field may be pitted against any other as "spiritual" vs. "material." All proper fields require thought *and* action. All exemplify the integration of mind and body.

By splitting apart thought and action, the doctrine of the mind-body dichotomy has subverted every rational virtue. But it has had perhaps its most corrupting influence in regard to productiveness, which it brushes aside as morally meaningless and ultimately as nonexistent. In place of the producer, the dichotomy offers a choice between two human archetypes: the spiritualist, who scorns the world; and the materialist, who scorns the mind. The first disdains business, technology, money as vulgar concerns of man's "lower nature" and holds that knowledge should not be tainted by being used. The second disdains theory, abstractions, science as useless and holds that material goods should be accumulated without reference to them. Both types agree that reason plays no role in the sustenance of human life. Both agree that man survives as animals do: not by the moral process of production, but by consuming mindlessly whatever material values he finds already formed around him. One type then concludes that self-preservation is an unspiritual chore and that producers are nothing but animals. Survival, this type complains, is a regrettable practical requirement without intellectual or moral significance—in effect, a necessary evil. To which the other type rejoins: "So much for thought and virtue. Let's be evil."

Ayn Rand is the first thinker to reject the mind-body dichotomy methodically, by reference to a theory of reality and of concepts. That is why she is also the first fully to practice the virtue of justice in the present context. She is the first to identify, in terms of a philosophic system, the source of wealth and, therefore, the proper estimate of those who create it.

A productive man is a *moral* man. In the more intellectually demanding and innovative fields, he is the epitome of morality. He deserves to be admired accordingly.

Such a man may be better in his work than in the rest of his life (a common occurrence today); but that is his contradiction and problem. It diminishes his character and his creative potential, but not what he has actually achieved. Nor do any problems of his alter the fact that, whatever the contribution of others, at the root of *his* achievement is his own will, action, and mind. As to the greatest of these—you already know it.

Turning now to a different aspect of the present virtue, productiveness is not only a necessary element of the good life, it is the good life's *central purpose*.[48] In developing this point, I must begin by considering an issue broader than productiveness, the second of the "supreme and ruling values": purpose.

The need of purpose is inherent in every cardinal aspect of human nature; it is inherent in life, in reason, in volition. Life is a process of goal-directed action. Reason requires a state of focus, i.e., of purposeful alertness. Volition, once one is in focus, can be exercised only within the context of values; one can choose among higher-level alternatives only by reference to some end one seeks to attain.

To regard purpose as a moral value is to acknowledge this essential need of man's life, to embrace its fulfillment as good, and then to fulfill it deliberately. One does this by adopting purpose as a *principle* of one's actions.

The principle of purpose means conscious goal-directedness in every aspect of one's existence where choice applies. The man of purpose defines explicitly his abstract values and then, in every area, the specific objects he seeks to gain and the means by which to gain them. Whether in regard to work or friends, love or art, entertainment or vacations, he knows what he likes and why, then goes after it. Using Aristotelian terminology, Ayn Rand often says that this kind of man acts not by efficient causation (mere reaction to stimuli), but by final causation ("fines" is Latin for "end"). He is the person with a passionate ambition for *values* who wants every moment and step of his life to count in their service. Such a person does not resent the effort which purpose imposes. He enjoys the fact that the objects he desires are not given to him, but must be achieved. In his eyes, purpose is not drudgery or duty, but something good. The process of pursuing values is itself a value.

The principle of purpose sanctions deliberate rest or relaxation, but condemns a course of drifting or of inaction. It condemns any form of being moved through one's days by the power of accident, such as a man's falling into a job, an affair, a philosophy, or even a movie theater simply because it or she happens to be there and to look further is too much trouble. The man who drops purpose turns himself into a cipher who evades his own nature, defaults on the responsibility of focus, and abdicates his power of choice. Such a man spends his time on throwing away his life.

The end of ethics, self-preservation, cannot be achieved

in a single stroke. It depends on a continuous, rational process, a process of pursuing derivative values that entail specific kinds of goals in every area of one's concern. The pursuit of purpose is thus what human life consists of concretely. In this sense, purpose is at once the essence of human life and the means of its preservation.

Like any value, purpose itself must be achieved by a specific course of action. If a man is to be purposeful, his goals must be interrelated. This in turn requires that they be integrated to a central purpose.[49]

A man with a hodgepodge of goals cannot achieve or even rationally pursue them. There is no way (besides caprice) for him to decide how to apportion his time and other assets among his concerns, or to decide how to resolve their conflicting demands in these regards. Such decisions require that one establish a hierarchy among one's goals, a scale of relative importance, by reference to which long-range action can be initiated and daily choices guided. This kind of hierarchy is possible only if a man defines a central purpose.

A central purpose is the long-range goal that constitutes the primary claimant on a man's time, energy, and resources. All his other goals, however worthwhile, are secondary and must be integrated to this purpose. The others are to be pursued only when such pursuit complements the primary, rather than detracting from it.

A central purpose is the ruling standard of a man's daily actions. In the philosophy of ethics, one must formulate an abstract standard of value to enable one to assess the various claimants to the title of "value." Similarly, in daily action, one needs a specific purpose as a standard to enable one to assess the various endeavors pressing themselves upon one as "important." The man without such a purpose has no way to tell what is important to him. However sincere he may be at the start, he has to end up as whim-ridden, erratic, directionless, i.e., as irrational. The man who defines his purpose, by contrast, knows what he wants from his time on earth. Since his concerns are hierarchically organized, his days add up to a total.

There is only one purpose that can serve as the integrating standard of a man's life: productive work.

The activity of productive work (if approached rationally) incorporates into a man's daily routine the values and virtues of a proper existence. It thus establishes and maintains his spiritual base, the fundamentals that are the precondition of all other concerns: the right relationship to thought, to reality, to values. A man doing productive work is a man exercising his faculty of thought in the task of perceiving reality and achieving values. Such an activity is independent of other men, in the sense that the mind is an attribute of the individual. It is also inherently long-range: each phase of creative endeavor makes possible the next, without limit. The producer moves through his days not in random circles, but in a straight line—which last, Ayn Rand writes, "is the badge of man, the straight line of . . . motion from goal to farther goal, each leading to the next and to a single growing sum. . . . "[50]

Nothing can replace productive work in this function. In particular, neither social relationships nor recreational pursuits can replace it.

One cannot substitute people for work. If a man defines his central purpose in terms of his relationship to others, this necessarily makes him a second-hander, no matter what form of the vice he chooses—whether he takes the path of a Keating who wants to be loved or of a con man who wants to deceive, of a dictator who wants to give orders or of an altruist who wants to take them. Anyone moved primarily by a social rather than a productive purpose thereby rejects reality, with everything this implies. That is why none of these types, however single-minded their behavior, qualifies as purposeful—assuming we mean by "purposeful" the value-oriented, effort-demanding existence described earlier. In fact, as Ayn Rand has observed, second-handedness in some variant is precisely what men resort to when they have dropped the discipline of purpose. Hoping to allay their anxiety and fill the void left by their own default, they have no recourse then but to run to others.[51]

A life of purpose is an expression of the virtue of rationality. As such, it requires that one practice independence and all of its fellow virtues, productiveness included. The majority of productive careers do involve regular contacts with other men. But this does not erase the distinction between professional function and social relationships. It does not turn work into a party.

Social relationships are an important value, but only within the appropriate context. First, a man must be committed to the development of his mind and must achieve the right relationship to reality. Then, as a form of reward, he can properly enjoy people (those who also achieve such a relationship and who share his values). First he must be pursuing a productive purpose. Only then, as a complement to such pursuit, is he fit for love, parties, or a social life.

Similarly, one cannot substitute recreation—games, sports, travel, hobbies, reading murder mysteries, watching TV, going shopping, going to the beach, and the like—for work. Recreation presupposes creation. Leisure activities are a form of rest and presuppose that which one is resting *from;* they have value only as relaxation and reward after the performance of work. A life devoted primarily to recreation is one lived with one's mind on hold, in disconnected snatches according to the spur of the moment—a game, a trip, a show, a purchase—with no long-range goal and no field for intellectual activity. This amounts to the stagnant, pointless life of a playboy. Any authentic human need, recreation included, can serve as the base of a legitimate profession. Ayn Rand is not, therefore, casting any aspersion on professional athletes, entertainers, or stamp dealers. The point is that all such fields qualify as work only if a man pursues them as work. Work involves continuity and disciplined creativity.

The fundamental validation of productiveness is man's need of material values. But, as should now be apparent, this is not the only reason why a man must be productive. Work is necessary not only materially, but also spiritually or psychologically: it is the sole means by which a person can sustain across his lifespan an active mind and a goal-directed course, and thereby remain in control of his brain and actions. Work is essential not only to wealth, but also to the three supreme values that are implicit in man's life as the moral standard; it is essential to reason, purpose, and (to anticipate) self-esteem.

Productiveness constitutes the main existential content of virtue, the day-by-day substance of the moral life; as such, it is a responsibility of every moral being, whatever his finances. Even if a man has already made a fortune, therefore, or inherits one or wins one in a lottery, he needs a productive career. A rich man may choose, if he has a legitimate reason, to pursue a kind of work that brings him no money. But he still must work. A bum is not a person living man's life, even if he has no trouble paying his bills.

So, let me add, must a woman work. Years ago, when women were demeaned as "homemakers," it was necessary to state that there is no double standard in morality—that a human being's need of work does not mean merely a male's need. Now, as cultural fashions change, we often hear that a woman should work, but that she must do it outside the home, in some capacity other than that of mother; this too is irrational. Motherhood, although certainly not obligatory, is a legitimate and extremely demanding career—if one pursues it as a career, with the requisite intellectual responsibility (and if the mother makes provision for her continuing purpose after her children are grown).

In evaluating an individual's productiveness morally, one must judge not by form or results, but by volitional essentials. The issue is not: what particular field do you select? because there are countless rational alternatives. Nor is the issue: how much do you achieve or how high do you rise? because, among other reasons, people differ in intelligence and, therefore, in the kind of work and scale of creativity open to them.

The moral issue is: how do you approach the field of work given your intellectual endowment and the existing possibilities? Are you going through the motions of holding a job, without focus or ambition, waiting for weekends, vacations, and retirement? Or are you doing the most and the best that you can with your life? Have you committed yourself to a purpose, i.e., to a productive *career?*[52] Have you picked a field that makes demands on you, and are you striving to meet them, to do good work, and to build on it—to expand your knowledge, develop your ability, improve your efficiency?

If the answers to these last questions are yes, then you are totally virtuous in regard to productiveness, whether you are a surgeon or a steelworker, a house painter or a painter of landscapes, a janitor or a company president.

It is often said that a career-minded individual, being selfish, is cold and unfeeling. Let us therefore state the actual nature of such a person's feelings, his feelings specifically toward his work, including its difficulties and its rewards. These feelings are captured in a brief exchange from *The Fountainhead*.

A friend of his, observing Roark's attitude to architecture, says: "After all, it's only a building. It's not the combination of holy sacrament, Indian torture and sexual ecstasy that you seem to make of it." To which Roark replies: "Isn't it?"[53]

This is the kind of inner state which every human being has the power to achieve, each on his own level. *This* is the state which gives meaning to life.

The philosophy which extols such creativity, and only that philosophy, is what men should honor by the title "the work ethic."

Pride as Moral Ambitiousness

"Pride" is the commitment to achieve one's own moral perfection.[54]

"Man," writes Ayn Rand,

> faces two corollary, interdependent fields of action in which a constant exercise of choice and a constant creative process are demanded of him: the world around him and his own soul. . . . Just as he has to produce the material values he needs to sustain his life, so he has to acquire the values of character that enable him to sustain it and that make his life worth living. . . . He has to . . . survive by shaping the world and himself in the image of his values.[55]

The virtue of productiveness is concerned with the former of these requirements; the virtue of pride is concerned with the latter.

A producer must struggle to create the best material products possible to him. Similarly, a proud man struggles to achieve within himself the best possible spiritual state. This means a state of full virtue, whatever the effort and discipline it involves. In regard to morality, nothing less than perfection will do.[56]

Since all the virtues are forms of rationality, the commitment to achieve moral perfection reduces ultimately to a single policy: the commitment to follow reason. As the laws of logic make clear, there is no middle ground in this issue: either a man makes such a commitment—or he does not.

In the Objectivist usage, "moral perfection" is a valid term, which is defined by reference to reality. To quote Ayn Rand: "Moral perfection is an *unbreached rationality*—not the degree of your intelligence, but the full and relentless use of your mind, not the extent of your knowledge, but the acceptance of reason as an absolute."[57] Perfection so conceived is not only possible, but also necessary; it is necessary to a person for the same reason that a code of morality is necessary. If man's life is the standard by reference to which virtue is defined, then vice is not a temptation or a tolerable option, but a mortal threat. Moral imperfection, in any area, means movement toward destruction.

Moral concepts, including "right," "good," and "perfect," are norms formulated to guide human choice. Such concepts can refer only to that which is within the power of choice. There is no excuse, therefore, for a man who resigns himself to flaws in his character. "Flaws" does not mean errors of knowledge, which involve no evasion; it means breaches of morality, which do involve evasion.[58] The moral man may lack a piece of knowledge or reach a mistaken conclusion; but he does not tolerate willful evil, neither in his consciousness nor in his action, neither in the form of sins of commission nor of sins of omission. He does not demand of himself the impossible, but he does demand every ounce of the possible. He refuses to rest content with a defective soul, shrugging in self-deprecation "That's me." He knows that that "me" was created, and is alterable, by *him*.

The essence of pride is *moral* ambitiousness.[59] If man is a being of self-made soul, then pride is the process of making it properly. Like all virtues, the process includes both an intellectual and an existential component.

Intellectually, pride requires that one work to grasp the truth in moral issues rather than settle for unvalidated bromides or feelings. The proud man deals with moral issues explicitly and *objectively,* using the method of logic. Only a code of objective principles—a code based on the facts of nature and of human nature—can be adhered to consistently, without opposition from reality. If one starts ethics by rewriting reality, then moral perfection is out of the question. If one demands that a virtuous act be devoid of personal motive (like the Kantians), or that man be emotionless (the Stoics), or that he be bodiless (Plotinus), then one will be led to condemn human beings for the fact of existing. Any variant of this primacy-of-consciousness approach negates the purpose of ethics.

Once one knows the right moral principles, the next step is to build them into one's soul by repeated rational action. One must make these principles "second nature," in the Aristotelian sense of the term, by practicing them as an absolute.

Since the moral is the volitional, moral absolutism does not require omniscience or omnipotence. The moral man does not undercut his character by accepting unearned guilt. He may not properly accept blame for a failure over which he had no control, for a desire that is inherent in his being alive, or for disobedience to a moral code that by its nature is impracticable. If, however, in a moment of weakness he does earn some moral guilt, he acts decisively to clean the slate and restore his moral purity. He condemns his improper behavior, analyzes its roots (identifying in the process the underlying evasions), makes reparation (where applicable), and works to reshape his mental policy; he thereby retrains his character for the future.

The man of pride despises the morally "gray." He does not practice the virtues selectively; he observes every moral principle—on principle. That is why Ayn Rand describes pride as "the sum of all virtues."[60] Aristotle similarly calls pride "the crown of the virtues" and notes that it presupposes all the others.

The rewards of the virtue of pride are all the values that a proper moral character makes possible. In particular, pride leads a man to the third of the "supreme values": *self-esteem.*[61]

Unbreached rationality produces self-confidence in a man; since his policy is to recognize reality, he has a sense of efficacy, a conviction of his power to deal with reality and achieve his goals. In addition, the moral character he creates is admirable; so the proud man has a sense of his own worth. This sense includes the feeling that he has a right to be the beneficiary of his actions, that he is entitled to the attention which self-sustenance demands, that he has earned the position of being his own highest value.

"Self-esteem" is a fundamental, positive moral appraisal of oneself—of the process by which one lives and of the person one thereby creates. It is the union of two (inseparable) conclusions, neither of which is innate: I am right and I am good—I can achieve the best and I deserve the best I can achieve—I am *able* to live and I am *worthy* of living.

An animal does not need self-appraisal; it is unconcerned with moral issues and cannot question its own action. But man, who survives by a volitional process, needs a moral code—*and* the awareness that he is conforming to it. He needs the knowledge of how to live, and the knowledge that he is living up to this knowledge. In Ayn Rand's formulation, man "knows that he has to be *right;* to be wrong in action means danger to his life; to be wrong in person, to be *evil,* means to be unfit for existence."[62] Self-esteem or its absence is an individual's verdict in this fundamental issue.

A positive verdict is a reward for having lived properly, and it gives a man the strength required to persevere in his course. It gives him the courage to be virtuous no matter what the obstacles in his path: to rely on his judgment, to fight for his goals, to pursue his happiness. A negative verdict—whether it takes the form of self-doubt or self-hatred—is a punishment for having lived one's days out of focus, and it turns one into a spiritual cripple, who spends his time primarily not on pursuing goals but on trying to cope with fear and guilt. Such a man feels fear, in Ayn Rand's words, "because he has abandoned his weapon of survival." He feels guilt, "because he knows he has done it volitionally."[63]

Most men seem to grasp *that* man needs self-esteem, but not *why.* Conventional moralities, such as altruism, are worse than useless in this regard; they devote themselves to fighting the need. Only the ethics of rational selfishness identifies the root of the need. The root is biological or metaphysical: a volitional being cannot accept self-preservation as his purpose unless, taking a moral inventory, he concludes that he is qualified for the task; qualified in terms of ability and value.

"Esteem" is a type of evaluation, and evaluation presupposes a standard of value. The state of a man's self-esteem, therefore, depends not only on his moral practice, but also on his moral theory; it depends on the standard (usually only implicit) that he uses to gauge self-esteem. Here arises a great divide among men: those who gauge self-esteem by the standard of rationality (of their commitment to full consciousness)—and those who do not so gauge it.

Since the self is the mind, self-esteem is mind-esteem. In Ayn Rand's definition, it is "reliance on one's power to think."[64] The commitment to consciousness is the directly volitional function of man; such commitment, moreover, is the source of human efficacy and of personal worth. The standard of rationality, therefore, is the only one based on the facts of reality. It is the only standard of self-esteem based on the nature of man and derived from the code of virtue required by man's life. No other code can be relevant to satisfying a need *of* man's life.

Judge yourself as good or evil, Ayn Rand concludes, hold yourself in esteem or contempt, by reference to a single criterion: your volitional use or misuse of your tool of survival.

Contrast this approach with the attempt, now epidemic, to gauge self-esteem by a standard other than rationality. An example would be the second-hander who judges his worth by the approval he receives, by the obedience he offers to the authorities, and/or by his willingness to sacrifice. In order to gain a sense of self-value, or at least a pretense at one, such a person must relegate to a secondary position any thinking he does. To feel good about himself, he must continually unfocus and subvert his mind—which action makes him feel out of control, inefficacious, no good. Thus the intractable inferiority complex of so many people today and their insolvable conflict: because they judge their soul by improper standards, they pit the requirements of their self-esteem against the requirements of their life. The ultimate result is to make both these values impossible to themselves.

Ayn Rand describes such a practice as setting one's "self-esteem against reality."[65] The practice on its current scale is a consequence of mankind's leading ethical theories and represents the utter perversion of a biological need. It is the surest method there is of turning oneself into an anxiety-ridden evader.

There are other, less devastating errors one can make in gauging self-esteem. A man committed to reason may, for example, undercut himself by demanding of himself the impossible. He may (implicitly) expect to be omniscient or omnipotent in some area, and therefore carry the burden of a chronic unearned guilt. As long as he continues to act morally, such a man does not lose his basic self-respect, but he does suffer some form of breach in self-esteem. The extent of the breach, along with the degree of danger it poses to his life and happiness, depends on the exact nature of his improper self-expectations.

A man suffering from invalid standards of self-esteem, whether irrational or honest but mistaken, needs to change his moral ideas. He must learn to judge himself not by his relation to others, nor by his knowledge or existential success, but by his maintenance of a certain mental state, one that depends on nothing but his own will: the state of being in full focus. In other words, he must learn to gauge his self-esteem by the standard of moral perfection as conceived by the Objectivist ethics.

Then he must live up to this standard by practicing the virtue of pride. Pride, in the Objectivist definition, is the only means there is to self-esteem and the only cure for a breach in it.

Like any moral attribute, pride and self-esteem are open to everyone. The heroes of Ayn Rand's novels possess a superlative intelligence; but they are still normal men, human beings and not another species; with "human" meaning "rational." Unfortunately, owing to false philosophy, to be human in this sense is so rare an attainment that most people regard it as impossible. The native endowment it requires, however, is commonplace: a functional intelligence on any scale. What such an intelligence then needs in order to function is liberation—by the proper moral code.

In our culture, every moral requirement of intelligence is relentlessly attacked. Rationality is castigated as heartless, intellectuality as arid, egoism as exploitative, independence as antisocial, integrity as rigid, honesty as impractical, justice as cruel, productiveness as materialistic. The sum of this approach—the crown of the creed of death worship—is the tenet that pride is evil.

If people believe that they should not aspire to be perfect, that self-esteem is a delusion and virtue consists in recognizing how vicious they are, then true virtue *is* impossible to them, and the trap is closed on the human race. The better men give up the exacting ambition to be good, and the rest give up any hope of reform. The result is the mass manufacture of despair. The despair takes the form of species-wide self-abasement and a centuries-long rule of immorality. Only a corrupt theory of morality can produce such rule.

On a historical scale, the doctrine of Original Sin is the *cause* of sin. Any ideology that preaches this doctrine in any variant is thereby removed from the status of reputable; any ideology that damns man is damned itself. Nor is it redeemed when its exponents offer their broken victims solace and love.

If a man is unworthy, his obligation is not to mope around castigating himself, but to correct his evil. If he is not unworthy, it is a monstrous injustice to try to convince him otherwise. Either way, there is no place in ethics for the idea of humility as a virtue.

Just as pride is the dedication to morality, so humility is the obliteration of morality—not only in practice, but also in theory. Many years ago, a devout Catholic, a distant relative of hers, told Ayn Rand that he was cheating on his wife. She asked him how he could justify his behavior. He replied: "If I lived up to every tenet of my religion, I would be guilty of a worse sin, the sin of pride."

An ethics that extols humility is a self-contradiction. It is the advocacy of a code of behavior, along with the demand not to practice it fully. Such an approach throws out moral principles and condemns any man who respects them. But it offers the perfect loophole for any would-be sinner, the escape clause for any shyster, the license to any whim-worshiper. The license is: "If you try to be too good, that makes you bad."

Religions present their humility creeds as stern codes of moral purity. This is a fraud. A stern code is one that demands to be practiced. It expects its adherents to earn the self-congratulation of being able to say: "I take right and wrong seriously, I live by what I preach, I am *good.*" By its nature, an absolutist approach demands pride and self-esteem.

If an ethics urges intrinsicist dogmas, then men do need to find a loophole or breathing space. They need to smuggle into their days some self-preserving behavior. If one upholds an ethics of life, however, he does not need to smuggle in any speck of its opposite.

One does not need a breathing space—from breathing.

The Initiation of Physical Force as Evil

Having covered the major virtues, I want to complete the present discussion by turning to a widespread vice: the initiation of physical force against other men. This vice represents the antithesis and destruction of the virtue of rationality—and therefore of every other virtue and every (nonautomatic) value as well.[66]

To refrain from force is not necessarily a mark of good character. One can be thoroughly evil, yet recoil from wielding a fist or club oneself (e.g., the coward who tries to destroy others by psychological or ideological, not physical, means). But to initiate force is to commit a major evil. In the long run, this evil *is* an inevitable result of irrationality.

Physical force is coercion exercised by *physical* agency, such as, among many other examples, by punching a man in the face, incarcerating him, shooting him, or seizing his property. "Initiation" means *starting* the use of force against an innocent individual(s), one who has not himself started its use against others.

Since men do not automatically come to the same conclusions, no code of ethics can escape the present issue. The moralist has to tell men how to act when they disagree (assuming they do not simply go their separate ways). In essence, there are only two viewpoints on this issue, because there are only two basic methods by which one can deal with a dispute. The methods are reason or force; seeking to persuade others to share one's ideas voluntarily—or coercing others into doing what one wishes regardless of their ideas. Objectivism countenances only the method of persuasion.

Not all persuaders are honest men; many are manipulators, even destroyers, who bypass logic and seek to get what they want from others by playing on their feelings. But these creatures, if they abstain from force, leave their victims free not to fall for the racket—free to think logically in solitude, to decide the question for themselves, and to act accordingly.

The man of force, however, in attacking a person's body (or seizing his property), thereby negates and paralyzes his victim's *mind*.

The mind is a cognitive faculty. Its function is to perceive reality by performing a process of identification, a process of gathering evidence and integrating it into a context in accordance with the rules of an objective methodology. As we have often seen, this process presupposes a sovereign, volitional consciousness and must be performed egoistically, individualistically, independently. It cannot, therefore, be forced.

"A rational mind," writes Ayn Rand,

> does not work under compulsion; it does not subordinate its grasp of reality to anyone's orders, directives, or controls; it does not sacrifice its knowledge, its view of the truth, to anyone's opinions, threats, wishes, plans, or "welfare." Such a mind may be hampered by others, it may be silenced, proscribed, imprisoned, or destroyed; it cannot be forced; a gun is not an argument. (An example and symbol of this attitude is Galileo.)[67]

To order a man to accept a conclusion against his own judgment is to order him to accept as true something that, according to everything he knows, is *not* true (is either arbitrary or false). This amounts to ordering him to believe a contradiction; it is like demanding his agreement that red is green or that 2 plus 2 equals 5. One can torture an individual, force him to mouth any words one says, even drive him insane, but one cannot make him believe such mouthings. Volition pertains to the act of initiating and sustaining the process of thought. If a man does choose to think, however, he has no choice in regard to the conclusions he reaches. No matter what the bribes dangled before him or the threats, a thinker has to follow the evidence wherever it leads. Even if he tries, he cannot will himself to accept as true that which he sees to be baseless or mistaken.

It is impossible for a man to engage in a cognitive undertaking or to reach a cognitive result, such as an idea, while brushing aside logic and reality. Yet this is what the criminal who seeks to force a mind demands of his victim. The victim, therefore, has only one recourse (if he cannot escape): to cease functioning as a cognitive entity. When reality is decreed, at gunpoint, to be out of bounds, a rational mind has no way to proceed.

This is why the greatest eras of human history have always been the freest; it is why science, art, invention, and every other expression of fresh human thought fail to arise or vanish in a dictatorship. Just as a man cannot abuse his own mind with impunity, just as he cannot without wrecking his cognition begin to evade, accept the arbitrary, default on integration, or defy his sense perceptions; so he cannot escape the consequences when others seek to force on his mind the same abuses.

The victim need not give his inner consent to the forcers' evil demands; he need not agree to start lying to himself. But there is one mental penalty he cannot avoid: if and to the extent that someone's gun becomes a man's epistemological court of final appeal, replacing the law of identity, then the man cannot think. This is not a matter of moral integrity on the victim's part, but of philosophical necessity. The point is not that a slave should choose to defy his captors (he should, if he can). The point is that, qua enslaved, he cannot perform the processes essential to human cognition; he *cannot* think. (He can still smuggle into his life an element of secret thought, if his captors leave him alone long enough and if he does not try to express his thought in reality.)

An eloquent example of the relationship between force and thought is offered in the climax of *Atlas Shrugged*. John Galt, the leader of the minds who have gone on strike, cannot come up with any plan to save the country; he cannot, even though a gang of thugs, terrified that their statist regime will collapse, is screaming for such a plan and, seeking to extract it from his brain by force, has strapped Galt to a torture machine. By Galt's knowledge, there is no way to achieve prosperity under a dictatorship—and neither torture nor death threat can alter this fact. Galt accordingly does not change his convictions. He does not consider them from some new angle, or try to think up any ideas to satisfy his torturers, or look for a compromise. He cannot reject his own convictions, nor will the thugs let him apply them. He has no alternative, therefore, but not to use his conceptual faculty further in regard to the issue. He does not use it because he cannot: nothing will make the political goal of these brutes practicable, and he knows it.

The brutes, therefore, are left helpless. They can kill him, but they cannot achieve what they desperately want: to start and direct a process of thought within their victim's mind. They cannot turn a volitional process into a deterministic response, or an action into a reaction. What they do achieve through coercion is the opposite of a new idea. Like autocrats throughout history, the thing they work to immobilize is precisely their victim's mind. They make their thrall, to the extent he is in thrall, *stop* thinking.

An irrational man functions differently under the rule of force. Through evasion and rationalization he can comply mentally with just about any decree of others; he can bring himself to "believe" any contradiction he chooses. But this sort of inner state flows from the rejection of reason. As such, it does not pertain to human knowledge or to the convictions of a rational person. In the cognitive sense of the terms, an irrational man's mental contents are not "beliefs" or "ideas." They are more like the jabbering of a parrot.

Since man is an integrated being of mind and body, any attempt to force his mind necessarily represents an attempt to rule his actions, and vice versa. To clarify this point, let me now consider force that aims to elicit from the victim not thought or belief, but existential action. A simple example would be a gunman who says: "I don't care what my prey thinks. I just want him to hand over his wallet."

Force in this aspect makes a man act *against* his judgment. The victim still sees what he sees, values what he values, knows what he knows. The forcer, however, bypasses the victim's cognition, making it useless in practice. When the gunman threatens: "Your money or your life," the owner still knows to whom the money belongs. But if he does not choose to risk death or physical harm, the threat is the factor that has to determine his action. His own conclusion—however clear, logical, compelling—becomes impotent.

The same applies to the conclusions of a teenage boy opposed to a particular war—or of a publisher dealing with sexual material or a physician dealing with the elderly or a person in a totalitarian country dealing with anybody—who has to act under the threats issued by some governmental agency. In all its forms and degrees, from private crimes to the incursions of the welfare state to full dictatorship, the principle is the same: physical force, to the extent it is wielded or threatened, denies to its victim the power to act in accordance with his judgment. Such treatment is tantamount, in Ayn Rand's words, to "forcing [a man] to act against his own sight," and it places the individual in an impossible metaphysical position.[68] If he does not act on the conclusions of his mind, he is doomed by reality. If he does, he is doomed by the forcer.

The virtue of rationality requires one to think, and then to be guided by his conclusions in action. Force clashes with both these requirements. Force used to change a man's mind acts to stop his mind (and thus make it inoperative as the source of his action). Force used to change a man's action shoves his mind (and thus its process of cognition) into the junkheap of the purposeless. In the one manifestation, the brute works to detach his victim's consciousness from reality and therefore from life; in the other, from life and therefore from reality.

Thus Ayn Rand's formal conclusion: "Whoever, to whatever purpose or extent, initiates the use of force, is a killer acting on the premise of death in a manner wider than murder: the premise of destroying man's capacity to live."[69] Or, as she states the principle in her next paragraph: "Force and mind are opposites. . . ."

Force is the antithesis not only of the primary virtue, but of every virtue. The brute attacks in his victims every aspect of the moral life, while at the same time rejecting each in regard to his own life. In unleashing a process of force, he acts to nullify his victims' independence—while himself becoming a second-hander, whose concern is the conquest not of nature, but of men. He seeks to prevent men from remaining loyal to rational principles—and he seeks it not on the grounds of a principle, but, as is true in every case of evil, without grounds; he seeks it through evasion and whim-worship. He orders his victims, when he feels like it, to accept and pass on to others any lie he commands. He throws out the concept of "desert"; his method of dealing with men is to extract the unearned for the sake of benefiting the undeserving, whether himself or others. As to the virtue of moral ambitiousness, I quote Ayn Rand: "[M]orality ends where a gun begins."[70]

There is another derivative virtue to consider. Since "force and mind are opposites," the brute stifles at the root the process on which his own survival depends, the process of men acting to create material wealth. At the same time the rule of force, once accepted by a society, breeds its own adepts. It replaces the creators with the kind of men who believe that what counts in life is not brainpower, but firepower. "Then the race goes," in Ayn Rand's words, "not to the ablest at production, but to those most ruthless at brutality. When force is the standard, the murderer wins over the pickpocket. And then that society vanishes, in a spread of ruins and slaughter."[71]

Such a denouement illustrates the fact that there is no dichotomy between value and virtue. Since virtue is man's means of achieving value, whatever destroys virtues necessarily destroys values as well. In judging any instance of the present evil, therefore—as in judging dishonesty or any act of evil—there is no trade-off to consider. No good is achievable under any circumstances or for anyone by means of the initiation of force.

Because "force and mind are opposites," *force and value are opposites,* too.

Values, in the objective interpretation, are facts—as evaluated by a mind guided by a rational standard. "Value" thus implies a valuer who concludes, by a process of cognition, that a given object will sustain his life. One cannot, therefore, sunder "value" from the requisite process of cognition; one cannot sunder it from the mind of one's intended beneficiary—from his consideration, thought, judgment. To force an individual, however, is to disdain and bypass this process of cognition. No result of the initiation of force, accordingly, can qualify as "good." It is not "good" in relation to the victim. (Since there are no conflicts of interest among rational men, it is not "good" in relation to anyone else, either.)

Value, as I have said, is a form of truth. Just as one cannot force truth on a man, so one cannot force values or virtues on him. Sounds uttered at gunpoint are not a "truth." An object embraced at gunpoint is not a "value." An action performed at gunpoint is not a "virtue." These three concepts denote not only the physical, but also an individual's recognition of reality. As such, they require a process of volitional consciousness; they require the individual's own choice and agreement.

Here is the crucial passage from Ayn Rand:

> . . . an attempt to achieve the good by physical force is a monstrous contradiction which negates morality at its root by destroying a man's capacity to recognize the good, *i.e.,* his capacity to value. Force invalidates and paralyzes a man's judgment, demanding that he act against it, thus rendering him morally impotent. A value which one is forced to accept at the price of surrendering one's mind, is not a value to anyone; the forcibly mindless can neither judge nor choose nor value. An attempt to achieve the good by force is like an attempt to provide a man with a picture gallery at the price of cutting out his eyes. Values cannot exist (cannot be valued) outside the full context of a man's life, needs, goals, and *knowledge.*[72]

A dictatorship provides the most obvious concretization of the above. The citizens' own understanding of reality, along with their own value-judgments, is irrelevant to their lives; state force, not individual cognition, is the principle governing their actions. To the extent that an individual is moral, therefore—i.e., is rational, independent, uncompromising, purposeful, proud—his life becomes unendurable. Such an individual has only three alternatives, which are defined in Ayn Rand's *We the Living.* He may attempt to flee the country, as Kira did. He may kill himself, as Andrei did. Or he may try to make the conflict between force and mind endurable, as Leo did, by nullifying one of the two clashing elements, the only one within his power. This means: drowning his mind, through promiscuity, drugs, alcohol, or some equivalent. To the extent that a person succeeds in this endeavor, he becomes the "forcibly mindless" of Ayn Rand's quotation; he becomes the living dead, who loses the capacity to know any longer what is being done to him or to care. No course of action that such a person takes can be "right," since he has renounced the root of virtue. Nor, for the same reason, can any object he goes through the motions of attaining be a "good."

The terminology of self-preservation is not applicable when the self has disappeared.

Now let us consider an even more instructive (though purely hypothetical) example. Let us suppose that the force-wielders restrict their coercion to only one significant issue, such as choice of career; and that they reach their verdict that a given boy should go into medicine, say, only after administering psychological tests to determine the boy's own interests and aptitudes. Suppose further that the boy himself is mistaken in his choice: although he thinks that some form of art is the right field for him, his basic (subconscious) value-judgments actually point to a career in medicine—except that he himself has not discovered this fact, does not believe it, and cannot be persuaded to accept the forcers' conclusion. Even granting all this, the point remains true. Even if medicine would be the right field for this boy were he to choose it himself, the act of forcing it on him makes it wrong.

If a boy goes into medicine by choice, he thereby brings a certain cognitive and emotional context to the assessment of his experiences in the field. Since he has decided to pursue specific objects, he can relish them when he reaches them; he can relish the new knowledge he gains, the new skills, the fascinating cases he encounters, the dramatic cures. He can also accept with equanimity, as the price of such positives, the boredom or other negatives with which any career is replete. (If his choice of career is mistaken, introspection will give him abundant evidence of the fact.)

But if a boy is forced into medicine under threat of jail or physical harm, the context he brings is reversed. The "positives" are no longer positive; they are not values *to him* because he has not evaluated them as such. And as to the negatives—the back-to-back emergencies, say, the litigious paranoids among his patients, the forty-eight-hour shifts, the relentless atmosphere of accident, disaster, blood, pus, and death—he can have only one feeling: "This is the nightmare men forced on me when they tore out of my life my passion for art!"

Can you think of a better recipe for manufacturing hatred of a career? Is there a better way to make a mind give up all ambition? Would you want to be treated by this kind of physician?

Is *this* the means of achieving "value" in human life?

Value, like truth, is contextual; neither one can be divorced from a mind's knowledge and judgment. That is why, whatever the force-wielders decree, it is wrong. No value can be achieved by an assault on the valuer; no creative result, by the agencies of destruction; no good, by the methods of evil. What the initiation of force can achieve is only the negative: frustration, resentment, despair, passivity, nonmotivation, nonevaluation, nonthought—along with the bloody existential results that ultimately flow from such negatives. This principle is universal. It applies not only to governmental coercion, but also to private crime; not only in regard to career, but also to marriage, friends, hobbies, even movies; not only to an isolated boy, but to any intended beneficiary, past or future, individual or social.

The above covers the essence of the Objectivist argument against the initiation of force. The concept of "force," however, is widely misused today. So I must now clarify in some detail what is—and is not—an act of force within the context of the present discussion. I want to begin by elaborating on the point that the evil is the initiation of *physical* force.

There is only one way to attempt to force a man's mind: by directing the force to his body (or property). By purely intellectual means, no one—neither an individual nor a society nor any part thereof, such as TV advertisers—can coerce a man. "Intellectual means" denotes statements or arguments, whether true or false, good or bad; this would constitute persuasion, not coercion. A man may be confused by the claims of others, but confusion does not have to breed mental passivity. A volitional being, left unmolested, is free to initiate a cognitive process. He can struggle to untangle his confusions and replace them ultimately with truth.

The only kind of "social pressure" that cannot be resisted by intellectual means is the kind that does not rely on intellectual means. If some group, governmental or private, tells a man: "Either you agree with us or we will clean out your bank account, break your legs, kill you," then a cognitive process on his part is ineffective; no such process avails in counteracting the threat. *This,* this category of threat or harm—physical force and nothing else—is what constitutes coercion. This is what sweeps into the discard the victim's mind.

Similarly, a man may be disappointed by others. Rightly or wrongly, he may be unable to persuade them to agree with his ideas or to satisfy his desires. But disappointment does not attack his body or negate his mind; it is not an indication that he has been coerced. A man cannot properly say: "Since no one will pay me a larger salary, my boss *forces* me to take this job at five thousand dollars per year." No employer is obliged to confer wealth or jobs on this individual; no one owes him a living. Nor, in a free society, can anyone stop him from looking further, from improving his skills, or from working to start his own enterprise. If an employer who offers a certain salary tells him to take it or leave it and he agrees to take it, for whatever reason (including desperate poverty), that is the opposite of force. It is an instance of a voluntary relationship between the men, an instance of trade.

Coercion is not coextensive with frustration caused by others. It pertains only to those frustrations that men cause by invoking the methods of brutality.

Turning to another point, we often hear denunciations not of force, but of violence. "Violence" names a particular form of force, force that is swift, intense, rough, and/or accompanied by fury. The moral issue we have been identifying, however, is not a matter of form. The evil is coercion and anyone who initiates it, whether he is a wild-eyed hit man brandishing a machine gun or a prim little bureaucrat with his weapons on call but discreetly out of sight. To denounce "violence" but not the initiation of force as such is to imply that only the first of these men is evil. This would mean that the rule of brutality is moral if carried out decorously, with the niceties of the electoral process observed, the right documents filled in, and the agony of the victims kept out of the newspapers. Such is what today's intellectuals do believe and what they are trying to insinuate into the public mind.

Just as "the physical" in the present issue is not limited to the violent, so it is not limited to the *direct* use of force.[73] An example of the indirect use of force would be the gaining of someone's property by fraud. In such a case, any consent the owner has expressed is nullified; the owner did not consent to the transfer of goods that actually occurred. Morally, the crime here is indistinguishable from plain robbery; the difference is only one of form. (The task of defining the many forms of physical force, direct and indirect, including all the variants of breach of contract, belongs to the field of law.)

Ayn Rand holds that to *initiate* force against others is evil. But to use force in *retaliation,* against the individual(s) or nation(s) that started its use, is completely proper. Using force in retaliation means using it not against the innocent, but to stop criminals or aggressors. The ethical difference is the same as that between murder and self-defense. As with lying, so with the use of force: the moral rule is not a sweeping commandment, but an absolute prohibition within a context.

Contrary to the claims of pacifists, forcible retaliation does not mean "sinking" to the brute's view of morality. One does not reason with a jungle beast; one cannot; but this does not mean "sinking" to an animal's viewpoint. It means recognizing the facts of reality and acting accordingly. The same applies in dealing with a man who, by his own behavior, declares that he can no longer be treated as a rational being. When men use force against such a self-made beast, they are treating him in the only manner he himself permits. Nor do the retaliators acquire values thereby; they merely protect what they already have. "A holdup man," Galt observes, "seeks to gain wealth by killing me; I do not grow richer by killing a holdup man. I seek no values by means of evil, nor do I surrender my values to evil."[74]

Objectivism's censure of the initiation of force is a conclusion. Its premises are all the basic principles of the Objectivist ethics and, beneath that, of the Objectivist metaphysics and epistemology. Similarly, the age-old brutality worship of mankind's intellectuals is a conclusion, which rests on a chain of premises. Most obviously, it rests on the theory of altruism.

Altruism demands the initiation of physical force. When the representatives of the needy use coercion, they regularly explain that it is obligatory: it is their only means of ensuring that some recalcitrant individual, whose duty is self-sacrifice, carries out his moral obligations—of ensuring that he gives to the poor the unearned funds he is born owing them, but is trying wrongfully to withhold. At the same time and with complete consistency, altruism (in its commonest forms) rejects the retaliatory use of force. The Bible, for instance, advises one to resist not evil, but to go with an aggressor an extra mile—which policy, it notes, is a form of sacrifice.

But altruism is not the basic cause of brutality worship. That cause lies in the fundamental philosophy of unreason. Specifically, it lies in the epistemology of intrinsicism and subjectivism and in the concept of "value" to which these viewpoints lead men.[75]

The epistemology of each school makes coercion a human necessity. Intrinsicism reduces cognition to revelation, in regard to which rational argument is futile. The only means of resolving men's disputes, accordingly, is force. In this view, force is the prerogative of the philosopher-kings, of the viceroy of God, or of whoever else possesses the ineffable insight denied to the masses. Subjectivism draws a similar conclusion from the premise that knowledge is impossible. In this view, there are no external facts or reality-based rules of logic to which disputants can appeal; there is only the dead end of "might makes right." By denying the objectivity of cognition, both these philosophies rule out in principle the path of persuasion as against coercion.

The concept of "value" inherent in these two viewpoints gives a moral sanction to the rejection of persuasion. By the nature of "the good," both schools believe, coercion of the innocent can be beneficent; it can be a form of moral idealism, an act of nobility, a virtue leading to the achievement of a *value*.

If value, as intrinsicism holds, is independent of human purpose or evaluation, then it is independent of human knowledge. If so, one can force "the good" on a man and benefit him thereby. To put the point another way: if virtue is obedience to commandments, then it is proper to compel such obedience; the thought processes of the victims are irrelevant. "Theirs not to reason why; theirs but to do and die." Subjectivism leads to the same conclusion by a different route. If value is a product of arbitrary human evaluation, then again value is independent of knowledge. In this version, there is no knowledge, whether of fact or value; so anyone is justified in ramming down the throat of others any object he feels is "good"; the object then *is* good, courtesy not of God's desire, but of the forcer's.

In both cases, the moral essence is the same. Whether in the name of self-abnegation and/or of "self-assertion," value is divorced from the mind and therefore is regarded as achievable not by means of reason, but by means of brutality.

As a rule, when the advocates of this creed see its consequences in practice, they are unmoved. Practicality had never been their motive. Consequences, shrugs the intrinsicist, are irrelevant to ethics; consequences, shrugs the subjectivist, are whatever I claim they are. Thus the professorial apologists of fascism and communism, who watched corpses piling up across continents, yet remained undeterred. The killing, they said, reflects the awesome "imperatives of history"; and anyway, they said, we *feel* that the Party is right.

The most popular argument in favor of the initiation of force, the one offered routinely by intrinsicists and subjectivists alike, declares that force is necessary because men will not listen to reason. This amounts to the claim that brutality is the antidote to irrationality. It is the same as telling a person: "I'm going to bash your brains in to assist you in using them."

If men are irrational (most are less so than the intellectuals who attack them), the cause is the ideas that dominate the world; the ideas, and the mind-destroying statism they promote. The solution is not force, but its opposite: a theory, and then a country, of reason.

If, by magic, men could abolish only a single vice and they selected the initiation of force, it would not make everyone moral or prevent every injustice. But it would transform the world. It would mean the end of crime, slavery, war, dictatorship. It would mean the Utopia that people so often fantasize or at least make speeches about: the reign of peace and human dignity.

Vice, however, is an effect, which cannot be ended by magic, but only by uprooting its cause. Just as evil (including brutality) on a world scale follows from one kind of philosophy, so good on the same scale will follow only from the opposite philosophy.

To abolish vice, establish virtue. To establish virtue, enshrine thought. To enshrine thought, identify its relationship to reality.

Nothing less will cut out the rot that has been spreading for decades from the heart of civilization to its farthest extremities.

Nothing less will prevent the fall not of Rome this time, but of New York.

■　　■　　■　　■

The principles of ethics, as of epistemology, are objective. Virtues and values, therefore, like concepts, involve an element of the *optional*. In the realm of thought, one must choose English, French, or some other language from an array of possibilities, each of which is consonant with the rules of conceptualization. Similarly, in the realm of action, one must choose a course of behavior from an array of possibilities which are consonant with the rules of morality.

For example, morality upholds the virtue of productiveness. But should one be a physician, an artist, a philosopher, a businessman? Each individual has to answer for himself, taking into account his own context—his interests, needs, opportunities. This does not mean that the decision is arbitrary. It is wrong to become a bank robber—or even an elevator operator if one has the mind and chance to do more. But the decision is not inscribed on some moral tablet, either ("Thou shalt not kill, thou shalt not bear false witness, Jones shall become a plumber, etc."). A moral principle, like any other, is an abstraction, not an itch or an order. It must be understood by means of reason, then applied in a particular situation through a process that recognizes the fact of choice.

Wealth, to give another example, is a moral value. But this does not imply any categorical imperatives, such as: "Amass as much money as possible," or "The richer you become, the more virtuous you are." A given individual may choose, for good reason, to pursue a line of work that brings in little money. This is an optional matter, as long as the individual does have a good reason. The reason might be the fact that, given his interests, it offers him the fullest scope for the creative use of his mind. He may not, however, properly forgo a lucrative career because he is lazy, or fears to provoke the jealousy of his friends, or wants to show off his *non*affluence to Francis of Assisi or John Kenneth of Cambridge.

The above applies in some form to all moral virtues and values, whether they pertain to career, love, or recreation. A proper morality is not a blank check *or* a straitjacket. There is every room for you to do what you choose with your life.

There is every room for you to be an individual—if what you want to be is a *rational* individual.

9

HAPPINESS

Having identified particular virtues, let us take an overview, looking at the fruits of the whole moral code we have been describing. In existential terms, the moral man's reward is life. In emotional terms there is another reward, a concomitant of the first, which also requires study: happiness. Happiness is man's—the good man's—experience of life. The achievement of this experience, writes Ayn Rand, is "the only *moral* purpose" of one's life.[1]

The discussion of happiness is in the nature of a coda to the symphony of morality. Today, when men associate morality with pain, it is advisable to begin by analyzing the relationship between virtue and the trait men call "practicality" or "realism." This will give us the proper context for a discussion of happiness.

I have saved for the end of ethics Ayn Rand's ideas in regard to a crucial human experience, the one that is the most intense and most philosophical of all the forms of happiness. The experience and form I mean is sex.

Virtue as Practical

The concept of "practical" is not restricted to the field of ethics. It pertains to the adapting of means to ends in any field. If knowledge is one's goal, observation is practical, prayer is not. If the conquest of typhoid is the goal, immunization is practical, the beating of tom toms is not. If human efficacy is the goal, the wheel or the computer is a practical invention, a perpetual motion machine is not.

The "practical" is that which reaches or fosters a desired result. Since the concept denotes a type of positive evaluation, it presupposes a standard of value. The standard is set by the result being pursued.

By extension, one may describe a man as practical, if the actions he takes work to achieve his goals. A man is impractical, by contrast, if his actions cause him to fail in his endeavors.

Moral codes, too, qualify as practical or impractical. Most of those that have been offered to the human race are impractical. These codes prescribe ends and/or means which clash with the requirements of man's life. To the extent that men obey such codes, they are led to contradiction, frustration, failure; the essence of their failure is their inability to eat their life and have it, too. The most blatant example is the theory of altruism. If the principle guiding one's actions is sacrifice— first to esteem an object, then to give it up—one's approach to the realm of choice enshrines the antithesis of practicality; it praises and guarantees the loss of values. Such a life seeks out defeat.

Despite the notions they espouse, men in the West are influenced by the unidentified remnants of a better (Aristotelian) heritage. People in the civilized world still want to live, to prosper, to be happy. By this standard, ethics, the ethics they officially profess, is hopeless. Hence the universal acceptance of a disastrous idea, one taken nowadays as self-evident: the idea that there is an inherent clash between the moral and the practical.

According to this idea, every man faces a basic alternative: to dedicate himself to the good, the right, the noble, to be an "idealist," in which case he must be unworldly, unrealistic, doomed to defeat—*or* to pursue success, prudence, that which works, to be a "realist," in which case he must dispense with ideals, absolutes, moral principles. (In philosophy, Platonism recommends the first of these choices, pragmatism recommends the second.) The alternative is: be good without earthly purpose, or seek ends while ignoring the necessary means. In other words: commit yourself to virtues *or* to values—to causes *or* to effects—to ethics *or* to life.

Objectivism rejects this dichotomy completely.[2]

The moral man's concept of the good, we hold, *is* his fundamental standard of practicality. Such a man experiences no conflict between what he thinks he ought to pursue (self-preservation) and what he wants to pursue. He defines all of his goals, fundamental and derivative alike, by reference to reality. As a result, he pursues only objects that are attainable by man, consistent with one another, and possible to him; he uses his mind to discover the means (including the principles) necessary to reach these objects; and he applies his knowledge in action, refusing to evade what he knows, to drift purposelessly, or to sacrifice his interests. This, in Ayn Rand's view, is the description of human nobility. What other policies could practicality require?

In the Objectivist approach, virtue is (by definition) the means to value. The notion of a dichotomy between virtue and efficacy is, therefore, senseless. To pursue rational goals by rational means is the only way there is to deal successfully with reality and attain one's goals. To be moral in the Objectivist definition *is* to be practical, and it is the only way to be practical.

This does not mean that success is guaranteed to a conscientious Objectivist. No philosophy can alter the metaphysically given fact that man is not omniscient or omnipotent. Regardless of a person's virtue, he may fail in an undertaking (or even die) through simple error. The pilot "wrong-way Corrigan," let us say, was conscientious and honest, but these qualities did not automatically point his plane in the right direction. Rationality is a virtue because action demands knowledge. If one does not acquire the necessary knowledge, then he cannot avoid suffering the consequences, even if he is in no way morally deficient.

Besides errors of knowledge, one must also reckon with the factor of other men. If one's goal in an undertaking involves the cooperation of others, his own virtue (or knowledge) cannot ensure success. The ideas, the motivation, the skills, the character traits that he needs in others depend on their choices, not his. An individual in a free society is free to search for the kind of men he wants or to try to persuade others to share his ideas. But no act of persuasion, however skillful, can nullify human volition. You cannot change a man's mind without his consent.

Then there is the factor of accident. It is possible, through no fault of anyone, for men to encounter illnesses, earthquakes, plane crashes, and the like, which can cut an individual down prematurely or cause him to fail in some endeavor. Proper human action can reduce the power of accident enormously (witness the ability of modern medicine and technology to prevent or deal with illness and disaster). But this does not mean that accident can be eliminated.

There is no cosmic overseer, who takes note of virtue and crowns it with success. Nor is this an injustice on reality's part; it is an expression of causality and identity—of causality, in that certain causes lead to certain effects, whether one desires them or not; of identity, in that man, like every other existent, is limited. The concepts of "justice" and "injustice" do not apply to the universe or to the lower forms of life. They apply only to certain choices and actions of human beings.

Virtue is not automatically rewarded, but this does not change the fact that it *is* rewarded. Virtue minimizes the risks inherent in life and maximizes the chance of success. Morality teaches one how to gain and use the full power of one's mind, how to choose one's associates, how to organize society so that the best among men rise to the top. It teaches one how to safeguard life and limb in principle and therefore against every danger that can be foreseen. This does not give men omnipotence; what it gives them is the means of preventing, mitigating, or counteracting innumerable evils that would otherwise be intractable.

In the context of an ethical discussion, the assessment of a course of action as "practical" or "impractical" can take into account only matters open to a man's choice. The question is: in such matters, does he act according to the principles necessary to achieve values, or does he introduce a breach between his mind and reality? In the first case, he and the ethics he follows deserve the accolade "practical"; in the second case, he and it do not. In this sense we may say that, despite man's limitations, morality *does* ensure practicality.

It is crucial here that one judge practicality from the long-range viewpoint. If one is concerned to evaluate a man's course, one must keep in mind the human time scale. Virtue does not promise instant value. If what you want is success TODAY—in work, in politics, in any field; if you demand peace, love, or any other such value NOW, without effort or the enactment of means across time; then nothing will give it to you (and you will soon give up your goal with a sigh or a curse, as the rebels of the 1960s did). "Practicality" in this usage is an invalid concept. The NOW disease is prevalent on today's campuses only because every inkling of a conceptual mode of existence has been bred out of the students.

Just as the moral and the practical go together, so do the immoral and the impractical. Just as the virtuous is the efficacious, so *the evil is the impotent.*[3]

Evil, for Objectivism, means the willful ignorance or defiance of reality. This has to mean: that which cannot deal with reality, that which is whim-ridden, context-dropping, self-contradictory. Evil is consistent in only one regard: its essence is consistently at war with all the values and virtues human life requires.

The antilife is barren. It achieves only the antilife.

As we have seen in discussing honesty, an irrational man qua irrational cannot achieve anything of value. His actions are necessarily self-defeating. There are unlimited further examples of this principle. There is the unjust employer in a free country who wants to make a business success (a legitimate value), but who is jealous of talented men and hires only mediocrities; as a result, his competitors put him out of business. There is the political candidate who seeks a reputation for eloquence through plagiarism, then sees his candidacy collapse when his sources are discovered. There is the relativist who seeks safety through uncertainty, urging men to make terms with anyone, who then sees the worst among men, thanks to that policy, rise to the top and turn his country into the opposite of a safe haven: a dictatorship. There is the dictator himself, who is after power, the power, he says, to be happier than any man, who proceeds to shackle the producers and devastate his nation, then spends his time fighting off terrors, real and imaginary, at home and abroad, outer and inner; in the end, if he lives long enough, he turns into a certifiable psychotic (e.g., Hitler and Stalin).

As with virtue, so with vice: one cannot judge its consequences properly if one takes a short-range viewpoint. The unjust employer or any other irrationalist need not reap the whirlwind the day or year he starts on his course. *The Fountainhead* provides an eloquent illustration. If you read the book only halfway through, then ask whether Roark or Keating is the practical man, you may well be tempted to decide in favor of Keating. At that point, Roark is friendless, unrecognized, condemned to work in a quarry, while Keating is at the top of his profession and surrounded by admirers. But if you continue reading and grasp the logic of the subsequent events, the principles dictating the outcome, you know why Roark ultimately wins out and why Keating has to fail. The same principles apply to every case of the apparent efficacy of evil.

An inverted moral code has so corrupted people that they associate evil with value rather than with loss—e.g., the mad scientist of the movies, who gains new knowledge because he is diabolical; or the "robber baron" of the historians, who gains wealth because he is an "exploiter"; or the lustful "materialist" of the preachers, who gains sexual joy because he is "only an animal." In actuality, the reverse is true. Virtue, not vice, leads to science, riches, and every other good, including sexual joy. The evil man taken pure, i.e., deprived of any assistance from the principle of virtue, is not the flamboyant value-achiever of our cultural mythology. He is a non-achiever, ignorant, impoverished, frustrated, resentful, and helpless, helpless to do anything about his condition. He is helpless by his own choice.

If the conventional ethics were correct, then so would be the conventional view of the rewards of evil. In that case, the religious symbolism of a powerful, glamorous devil wreaking havoc with the humble forces of virtue would be appropriate. From the Objectivist perspective, however, this symbolism is a travesty. Men, as Dominique Francon thinks in *The Fountainhead,* "had been so mistaken about the shapes of their

Devil—he was not single and big, he was many and smutty and small." Or, as Stepan Timoshenko puts it in *We the Living,* the forces of evil are "not an army of heroes, nor even of fiends, but of shriveled bookkeepers with a rupture who've learned to be arrogant." The proper symbol of evil, he says, is not "a tall warrior in a steel helmet, a human dragon spitting fire," but "a louse. A big, fat, slow, blond louse."[4]

Evil does have one power. It has not the power to create, to set positive goals and achieve them, but the power to destroy: to destroy itself and its victims.

Whatever the human value involved, its achievement requires the use of the mind; its destruction requires the opposite. To turn oneself into a self-confident, rational being takes a sustained effort of thought and will; to turn oneself into a stuporous puppet takes only, say, some snorts of cocaine. To build a happy marriage, one must know one's values and one's partner, one must work to identify, cooperate, communicate; to wreck one's marriage, one need merely take it for granted and give one's partner no thought at all. To sculpt the *David,* one needs the genius of Michelangelo; to smash it, only some rampaging barbarians. To create the United States required the intellect and the painstaking debates of the Founding Fathers; to run it into the ground, only the crew of anti-intellectuals now ensconced in Washington.

"No thought, knowledge, or consistency is required in order to destroy," writes Ayn Rand,

> unremitting thought, enormous knowledge, and a ruthless consistency are required in order to achieve or create. Every error, evasion, or contradiction helps the goal of destruction; only reason and logic can advance the goal of construction. The *negative* requires an absence (ignorance, impotence, irrationality); the *positive* requires a presence, an existent (knowledge, efficacy, thought).[5]

Evil men, though impotent, *can* disappoint, deceive, and betray the innocent; if they turn to crime, they can rob, enslave, and kill. This is one reason that man needs to practice the virtue of justice (to distinguish between the good and the evil). It is also a reason why man needs to live in a proper society, one designed to protect individual rights. Some evil and thus some harm to the innocent are unavoidable; no philosophy can guarantee virtue, since virtue is a matter of choice. In a proper society, however, evil is a marginal element. When men live by rational principles, the evil, so far as men can identify its presence, is ostracized and stopped. Under these conditions, even its power to destroy is largely nullified—except in regard to the evildoer himself.

Unfortunately, men have not dominantly lived by rational principles. One way or another throughout the centuries, the men who embody the good, or who represent it in a given issue, have aided, not stopped, the evil. They have paved the road for it, letting (or helplessly watching) it profit from the achievements of virtue.

There are countless forms of this road-paving. The forms include the serfs of statist regimes, whose unrewarded toil builds the palaces or dachas of their indolent monarchs or commissars—the honest businessmen and workers of a mixed economy, whose "excess" profits and wages are siphoned into the pockets of sundry incompetents—the self-made man who, whether out of guilt or reckless generosity, agrees to carry on his back a gang of loafing relatives—the amoral genius in science who discovers a new force of nature, then turns his knowledge over to all comers, including avowed killers—the great artists of the past, whose works are interspersed in today's museums, concert halls, and English classes amongst the nonobjective trash of our era, thereby conferring stature by association on the trash—the better man in any field who, fearing to stand alone against his colleagues, agrees to lend their latest aberration the prestige of his own hard-won name—the representatives of any good cause who have had the cult of compromise pounded into them and end up making deals with the devil—the man like Gail Wynand in *The Fountainhead,* who observes the whole spectacle, sees the seemingly universal rule of evil, and concludes that he must gain power over the irrational by pandering to the lowest instincts of the mob, and who thereby turns his own brilliant mind into an instrument of that mob.

Some of these men know that they are road-pavers of evil; some do not. Some act by choice; some, by force. Some suffer from an error of knowledge; others, from a breach of morality. But whatever the motive or the form, the common denominator is the same: a donation to the irrational of the fruits of virtue, a blood transfusion from the good to the evil.[6] This means: the pumping of life into the forces of death.

The success of evil, to the extent such a phenomenon exists, flows not from any inherent efficacy on the part of evil, but from the errors or flaws of men who are essentially (or in some issue) good. Above all, such success flows not from any individual's compromise or weakness, but from the fact that throughout history the good has failed to recognize itself or to assert its rightful claims.

In the ethics that so far has ruled the world, the transfusion of value from the deserving to the undeserving is regarded as the essence of virtue; the virtuous man, by definition, must work to bring about the success of parasites. This theory is the formal demand for the arming of evil. In Ayn Rand's historic identification, it is the demand for *the sanction of the victim*.[7]

The "sanction of the victim" means the moral man's approval of his own martyrdom, his agreement to accept—in return for his achievements—curses, robbery, and enslavement. It means a man's willingness to embrace his exploiters, to pay them ransom for his virtues, to condone and help perpetuate the ethical code which feeds off those virtues, which expects them and counts on them at the very moment it is damning them as sin and condemning their exponents to hellfire (supernatural or secular).

This is the moral issue in John Galt's strike: to say no to this code for the first time. Galt refuses to sanction the immolation of the creators. He withdraws the power of the good from the hands of the evil. He quits the world and lets the evil confront the full reality of its own impotence.

Ayn Rand demands of men unbreached integrity, justice, and *selfishness*. This demand is not "too extreme." Nothing less will put an end to the obscene blood transfusion that has wrecked most of human history.

In the rational society envisioned by Objectivism, the evil has no foothold on the living power of the good and no way to offer it torture as recompense. On the contrary, the evil is both damned and dammed, while the good is left free to achieve values and enjoy them. In this kind of society, the rewards of morality, its preeminent *practicality,* will become obvious to everyone.

Why have men for centuries been content to live with so insufferable a contradiction as the moral-practical dichotomy? Why have they not indignantly rejected the conventional ethics precisely because it is impractical? The answer points us to the roots of ethics in metaphysics and epistemology.

The most obvious of the deeper issues at work here is the soul-body dichotomy. An advocate of this viewpoint shrugs resignedly when he sees that the morality he preaches leads to disasters in practice. Everyone knows, he says, that morality is a spiritual concern and that the spiritual is opposed to the physical. The choice facing a person, he says, is to cling to the soul, retire idealistically from the world into the Church or the desert, and be canonized as a man that "hateth his life"; or to cling to the world by retiring from morality.

Whatever their differences, both sides in this choice agree about the role of morality. They agree that morality, by its nature, is harmful. It is harmful in regard to "this" life, says the one; it is harmful in "real" life, says the other. Life, accordingly, requires not virtue (in any definition), but expediency. In other words, *principles* to guide one's choices are not a necessity of successful action here on earth; rather, they are an otherworldly impediment, a spiritual thorn in one's flesh, to be masochistically endured or amorally plucked out.

In the standard philosophy of our era, the vital power of principle is set in reverse. The power is detached from the work of self-preservation and is *moved to the side of the antilife.* What makes such a perversion possible?

Principles are a form of conceptualization. Pitting principles against life is equivalent to pitting theory against practice. In both formulations, one is pitting concepts against life and practice, which means: one is accepting a breach between concepts and reality. This in turn presupposes a certain view of concepts.

Nothing but a false theory of concepts can explain the worldwide scorn today for the conceptual guidance offered by principles. Such scorn would be impossible to a man who regarded conceptualization as the means of knowing existence; but it is necessary to the disciples of intrinsicism and subjectivism, who make abstractions useless by detaching them from percepts. The intrinsicists have the effrontery to build on this uselessness: be loyal to principles apart from reality, they say, and suffer the consequence, which is misery here on earth. To which the subjectivists reply: that *is* the price of being principled and it is too high; so, they conclude, anything goes. The one mentality tells us: abstractions including those of the evaluative variety, do not pay off in this world—which they don't, not in his kind of interpretation. The other shrugs: so much for abstractions, let's be "practical." Thus the awesome spectacle created by both sides: the spectacle of man, the rational being, asserting as a truism the incredible notion that his cognitive faculty is an obstacle to his survival.

As long as men reject reason in epistemology, they will necessarily reject it in ethics. If they introduce a breach between consciousness and existence at the base of their thinking, they will carry that breach into their thinking on value questions as well. Such an approach will lead them inevitably to some form of the moral-practical dichotomy.

This dichotomy, despite its historical prevalence, reveals nothing about values or about life. It is not a truth, but the culmination of error, the telltale symptom of lethal falsehoods at the heart of the prevalent world view.

Ayn Rand's principle of the harmony between the moral and the practical is also a culmination. She upholds the principle because, long before she reaches ethics, she upholds the objective view of concepts and the primacy of existence.

Morality, she says, is practical because consciousness is practical. And consciousness is practical because it is "the faculty of perceiving that which exists."

Happiness as the Normal Condition of Man

Pleasure—using the term for a moment to designate any form of enjoyment—is an effect. Its cause is the gaining of a value, whether it be a meal when one is hungry, an invitation to a party, a diamond necklace, or a long-sought promotion at work. The root of values, in turn, is the requirements of survival. Self-preservation, in other words, entails goal-directed action, success at which leads (in conscious organisms) to pleasure. Metaphysically, therefore, pleasure is a concomitant of life. Pain is a concomitant of the opposite; its cause is an organism's failure or injury in some respect.[8]

On the physical level, Ayn Rand observes, the pleasure-pain mechanism is a "barometer" of one's basic alternative. The sensation of pleasure indicates that one is satisfying in some form a biological need and, to that extent, is following a right course of action. The sensation of pain is a warning that something is wrong; it indicates some lack or damage that requires corrective action. On this level, the mechanism is automatic: the standard of value that determines bodily "right" and "wrong" is set innately. That standard is the organism's life.

A sensation does not necessarily indicate long-range consequences. Too many sweets, to take the standard example, may give pleasure in the moment, but then lead to the pains of stomachache and tooth decay. This kind of case is no exception to the pleasure-life correlation. The pleasure here derives from the fact that sugar does satisfy a biological need; and because the excessive intake *is* harmful, its eventual consequence is pain. Similarly, the pain from the dentist's drilling indicates that some (nerve) tissue is being destroyed—which in this instance serves the organism's life. The long-range result, other things being equal, is the sensory glow that accompanies unimpaired vitality.

Just as the body has pleasure-pain sensations to protect it, so consciousness has two *emotions,* joy and suffering, as a barometer of the same alternative, life or death. Joy is the result of gaining a chosen value, one held on the conceptual level (as against an innate, physiologically set value). Suffering is the result of loss or failure on this level.

This brings us to happiness, which is a fundamental and enduring form of joy. "Happiness," in Ayn Rand's definition, "is that state of consciousness which proceeds from the achievement of one's values."[9]

On the conceptual level, the standard of value determining human responses is not automatic. Men's chosen values are not necessarily in harmony with the requirements of survival. On the contrary, a man can avidly pursue irrational values and thereby gain pleasure (of a sort) from the process of harming himself. Such a man inverts his emotional barometer, turning it into an agent of death; the mechanism becomes not his protector, but a siren urging him to self-destruction.[10] For example: the people whose pleasure in life comes from crime or drugs or idleness or power lust or being accepted by the group or from any other form of being out of focus.

Pleasure, however, *is* a concomitant of life; so one cannot reach happiness by any of these means. One cannot, because a course of self-destruction is an antivalue course, i.e., a course incompatible with successful goal-directed action.

Only the moral man, as we know, the exponent of self-preservation, uses his cognitive faculty to make the countless decisions involved in choosing values and pursuing goals. Only he selects ends and means consonant with the nature of existence and with the integrity of his own consciousness. Only he refuses to sabotage his person or his goals by indulging in out-of-context desires or fears. In the terminology of the last section, only he is practical, i.e., able to achieve his values. Only he, therefore, can reach the emotional result and reward of such achievement.[11]

The moral, the practical, and the happy cannot be sundered. By their nature, the three form a unity: he who perceives reality is able to gain his ends and thus enjoy the process of being alive. Similarly, the evil, the impractical, and the unhappy form a unity. He who evades renders himself impotent in action and thus experiences life as suffering.

When happiness is said to proceed "from the achievement of one's values," this does not mean that it follows from the gaining of *any* ends, rational or otherwise. If a man holds and achieves rational values, he will be happy as a result, and his happiness will reflect the fact that his course of action is pro-life. If he holds irrational values, however, he may attain a particular, out-of-context goal(s); but he cannot "achieve *his* values," because irrational values, involving as they do inbuilt contradictions and chronic clashes with reality, cannot *be* achieved.

The irrational man is inevitably tortured. To him, failure means suffering—and so does success. Success of his kind (at blanking out reality) is a threat, attainment brings anxiety, desire is guilt, self-esteem is self-loathing, pleasure is laced with hangover, joy is overcome by pain. Whatever the name of such a state, it is not "happiness."

"Happiness," writes Ayn Rand, in an important elaboration of her definition,

> is a state of noncontradictory joy—a joy without penalty
> or guilt, a joy that does not clash with any of your values
> and does not work for your own destruction, not the joy
> of escaping from your mind, but of using your mind's full-
> est power, not the joy of faking reality, but of achieving
> values that are real, not the joy of a drunkard, but of a
> producer.[12]

Since joy of this kind involves the achievement of values,
it demands *values* (as against whims); a passion to attain goals
one is convinced are right (as against uncertainty about goals
that are arbitrary); in a word, purpose (as against drifting).
The rational man fulfills this requirement. The irrational man
does not. Qua irrationalist, what moves him is not the quest
for positives, but the avoidance of negatives. In psychological
terms, he exhibits not healthy self-assertion, but neurotic de-
fensiveness. In Ayn Rand's words, he exemplifies not "motivation by love," but "motivation by fear."[13]

"Love" in this context means the desire to gain and enjoy
a value; "fear" means the desire to escape a disvalue. The
distinction pertains to a man's *primary* motive in a given undertaking. As examples: the man who struggles to create
something new in his work (and who may, as part of the process, have to fight many obstacles placed in his path) vs. the
man who wants primarily *not* to get blamed by the boss or
fired—the man who seeks a passionate romance with a kindred spirit vs. the man who sleeps with anyone because what
he wants is not to be left alone—the man who tends to his
health in order to be free to live and act vs. the hypochon-
driac obsessed with not being sick—the man who turns to
Rachmaninoff for melody and inspiration vs. the man who
turns to Schönberg in order not to be passé and not to be too
awake—the presidential candidate who has something to say
in a TV debate, who wants to make a case to the country and
win the argument vs. the candidate who wants only *not* to
make any mistakes onscreen and *not* to lose.

In one sense, both the above types of men are "purpo-
sive"; both are "after something." They are not both "pur-

posive" in the moral sense, however, because morality is a means to survival, and the goal of life, as Ayn Rand points out, cannot be attained by the zero-seeking method:

> . . . achieving life is not the equivalent of avoiding death. Joy is not "the absence of pain," intelligence is not "the absence of stupidity," light is not "the absence of darkness," an entity is not "the absence of a nonentity." Building is not done by abstaining from demolition; centuries of sitting and waiting in such abstinence will not raise one single girder for you to abstain from demolishing. . . . Existence is not a negation of negatives. Evil, not value, is an absence and a negation. . . .[14]

Happiness is not an absence, either; nor is it some guilty pleasures that serve merely to lessen anxiety. It is not what you feel when you stop beating your head against a wall. It is what you feel when you refuse ever to engage in such beating, when you esteem and protect your head as a matter of principle. Happiness, the reward of life, is an aspect of life. It too requires values, not merely avoidance; and, therefore, a functioning mind.

Just as man cannot achieve self-preservation arbitrarily, but only by the method of reason, so he cannot achieve happiness arbitrarily, but only by the same method. The method is the same because self-preservation and happiness are not separate issues. They are one indivisible fact looked at from two aspects: external action and internal consequence; or biological cause and psychological effect; or existence and consciousness.[15]

Even though rationality does not lead to success automatically, it is more than a necessary condition of happiness. It is also a sufficient condition. Virtue does ensure happiness in a certain sense, just as it ensures practicality.

Consider here a moral man who has not yet reached professional or romantic fulfillment—an Ayn Rand hero, say, like Roark or Galt, at the point when he is alone against the world, barred from his work, destitute. In existential terms, such a man has not "achieved his values"; he is beset by problems and difficulties. Nevertheless, if he *is* an Ayn Rand hero, he is confident, at peace with himself, serene; he is a happy person even when living through an unhappy period. He does experience deprivation, frustration, pain; but, in Ayn Rand's memorable phrase, it is pain that "goes only down to a certain point,"[16] beneath which are the crucial attributes such a man has built into his soul: reason, purpose, self-esteem.

A man of this kind *has* "achieved his values"—not his existential values, but the philosophical values that are their precondition. He has achieved not success, but the ability to succeed, the right relationship to reality. The emotional leitmotif of such a person is a unique and enduring form of pleasure: the pleasure that derives from the sheer fact of a man's being alive—if he is a man who feels able to live. We may describe this emotion as "metaphysical pleasure," in contrast to the more specific pleasures of work, friendship, and the rest. Metaphysical pleasure does not erase the pains incident to daily life, but, by providing a positively toned context for them, it does blunt them; in the same manner, it intensifies one's daily pleasures. The immoral man, by contrast, suffers metaphysical pain, i.e., the enduring anxiety, conflict, and self-doubt inherent in being an adversary of reality. This kind of pain intensifies the man's every daily defeat, while turning *pleasure* for him into a superficiality that "goes only down to a certain point."

Metaphysical pleasure depends only on one's own choices and actions. Virtue, therefore, does ensure happiness—not the full happiness of having achieved one's values in reality, but the premonitory radiance[17] of knowing that such achievement is possible. The one state is represented by Roark at the end of the novel, standing triumphant atop the Wynand Building, looking down at Dominique. The other is Roark at the start and throughout, even when toiling in the granite quarry.

The ability to achieve values, I must add, is useless if one is stopped from exercising that ability—e.g., if an individual is caught in a dictatorship; or is suffering from a terminal illness; or loses an irreplaceable person essential to his very existence as a valuer, as may occur in the death of a beloved wife or husband. In such situations, suffering (or stoicism) is all that is possible. Morality is a means to action in the world; the soul by itself is not an entity, an end, or a fulfillment. Character alone, therefore, deprived of the necessary existential context, will not produce happiness, not even metaphysical pleasure. There is no joy in being alive if one cannot live.

Virtue does ensure happiness, at least in the metaphysical sense—except when life itself becomes impossible to a man, because, for some reason, the pursuit of values becomes impossible.

The Objectivist view of happiness differs in every essential from the two views dominant in today's culture. One of these, the intrinsicist approach, regards happiness as low or evil. The other, a subjectivist approach, is hedonism.

Intrinsicism, whatever its promises in regard to another life, leads in this one to suffering. Enjoyment as such thus becomes suspect; it becomes a sign of ethical dereliction—of selfishness, ambition, "materialism." There can be no question, therefore, of pursuing happiness; one's moral destiny is the opposite: duty, loss, sacrifice. This kind of philosophy urges on men the adoration of pain, a condition eloquently symbolized in the West by the acceptance of crucifixion as an ideal. Such adoration reached unprecedented virulence in the modern, Kantian era.

To an Objectivist, the adoration of pain is literally unspeakable. Morally, there is nothing to say about it beyond noting that its cause is the worship of death.

Hedonism, at first glance, may seem to be an opposite viewpoint. Hedonism is the theory that pleasure (or happiness) is the *standard* of value. In order to determine values and virtues, the theory holds, one must ask whether a given object or action maximizes pleasure (one's own and/or that of others). The emotion of pleasure, however, is a consequence of a man's value-judgments, so the theory is circular. It amounts to the advice: value that which you or others, for whatever reason, already value. This means, in practice: do whatever you feel like doing.

Happiness is properly the purpose of ethics, but not the standard.[18] One must choose values by reference not to a psychical state, but to an external fact: the requirements of man's life—in order to achieve the state of enjoying one's life. It is self-defeating to counsel the pursuit of pleasure as a primary ethical guide, because only the pleasure attendant on the achievement of rational values leads to happiness. The pleasure-seeker, therefore, must first distinguish the rational from the irrational in this field—by means of an *objective* approach to ethics.

The intrinsicist says: give up your happiness. The subjectivist replies: no, go after it—by any random means you choose. The one says: pleasure is animalistic, unspiritual, immoral. The other, at least in its popular version, replies: you're right, so let's be animals and grab any "kicks" we can. Whatever their disagreements, the two schools lead to the same result, the same deflection. Just as, in epistemology, the two theories knock mankind off the road of knowledge, so, in ethics, they knock mankind off the road of joy, into the gutter of suffering. This leads most men to conclude that happiness is impossible, that life by its nature is hell.

Ayn Rand, by contrast, advocating as she does an objective approach to ethics, holds that pleasure is moral. Happiness, therefore, is not only possible, but more: it is the normal condition of man. Ayn Rand calls this conclusion, which is essential to the Objectivist world view, the "benevolent universe" premise.

"Benevolence" in this context is not a synonym for kindness; it does not mean that the universe cares about man or wishes to help him. The universe has no desires; it simply is. Man must care about and adapt to it, not the other way around. If he does adapt to it, however, then the universe is "benevolent" in another sense: "auspicious to human life." If a man does recognize and adhere to reality, then he can achieve his values in reality; he can and, other things being equal, he will. For the moral man, failures, though possible, are an exception to the rule. The rule is success. The state of consciousness to be fought for *and expected* is happiness.

The rejection of this viewpoint is what Ayn Rand calls the "malevolent universe" premise (others have called it the "tragic sense of life"). This premise states that man *cannot* achieve his values; that successes, though possible, are an exception; that the rule of human life is failure and misery.

Like any conscious creature, a man on the benevolent-universe premise is well acquainted with pain. His insignia, however, is his refusal to take pain seriously, his refusal to grant it metaphysical significance. To him, pleasure is a revelation of reality—the reality where life is possible. But pain is merely a stimulus to corrective action, and to the question such action presupposes. The question is not "What's the use?" but "What can I do?"

> We do not think that tragedy is our natural fate and we do not live in chronic dread of disaster [explains a character in *Atlas Shrugged*]. We do not expect disaster until we have specific reason to expect it—and when we encounter it, we are free to fight it. It is not happiness, but suffering that we consider unnatural.[19]

This view of the world becomes in due course a self-fulfilling prophecy (as does its opposite). The man who refuses to blame his problems on reality thereby keeps alive his only means of solving them.

The benevolent-universe premise has nothing to do with "optimism," if this means Leibniz's idea that "all is for the best." A great many things in the human realm are clearly for the worst. Nor does the premise mean that "the truth will prevail," unless one adds the critical word "ultimately." Nor is benevolence the attitude of a Pollyanna; it is not the pretense that there is always a chance of success, even in those situations where there isn't any. The corrective to all these errors, however, is not "pessimism," which is merely another form of pretense.

The corrective is realism, i.e., the recognition of reality, along with the knowledge of life that this brings: the knowledge that happiness, though scarce, is no miracle. It is scarce because it is a culmination that only a demanding cause, moral and philosophical, can produce. It is no miracle because, when the cause is enacted, its effect follows naturally—and inevitably.

Sex as Metaphysical

I shall consider sex first as it functions in the life of a rational man.

A rational man needs not merely to know intellectually that he is good and the universe auspicious, but to experience in the form of a consummate emotion the full reality of these two facts, which are essential to his action and survival. Happiness in the sense of metaphysical pleasure, we have said, is an enduring affective leitmotif, a positive background conditioning one's daily joys and sorrows. This kind of pleasure is too vital to remain always a mere background. Sometimes, as an intense state of exultation, it itself becomes the focus of consciousness.

Sex, in Ayn Rand's identification, is "a celebration of [one]self and of existence"; it is a celebration of one's power to gain values and of the world in which one gains them. Sex, therefore, is a form of feeling happiness, but from a special perspective. Sex is the rapture of experiencing emotionally two interconnected achievements: self-esteem and the benevolent-universe conviction.[20]

Sexual feeling is a sum; it presupposes all of a rational man's moral values and his love for them, including his love for the partner who embodies them. The essential meaning of such a feeling is not social, but metaphysical; it pertains not to any single value or love, but to the profound concern involved in all value pursuit: the relationship between a man and reality. Sex is a unique form of answering the supreme question of a volitional being: can I live? The man of self-esteem, using cognitive, conceptual terms, concludes in his own mind that the answer is yes. When he makes love, he knows that yes without words, as a passion coursing through his body.

Sex is a physical capacity in the service of a *spiritual* need. It reflects not man's body alone nor his mind alone, but their integration. As in all such cases, the mind is the ruling factor.

There is a biological basis of human sexuality and a counterpart in the animal world. But all animal needs and pleasures are transfigured in the context of the rational animal. This is apparent even in regard to such simple needs as food and shelter. Human beings, precisely to the extent that they have attained human stature, gain comparatively little enjoyment from the mere sensation of satisfying these needs. Their pleasure comes mostly from the accompanying emotions. It comes from the constellation of conceptually formulated values that define the needs' *human* satisfaction. Thus the joys of haute cuisine with special friends amid crystal and tapestries in a fine restaurant, or of beef stew and a glass of wine with a loving wife in one's own dining room, as against the act, equally nutritious and shielded from the elements though it may be, of chewing a piece of meat in a vacant cave somewhere. The principle is that a pleasure which was once purely biological becomes, in the life of a conceptual being, largely spiritual. The principle applies preeminently to sex. No human pleasure as intense as that of sex can be dominantly a matter of physical sensation. Dominantly, sex is an emotion; and the cause of emotion is intellectual.

The fact that a man's sex life is shaped by his conclusions and value-judgments is evident in every aspect. It is evident in the setting he prefers, the state of dress, the caresses, positions, and practices, and the kind of partner. This last is particularly eloquent.

No man desires everyone on earth. Each has some requirements in this regard, however contradictory or unidentified—and the rational man's requirements, here as elsewhere, are the opposite of contradictory. He desires only a woman he can admire, a woman who (to his knowledge) shares his moral standards, his self-esteem, and his view of life. Only with such a partner can he experience the reality of the values he is seeking to celebrate, including his own value. The same kind of sexual selectivity is exercised by a rational woman. This is why Roark is attracted only to a heroine like Dominique, and why Dagny Taggart in *Atlas Shrugged* is desperate to sleep with John Galt, not with Wesley Mouch. Romantic love is the strongest positive emotion possible between two individuals. Its experience, therefore, so far from being an animal reaction, is a self-revelation: the values giving rise to this kind of response must be one's most intensely held and personal.

When a man and woman do fall in love—assuming that each is romantically free and the context otherwise appropriate—sex is a necessary and proper expression of their feeling for each other. "Platonic love" under such circumstances would be a vice, a breach of integrity.[21] Sex is to love what action is to thought, possession to evaluation, body to soul. "We live in our minds," Roark observes, "and existence is the attempt to bring that life into physical reality, to state it in gesture and form."[22] Sex is the preeminent form of bringing love into physical reality.

The subject of sex is complex and belongs largely to the science of psychology. I asked Ayn Rand once what philosophy specifically has to say on the subject. She answered: "It says that sex is *good.*"

Sex is moral, it is an exalted pleasure, it is a profound value. Like happiness, therefore, sex is an end in itself; it is not necessarily a means to any further end, such as procreation. This uplifted view of sex leads to an ethical corollary: a function so important must be granted the respect it deserves.

To respect sex means to approach it objectively. The guiding principle should be: select a partner whom you love on the basis of *values* you can identify and defend; then do whatever you wish together in bed, provided that it is mutually desired *and* that your pleasures are reality-oriented. This excludes indiscriminate sexual indulgence and any form of destructiveness or faking—such as, among other examples, the chaser's promiscuity, the rapist's coercion, the adulterer's pretense of fidelity, and the sadist's pretense that his power to cause suffering is a mark of efficacy. (Fantasy, in sex as in other departments of life, is a form of imagination and thus legitimate, as long as one does not drop the distinction between fantasy and reality.)

The guiding principle in sex should be: esteem sex as an expression of reason and of man's life in the full, moral sense of the term; then, keeping this context in mind, pursue the value greedily.

Such a viewpoint is the opposite of today's dominant philosophy on the subject.

Intrinsicism damns sex outright. It holds that love is a relationship between two souls that is not to be sullied by connection to the body. In this view, sex—like wealth, pleasure, and life itself—has nothing to do with reason or the conceptual faculty; it is selfish, "animalistic," "materialistic." Such a function can be justified only as a necessary evil, a means to procreation. The true idealists among men, accordingly, such as priests and nuns, will stay morally pure by practicing celibacy. As to the rest of humanity, the guidance it needs is a scroll of prohibitions: no premarital sex, no divorce, no oral intercourse, no masturbation, no contraception, no abortion.

These prohibitions are an act of war against mankind. They are the formal declaration that joy is a crime.

"Only the man who extols the purity of a love devoid of desire," writes Ayn Rand, "is capable of the depravity of a desire devoid of love."[23] This brings us to the typical subjectivist approach to sex. The subjectivist, too, severs concepts from percepts and holds that sex is a mere sensory reaction, devoid of intellectual cause. But he tells men to go ahead and revel in it, to grab whatever animalistic sensations they want without reference to principles or standards. In this theory, love is a myth, and sex is merely a wriggling of meat. So anything goes that satisfies anybody's whim—whenever he feels like it, wherever, however, and with whomever or whatever he decides to pick up.

The basic identity of these two viewpoints is obvious. I do want to note, however, the glee with which both schools, pursuant to their basic interpretation, consign sexual attraction to the domain of chemistry, hormones, an inexplicable "spark," or something else, something—anything—which is not man's chosen values, anything which allows people to go on insisting that "love is blind." This glee is a form of triumph; it is the irrationalist's pleasure at the supposed impotence in a crucial realm of his enemy: man's mind.

People whose souls are formed by such philosophies—along with those who reach the same moral dead end on their own, without benefit of explicit ideas—approach sex differently from the rational man. If one lacks self-esteem and regards the universe as malevolent, he has no cause for metaphysical celebration. But his need for self-esteem remains. Such an individual may pretend that compliance with sexual taboos indicates a higher virtue on his part. Far more often in the modern West, however, his kind practices sex uninhibitedly, but seeks to reverse cause and effect while doing so. These men seek to make sex not the expression of self-esteem, but the means of gaining it (usually through the partner's approval or submission).[24] One cannot, however, gain self-esteem by such means, so sex becomes an act of faking and of escapism. It becomes not the joy of affirming a benevolent universe, but a momentary diminution of the anxiety caused by a malevolent-universe premise. In this sort of approach, too, sexual desire is a self-revelation. The man who attempts such a fraud with an uncoerced partner has to feel that she will go along with it, that she is on his spiritual level or even lower.

Proper human sex, by contrast, requires men and women of stature, in regard both to moral character and metaphysical outlook. It is to such individuals that Ayn Rand is referring when she writes, in summation, that man's spirit "gives meaning to insentient matter by molding it to serve one's chosen goal." This kind of course, she continues, leads one

> to the moment when, in answer to the highest of one's values, in an admiration not to be expressed by any other form of tribute, one's spirit makes one's body become the tribute, recasting it—as proof, as sanction, as reward—into a single sensation of such intensity of joy that no other sanction of one's existence is necessary.[25]

This is what should come to your mind when you think of "morality"—this kind of ecstasy and the intellectual creativity at its root and the thing at *its* root: the fact of man the hero facing nature as a conqueror; not chastity and poverty and groveling before ghosts.

The individual who gains these Objectivist values does not say "There but for the grace of God go I." He earned what he has, and he knows it.

▪   ▪   ▪   ▪

Practicality, happiness, the sexual celebration of life—all these are effects, which presuppose the necessary cause. To attain any of them in unbreached form, one must be guided by a certain philosophy.

In metaphysics, one must regard this world as real and as the only reality; otherwise one will undercut one's ability to deal with the world and will build into one's soul a sense of impending defeat. In epistemology, one must regard reason as unqualifiedly valid; otherwise one will lose confidence in one's only means of reaching one's goals. In ethics, one must hold values compatible with man's life as the standard; otherwise one cannot believe that values are achievable.

Every system of philosophy, admittedly or not, leads to some kind of emotional summation, some culminating feeling about man and life. This feeling may be regarded as a litmus test, which reveals the system's relation to reality and thus its essence and merit.

On the negative side, one thinks here of the catalogue of woes that Augustine offers in the *City of God,* the litany of diseases, disasters, and calamities that fills his mind and his pages when he considers the subject of man's life on earth. As to our own century, one thinks of his agonized heirs, the Existentialists—of their preoccupation with fear and trembling, *Ängst,* death, nothingness, nausea. The emotional outlook of this whole axis, whether religious or secular, ancient or modern, is captured eloquently in a remark of Schopenhauer (an avowed mystic and altruist). "Whatever one may say," he writes, "the happiest moment of the happy man is the moment of his falling asleep, and the unhappiest moment of the unhappy that of his waking. . . . Human life must be some kind of mistake."

There is surely a mistake here. But it is not life.

An opposite kind of philosophy exists and leads to the opposite feeling about man and life. The outstanding classical exponent of this philosophy is Aristotle. I am thinking specifically of the serenity of his "great-souled man" and of Aristotle's conviction that eudaimonia is the human entelechy. The natural and proper human end, to which all rational endeavors contribute, Aristotle holds, is a state of rich, ripe, fulfilling earthly happiness.

The litmus test indicating Ayn Rand's approach in this issue is the heroes of her novels—the heroes, and the joyous, sunlit world they inhabit.

A rational philosophy, like a process of virtue, actually works. It *is* practical—if the thing one wishes to reach is that which is man's birthright: the gaiety of an innocent, soaring spirit reveling in a benevolent universe.

10

GOVERNMENT

Politics, like ethics, is a normative branch of philosophy. Politics defines the principles of a proper social system, including the proper functions of government.

Living in society is a value to man if it is the right kind of society. The wrong kind, like any wrong course of action, is a threat to man, and can be fatal.

There is only one standard to guide a thinker in defining the "right" social system: man's code of moral values, i.e., the principles of ethics. Politics rests on ethics (and thus on metaphysics and epistemology); it is an application of ethics to social questions. Politics, therefore, is a conclusion drawn from all the fundamentals of a philosophic system; it is not the system's start or any kind of primary. This is true of every theory of politics, no matter where it stands in the ideological spectrum.

What type of society conforms to or reflects the principles of morality?—this is the question asked by philosophical politics. Given the Objectivist morality, the question becomes: what type of society conforms to the requirements of man's life? What type makes possible the virtues we have been studying? What type represents the supremacy of reason?

Individual Rights as Absolutes

The basic principle of politics, according to Objectivism, is the principle endorsed by America's Founding Fathers: individual *rights*.

"Rights," states Ayn Rand,

> are a moral concept—the concept that provides a logical transition from the principles guiding an individual's actions to the principles guiding his relationship with others—the concept that preserves and protects individual morality in a social context—the link between the moral code of a man and the legal code of a society, between ethics and politics. *Individual rights are the means of subordinating society to moral law.* [1]

A "right," in Ayn Rand's definition, "is a moral principle defining and sanctioning a man's freedom of action in a social context." A right is a sanction to independent action; the opposite of acting by right is acting by *permission*. If someone borrows your pen, you set the terms of its use. When he returns it, no one can set the terms for you; you use it by right. [2]

A right is a prerogative that cannot be *morally* infringed or alienated. Factually, criminals are possible; innocent men can be robbed or enslaved. In such cases, however, the victim's rights are still inalienable: the right remains on the side of the victim; the criminal is *wrong*.

If a man lived on a desert island, there would be no question of defining his proper relationship to others. Even if men interacted on some island but did so at random, without establishing a social system, the issue of rights would be premature. There would not yet be any context for the concept or, therefore, any means of implementing it; there would be no agency to interpret, apply, enforce it. When men do decide to form (or reform) an organized society, however, when they decide to pursue systematically the advantages of living together, then they need the guidance of principle. That is the context in which the principle of rights arises. If your society is to be moral (and therefore practical), it declares, you must begin by recognizing the *moral requirements* of man in a social context; i.e., you must define the sphere of sovereignty mandated for every individual by the laws of morality. Within this sphere, the individual acts without needing any agreement or approval from others, nor may any others interfere.

In content, as the Founding Fathers recognized, there is one fundamental right, which has several major derivatives. The fundamental right is the right to life. Its major derivatives are the right to liberty, property, and the pursuit of happiness.

The right to life means the right to sustain and protect one's life. It means the right to take all the actions required by the nature of a rational being for the preservation of his life. To sustain his life, man needs a method of survival—he must use his rational faculty to gain knowledge and choose values, then act to achieve his values. The right to liberty is the right to this method; it is the right to think and choose, then to act in accordance with one's judgment. To sustain his life, man needs to create the material means of his survival. The right to property is the right to this process; in Ayn Rand's definition, it is "the right to gain, to keep, to use and to dispose of material values." To sustain his life, man needs to be governed by a certain motive—his purpose must be his own welfare. The right to the pursuit of happiness is the right to this motive; it is the right to live for one's *own* sake and fulfillment.[3]

Rights form a logical unity. In the words of Samuel Adams, all are "evident branches of, rather than deductions from, the duty of self-preservation, commonly called the first law of nature." It would be a crude contradiction to tell a man: you have a right to life, but you need the permission of others to think or act. Or: you have a right to life, but you need the permission of others to produce or consume. Or: you have a right to life, but don't dare pursue any personal motive without the approval of the government.

The rights to life, liberty, and the pursuit of happiness, though misinterpreted and implicitly denied by today's intellectuals, are still given some lip service in the West. The right to property, however, is regularly opposed; private property, the intellectuals claim, clashes with the very principle of human rights. Ayn Rand answers this claim eloquently:

> Just as man can't exist without his body, so no rights can exist without the right to translate one's rights into reality—to think, to work and to keep the results—which means: the right of property. The modern mystics of muscle who offer you the fraudulent alternative of "human rights" versus "property rights," as if one could exist without the other, are making a last, grotesque attempt to revive the doctrine of soul versus body. Only a ghost can exist without material property; only a slave can work with no right to the product of his effort. The doctrine that "human rights" are superior to "property rights" simply means that some human beings have the right to make property out of others; since the competent have nothing to gain from the incompetent, it means the right of the incompetent to own their betters and to use them as productive cattle. Whoever regards this as human and right, has no right to the title of "human."[4]

Since man is an integrated being of mind and body, every right entails every other; none is definable or possible apart from the rest. There can be no right to think apart from the right to act: thinking (for a rational man) is a guide to action; the process consists in setting the ends and the means of one's action through the identification of facts and of values. Similarly, there can be no right to act apart from the right to own: action requires the use of material objects (even the act of speaking requires a patch of ground on which to stand). Freedom—like man—*is* indivisible. Or, in Ayn Rand's words: *"Intellectual* freedom cannot exist without *political* freedom; political freedom cannot exist without *economic* freedom; *a free mind and a free market are corollaries."*[5]

Turning now to the question of logical validation: since they are not primaries, man's rights require proof through the appropriate process of reduction. In the Objectivist approach, the nature of such reduction is readily apparent. Each of man's rights has a specific source in the Objectivist ethics and, beneath that, in the Objectivist view of man's metaphysical nature (which in turn rests on the Objectivist metaphysics and epistemology). Man is a certain kind of living organism—

which leads to his need of morality and to man's life being the moral standard—which leads to the right to act by the guidance of this standard, i.e., the right to life. Reason is man's basic means of survival—which leads to rationality being the primary virtue—which leads to the right to act according to one's judgment, i.e., the right to liberty. Unlike animals, man does not survive by adjusting to the given—which leads to productiveness being a cardinal virtue—which leads to the right to keep, use, and dispose of the things one has produced, i.e., the right to property. Reason is an attribute of the individual, one that demands, as a condition of its function, unbreached allegiance to reality—which leads to the ethics of egoism—which leads to the right to the pursuit of happiness.

Since a proper philosophy is an integrated system, each right rests not merely on a single ethical or metaphysical principle, but on all the principles just mentioned (and ultimately on all the principles, from every branch of philosophy, which precede the issue of rights).

All rights rest on the fact that man's life is the moral standard. Rights are rights to the kinds of actions necessary for the preservation of human life. Just as "it is only the concept of 'life' that makes the concept of 'value' possible," so it is only the requirements of *man's* life that make morality, and thus the concept of "rights," possible.

All rights rest on the fact that man survives by means of reason. Rights are rights to the actions necessary for the preservation of a *rational* being. Only an entity with a conceptual faculty has judgment on which to act, volition with which to select goals, and intelligence with which to create wealth.

All rights rest on the fact that man is a productive being. Rights presume that men can live together without anyone's sacrifice. If man merely consumed objects provided in a static quantity by nature, every man would be a potential threat to every other. In such a case, the rule of life would have to be that which governs the lower species: seize what you can before others get it, eat or be eaten, kill or be killed.

All rights rest on the ethics of egoism. Rights are an individual's *selfish* possessions—his title to *his* life, his liberty, his property, the pursuit of his own happiness. Only a being who is an end in himself can claim a moral sanction to independent action. If man existed to serve an entity beyond himself, whether God or society, then he would not have rights, but only the duties of a servant.

Whoever understands the philosophy of Objectivism (or implicitly accepts an Aristotelian morality of self-interest, as was done by the political thinkers of the Enlightenment), can read off the proper human rights effortlessly; this may cause him to regard such rights, in the wording of the Declaration of Independence, as "self-evident." Rights, however, are not self-evident. They are corollaries of ethics as applied to social organization—if one holds the right ethics. If one does not, none of them stands.

The rights to life, liberty, property, and the pursuit of happiness are the only rights treated by philosophical politics. They are the only rights formulated in terms of broad abstractions and resting directly on universal ethical principles. The numerous applications and implementations of these rights, such as freedom of the press or trial by jury or the other prerogatives detailed in the Bill of Rights, belong to the field of philosophy of law and require for their validation a process of reduction to man's philosophic rights.

By its nature, the concept of a "right" pertains, in Ayn Rand's words, "only to action—specifically, to freedom of action. It means freedom from physical compulsion, coercion or interference by other men." Since each man is obliged to be self-sustaining, no one has a right to the actions or products of *other men* (unless he earns that right through a process of voluntary trade). A right is not a claim to assistance or a guarantee of success; if what one seeks involves the activity of other men, it is their right to choose whether to cooperate or not. A man's rights impose no duties on others, but only a negative obligation: others may not properly violate his rights.[6]

The right to life is the right to a process of self-preservation; it does not mean that other people must give a person food when he is hungry, medicine when he is sick, or a job when he is unemployed. The right to liberty does not mean that others must satisfy a person's desires or even agree to deal with him at all. The right to property does not mean the right to be given property by the government, but to produce and thereby earn it. The right to the *pursuit* of happiness is precisely that: pursuit is not necessarily attainment. Otherwise, one could claim that his fellows, by withholding their favors, are destroying his happiness and thereby infringing his rights. What then would become of *their* rights?

If rights are defined in rational terms, no conflict is possible between the rights of one individual and those of another. Every man is sovereign. He is absolutely free within the sphere of his own rights, and every man has the same rights.[7]

If one detaches the concept of "rights" from reason and reality, however, then nothing but conflict is possible, and the theory of "rights" self-destructs. Just as bad principles drive out good, so false rights, reflecting bad principles, drive out proper rights—a process that is running wild today in the proliferation of such self-contradictory verbiage as "economic rights," "collective rights," "fetal rights," and "animal rights."

"Economic rights" in this context means a man's right, simply by virtue of existing, to man-made goods and services, such as food, clothing, a home, a job, education, day care, medical care, a pension. All such claims involve a contradiction: if my right to life entails a right to your labor or its product, you cannot have a right to liberty or property. If my unearned claim is not satisfied, my "right" is violated; if it is satisfied—as a matter of right, regardless of your choice—then your right to life is violated; you become a rightless creature, who functions by my or society's permission. Free milk for part of the population, as one political theorist puts the point, means slave labor for the rest. The "right to enslave," Ayn Rand observes, is a contradiction in terms; it means the right to infringe rights.[8]

The rights of man subsume "economic" prerogatives only in the form of the right to property, and of the rights to free association and free trade (as aspects of liberty). "Economic rights" in any other sense means the destruction of the concept "rights." Such a notion represents the attempt, deriving from the ethics of self-sacrifice, to turn a man's *needs* into duties imposed on others; this is an inversion that in a single stroke wipes out the essence of virtue for both parties, needer and needed. Virtue, as we know, is self-generated, self-sustaining action.

"Collective rights" means rights belonging to a group qua group, rights allegedly independent of those possessed by the individual. Thus we hear of the special rights of businessmen, workers, farmers, consumers, the young, the old, the students, the females, the race, the class, the nation, the public. The spokesmen of such groups present demands that violate legitimate rights, either of individuals outside the group and/or of those inside it. The demands range from financial favors to special powers to outright slaughter. Like the theory of "economic rights," all such collectivist variants reflect the ethics of self-sacrifice; all the variants divide men into beneficiaries and servants, masters and slaves, and thus negate the concept of "rights," substituting for it the principle of mob rule.[9]

"A group," Miss Rand observes,

> can have no rights other than the rights of its individual members. In a free society, the "rights" of any group are derived from the rights of its members through their voluntary, individual choice and *contractual* agreement, and are merely the application of these individual rights to a specific undertaking. . . .
>
> A group, as such, has no rights. A man can neither acquire new rights by joining a group nor lose the rights which he does possess. The principle of individual rights is the only moral base of all groups or associations.

"Individual rights," in short, is a redundancy, albeit a necessary one in today's intellectual chaos. Only the individual has rights.[10]

Just as there are no rights of collections of individuals, so there are no rights of *parts* of individuals—no rights of arms or of tumors or of any piece of tissue growing within a woman, even if it has the capacity to become in time a human being. A potentiality is not an actuality, and a fertilized ovum, an embryo, or a fetus is not a human being. Rights belong only to man—and men are entities, organisms that are biologically formed and physically separate from one another. That which lives within the body of another can claim no prerogatives against its host.[11]

Responsible parenthood involves decades devoted to the child's proper nurture. To sentence a woman to bear a child against her will is an unspeakable violation of *her* rights: her right to liberty (to the functions of her body), her right to the pursuit of happiness, and, sometimes, her right to life itself, even as a serf. Such a sentence represents the sacrifice of the actual to the potential, of a real human being to a piece of protoplasm, which has no life in the human sense of the term.[12] It is sheer perversion of language for people who demand this sacrifice to call themselves "right-to-lifers."

The climax (to date) of the campaign against "rights" is the detachment of the concept from the human species altogether, i.e., the claim that *animals* have rights.

Rights are moral rules enjoining persuasion as against coercion, and there is no way of applying morality to the amoral or persuasion to the nonconceptual. An animal needs no validation of its behavior; it does not act by right or by permission; it perceives objects, then simply reacts as it must. In dealing with such organisms, there is no applicable law but the law of the jungle, the law of force against force.

An animal (by nature) is concerned only with its survival; man (by choice) must be concerned only with *his*—which requires that he establish dominance over the lower species. Some of these are threats to his life and must be exterminated; others serve as sources of food or clothing, as subjects of medical research, even as objects of recreation or surrogate friendship (pets). By its nature and throughout the animal kingdom, life survives by feeding on life. To demand that man defer to the "rights" of *other* species is to deprive man himself of the right to life. This is "other-ism," i.e., altruism, gone mad.

A man must respect the freedom of human beings for a selfish reason: he stands to benefit enormously from their rational actions. But a man gains nothing from respecting the "freedom" of animals; on the contrary, such a policy would seriously jeopardize his survival. How can man morally inflict pain on other species or treat them as means to his own ends? He can do it, Objectivism replies, when such treatment is necessary or advisable as judged by the standard of morality; he can do it because *man's* needs are the root of the concept "moral." The source of rights, as of virtues, is not the sensory-perceptual level of consciousness, but the conceptual level. The source is not the capacity to experience pain, but the capacity to think.

There are no rights *to* the labor of other men, and no rights *of* groups, parts, or nonhumans. There are only the rights of man, his right to pursue on his own a certain course of action.

The rights of man, Ayn Rand holds, can be violated by one means only: by the initiation of physical force (including its indirect forms, such as fraud). One cannot expropriate a man's values, or prevent him from pursuing values, or enslave him in any manner at all, except by the use of physical force. Whoever refrains from such initiation—whatever his virtues or vices, knowledge or errors—necessarily leaves the *rights* of others unbreached.[13]

Although earlier thinkers, including the Founding Fathers, often implied the above, they did not identify it explicitly. This represented a lacuna in the theory of rights that made its consistent application to reality impossible. Thus, if a man has no education, no formal training in how to choose or act, many Enlightenment thinkers believed, he will not know how to exercise his right to liberty; this belief led to the advocacy of state schooling as a means of protecting rights. Or, a century later: if a man cannot compete in a field because of the economic power of those already established in it, conservative Republicans declared, his liberty is thereby reduced; this belief led to the major forerunner of twentieth-century American statism: the Sherman Antitrust Act of 1890. The supposed defenders of liberty in these cases made no attempt to point to anyone's use of physical force; there was *no* recognized principle to guide them in their momentous interpretations, no principle to define what constitutes the infringement or protection of rights. Hence the door was open to the Hegelian idea that compulsion—compulsory schooling, compulsory taxation, compulsory competition, and so on—is the means to freedom; i.e., the door was open to the destruction of the concept of "rights."

Ayn Rand's discovery that rights can be violated only by the use of physical force is historic. It is essential to the proper completion of the theory of rights, giving men, for the first time, the means to implement the theory *objectively*. The violator of rights, in her view, is not to be detected by "intuition," feeling, or vote; his action is a tangible fact, available in principle to sense perception. The protection of rights, accordingly, involves a single function: protecting the innocent from such action.

Ayn Rand's grasp, in politics, of the relationship between rights and force flows from her grasp, in ethics, of the *moral* evil of physical force. Force, her ethics teaches, is a form of action—the only one—which paralyzes and negates the victim's mind. It is thus the only evil one man can perpetrate against another which negates the victim's tool of survival, i.e., which literally stops the action of human self-preservation, i.e., which contradicts the *right* to live.

An individual can be hurt in countless ways by other men's irrationality, dishonesty, injustice. Above all, he can be disappointed, perhaps grievously, by the vices of a person he had once trusted or loved. But as long as his property is not expropriated and he remains unmolested physically, the damage he sustains is essentially spiritual, not physical; in such a case, the victim alone has the power and the responsibility of healing his wounds. He remains free: free to think, to learn from his experiences, to look elsewhere for human relationships; he remains free to start afresh and to pursue his happiness. Only the crime of force is able to render its victim helpless. The moral responsibility of organized society, therefore, lies in a single obligation: to banish this crime, i.e., to protect individual rights.

Reason has one and only one *social* requirement: freedom—such is the essence of the case for man's rights. Metaphysically, the individual is sovereign (he is a being of self-made soul). Ethically, he is obliged to live as a sovereign (as an independent egoist). Politically, therefore, he must be able to act as a sovereign.

Men can choose not to recognize rights, just as they can choose to discard morality or evade reality; but they cannot choose it with impunity. Both in theory and in blood-soaked practice, there is only one alternative to freedom: men's attempt to live while defying reason's requirements. This means the attempt to survive without a tool of survival.

Rights are *objective* principles; they are objective in regard both to content and to validation. "[T]he source of man's rights," states Ayn Rand,

is not divine law or congressional law, but the law of identity. A is A—and Man is Man. *Rights* are conditions of existence required by man's nature for his proper survival.

> If man is to live on earth, it is *right* for him to use his
> mind, it is *right* to act on his own free judgment, it is *right*
> to work for his values and to keep the product of his work.
> If life on earth is his purpose, he has a- *right* to live as a
> rational being: nature forbids him the irrational.[11]

Here again we see at work the primacy-of-existence orientation. The world, including man, *is* a certain way; therefore,
if man wishes to survive, he must act accordingly.

In a primacy-of-consciousness philosophy, by contrast,
rights, if endorsed at all, are derived from the edicts of consciousness.

The individual, says the intrinsicist who accepts rights, is
God's creation and therefore His property, not the collective's. Such an approach implies a denial of rights; it means
that only God is morally sovereign. In practice, this leads to
the conclusion that man on earth may be used and disposed
of by God's representatives on earth.

No religious society has ever cherished or protected individual freedom, which is a purely secular value and achievement. Rights, contrary to a formulation common during the
Enlightenment, do not derive from man's source or "creator." They derive from the fact of man's existence and the
requirements of his survival, however he came into being.

In the (social) subjectivist variant, the source of rights is
the feelings or laws of the group. This represents an explicit
denial of rights. In this view, a man's "rights" are nothing but
permissions granted to him (temporarily) by other men.

In truth, rights are earthly and absolute at the same time,
because their source is neither God nor the group, but reality;
reality, plus the choice to remain in it.

"Individualism" means emphasis on the individual. Subjectivists of the personal variety use the term to denote and
sanction whim-worship. Ayn Rand, however, uses the term
within the context of her basic premises. "Individualism" is
the view that, in social issues, the individual is the unit of
value; this is a moral corollary of the principle that each man
is an end in himself. Politically, as an expression of this approach, an "individualist" social system is one that upholds
individual rights.

The opposite of individualism is any morality that values

something—anything—above man the individual, and any politics that places any consideration above individual rights. If we set aside the alleged claims of God, animals, or the ozone layer to preeminence in this connection, then the philosophical competitor of individualism is collectivism. Collectivism is an application to politics of the ethics of altruism. Since man exists only to serve other men, it says, individual rights are a myth; the group is the unit of value and the bearer of sovereignty.

No one can turn man into a cog of society; not into a *thinking* cog. All that one can accomplish by the attempt is to destroy man. A collectivist system, therefore, like any form of irrationality, is necessarily self-defeating, no matter what its specific policies or leaders. Evil is impotent in every version and in every field, politics included.

Ayn Rand is more realistic than the panicky anti-communists of the Cold War era, who trembled before the alleged practicality of dictatorship. The best symbol of this issue is the contrast between two projections of a collectivist future: George Orwell's *1984* vs. Ayn Rand's *Anthem* (which was published more than a decade earlier, in 1938). Orwell regards freedom as a luxury; he believes that one can wipe out every vestige of free thought, yet still maintain an industrial civilization. Whose mind is maintaining it? Blank out. *Anthem,* by contrast, shows us "social cogs" who have retrogressed, both spiritually and materially, to the condition of primitives. When men lose the freedom to think, Ayn Rand understands, they lose the products of thought as well.

The historical evidence in support of Ayn Rand's position keeps piling up. The latest piece (1990) is the worldwide shambles of communism. The victims of Marx, without understanding or ideology, are fleeing for their lives to some form of market economy. Without freedom, even the Soviet leaders now admit, a country has no future but starvation.

For seventy-five years, when confronted by the failures of collectivism, the intellectuals of the West have taken refuge in the mind-body dichotomy. Socialism or communism, they say, is noble in theory, but it is not practical. It surely is not practical. The reason is that it is false and vicious *in theory*.

The individual is an autonomous entity, whose rights are an absolute. This is a fact which cannot be rewritten. It is the fact with which any true and noble political theory must begin.

Government as an Agency to Protect Rights

If society as an organized body is to protect man's rights, the citizens must create an agency with the power to do the job. Since force can be stopped only by force, such an agency must banish coercion by itself using force against the force-wielders. This agency is the *government*.

"A government," in Ayn Rand's definition, "is an institution that holds the exclusive power to *enforce* certain rules of social conduct in a given geographical area."[15] In reason, such a power cannot be a primary. Government is a social creation, and society consists of individuals. Any powers of government, therefore, must derive from those of the individuals who create it.

In a proper society, the government is the servant of the citizens, not their ruler. Specifically, it is the agent of man's self-defense. An agent of self-defense may not initiate force against innocent men. It has a single power, one inherent in the individual's right to life: the power to use force in *retaliation* and only against those persons (or nations) who start its use.

By its nature, government has a monopoly on the use of force. In a rational society, individuals agree to delegate their right of self-defense; they renounce the private use of physical force even in self-protection (except during those emergencies that require action at once, before the police can be summoned). If a society is to uphold man's rights, such delegation is essential.[16]

If men did not delegate the task of self-defense to a central agency, every individual would have to live and work armed, ready to shoot any stranger who looked suspicious (and who in turn would be ready to shoot him)—or, much more likely, men would form packs to protect themselves from other, similar packs, and the result would be gang wars and mob rule. In either case, peaceful coexistence among men would be impossible.

Physical force is the power of destruction. A rational society cannot exist if a man is free to unleash such a threat against others as and when he chooses. This applies whatever the threatener's knowledge and character, whether he is informed or ignorant, judicious or rash, just or unjust. The "use of force against one man," states Ayn Rand, "cannot be left to the arbitrary decision of another."[17]

A society must remove the retaliatory use of force methodically from the realm of whim. Every aspect of such use must be defined in advance, validated, codified: under what conditions force can be employed, by whom, against whom, in what forms, to what extent. The nonarbitrary use of force requires, in Ayn Rand's words,

> *objective* rules of evidence to establish that a crime has been committed and to *prove* who committed it, as well as *objective* rules to define punishments and enforcement procedures. Men who attempt to prosecute crimes, without such rules, are a lynch mob. . . .
>
> *A government is the means of placing the retaliatory use of physical force under objective control*—i.e., under objectively defined laws.
>
> . . . [A government] should be an impersonal robot, with the laws as its only motive power.[18]

If men are to be free, they need a government of a definite kind. Such a government is a government of laws and not of men.

The laws of a proper society are objective in regard to their validation and, as a result, in regard to their interpretation as well.[19] Since rational laws prohibit only crimes defined in terms of specific physical acts (physical force), the individual is able to know, prior to taking an action, whether or not the law forbids it and what the consequences of disobedience will be. The meaning of such laws is independent of the claims of any interpreter, in any branch of government; it can be grasped from the statement of the law itself. This stands in stark contrast to laws forbidding crimes that are not defined in terms of specific physical acts; e.g., laws against "blasphemy," "obscenity," "immorality," "restraint of trade," or "unfair profits." In all such examples, even when the terms are philosophically definable, it is not possible to know from the statement of the law what existential acts are forbidden. Men are reduced to guessing; they have to try to enter the mind of the legislator and divine his intentions, ideas, value-judgments, philosophy—which, given the nature of such legislation, are riddled with caprice. In practice, the meaning of such laws is decided arbitrarily, on a case-by-case basis, by tyrants, bureaucrats, or judges, according to methods that no one, including the interpreters, can define or predict.

Some concrete-bound laws are indefensible, yet still objectively definable; e.g., a law forbidding the sale of alcoholic beverages. But a government prone to such laws cannot legislate an infinite number of concretes; it has to rely at critical points on abstract formulations that derive ultimately from a nonobjective standard of ethics, such as the "will of God" or the "public welfare." In essence, therefore, the law of such a country is nonobjective in regard both to validation and to interpretation. The only *system* of laws that excludes every element of the nonobjective—of the indefensible *and* the unknowable—is one that confines legislation to the protection of rights.

Nonobjective law contradicts and defies the whole reason man needs government. Such law—in any variant, religious or social—represents a monopoly on the use of force granted to an agency ruled by whim. This means a government of men and not of laws, i.e., a formal authorization for the state to swallow up the citizens. In such a society, the right to life is discarded; men act by permission—and in terror.

Totalitarian theorists and leaders, understanding this point, insist on nonobjective legal codes. These men do not demand obedience only to knowable edicts, however vicious; they understand that an individual can still struggle to remain sovereign internally in such a case and conform only outwardly. The totalitarian goal is to inculcate servility—to make the citizens spend their lives trying to anticipate the government's next whim—to make men beat the ruler to the punch and obey his decrees before he gets around to decreeing them. This is a more potent method of breaking men's spirit than the policy of enacting cruel but clear-cut laws.

Coming back to a proper society: man's need for a "government of laws" extends beyond the issue of stopping criminals. Even if everyone were completely virtuous, disagreements among men would still be possible, because man is not omniscient or infallible. Two individuals can contract to trade their products yet, innocently, fail to understand the terms of their agreement in the same way. One person can then act on his understanding, honestly believing that justice is on his side, while the other honestly believes that the action violates his own rights. The immense field of civil law indicates the range and kinds of disagreements possible to noncriminals.

This leads to an essential function of government: the protection and enforcement of contracts, including the resolution of disputes that arise therefrom—their impartial resolution, in accordance with objectively defined laws. Under such a system, none of the parties needs to (or may) decide unilaterally that he is a victim with the onus of taking physical action to repair his interests. Here again the government acts to defend men's rights and thus to prevent any arbitrary use of physical force. Proper civil courts, Miss Rand observes, are "the most crucial need of a peaceful society." Criminals are a small minority; contractual protection for honest undertakings, however, is a daily necessity of civilized life.[20]

The purpose of government is to bar men's use of physical force against others for any reason—in part, by protecting men from aggressors, domestic or foreign; in part, by settling impartially disputes that involve men's rights.

This purpose entails three and only three governmental functions. In Ayn Rand's statement, these are: *"the police,* to protect men from criminals—*the armed services,* to protect men from foreign invaders—*the law courts,* to settle disputes among men according to objective laws."[21] Any additional function would have to involve the government initiating force against innocent citizens. Such a government acts not as man's protector, but as a criminal.

Government is inherently negative. The power of force is the power of destruction, not of creation, and it must be used accordingly, i.e., only to destroy destruction.[22] For a society to inject this power into any creative realm, spiritual or material, is a lethal contradiction: it is the attempt to use death as a means of sustaining life.

The above means, first of all, that the state must not intervene in the intellectual or moral life of its citizens. It has no standards to uphold and no benefits to confer in regard to education, literature, art, science, sex (if adult and voluntary), or philosophy. Its function is to protect freedom, not truth or virtue.

The right to think and act as one chooses necessarily includes the right to choose incorrectly, whether through ignorance or evasion (and then to suffer the consequences). An individual free to choose only what the government authorizes as correct has no freedom. A proper government is based on a definite philosophy, but it can play no role in promoting that philosophy. Such a responsibility belongs to private citizens, who can keep the right system only by exercising "eternal (ideological) vigilance." If the agency with a monopoly on coercion undertakes to enforce ideas, any ideas, whether true or false, it thereby reverses its function; it becomes the enemy, not the protector, of the free mind and thus loses its moral basis for existing.

In an intrinsicist or subjectivist approach to philosophy, virtue (along with truth, beauty, and all other human values) is divorced from the mind and therefore is attainable by means of force. In an objective approach, force and value are opposites. The goal of a proper society, accordingly, is not to compel truth or virtue (which would be a contradiction in terms), but to make them *possible*—by ensuring that men are left free.

For the same reason, the state must not intervene in another aspect of men's intellectual life: the realm of production and trade. The state must not undertake to provide men with economic standards or benefits, whether in regard to goods, services, or conditions of trade. A proper government offers freedom from coercion (including fraud), not from the responsibility of self-sustenance. It protects men from thieves, swindlers, and killers, not from reality or the need to create one's values by one's own mind and labor. Politicians, therefore, must have nothing to do with production or distribution; they may not build, manage, or regulate schools, hospitals, utilities, roads, parks, post offices, railroads, steel mills, banks, and the like, nor may they hand out subsidies, franchises, tariff protection, social insurance, minimum-living standards, minimum-wage laws for workers, parity laws for farmers, insider-trading laws for investors, fair-price laws for consumers, and so on. No one but the creator may dispose of the products of his thought or determine the process of creating them. In this field as in every other, the goal of a proper society is the opposite of compulsion. Here, too, the goal is to make value (in this instance, wealth) possible—through the protection of freedom.

Even in regard to its legitimate functions, a government may not justifiably initiate force. It must operate jails and military installations, but it may not demand that men serve in the police or the army against their own judgment, nor may it finance its activities by seizing property without the consent of the owners. (Rational methods of financing a government are discussed by Ayn Rand in chapter 15 of *The Virtue of Selfishness*.)

In a proper society, the citizens have rights, but the government does not. The government acts by permission, as expressed in a written constitution that limits public officials to defined functions and procedures. The first and best example of this approach was the original American system, with its brilliantly ingenious mechanism of checks and balances. There are some contradictions in the Constitution; in essence, however, its purpose was to protect the individual from two potential tyrants: the government and the mob. The system was designed to thwart both the power lust of any aspiring dictator and any momentary, corrupt passion on the part of the general public.

The Declaration of Independence and the Constitution are the greatest achievements in political history, and they dazzled the world for well over a century, until they were scuttled by an alien ideology. No political system, whatever its built-in safeguards, can survive the atrophy in the mind of the intellectuals of its basic philosophy.

The American system, as has often been stated by conservatives, was not a democracy, whether representative or direct, but a republic. (I use these terms as the Founding Fathers did.) "Democracy" means a system of unlimited majority rule; "unlimited" means unrestricted by individual rights. Such an approach is not a form of freedom, but of collectivism. A "republic," by contrast, is a system restricted to the protection of rights. In a republic, majority rule applies only to some details, like the selection of certain personnel.

Rights, however, remain an absolute; i.e., the principles governing the government are not subject to vote.

The "consent of the governed" is the source of a government's power, since government is an agent of its citizens.[23] But this does not mean that the citizens can delegate powers they do not possess. It does not mean that anything to which the governed consent is thereby proper or a proper function of government—which would be pure subjectivism and collectivism. In a republic, the governed may not rightfully strike down an innocent fellow-citizen, not in any form, even if the nation consents to it without a dissenting voice.

The source of a government's power is not arbitrary consent, but *rational* consent, based on an objective principle. The principle is the rights of man.

Statism as the Politics of Unreason

"Statism" means any system that concentrates power in the state at the expense of individual freedom. Among other variants, the term subsumes theocracy, absolute monarchy, Nazism, fascism, communism, democratic socialism, and plain, unadorned dictatorship. Such variants differ on matters of form, tactics, and/or ideology. Some statists nationalize the means of production; others allow the façade of private ownership but give the state control over the use and disposal of property. Some righteously practice a caste system; others, who also practice it, deny that they do. Some hold that free countries should move toward omnipotent government peacefully, by "evolution"; others cry for revolution. Some uphold statism on intrinsicist grounds (e.g., the divine right of kings, ayatollahs, or witch doctors); others invoke social subjectivism, citing the needs of the race, the nation, the class, mankind, or the tribe.

Some rulers oversee their subjects' every move. Others allow men a long leash. But all insist on *some* leash and on their right to set its length at will.

Some rulers concentrate on attaining thought control, deeming men's obedience in regard to action to be an inevitable but secondary consequence. Some, especially the types who despise thought as useless, concentrate on controlling men's actions through sheer brutality (and thereby *make* their subjects' thought useless). Still others concentrate on establishing public ownership of the means of production, and thereby outlaw independent action *and* thought.

Whatever the point of entry of such governments, the essence of their policy is the same: war against man—against his mind, body, and property alike. The result of such war has always been the manufacture of corpses. The corpses are an expression, in negative terms, of the principle that freedom is the social requirement of man's tool of survival.

Just as individualism is the politics demanded by reason, so statism is the politics of unreason. Just as a free system of government flows from and then fosters in its citizens a philosophy that accepts reality, the conceptual level of consciousness, egoism, productiveness, and man the self-made sovereign; so an unfree system flows from and fosters the opposite of such a philosophy.

Forty years ago, the identification of statism with unreason would have been hotly contested, especially by the political left. Not any more, as the heirs and admirers of the New Left of the 1960s make eloquently clear.[24]

The Old Left claimed to represent science and logic (albeit "dialectic" logic); the New Left opts for unabashed mysticism, such as religious revivals, parapsychology, Orientalism. The Old Left, deriding "pie in the sky," avowed its concern for men's physical well-being; the New Left, disdaining physical reality, pursues a new kind of pie in the sky: "consciousness expansion" through drug addiction. The Old Left admired machinery, material wealth, the conquest of nature (even if by and for the collective); the New Left, crying "Back to nature" and "Down with economic growth," regards human invention as unnatural, automobiles as "pollutants," and factories as a threat to the "fragile ecology" of the planet. The Old Left upheld the dignity of labor (physical labor) and demanded justice for the worker; the New Left turns a fondly nostalgic gaze not on any kind of worker, but on "polymorphous perverse" hippies.

The Old Left defended an ideology, a system, a long-range answer (however false) to social questions; the New Left, flaunting *anti*-ideology, is concrete-bound, NOW-worshiping, perceptual-level. The Old Left sought a government of law (as against a government of so-called "economic royalists"); the New Left regards law as exploitation and is calling for a government not of law, but of equalized pressure groups. The Old Left, invoking the value of fairness, legislated "equality of opportunity" (i.e., the welfare state); the New Left, dropping any pretense at fairness, wants "equality of results" (i.e., egalitarianism). The Old Left conveyed a certain breadth of vision (it spoke of "One World" or of the united proletariat); the New Left, unable even to daydream in such terms, wants neighborhood socialism; it wants the tribalism of *local* gang warfare, with one gang running the Bedford-Stuyvesant district in Brooklyn, another running Columbia University, and so on. *This* is the political bottom, which America's onetime "idealists" and "progressives" have finally hit.

The Old Left transmuted in this fashion because it was a solid philosophic contradiction, which could not be sustained. When confronted by this contradiction in inescapable terms in the 1960s, its members—those who did not retreat into a mumbling "moderation" or an embarrassed "neoconservatism"—chose according to their deepest premises. Being statists, they chose according to the actual philosophic meaning of statism. In Ayn Rand's summary:

> Confronted with the choice of an industrial civilization or collectivism, it is an industrial civilization that the liberals discarded. Confronted with the choice of technology or dictatorship, it is technology that they discarded. Confronted with the choice of reason or whims, it is reason that they discarded.[25]

Whoever, at this stage of the twentieth century, having seen the history of Russia, Germany, China, Iran, *and America,* still does not understand the philosophy, the cause, or the effect of statism will never do so. Such an individual does not choose to understand.

This brings me to another topic: to an alleged opposite of statism that, in fact, entails it. I mean *anarchism.*

Anarchism is the idea that there should be no government. In Objectivist terms, this amounts to the view that every man should defend himself by using physical force against others whenever he feels like it, with no objective standards of justice, crime, or proof.[26]

"What if an individual does not *want* to delegate his right of self-defense?" the anarchist frequently asks. "Isn't that a legitimate aspect of 'freedom'?" The question implies that a "free man" is one with the right to enact his desire, any desire, simply *because* it is his desire, including the desire to use force. This means the equation of "freedom" with whim-worship. Philosophically, the underlying premise is subjectivism (of the personal variety).

The citizens of a proper society should reply to such a subjectivist as follows: "Don't delegate your right of self-defense, if that is your choice. But if you act on your viewpoint—if you resort to the use of force against any of us—we will answer you by force. Our government will answer you, in the only terms you yourself make possible."

It is a contradiction to assert one's right to use force as one chooses, while demanding that others refrain from organizing to protect themselves. Whoever breaks the laws of a proper government, no matter what his philosophic reasons, becomes thereby a criminal, and men are morally bound to treat him as such.

Anarchists in America pretend to be individualists. Philosophically, however, anarchism is the opposite of individualism; as its main modern popularizer, Karl Marx, makes clear, anarchism is an expression of Utopian collectivism. In the Utopian view, the state by its nature is an exploitative, but temporary, aberration; after men are properly reconditioned, this aberration will disappear, along with all disputes and injustices; mankind will be suffused by loving harmony. The harmony will come when men learn at last to blend into the "organic" One or Whole that they really are. In other words, social problems and the need of government will wither away when individuality withers away.

The theory of anarchism does not recognize that honest disagreement and deliberate evil will always be possible to men; it does not grasp the need of any mechanism to enable real human beings to live together in harmony. The reason is that the theory has no place for real human beings, i.e., for individuals.

Leaving aside some close-knit, short-lived communes, an-

archism cannot even be tried in practice. *Anarchy,* the breakdown of law and order, is possible for a brief time, but not
anarchism as a guiding philosophy. The immediate result of
anarchy, assuming a society has no rational leadership, has to
be men's establishment of some semblance of order by means
of gang rule and/or the rule of a strongman. Even savages on
the perceptual level understand that lawless chaos is incompatible with survival.

If words have to stand for objects in reality, then the only
referent of "anarchism"—the only possible political system it
designates—is some variant of statism. This is why Objectivism dismisses as foolish the notion that republican government is a "middle of the road" between statism and
anarchism. Statism is one extreme; individualism is the other.
Anarchism is merely an unusually senseless form of statism; it
is not an extreme of "freedom," but the negation of the concept.

There *are* middle-of-the-road'ers in politics, who advocate a union of individualism and statism. This brings us to
the system that rules the West today: the *mixed economy.*[27]

A mixed economy is a mixture of freedom and controls.
Such an approach, its defenders argue, rejects absolutes and
thereby offers "the best of both worlds": it combines self-
interest and duty; independence for the individual and compulsion in the service of a higher cause; private property as
the engine of production and a compassionate government to
regulate the producers and redistribute their products.

The theory of the mixed economy is a blatant contradiction. It advocates rights and no rights, i.e., an unphilosophical, unprincipled approach to political questions. How is a
"mixed" society to determine its proper course in any given
issue? How is it to know when to respect rights and when to
infringe them? In the absence of principle, men act without
knowledge or vision. They act short-range and by feeling,
their own or their gang's, struggling to trample on others before others trample on them, guessing case by case what policy will "work" for the nonce. This spectacle is what people
now decry as "pressure-group warfare" (and ascribe to too
much "selfishness"). The solution offered by our press and
politicians, the imperative they urge on every group, no mat-

ter what the justice of its claims, is: "Don't be rigid; compromise."

The mixed economy obviously rests on the philosophy of pragmatism, and thus on subjectivism. If subjectivism or intrinsicism is embraced as a matter of principle, it leads in politics to pure statism. But if subjectivism or intrinsicism, as happens regularly for perfectly logical reasons, causes men to disdain principles, it leads in politics to eclecticism. Eclecticism is the attempt to combine in one system essentials taken from contradictory approaches.

Since pragmatism dispenses with the idea of an external world and with objective rules of conceptualization, its exponents see no reason for context-keeping or for restraint. They feel free to assert any social demand or daydream that wells up from their subconscious or their subculture. These are the kind of people who specialize in manufacturing false rights. Everyone, they tell us, is entitled to have a satisfying job, or better medical care, or higher education, or highbrow TV programs, or a lifetime supply of condoms, or a knowledge of famous people's secrets, or a smoke-free workplace, or an obscenity-free library, or an evolution-free curriculum, or a sodomy-free bedroom, or an abortion-free hospital, or a free abortion, or moral regeneration through public prayer—and the government, therefore, ought to pass a law. By what means will all these values or alleged values be provided? At what cost? Which men, women, and children are to become rightless, defenseless victims? Our goals are noble, the dreamers reply, and noble goals should not be sullied by grubby discussions of means.

The terminal stage of a mixed economy is implicit in the system's definition. As the virtue of integrity tells us, compromise between good and evil leads to the triumph of evil. This applies to every field of human action, politics included. If one believes that individual rights may be overridden by government sometimes, "when the public welfare (or God) necessitates it," then one has conceded that rights are not inalienable, but are conditional on the requirements of a higher value. This means that man exists not by right, but by the permission of society or God. If so, the principle of individual rights has not been "moderated"; it has been thrown out in theory—in favor of the principle of statism, which, therefore, wins out in practice.

Within certain limits, the course of a mixed economy is erratic. The country may waver between freer and more controlled periods; it may take statist, then antistatist, then superstatist lurches; it may reach its ultimate outcome slowly or rapidly—but the nature of the outcome is unaffected. If the statist element is not rejected in principle and repealed in total, it eventually consumes the last remnants of the individualist element. (The *economic* mechanism ensuring this result is the principle that controls necessitate further controls.)

As the history of the West in the past century demonstrates, the mixed economy is not a "third way" between capitalism and socialism. It is merely a transition stage, a disintegrating antisystem, careening drunkenly but inexorably from freedom to dictatorship.

As a rule, the calls within a mixed economy for more controls are originated not by the people (who are busy earning a living), but by two groups of intellectuals. In America, these groups are referred to as the "liberals" and the "conservatives" (the term "liberal," it seems, is now being replaced by "moderate"). Both groups are opposed to capitalism; both endorse Bismarck's welfare state, i.e., a highly controlled stage of the mixed economy; both reject "extremes" of any kind, including the principle of individual rights. Their disagreement pertains to a single question: what kind of rights should the government violate next?

The liberals tend to advocate intellectual freedom, while demanding economic controls. The conservatives (though they endorse many economic controls) tend to advocate economic freedom, while demanding government controls in all the crucial intellectual and moral realms. Both groups obviously subscribe to and reflect the mind-body dichotomy. The conservatives, whose roots lie in religion, are mystics of spirit. The liberals, whose roots lie in Marx, are mystics of muscle.

> The conservatives [writes Ayn Rand] see man as a body freely roaming the earth, building sand piles or factories—with an electronic computer inside his skull, controlled from Washington. The liberals see man as a soul freewheeling to the farthest reaches of the universe—but

wearing chains from nose to toes when he crosses the street to buy a loaf of bread.[28]

Is it a paradox that the spiritualists advocate economic freedom, while the materialists advocate intellectual freedom? Ayn Rand holds that such a development is logical:

> . . . each camp wants to control the realm it regards as metaphysically important; each grants freedom only to the activities it despises. . . . Neither camp holds freedom as a value. The conservatives want to rule man's consciousness; the liberals, his body.[29]

There is nothing more to be said here about the liberals; no one can confuse Franklin D. Roosevelt or Edward M. Kennedy with Objectivism. About the conservatives, however, who pretend to be defenders of "free enterprise" or "the American way of life" while spreading all the opposite ideas and laws, something remains to be said.

Precisely because of their pretense, the conservatives are morally lower than the liberals; they are farther removed from reality—and, therefore, they are more harmful in practice. Since they purport to be fighting "big government," they are the main source of political confusion in the public mind; they give people the illusion of an electoral alternative without the fact. Thus the statist drift proceeds unchecked and unchallenged.

Historically, from the Sherman Act to Herbert Hoover to the Bush Administration, it is the conservatives, not the leftists, who have always been the major destroyers of the United States.

"Conservative" here must be construed in philosophic terms. It subsumes any "rightist" who attempts to tie the politics of the Founding Fathers to unreason in *any* form— whether he is a Protestant fundamentalist, a Catholic invoking Papal dogma, a neoconservative invoking Judaic dogma, a Republican invoking "states rights" (i.e., a man seeking fifty tyrannies instead of one), a libertarian invoking anarchism, or a Southerner invoking racism.

Freedom is the opposite of every one of these creeds— and so is Objectivism their opposite.

Objectivists are not "conservatives." We do not seek to preserve the present system, but to change it at the root. In the literal sense of the word, we are *radicals*—radicals for freedom, radicals for man's rights, radicals for capitalism.

We have no choice in the matter.

We have no choice because, in philosophy, we are radicals for reason.

11

CAPITALISM

Politics is to economics as mind
is to body, or as an abstraction is to one of its concretes.
Politics identifies the principles that should govern every social field. The right political system thus includes as one of its
aspects the right economic system. Morality determines politics, as its application to organized human interaction—and
politics then determines economics, as *its* application to the
field of production and trade.

The purpose of the science of economics is to identify
how the principles of a proper politics actually work out in
regard to men's productive life (and what happens to production under an improper system). Politics tells us that man has
the right to property. But how will private owners decide
what to do with their property—what to create, consume,
trade? Will the mechanisms governing such decisions function
to promote man's life? Can a free man legally use his wealth
in such a manner that other men, however rational, are left at
his arbitrary mercy? By defining the laws of a free market, a
proper economist answers all such questions; in regard to the
virtue of productiveness, he explains why nothing but good
can come to everyone from the principle of freedom (and

nothing but evil from its abrogation). In essence, he completes the case for man's rights by showing that, here as elsewhere, the moral *is* the practical.

Hierarchically, the science of economics is a derivative, which succeeds philosophy; since economics presupposes politics, it also presupposes morality and, beneath that, metaphysics and epistemology. This is why economics cannot alter philosophic truths and why an economist without the right philosophy (at least in implicit terms) is doomed to failure; such a man can neither identify economic laws nor predict a country's long-range economic future. Despite its intimate relationship to philosophy, however, economics is not a part of philosophy; its concern is not universal principles of human action, but a specialized subject matter.

Although I am assuming certain economic principles, therefore, my purpose in this chapter is to continue the discussion of politics by offering a philosophic analysis of capitalism. What philosophic and *moral* principles does the capitalist system embody? And what, therefore, must be the effect of the system on man's life?

As to specifically economic questions, along with all the economic objections to capitalism that have been raised by statists, I leave them as a rule to rational economists to answer. Anyone familiar with procapitalist literature, Objectivist or otherwise, knows that these questions have already been answered, at least in essence. He also knows that every economic objection to capitalism ever uttered has been refuted a thousand times, with enough theory, facts, proofs, historical references, graphs, and footnotes to convince anyone, except the kind of intellectual I will consider at the end of the chapter.

There are flaws in classical economics, to be sure, and even in its best modern heir, the Austrian school as represented by Ludwig von Mises. But capitalism is not perishing from such flaws. It is perishing from the absence of a rational philosophy. This absence alone explains why the abundance of economic answers offered to our century by a better past has been ignored by the world and will go on being ignored.

Economics is invaluable as a supplement to philosophy. Like a body without a mind, however, it is worthless and impossible apart from philosophy.

Capitalism as the Only Moral Social System

"Capitalism," in Ayn Rand's definition, "is a social system based on the recognition of individual rights, including property rights, in which all property is privately owned."[1] This is a definition in terms of fundamentals and not of consequences. "Capitalism," by contrast, may not be defined as "the system of competition." Competition (for power and even for wealth) exists in most societies, including totalitarian ones. Capitalism does involve a unique form of competition, along with many other desirable social features. But all of them flow from a single root cause: freedom.

Under capitalism, state and economics are separated just as state and church are separated and for the same reasons.[2] Producers must obey the criminal law and abide by the decisions of the courts; but otherwise the policy of the government is: hands off! The term "laissez-faire capitalism," therefore, is a redundancy, albeit a necessary one in today's linguistic chaos. Capitalism *is* the system of laissez-faire; it is not the mixture of political opposites that now rules the West. In a free market, there are no government controls over the economy. Men act and interact voluntarily, by individual choice and free trade.

Historically, pure capitalism has never existed. It was, however, approached by the West during the period of the Industrial Revolution; the best example was America in the nineteenth century. That was the closest men have yet come to an unbreached recognition of rights and, therefore, to a free market.

Since rights are the means of subordinating society to the moral law, capitalism is the only *moral* social system.[3] The virtue of rationality involves both a process of consciousness and a corresponding course of physical action. In a statist society, a handful of heroes are able, for a while, to preserve certain elements of rationality in their own mind, though it takes an unusual psychological struggle for them to achieve even this much. When a thinker is ruled by force, however, he cannot act on his conclusions. Thus his virtue and his mind, even if he had fought to sustain them internally, ultimately come to seem to him exactly what they are under the circumstances: useless.

What capitalism guarantees is that, if a man does choose to think, he *can* act accordingly. No one has the power to neutralize the mind; no one can force on another his ideas, his values, or his errors. A system geared to the basic social need of reason, freedom, is geared thereby to all the needs of man's life. Capitalism is the only system that makes possible the achievement of virtue—of *any* proper virtue and, therefore, of every moral value.

A free market, as we know, is a corollary of a free mind. The point here is the converse: a free mind is a corollary of a free market. Every other social system clashes with every essential aspect of the mind's function.

Let us concretize the above by identifying the relationship between capitalism and the most important expressions of rationality covered in the chapters on morality: the six derivative virtues and the principle of egoism.

The virtue of independence consists in a man's primary orientation to reality, not to other men. In fundamental terms, we said, the independent man is as alone in society as on a desert island. Such a mode of life demands freedom. In order to *be* alone in the requisite sense, a man must be *left* alone.

A man yoked by law to the decisions of others, any others, whether his family, his race, his nation, or the entire world, must place people first in his mental hierarchy, above reason and reality. He must devote himself to imitating, cajoling, obeying (or forcing) the others in power, whatever they believe. By the nature of the system, those others are his means of survival: directly or indirectly, they control his intellectual tool, the means of cognition, and his material tools, the means of production.

Under any variant of statism, conformity to the man-made replaces conformity to the metaphysically given; because now the man-made, right or wrong, sets the terms of behavior. The rulers demand obedience at the point of a gun. Dissenters face fine, imprisonment, or death.

Degrees are irrelevant here. From the moment of a free society's first conscious breach of individual rights, the principle of independence has been dropped in favor of the principle of social conformity. The arena open to independence, therefore, starts to shrink and goes on shrinking (barring a fundamental change in the society's philosophy). Either independence, like every other virtue, is upheld as an absolute or not at all. The only system that can uphold it as an absolute is one that respects freedom as an absolute.

Intellectually, independence requires that one form one's own judgments. But a paternalistic society accepts the opposite premise: since men are incompetent to think for themselves, its advocates say, the government will do the thinking for them, by defining the right ideas and behavioral standards, then sending out the appropriate enforcement squads. The independent thinker is a potential innovator; he is the man willing if necessary to provoke opposition, to suffer unpopularity, to defy the mob. Who in his senses would do it if the political system delivers him rightless into the hands of that mob? Only a handful of righteous rebels will rebel—until they are hunted down (or overturn the system).

Materially, independence requires that one support himself by the work of his own mind. This presupposes a political system without government favors or favorites—without looters or moochers, rulers or ruled. The character of the rulers is irrelevant; it makes no moral (or practical) difference whether they are kind or cruel, benevolent or malevolent, responsible (by their own lights) or irresponsible.

If, for example, the planners running a socialist economy are responsible individuals, they will have to set terms for the legitimate use of public property; this will require them to define men's permissible course of thought and action. They will have to specify the scientific theories worthy of laboratory research, the inventions worthy of economic investment, the art worthy of public funding, the men worthy of employment and promotion in every field from ditchdigging to college teaching, the dissent worthy of being aired on the (publicly owned) streets, in the (publicly owned) meeting halls, and in the (publicly owned) press. (For a partial example of this approach, in a semisocialist country, study the volumes of regulations issued by Washington, the volumes defining what businessmen, physicians, educators et al. must, can, and cannot do when they spend federal funds.) If the planners are irresponsible men, however, independence on the citizen's part is equally impossible: such men will demand anything or nothing and then switch the setup the next hour or month. They will act according to their whim of the moment, which thus becomes the basic law of the citizen's life. (For example, study the ceaseless, senseless changes through the years in all the above federal regulations.) Either way, the planners in matter become totalitarian dictators. To the men whose lives are being thus planned, independence is not a life-sustaining virtue. It is a threat when confined to the soul and, in action, a crime.

The common man, we often hear, could never attain independence under capitalism because of the power held by employers, corporations, "monopolists." The truth is that no private individual or group, criminals aside, can affect the independence of any other individual or group. Given the size of the earth (and the need for private property to be earned, then objectively demarcated), it is physically impossible for anyone, whether alone or in voluntary association with others, to own the planet or any meaningful fraction thereof. Under capitalism, as reputable economists have demonstrated repeatedly, a private monopoly can be gained and kept only through merit; without government favors, it is impossible for anyone to monopolize even a single commodity and then, enjoying a life of stagnant ease, use his property to "exploit" others. The moment a person attempts to set prices above (or wages below) the market level, he invites competition— competition on the consumer's level, as men turn to other commodities (or employers); and/or, what is ultimately more important, competition on the producer's level, as capitalists move money into the stagnant field in order to compete for the higher profits.[4]

If the boss or the CEO in a free system does try the irrational in his business, the result is a temporary inconvenience to the rational worker, consumer, or investor, who must look elsewhere to satisfy his need; the long-range harm is suffered by the irrationalist himself, when the lookers find or create by themselves what they are seeking. In a publicly owned system, by contrast, there is no "elsewhere" for men to look: jobs, wages, hours, consumption, and production are set by a single entity, the state. How in logic can an anticapitalist thinker claim to detest men's "dependence" on an "excessively powerful" private employer or supplier, then propose as a solution that everyone be forced by law to deal with a single, omnipotent employer-supplier?

The statist replies that such a monopoly is no threat to independence; government edicts are not force, he explains, because the people themselves, if it is a "people's republic" or a democracy, are the source of the government, which represents them. Tell it to the individual who is not represented by the government and does not agree with its plan for his life. Tell the kulak under Stalin, or the student in Tienanmen Square, or the physician in Massachusetts that he is "really" the source of the laws (or tanks) being unleashed against him, appearances to the contrary notwithstanding. Historically, the modern root of this obscene notion is not, as is often said, Hegel, but his mentor, Kant. Kant postulated as man's essence a "noumenal" self, an unknowable entity that imposes on men an austere life of duty—but this is not an unjust imposition, Kant insists; a man is obligated to do his duty because he *himself*—himself in itself—is the author of the duty; even though his apparent or "phenomenal" self may be too superficial to understand this truth. Of course, only philosophers talk in such terms; politicians and journalists are content to cash in on the terms without mentioning them.

Throughout history, the great innovators always flourished in the freer periods. Contrast the epochal achievements of the freer cities of ancient Greece with the stagnation across millennia of the theocracy of ancient Egypt; or the dazzling progress of the Renaissance with the retrogression under Church rule in the Middle Ages; or the beauty and wealth pouring from the cornucopia of the nineteenth century with the death-laden insignia of the twentieth. Observe also the fate of the independent man even in the semistatist countries today. The most eloquent evidence of it is called the "brain drain," as people from around the world, England included, flee to the United States. Within the United States, there is a similar flight—away from all-but-socialized fields like manufacturing and medicine to the less controlled professions.

Individualism and independence rise and fall together. Any other politics represents the opposite of the virtue of independence; it represents a form of slavery.

Justice is the virtue of judging men morally and of granting to each that which he deserves. Like every other virtue, this is a form of fidelity to reality, of independent thought, and of self-protection. It requires, therefore, a political system consonant with all these values; the system is capitalism.

To the statist, moral judgment by the individual is intolerable. The authorities must have men who will heed them in all matters, including human interaction and association; it is impossible to plan a person's actions for him if he retains the power to veto social arrangements by reference to his personal moral code. Similarly, the politicians of a mixed economy count on pressure groups who agree to eschew moral judgment and compromise on anything. What statists of every kind need is not the cognitive self-assertion implicit in virtue, but the opposite; in this instance, they need a man's willingness *not* to judge others independently, but to praise, blame, "negotiate," or stay neutral, according to the requirements of "the community." As to the self-protection afforded by justice, many statists add, the individual need not concern himself with it; since the government educates the citizens morally, it thereby assures everyone's well-being. Other statists go further: it is wrong, they hold, to consider one's well-being at all; one must love one's fellows however hurtful they are—because one's fellows are the moral beneficiary, for whose sake the individual is living and toiling.

Since an individual under freedom chooses his own actions, he can be held responsible for them. Moral judgment of such a man is necessary and *possible*. If a man acts under compulsion, however, he cannot be held responsible. How, under statism, is a moral judge to differentiate? How is he to know which actions of others reflect choices untainted by the state's power, and which actions, however wrong, are the helpless reactions of a man who sees a gun at his (or his family's) head and an abyss of despair at his feet? Even if a citizen under statism rejects his leaders' rejection of morality, therefore, it is difficult—and in countless cases impossible—for him to pronounce moral judgment himself. As with rationality and independence, the most he can attempt is to smuggle in some crumbs of virtue within the privacy of his own mind—after which, he is not free to act on the crumbs anyway.

In regard to action, justice consists in seeking and granting the earned, both in spirit and in matter; the essential rule is the trader principle. "Trade," however, denotes a voluntary exchange of values; you do not "trade" your wallet to a hold-up man in exchange for him letting you flee for your life. The trader principle requires a system of voluntary relationships; it requires a government that is forbidden to emulate hold-up men.

In a free-market system, every man must pay his own way; he can claim from others only what he has earned, as judged by the parties' mutual, uncoerced evaluations. As to the nonearners and nontraders, the system is fully as "cruel" (i.e., as just) as its enemies say: it offers people no alibis, no welfare workers, no booty. Under capitalism, no man's achievements or troubles, whatever their nature or source, are assets or liabilities belonging to other men. Thus, in Ayn Rand's words, "an end will be put to the infamy of paying with one life for the errors [or even accidents] of another."[5]

In a capitalist system, a producer can do with his wealth what he chooses. He can invest it, spend it on himself and his loved ones, or give it away. He can give a reasonable amount of help to unfortunates who cannot support themselves (this is moral if his help is consistent with a proper hierarchy of values). He can bleed himself dry by a course of self-sacrifice. He can will his possessions to any heirs he picks, deserving or otherwise. Under capitalism, however, the man who bleeds himself dry gets no transfusion from the state; while any undeserving recipient finds the market system set against him. The most eloquent example of this last is the playboy in a free country who inherits a fortune; he does not keep it long. "From shirtsleeves to shirtsleeves in three generations," Americans used to say at the turn of the century. If a poor man rose to wealth, then left his money to worthless heirs, his grandson was back on the street without a suit to his name. Project how widespread this phenomenon had to be to give rise to a popular aphorism, then observe what happens to the worthless children of the rich under our present policies. (Most end up in Washington demanding a redistribution of suits.)

The opposite of justice is the principle of penalizing virtue while rewarding evil—which is precisely the principle of statist societies. If an individual is rational, independent, proud, he is denounced. If an individual expends effort in docile, authorized form, his product is seized, while his docility is praised. But if an individual represents the vilest of evils, if he is a power-luster who dared to covet other men's souls and who succeeded in his quest, he receives impassioned accolades and the showiest material perquisites. Thus the highest of the high, morally speaking, is vilified and crushed, while the lowest of the low, ensconced in his palace, savors the fawning homage beamed to him hourly by the state television network.

Whoever mutters that socialism is unjust in practice, but idealistic in theory, knows nothing about theory or about justice. Every statist regime is unjust in practice. The reason is that injustice is the essence of its theory.

Productiveness is the virtue of creating material values. In a free market, such a virtue is a necessity; there are no governmental bonuses for parasites. Contrary to another Big Lie, the rule of *capitalist* society, as of nature, is: he who does not work shall not eat. Capitalism is the system of productiveness; it is the system of and for producers. As to consumers under such a system, they are men who pay for what they consume, i.e., men who themselves earned the means of payment (or received it from someone who did). In a free society, *only* producers are consumers.

The root of capitalism's productiveness is the fact that it is the system of free thought and thereby of creativity. Among other things, a creative life, as we have seen, entails a private career chosen as a long-range purpose; this demands an individualist politics. Privacy without the principle of egoism to sanction it is impossible, and so is a long-range approach without freedom from interference. There can be no personal career for a creature whose destiny is public service, and there can be no chosen, sustained course of action for a creature at the mercy of clashing pressure groups (or of a dictator's switching orders). There can be no purposefulness in the moral sense apart from the right to *set* one's purposes, i.e., the right to the pursuit of happiness. A person obliged to satisfy the desires of others has to become whim-ridden—because he *is* ridden by whim, the whim of whoever happens to be his moral master.

Since no one in a free society has a customer, a supplier, a job, an insurance policy, or a bank loan by force, since there are no laws to entrench mediocrity (or worse) and bar the path of talent, every chance exists for the innovator, the fountainhead in any field, to be heard, to place on the market the work of his mind, to fight slothful opposition, to rise to the top and be rewarded. The source of capitalism's creativity, therefore, may be described as "competition"; but it is the kind which rests on the fact that each man is free to offer his best and that other producers are free to decide whether or not to buy it. The real source, in a word, is freedom, which clears the road for the active mind.

Because it is the system geared to the requirements of the creative process, capitalism is the system of wealth. It is a system that has no competition at all in regard to the achievement of material abundance—a fact that the enemies of capitalism turn into an objection. Capitalism, the advocates of the mind-body dichotomy say, gives too much importance to "materialistic concerns." Economic growth under capitalism, the anti-effort mentalities add, is excessive; someone is always revolutionizing the methods of production; there is never time to "rest." In essence, both these objections are true: capitalism *is* the system of this material world, and it *is,* as we hear, a "rat race"—but so is life. Life is motion, one way or the other, forward or backward, in the direction of self-preservation or of destruction. Capitalism is the forward system; it is the "progressive" system, using "progress" for once in the literal sense.

The historical evidence in regard to the present virtue is as abundant as wealth under capitalism. The state of a country's freedom has always been correlated with its standard of living. The richest country in history was the United States at the time when it was also the freest. As to the other direction, look around the globe. Virtually no one, not even the highest-ranking Ivy League professors any longer, tries to pretend that dictatorship leads to prosperity.

Virtue, as our analysis so far reaffirms, *is* one. If the virtues already covered require capitalism, the others do, also.

Integrity, the refusal to permit a breach between thought and action, presupposes an individual's freedom in regard to both man's attributes: mind and body. A breach between the two is inherent in statism; leaving aside torture or brainwashing, dictatorships do not try directly to crush the subject's mind; what they do is take over a country's physical resources, making it impossible for an individual to act on his conclusions. Integrity demands men of principle, who spurn any plea for a moral compromise. Who can be anything but "flexible" in the most mealy-mouthed, pragmatist sense, when the pleaders express their viewpoint not only with words, but also by pointing to the paraphernalia of compulsion waiting mutely to back the words up?

Honesty, the selfish refusal to fake reality, requires a system geared to selfishness and to reality. Under statism, some form of faking is unavoidable. Since the opinions of others, right or wrong, are elevated to the position of metaphysical primacy, survival entails some public adherence to those opinions, no matter what the pretense, the flattery, the hypocrisy, or the plain lying this involves. Even honesty within the privacy of one's own mind eventually becomes impossible. Whoever tries to live "a normal life" in a dictatorship (as against going crazy, killing himself, killing his mind, starting a rebellion, escaping, or joining the rulers) cannot avoid lying to himself. He must learn to tolerate the unendurable by rationalizing the system. The naked admission that there is no good reason behind any of it, that he is a pawn of killers as an end in itself, would destroy his ability to act obediently. It is possible to be an unprotesting slave, if one can make oneself semibelieve a suitable moral cover-up; but not if one cannot.

Pride, the sum of the virtues, requires the moral ambitiousness of seeking to observe every moral principle. This presupposes a system in which moral principles can be practiced. As to the value of self-esteem, who can achieve it in a system that degrades him to the status of helpless social atom? Who can feel that he is *able* to live—when in fact he isn't?

This brings me to the final moral issue to be considered here: the principle of egoism. Since egoism is a requirement of life and a presupposition of rights, it is inherent in the system of life and rights. Under capitalism, as a matter of fundamental law, man *is* an end in himself. Though he is free to live for others, each is expected by the nature of the system to be the beneficiary of his own actions: he gains values by pursuing his own life, property, and happiness. This is the opposite of any system that upholds self-denial.

Capitalism rewards the pursuit of *rational* self-interest.

Since rights are inalienable, a man can succeed ultimately only by creative thought and action, not by sacrificing others through the use of force or fraud. Nor can he succeed by sacrificing himself—whether through selfless service or plain irrationality, such as being irresponsible, context-dropping, and short-range. Criminality aside, a man *can* act irrationally under capitalism; but he cannot run to the government for any recompense or bailout. In a system based on adherence to nature, there are no "no fault" clauses. Either one adheres to nature or, in due course, nature takes care of the matter.

The relationship between capitalism and egoism is manifest in every area of human life, spiritual and material. Romantic love, for instance, being a selfish phenomenon, developed into a Western ideal only with the rise of individualism. To this day, logically enough, collectivists scorn such love as "bourgeois." The most obvious expression of capitalism's egoism, however, occurs in the material realm. Capitalism counts on the *profit motive*.

The "profit motive," speaking broadly, means a man's incentive to work in order to gain something for himself—in economic terms, to make money. By Objectivist standards, such a motive, being thoroughly just, is profoundly moral. Socialists used to speak of "production for use" as against "production for profit." What they meant and wanted was: "production by one man for the unearned use of another."

In a specialized sense, "profit" means the financial return to the owner of a business enterprise; it is the difference between a businessman's costs and his income. If there are to be business enterprises, someone has to accumulate capital through production and saving, someone has to decide in what future products his savings should be invested, someone has to organize and manage the enterprise and/or choose and oversee the men competent to do it (management includes the crucial task of productively integrating natural resources and human labor). These are the effort-demanding, risk-laden decisions and actions on which abundance depends. Profit represents success in regard to such decisions and actions; loss represents failure. Profit, therefore, may be described as a payment earned by moral virtue, the virtue of a specific group within the economy; it is a payment for the thought, the initiative, the long-range vision, the courage, the efficacy of an economy's prime movers. (Profit is "exploitation" only in a mystic viewpoint, such as Marxism; if wealth is the product of muscular labor, then anyone not turning cranks on the assembly line is a parasite.)

The amount of a businessman's profit indicates how much his customers value his product over the factors constituting the input to the enterprise. Profit thus measures exactly the *creation* of wealth by the profit-maker. Loss indicates people's lower evaluation of the output than of the input; loss thus measures the destruction of wealth. As Isabel Paterson words the point in *The God of the Machine:* "Production *is* profit; and profit *is* production. They are not merely related; they are the same thing. When a man plants potatoes, if he does not get back more than he put in, he has *produced nothing.*"[6]

It is needless to discuss further the relationship between egoism and capitalism. Leaving aside the conservatives, who are committed to evading the subject, everyone else, whatever his politics, understands the relationship perfectly.

Morally, I conclude, capitalism emerges triumphant: it is the system of and for the good. For which reason, evil men under capitalism cannot succeed, not in the long run. No system can guarantee rationality. What a proper system can do, however, is to de-fang the evil. By safeguarding innocents from force, capitalism does the possible in this regard. To be free from the machinations of the wicked, all that a man needs is freedom. The only protection virtue needs from vice is a single rule: hands off! Thereafter, the worst that the exponents of unreason can achieve is to make the path of the moral man more difficult—for a while.

Since capitalism is the precondition of all proper moral principles, any statist system is incompatible with them. As a rule, statists do not avow their rejection of morality. Just as the moderns characteristically invoke "pure reason" to invalidate reason and "true existence" to undercut reality, so they use the terminology of the life-sustaining virtues to defend a politics that destroys those virtues.

We demand a rationally planned economy, the statists say (or said), let us plan the future—while denying the social condition (freedom) required for man to act long-range or to function rationally. Let us have true independence, they say, the independence of the poor from the rich—by making it necessary for everyone, rich and poor alike, to become a second-hander. Let us protect our integrity from the seductions of the moneyed elite, they say—by making men's abandonment of principle a condition of survival. Let us sweep aside the lies of advertisers and hucksters, they say—by founding a new society on the supremacy of the group, i.e., on one of the greatest lies of all. Give us justice, they plead, social justice—which consists in sacrificing the Atlases of the world to the Roosevelts and the Stalins. Let us have abundance for everyone, they (used to) plead—by making production impossible. Let us start to take moral pride in our species, they cry—by enacting into law the antimorality of sacrifice.

It is bad enough to hate this life openly, like a medieval saint or a Middle Eastern fanatic. It is worse—more dishonest—to proclaim one's love of life while acting methodically to thwart its every requirement.

On one moral issue, most statists do not dissemble. They tell us loudly that when they come to power, they will eradicate selfishness. This is precisely what they have struggled to accomplish when in power, with results on a world-wide scale that are by now self-evident.

"Public ownership of the means of production," states Ayn Rand, denotes "public ownership of the mind."[7] Since thought is an attribute of the individual, this in turn denotes the death of the mind.

The moral justification of capitalism is *not* that it serves the public. Capitalism does achieve the "public good" (appropriately defined), but this is an effect, not a cause; it is a secondary consequence, not an evaluative primary. The justification of capitalism is that it is the system which implements a scientific code of morality; i.e., which recognizes man's metaphysical nature and needs; i.e., which is based on reason and reality. A secondary consequence of such a system is that any group who lives under it and acts properly has to benefit.

The distinction between primary and secondary—in other words, one's hierarchy of values—is critical here, as it is throughout the realm of evaluation. A simple example is furnished by a man swimming in a lake. If reaching a distant shore is his evaluative primary and swimming is merely a means to it, the man will husband his energy, take periodic rests, move in a straight line, keep his body as tranquil as he can; he will do what he must to reach his goal, but no more—especially if he is a reluctant swimmer, who generally shuns the activity. But if he is primarily interested in the swimming, if his motive, say, is aerobic exercise and reaching the shore is merely a result (albeit an imperative one), he will go out of his way, other things equal, to expend energy, avoid rests, swim in zigzag fashion, make his heart pound fiercely. One's priorities make a difference; they may drastically affect one's behavior even in regard to enacting the same causal sequence. Assuming that there is any room in which to maneuver, one's *primary* value in a given context is the thing one will focus on, emphasize, lionize.

From Adam Smith to the present, the value standard upheld by capitalism's champions has been the "public good." Individual freedom has been defended either as an ethically neutral means to this end (a common Enlightenment attitude) or, after Kant, as a necessary evil. Capitalism's virtue, in this interpretation, is that it converts the amorality of "prudence" or the wickedness of greed into the nobility of social work. Men who hold this viewpoint, like the reluctant swimmer, are impelled to minimize one aspect of the causal sequence they uphold here and to emphasize the other. They minimize the individualist cause and emphasize the social effect, which, to them, is the moral primary. Thus they find themselves drawn irresistibly to compromise, cutting back one step at a time on the element they regard as neutral or worse, allowing "some controls" and then more and still more.

The reluctant swimmer of our example has to swim; in his case, the cause-effect sequence is physical and even perceptual. The reluctant individualist, however, does not have to cling to individualism as a means. On the contrary, after a certain point his altruism requires him to rethink the causal laws involved.

In the political field, the identification of a causal relationship is a conclusion drawn from philosophical premises. Those who hold an objective view of values can demonstrate what are the means (the principles) necessary to achieve values; they can, therefore, identify causal laws in politics that are objective. Altruists, however, being nonobjective in ethics, have to be nonobjective in politics, also. Since their ultimate end is not based on reality, they cannot define a code of principles necessary to reach it; they cannot know what policies lead to the "public good." Hence the contradictory schemes urged by do-gooders through the centuries, as fads, philosophic or otherwise, come and go.

In this situation, the (post-Kantian) altruist has only two choices: to tolerate an unequivocal evil, selfishness, because of its alleged positive results (today's conservative viewpoint), or to reject the evil on the grounds that a depraved cause cannot be the means to a beneficent end (the liberal viewpoint). Since neither group of men can demonstrate an objective causal sequence in this matter, the choice comes down to the following: should we endorse a vice without understanding why we must, or should we try the path of virtue and see where it leads? On its face, the conservative position is morally bankrupt. In the end, therefore, the conservative, like the liberal, comes to *deny the causal sequence itself:* individual freedom, he comes to agree, is *not* the means to the public welfare. On the contrary, he starts to say, I see now that unrestrained capitalism "sometimes" (then "often") hurts the public.

Thus the famous and entirely accurate remark made in his later years by John Stuart Mill, the Utilitarian who had once been an ardent supporter of laissez-faire: "We are all socialists now." (A fuller discussion of this issue is offered in the final sequence of the present chapter.)

We Objectivists are *not* socialists. Whoever accepts our code of values can harbor no doubts in regard to the necessity or efficacy of freedom. For us there can be no question of "tempering" capitalism or of tampering with it. There can be no temptation to sacrifice any particle of the moral primary—which in this context is man's rights—for the sake of any "social gains" whatsoever, whether imagined *or real.*

The most eloquent statement of this last point is given by Hank Rearden, the industrialist in *Atlas Shrugged,* during his trial before a panel of judges in a mixed-economy courtroom. He has been charged (correctly) with breaking an economic regulation which, the court stated, was designed to promote the "public good." Rearden answers, in part:

I could say to you that you do not serve the public good—
that nobody's good can be achieved at the price of human
sacrifices—that when you violate the rights of one man,
you have violated the rights of all, and a public of rightless
creatures is doomed to destruction. I could say to you that
you will and can achieve nothing but universal devasta-
tion—as any looter must, when he runs out of victims. I
could say it, but I won't. It is not your particular policy
that I challenge, but your moral premise. If it were true
that men could achieve their good by means of turning
some men into sacrificial animals, and I were asked to im-
molate myself for the sake of creatures who wanted to
survive at the price of my blood, if I were asked to serve
the interests of society apart from, above and against my
own—I would refuse. I would reject it as the most con-
temptible evil, I would fight it with every power I possess,
I would fight the whole of mankind, if one minute were
all I could last before I were murdered, I would fight in
the full confidence of the justice of my battle and of a
living being's right to exist. Let there be no misunderstand-
ing about me. If it is now the belief of my fellow men,
who call themselves the public, that their good requires
victims, then I say: The public good be damned, I will
have no part of it![8]

The above constitutes Ayn Rand's validation of capitalism. She does not justify laissez-faire as a practical means to a
social purpose.

For the first time in history, she offers a selfish—i.e., a
moral—defense of capitalism.

Capitalism as the System of Objectivity

Capitalism implements the right code of morality because it is
based on the right view of metaphysics and epistemology. It
is the system of virtue because it is the system of objectivity.

In essence, "virtue" and "objectivity" denote the same
phenomenon: the proper volitional relationship between consciousness and existence. "Virtue" denotes this relationship
considered as the principle governing a man's actions; "objectivity" denotes it as the principle governing his cognition.

Each of these concepts, accordingly, entails the other; but "objectivity" is the more fundamental of the two.

The validation of the capitalist system follows the method of objectivity: certain political conclusions are reduced to the principles of a scientific morality, which are themselves reduced ultimately to perceptual data. Such a system is geared to the requirements of a reality-oriented consciousness: capitalism protects objective rights by means of objective laws.

Capitalism is incompatible with any version of intrinsicism. It is a system of and for mentally active, this-worldly valuers, not of passive self-abnegators. Nor does the system permit any intrinsicist to enforce his commandments through the power of law. Similarly, because it *is* geared to the reality orientation, capitalism is incompatible with any version of subjectivism, whether personal or social. Nor does "laissez-faire" mean that "anything goes"; in a republic, "nothing goes" that infringes man's rights.

The principle of objectivity applies to every feature of capitalism: it applies to all values and all forms of human relationship that are inherent in the system.[9] (Individuals, of course, are left free to be objective or nonobjective.) Let us start by discussing the objectivity of *economic value*.

The economic value of goods and services is their *price* (this term subsumes all forms of price, including wages, rents, and interest rates); and prices on a free market are determined by the law of supply and demand. Men create products and offer them for sale; this is supply. Other men offer their own products in exchange; this is demand. (The medium of exchange is money.) "Supply" and "demand," therefore, are two perspectives on a single fact: a man's supply *is* his demand; it is his only means of demanding another man's supply. The market price of a product is determined by the conjunction of two evaluations, i.e., by the voluntary agreement of sellers and buyers. If sellers decide to charge a thousand dollars for a barrel of flour because they feel "greed," there will be no buyers; if buyers decide to pay only a nickel a barrel because they feel "need," there will be no sellers and no flour. The market price is based not on arbitrary wishes, but on a definite mechanism: it is at once the highest price sellers can command and the lowest price buyers can find.

Economic value thus determined is *objective*.

An objective value is an existent (in this instance, a product) as evaluated by a volitional consciousness pursuing a certain purpose in a certain cognitive context; the evaluation (including the purpose) must be rational, i.e., determined ultimately by the facts of reality. To quote again Ayn Rand's formulation: "Values cannot exist (cannot be valued) outside the full context of a man's life, needs, goals, and *knowledge*."[10] The above describes precisely how economic evaluations are made on a free market. Men are left free to judge the worth of various products, the worth *to them;* each judges in accordance with his own needs and goals as he himself understands these to apply in a particular context. Market value thus entails valuer, purpose, beneficiary, choice, knowledge—all the insignia of objective value as against the revealed variety. At the same time, men's evaluations, economic or otherwise, cannot with impunity be capricious; under capitalism irrational men suffer the consequences, one of which is their eventual loss of economic power and thus of the ability to influence the market price. Market value, therefore, is objective in the full, technical meaning of the term. It is specifically objective, as against being intrinsic or subjective.

It is essential here to grasp Ayn Rand's distinction between two forms of the objective: the *philosophically* objective and the *socially* objective. "By 'philosophically objective,' " she writes,

I mean a value estimated from the standpoint of the best possible to man, *i.e.,* by the criterion of the most rational mind possessing the greatest knowledge, in a given category, in a given period, and in a defined context (nothing can be estimated in an undefined context). For instance, it can be rationally proved that the airplane is *objectively* of immeasurably greater value to man (to *man at his best)* than the bicycle—and that the works of Victor Hugo are *objectively* of immeasurably greater value than true-confession magazines. But if a given man's intellectual potential can barely manage to enjoy true confessions, there is no reason why his meager earnings, the product of *his* effort, should be spent on books he cannot read—or on subsidizing the airplane industry, if his own transportation needs do not extend beyond the range of a bicycle. (Nor is there any reason why the rest of mankind should be held down to the level of his literary taste, his engineering capacity, and his income. Values are not determined by fiat nor by majority vote.)

Just as the number of its adherents is not a proof of an idea's truth or falsehood, of an art work's merit or demerit, of a product's efficacy or inefficacy—so the free-market value of goods or services does not necessarily represent their philosophically objective value, but only their *socially objective* value, *i.e.,* the sum of the individual judgments of all the men involved in trade at a given time, the sum of what *they* valued, each in the context of his own life.[11]

The philosophically objective value of a product is the evaluation reached by the men with the best grasp of reality (in a specific category and context), regardless of whether or not they are involved in buying and selling the product. The socially objective value is the evaluation reached by the actual buyers and sellers. These two evaluations are not necessarily the same, because the buyers and sellers may lack the requisite grasp of reality; they may lack the knowledge which would make the product, as judged by their own mind, a need, a pleasure, a *value* (or, conversely, which would make the product a disvalue).

The free market, however, is the greatest of all educators. It continually raises the knowledge of the citizens, the caliber of their tastes, the discrimination of their pleasures, the sophistication of their needs.

A free market [writes Ayn Rand] is a *continuous process* that cannot be held still, an upward process that demands the best (the most rational) of every man and rewards him accordingly. While the majority have barely assimilated the value of the automobile, the creative minority introduces the airplane. The majority learn by demonstration, the minority is free to demonstrate. . . .

Within every category of goods and services . . . it is the purveyor of the best product at the cheapest price who wins the greatest financial rewards *in that field*—not automatically nor immediately nor by fiat, but by virtue of the free market, which teaches every participant to look for the *objective* best within the category of his own competence, and penalizes those who act on irrational considerations.[12]

Any given person in a free society can choose to brush reason aside but, since there is no agency to deflect the principle of justice, such persons do not set the long-range economic terms of the society. If a man blows his pay on liquor and has nothing left for rent; if he succumbs to a buying spree in a bull market while ignoring a company's fundamentals; if he invests his cash in the horse and buggy while sneering at the automobile—he loses out, and he continues to lose unless he learns a better approach. The system thus institutionalizes, though it cannot compel, respect for reality—and men's economic (and other) evaluations are set accordingly. (Similarly, the growing statism of a mixed economy promotes the increasingly debased mass tastes we see today in such fields as art, literature, and entertainment.)

Market value, in essence, is the most rational assessment of a product that a free society can reach at a given time; and there is always a tendency for this assessment to approach the product's philosophically objective value, as people gain the requisite knowledge. In time, barring accidents, the two assessments coincide. The creative minority grasps the philosophically objective value of a good or service, then teaches it to the public, which is eventually lifted to the creators' level of development. "It is in this sense," Miss Rand concludes, "that the free market is not ruled by the intellectual criteria of the majority, which prevail only at and for any given moment; the free market is ruled by those who are able to see and plan long-range—and the better the mind, the longer the range."[13]

The dominant view today is that economic value (like every other kind) is not objective, but arbitrary. Monopolists or other "exploiters," subjectivists claim, charge any amount they feel like charging; landlords and bankers set rents or interest rates at whim; employers pay whatever niggardly wage their avarice decrees. Economic theory and history alike prove that capitalism does not work this way; both theory and history make clear what happens in a free market to overchargers, underpayers, and any other would-be fiat-mongers (they lose their customers, their workers, and ultimately their shirts). Subjectivists, however, cannot heed any such proof; since they do not acknowledge the possibility of consciousness perceiving existence, they cannot accept the possibility of an objective economy.

The standard cure for capitalism's "arbitrary prices" is recourse to the state; the government, we are told, must legislate an inherently "fair price" independent of market conditions. This represents intrinsicism posing as the solution to subjectivism. "Fairness" in an economic context, however, means honest free trade; the "fair" price is the price men agree to pay. Since force and mind are opposites, the government under capitalism does not legislate prices; it does not legislate any value-judgments, economic or otherwise. But intrinsicists have no compunctions about unleashing force against a mind and no qualms about the means they employ to discover what price is "fair." As always, they count on revelation—in this instance, emanating not from the will of God, but from the caprice of politicians reacting to the caprice of pressure groups.

The subjectivist intellectual, in effect, causes people to turn in self-defense to the intrinsicist leader, who acts as a spokesman for a different group of subjectivists. This kind of vicious circle extends far beyond the realm of politics and economics.

Since economic value under capitalism is objective, *profits* are objective, also.

Profit is the difference between two prices, the price of the input (including labor) to a business and the price of its output. There is, therefore, no such thing as an intrinsically "fair" profit, and there is no such thing as an "excess" or "arbitrary" profit. There is only the profit men *earn.*

In general, since material goods and services in every category are evaluated objectively, their creators' (long-range) financial compensation is equally objective. Whatever its form, income under capitalism is not determined "intrinsically" or "subjectively"; it cannot be too high or too low; all earnings *are* earned. "[T]he degree of a man's productiveness," writes Ayn Rand, "is the degree of his reward."[14]

A man's wealth under capitalism depends on two factors: on his own creative achievement, and on the choice of others to recognize it. Since the system promotes such recognition, however, a man's wealth depends in the end only on his exercise of his creative faculty. The more active a mind, within any given field of production, the richer its possessor eventually becomes. Such is the harmony between mind and body attained in practice by a system that is based from the start on a correct view of these two attributes of man.

Some highly specialized creators, however mentally active, do not grow rich under capitalism (or under any system). Thus even the best epistemologist will never attain the market or income available, say, to a novelist or a shoe manufacturer. Their money, however, is not taken from him. Moreover, a rational epistemologist in a country with an unsubsidized (and untenured) professorate will in time outearn an irrational one. As to the income of epistemologists in a free country if none of them is rational, none of them makes money for long—because then freedom does not last long; after which, novels, shoes, and professors disappear, too.

The so-called "Protestant ethic" taught our forefathers that riches are a sign of virtue, a prize to the diligent conferred by the justice of God. It is true that riches in a free country are a sign of virtue. The agent of justice, however, is not an otherworldly overseer, but a worldly creation—not a supernatural entity, but an objective social system.

Money is a medium of exchange—and in principle one makes it under capitalism not by vote, pull, or luck, but by a process of rational work. In this sense, money is an objective measure and reward of objective behavior, intellectual and then existential. For Ayn Rand, the love of money is not "the root of all evil," as the moralists of sacrifice and the mind-body dichotomy insist. On the contrary, the love of money is more aptly described as the root of all good—which is the theme of a famous speech in *Atlas Shrugged* delivered by the copper king Francisco d'Anconia.

"Have you ever asked what is the root of money?" the speech begins. "Money is a tool of exchange, which can't exist unless there are goods produced and men able to produce them." Such a tool presupposes everything on which goods and their exchange depend. America, d'Anconia observes, is a country of money. Philosophically, this means that it is "a country of reason, justice, freedom, production, achievement."

If you ask me to name the proudest distinction of Americans, I would choose—because it contains all the others—the fact that they were the people who created the phrase "to *make* money." No other language or nation had ever used these words before; men had always thought of wealth as a static quantity—to be seized, begged, inherited, shared, looted or obtained as a favor. Americans were the first to understand that wealth has to be created. The words "to make money" hold the essence of human morality.[15]

(Money itself must be a freely chosen material value, a commodity such as gold, which is an objective equivalent of wealth. Under capitalism, money is not worthless paper arbitrarily decreed to be legal tender by men in positions of political power.)

Like sex, art, and happiness, money in its own way is a kind of summation and is widely taken as such. It is a token of an entire philosophy, a philosophy of selfishness, worldliness, and cold calculation (i.e., thought). This is why the apostles of unreason denounce the "almighty dollar"—and why the heroes of *Atlas Shrugged* adopt the dollar sign as their trademark. The dollar, Ayn Rand holds, as the currency of a free country, is a symbol of free trade and therefore of a free mind.

Under capitalism, critics complain, the rich man has too much power; "money talks." So it does. When it doesn't, something else does. The money speech ends with: "When money ceases to be the tool by which men deal with one another, then men become the tools of men. Blood, whips and guns—or dollars. Take your choice—there is no other—and your time is running out."[16]

This brings us to the difference between *economic power* and *political power.*

Economic power is the power resulting from the possession of wealth. Political power is the power resulting from the government's monopoly on coercion. In essence, the difference is that between purchase and plunder. "[E]conomic power," in Ayn Rand's words, "is exercised by means of a *positive,* by offering men a reward, an incentive, a payment, a value; political power is exercised by means of a *negative,* by the threat of punishment, injury, imprisonment, destruction.''[17] The first is aimed at man's faculty of choice; the second (in a statist context) aims to negate the faculty of choice. The first appeals to motivation by love; the second, to motivation by fear.

Those who believe that riches are causeless, however, see no fundamental difference between the two kinds of power; to them, there is only a difference between two kinds of whim, the businessmen's or ''the people's.'' (Hence such a bromide as ''A hungry man is not free.'') This viewpoint, Ayn Rand observes, is tantamount to the claim that there is no reality, no objectivity, and no difference between life and death.

Economic power *is* power. Any proper value is a form of power; it endows its possessor with capabilities that nonpossessors lack. If this were not so, the object would not be a value. In a free society, however, no man's powers, however great, are a hindrance to anyone else; they are a benefit to others.

Economic power is not unique in this regard. Consider, for example, a spiritual value, such as knowledge. If a man enjoys ''cognitive power,'' he can achieve his goals better than an ignorant person; he can choose a better course to pursue, then influence his fellows in a way that ignoramuses cannot hope to match. This does not mean that knowledgeable men succeed by exploiting fools. Nor does it mean that ''An ignorant man is not free.'' If a fool wants to shape the destiny of society, but experts convince people to take an opposite direction, is this a case of ''coercive'' cognitive power? Only an egalitarian would say so; since it is impossible for everyone to be equally wise, he adds, we must see to it that everyone is equally stupid. (The name of this program is progressive education.) In this approach, any value—economic, cognitive, amatory, athletic, esthetic, or otherwise—is unfair. The only solution is the equality of a graveyard.

Knowledge—to continue the example—like material wealth, can be acquired and used to achieve one's ends only by objective means; this requires that men judge freely whether to accept a given idea, just as they must judge freely whether to buy a given product. Further: knowledge is not a static quantity; it has to be discovered and, practically speaking, the sky is the limit. One man's knowledge is not looted from the brain of his neighbor, nor does it harm his neighbor; it helps him. The cognitive beginner in the era of Galileo or Einstein enjoys an incomparably greater return for the same mental effort than his counterpart did in the era of Ptolemy or Bernard of Clairvaux. Wealth is not a static quantity, either; it, too, has to be created; and the more wealth there is in the world, the easier it is for everyone to flourish economically. Thus the relative riches of the poorest Western drone today, thanks to the "robber barons," as against the standard of living of the most industrious serf under Pope Gregory VII or King Louis IX.

In a capitalist system, the greater a man's power to think and thereby to satisfy his "materialistic greed," the greater the benefits he confers on his fellows (although this is not the justification of the system). The less a man's power to satisfy his "greed" or even his needs, the more he depends on the minds above him. This human continuum is what Ayn Rand describes, in a crucial identification, as the *pyramid of ability:*

Material products can't be shared, they belong to some ultimate consumer; it is only the value of an idea that can be shared with unlimited numbers of men, making all sharers richer at no one's sacrifice or loss, raising the productive capacity of whatever labor they perform. It is the value of his own time that the strong of the intellect transfers to the weak, letting them work on the jobs he discovered, while devoting his time to further discoveries. This is mutual trade to mutual advantage; the interests of the mind are one, no matter what the degree of intelligence, among men who desire to work and don't seek or expect the unearned.

In proportion to the mental energy he spent, the man who creates a new invention receives but a small percentage of his value in terms of material payment, no matter what fortune he makes, no matter what millions he earns. But the man who works as a janitor in the factory producing that invention, receives an enormous payment in proportion to the mental effort that his job requires of *him*. And the same is true of all men between, on all levels of ambition and ability. The man at the top of the intellectual pyramid contributes the most to all those below him, but gets nothing except his material payment, receiving no intellectual bonus from others to add to the value of his time. The man at the bottom who, left to himself, would starve in his hopeless ineptitude, contributes nothing to those above him, but receives the bonus of all of their brains. Such is the nature of the "competition" between the strong and the weak of the intellect. Such is the pattern of "exploitation" for which you have damned the strong.[18]

"Strength" in this context does not mean bodily strength, since capitalism bars the initiation of force; it means efficacy in regard to production. "Weakness" means inefficacy at production, whatever the cause, whether it be bad genes, bad luck, or bad character. It is, therefore, absurd to claim that the strong succeed by "trampling on" the weak. When the strong are left free to function, everyone benefits. When the strong are enslaved or regulated, everyone is doomed.

As a rule, the defenders of capitalism have been worse—more openly irrational—than its attackers. The man who spread the notion that capitalism means death for the weak was the system's leading nineteenth-century champion, Herbert Spencer; capitalism, he held, permits only the "survival of the fittest." This is the conclusion Spencer reached by attempting to deduce capitalism from the intellectuals' fad of the period, Darwin's theory of evolution.[19] Since animals survive by fighting over a limited food supply, Spencer argued in essence, so does man. This "defense" of laissez-faire has been incomparably more harmful than anything uttered by Marx. The wrong arguments for a position are always more costly than plain silence, which at least allows a better voice to be heard if such should ever speak out.

There is no clash in a free society among any groups who choose life as their standard. The welfare of all alike depends on the same social condition. When men's rights are respected, all men are equal before the law and, therefore, equal before nature and equal before the marketplace. They are "equal" in the sense of each being free.

Under capitalism, men enjoy "equality of opportunity" in the only legitimate sense of that vague, usually statist term: each has the right to act on his mind's conclusions and keep its products. This is the only "opportunity" a person needs or has any grounds to demand. Accidents aside, the result of this social condition, for every individual, strong or weak, who struggles to make something of himself, is the pursuit of happiness—and then in due course its achievement.

The ultimate validation of capitalism is that it institutionalizes not only the right values and virtues, but also the deepest truths. It is the system built on the proper relationship between existence and consciousness, i.e., between the axioms of philosophy themselves—the system that recognizes this relationship, permits it to men, and, like reality, demands it of them.

Capitalism is a corollary of the fundamentals of philosophy. Whoever understands capitalism sees it as the social system flowing from the axiom that "Existence exists"—just as whoever understands the axiom sees it ultimately as the principle entailing capitalism.

Opposition to Capitalism as Dependent on Bad Epistemology

The opposition to a political system involves the same category of thought as the defense. Although the opposition to capitalism often claims to be purely economic or practical in its concerns, it is in essence philosophical. It derives from a certain moral and, above all, epistemological approach.

The moral issue, by now obvious, is that one cannot combine the ethics of sacrifice with the politics of individualism. In addition, morality in this context is what gives content to "practicality." The "practical" is that which fosters a desired result, and morality is what specifies the results a social system should aim to reach. In Ayn Rand's words, "The evaluation of an action as 'practical' . . . depends on what it is that one wishes to practice."[20] If what one wishes to practice is power lust, going "back to nature," sacrificing the able, and/or sacrificing everybody (egalitarianism), then capitalism is not practical; it represents the opposite of all such practices.

The deepest root of politics, however, is not morality, but *its* root, epistemology (combined with metaphysics).

Truth—in regard to social problems, as to all others—does not force itself on men's minds; intrinsicism is false. If men are to grasp truth, they must perform a definite cognitive process. Just as capitalists, if they are to succeed in their (financial) goal, must function on the *conceptual* level of consciousness, with everything this implies, so must the defenders of capitalism, if they are to succeed in their (intellectual) goal. In an irrationalist era, neither group has any chance; capitalism could not last even if, by miracle, it were legislatively enacted—and it could never be enacted because no one, least of all the intellectuals, would be able to hear the reason why it *should* be enacted. Today, social scientists can write tomes cataloguing minutiae yet, in regard to any issue that matters, never suspect the obvious.

The opposition to capitalism often involves an element of evasion. But often it does not; the opponents are sincere; they are, one must say, honestly stupid—and it is a self-made, epistemologically induced stupidity. Intellectuals of this kind are deaf to facts (though unfortunately never dumb); they come to political conclusions by the same means they impute to capitalists in regard to the setting of prices: they do it by whim.

To illustrate the pattern, let us consider the Marxist charge, already answered, that capitalism leads to coercive monopolies. The point here is to demonstrate that the answer, like any rational idea, involves a certain kind of cognitive process and, therefore, relies on a certain kind of epistemology.

Suppose, plunging into an imaginary discussion, we start to answer an opponent by offering a definition of "monopoly." "Definitions," the modern mentality replies, "are a matter of semantics." Or: "Definitions are a matter of authority, and mine is endorsed by three Nobel laureates." Or: "Why do we need *any* rigid definition? I know what a monopoly is even if I can't state it in a cut-and-dried formula. I just saw the corner grocer go out of business because Safeway moved in. That's enough for me." The translation of these replies is: we can dispense with definitions, essentials, clarity, objectivity, concepts—all we need are percepts and feelings.

Suppose we try another tack. To refute the charge that "monopolies" have "too much power," we distinguish economic from political power. In order to explain the distinction, however, we have to indicate its basis by clarifying the essential difference between business and government. "Government," we begin, "if we are to grasp it correctly, requires us to turn to the question of man's rights, which takes us back to ethics; just as the nature of business requires us to turn to the cause of wealth, which takes us back to the role of the mind in man's life." Long before we have uttered even the outline of such a cognitive program, we will hear the modern answer: "That's theory, that's system-building, that's ideology! Who needs it? I *see* the robber baron's sweating workers, I've met some guys in the antitrust department, and I know they have the people's welfare at heart." Translation: we can dispense with abstractions, hierarchy, context, integration.

Suppose we try one last time. We distinguish monopolies achieved under capitalism (which depend on merit and harm no one) from monopolies granted under a mixed economy (which are a form of coercion dependent on government favors, such as tariff protection, subsidies, franchises); we conclude indignantly that the Marxist objection blames capitalism for evils that derive not from capitalism but from statism. "There are no sweeping, black-and-white social laws," we hear in reply. "How can you say that *every* governmental monopoly has bad consequences, and every free-enterprise monopoly, good ones? We must study each case on its own merits and remember that our conclusions are only tentative." Translation: we can dispense with principles, absolutes, causality, knowledge—nothing is certain but death, taxes, and the evil of capitalism.

Who can talk to mentalities like these? They cannot be convinced by a process of logic because they have no inkling of the nature of such a process. Thanks to the epistemology they practice (and probably preach), they are not open to reason.

All the objections raised against capitalism depend on the above kind of epistemology. And as in the issue of monopolies, all the evils widely ascribed to capitalism flow not from capitalism, but from its opposite. This includes such evils as depression, child labor, racism, adulterated food and drugs, pollution, war, and pornography.[21]

A depression is a major, nationwide economic decline, which can be caused only by an agency with nationwide power: the government—in this instance by using its (statist) power to manipulate the money supply. Child labor was necessitated by the poverty inherited from feudal economies; it was wiped out in the nineteenth century not by laws or labor unions, but by capitalism's productivity. Racism is a primitive form of collectivism that has been entrenched worldwide throughout history—except under capitalism; witness the fact that the American system led to a civil war which eradicated slavery.

Adulterated food and drugs are rare on a free market, because a seller's reputation for quality is essential to his long-range profits and because fraud is a crime; but decline in quality (of everything) is normal in a mixed economy, as businessmen with political pull move in to fleece a public lulled into the delusion that, since inspectors from Washington are overseeing everything, individual judgment is unnecessary. Pollution is a minor side effect of industrialization, one that only an unfettered industry has the financial and technological means to clean up. War is a product of dictatorships, which survive by looting; "the major wars of history," Ayn Rand observes, "were started by the more controlled economies of the time against the freer ones."[22] Pornography (along with drug addiction) spreads across a nation not because of liberty, but because of despair, the despair of semifree men in a collapsing world terrified by an unknowable future.

Most of the anticapitalist charges, absurd as they are taken singly, are presented to the public in pairs, both sides of which are wrong. We are bombarded by a stream not only of falsehoods, but of contradictory, self-cancelling falsehoods, such as:

"Capitalism is the system of coercive monopolies" and, from the same man or professor the next hour or month, "Capitalism is the system of cutthroat competition."

"Capitalism debases men by creating hunger" and "Capitalism subverts morality by creating affluence."

"Capitalist greed causes inflation" and "The gold standard leads to an inadequate supply of money and credit."

"Capitalism is another name for militaristic imperialism" and "Conscription is necessary because no one would fight even a war of self-defense under a free system."

"Capitalism is hostile to invention [followed by stories about industrialists allegedly suppressing new discoveries]" and "Capitalism leads to an intolerable rat-race of inventions."

"Capitalism is fine for the productive genius, but what about the common man?" and "Capitalism is fine for the common man, but what about the genius? [because a rock star makes more money than a physicist]."

"Capitalism is impracticable in our complex modern world—we are too advanced" and "Capitalism is impracticable in the undeveloped world—they are not advanced enough."

Some men have the grace to blush when the above pairs are pointed out. Others see no need to blush; having rejected every requirement of the conceptual faculty, they do not hesitate to throw out explicitly its method. "Aristotelian logic is old-fashioned," they say. "We use a dynamic, dialectic, and/or multivalued approach to thought."

Men who are immune to facts and logic have no alternative but to traffic in fantasy. Hence the senseless projections we hear today about life under pure capitalism: "What if roads were private property and the owners refused to let people drive on them?" "What if commercial firefighters charged a million dollars to put out a fire?" "What if unregulated television networks aired nothing but commercials and genitalia?" All of this is like asking: "What if bakers refused to let people buy their bread?" "What if surgeons charged a million dollars for an appendectomy?" "What if an unregulated press brought out papers filled only with ads and obscenities?" (One rarely hears anybody ask: "What if, under socialism, a clerk in the People's Planning Commission nurses a hatred for some helpless worker?" or "What if the top leader turns into a monster?"—yet these are daily realities under every version of collectivism.)

The most ludicrous of all the projections we hear is: "What if, under capitalism, no one volunteers to help the truly helpless?" Such callousness never existed in early America; it is possible on a large scale only when men are crushed by poverty, thanks to statism; and/or when men feel mutual hatred, thanks to being forced to subsist as prisoners in collectivist chain gangs.

Without a proper epistemology, men do not use their minds properly, and their political conclusions are correspondingly worthless. In today's culture, this principle works out as follows. Irrationalism leads the intellectuals to discard the possibility of independence (of the reality orientation) in favor of altruism, which leads them to conclude that capitalism is evil. Thereafter, however scandalously they drop context, rewrite history, or contradict themselves, they feel no shame; so long as they are anticapitalist, they feel noble. Their epistemology, in short, permits them to manipulate the data as they choose—to reach any conclusions they like in regard to any matter of fact; and their ethics programs them to reach only statist conclusions.

The above is why the intellectuals have never grasped the virtue of capitalism. They did not grasp it a century ago, and they are worse (and factually more ignorant) today. In every branch of the social sciences now, our intellectuals are literal "know-nothings," especially in the field of their own specialization. They are know-nothings *because* of their specialization, i.e., because of the kind of philosophy their years of academic training have instilled in them.

Man needs a philosophy to enable him to reach an integrated understanding of facts and a rational standard of evaluation. Without a proper philosophy, therefore, facts galore can be available, but men will not be able to grasp, connect, estimate, or learn from them. I am speaking here not only of corrupt intellectuals, but also of plain, decent men.

An honest but nonphilosophical man can recognize the rising prosperity of nineteenth-century America. But he will not know the implication of his observation for today's world. He will not know why freedom is essential to prosperity, or what it has to do with man's mind, or how to answer the people telling him that the cause of the wealth was natural resources, government subsidies, or the unlimited frontier, that "It's a changing world," and that capitalism does not apply any longer.

An honest man can see the worldwide failure of statism. But without philosophy he will not know how to answer the people telling him that the failure stems not from the nature of statism, but from its perversion, from the wrong leaders or the wrong tactics—the people who say that "Our gang would do it better."

An honest man can see that America is now on the brink of chaos and even suicide. But without philosophy he cannot identify the opposite principles at work in our mixed economy or even know that the system *is* a mixture of opposites. If a man understands only that "Something is wrong," he is vulnerable to those who clamor that what is wrong is that there is still too much capitalism in the country.

History, economics, journalism are not to be disparaged. But no amount of historical, economic, or journalistic data by themselves will change men's mind on the issue of capitalism vs. statism.

The battle for the world is not a battle between two political ideals. It is a battle between two views of the nature of thought.

▪　▪　▪　▪

Capitalism is practical. Capitalism is moral. Capitalism is *true*. But men will never know it until they understand these three concepts, along with everything on which they hierarchically depend.

If men are ever to reach a world where man is free, free not by permission but on principle, they must first enact the cause of freedom: they must grasp and accept the intellectual base it requires.

If they do so, the next American Revolution—in whatever land it occurs—will be more than a historic interlude. Next time, it will have a chance of lasting.

12

ART

The last of the five branches that make up a full system of philosophy is esthetics, the philosophy of art.

Philosophy as such does not deal with the problems of a specialized professional field, such as law, education, psychology, or physics. Each of these fields does need philosophy: it needs not only broad philosophic guidance, but also the application of philosophy (especially, epistemology) to its own special problems and methods. Thus the importance of subjects such as the philosophy of law, of education, or of science.

These subjects presuppose a division of intellectual labor; each addresses the needs of a specific group of professionals. A *branch* of philosophy, by contrast, is universal and timeless. It deals with an intellectual need of man qua man.

Besides the need of a view of the universe (covered by metaphysics), a method of knowledge (epistemology), and a code of values (ethics and politics), the only other need within the province of pure philosophy is *art*.

Even so philosophical a need as sex is not a subject for purely philosophical study (among other reasons, a scientific understanding of sex has to include a study of anatomy and physiology). But art pertains to man precisely qua subject of philosophy: art is a need of the mind, i.e., of man qua thinker and valuer. That is why, like philosophy itself, art has always existed among men, from prehistory to the present, and why animals have neither art nor any equivalent of it.

Esthetics asks: what is art? what is its role in man's life? by what standards should an art work be judged?

To answer these questions, a knowledge of fundamentals is necessary. Hierarchically, esthetics, like politics, is a derivative, which rests on the three basic branches of philosophy. Politics, as the application of ethics to social questions, is the narrower of the two fields. Esthetics is more profound: art's special root and concern is not ethics, but metaphysics.

Art as a Concretization of Metaphysics

A work of art is an end in itself, in the sense that it serves no purpose beyond man's contemplation of it. When one differentiates art from other human products, this fact is an essential. A scientific treatise, a machine, a busy signal on the telephone are a means to a utilitarian goal; a novel, a statue, a symphony are not.

The materialist mentality typically concludes that art is a frill, an indulgence unrelated to reason or to man's life in this world. The spiritualist mentality, in full agreement, takes off for points unknowable: he concludes that art is the prerogative of a mystic elite oriented to a supernatural dimension.

In opposition to both views, Objectivism holds that art does have a purpose, a *rational,* worldly, practical purpose. Art fulfills an essential need of human life, not a material need, but a spiritual need. "Art," writes Ayn Rand, *"is* inextricably tied to man's survival—not to his physical survival, but to that on which his physical survival depends: to the preservation and survival of his consciousness."[1]

The root of man's need of art lies in the fact that human consciousness is conceptual—and that a conceptual being needs the guidance of *philosophy.*

Since a conceptual consciousness is an integrating mechanism, it requires the ultimate integration of its contents that is provided by philosophy. A conceptual being needs context, principles, and long-range direction; he needs connection among his goals, coherence among his days, a broad overview uniting his disparate experiences, conclusions, and actions into a sum. To achieve such integration, a man needs a code of ethics and, above all, that on which ethics rests: a perspective on existence as such. He needs a view not only of work, of friends, or of food, but of life. He needs *metaphysical* conclusions. He needs them precisely to the extent that he does function as a man, rather than as an animal, or as close to such as a man can come: as an unthinking, concrete-bound, habit-driven drone.

A man may not deal with philosophic issues in conscious terms. But explicitly or implicitly he needs to know: what is the nature of the world in which I am acting and what kind of being am I the actor? (This latter includes the question: what are my means of knowledge?)

Ayn Rand illustrates as follows the kind of issues that are crucial in some form to everyone:

> Is the universe intelligible to man, or unintelligible and unknowable? Can man find happiness on earth, or is he doomed to frustration and despair? Does man have the power of *choice,* the power to choose his goals and to achieve them, the power to direct the course of his life— or is he the helpless plaything of forces beyond his control, which determine his fate? Is man, by nature, to be valued as good, or to be despised as evil?[2]

This category of questions is metaphysical: it pertains to a view of man in relation to the universe—or, what amounts to the same thing, a view of the universe in relation to man. Although an estimate of man's metaphysical nature is involved in these questions, ethics is not. The issue raised is not: "By what rules should a man live?" but, in effect, "Can man live?"—which is logically prior and which affects all of a man's specific choices and rules. If man is an efficacious being in a benevolent universe, then certain choices and actions (expressing self-assertion, ambition, idealism) are appropriate to him; if not, not. In either view (and in all the mixtures in between), metaphysics acts as man's *value conditioner*. By specifying in advance the nature of that to which he can realistically aspire, it tells him, in essence, how to approach the field of morality.

This category of questions, Miss Rand concludes, is "the link between metaphysics and ethics. And although metaphysics as such is not a normative science, the answers to this category of questions assume, in man's mind, the function of metaphysical value-judgments, since they form the foundation of all of his moral values."[3]

In any human activity—whether one is performing surgery, building a skyscraper, or defining abstract principles—two types of cognition are involved. In some form, a rational being must know not only the nature of his activity, but also the philosophic context on which it rests: why the activity is proper, how it relates to his code of values, how his values relate to reality. Thus a man's metaphysical value-judgments, as Ayn Rand puts the point, "are involved in every moment of his life, in his every choice, decision and action."[4] The basic orientation underlying the concretes of one's daily endeavors must be continuously operative in one's mind as one's basic guide. For this purpose, it need not (and cannot) be a continuous object of conscious awareness; but a rational being cannot afford to leave so vital an issue purely to subconscious implication. If he is to be in control of his life, he must have the power to know his metaphysics, i.e., to summon it into focus, to make it the specific object of his awareness. In this sense, a man's view of life must be available to him at all times—and available *as a sum*.

Metaphysical principles are the widest of all; they involve the total of human experience, subsuming a vast range of concretes by means of long chains of abstractions. Any given principle, once identified consciously, can be assessed as true or false (and if necessary revised) by applying the method of logic; this task belongs to the science of philosophy. But no one, philosophers included, can hold such a complexity of experiences and abstractions within the focus of his awareness as a sum. Yet a sum is precisely what a man needs. For cognitive purposes in this context, a thinker needs analysis, i.e., separately identified abstractions. For action, a man needs the integration, the all-embracing sweep, the vision of the universe.

If this kind of vision is to be available to a man's consciousness, his fundamental conclusions must be condensed into a unit on which he can choose to focus. He needs a concrete that can become an object of direct experience while carrying with it the meaning of his whole view of life. This is the role of art.

"Art," in Ayn Rand's definition, "is a selective re-creation of reality according to an artist's metaphysical value-judgments."[5]

The artist, Ayn Rand holds, makes a specialized use of the two basic processes of human consciousness. He uses isolation and integration in regard to

> those aspects of reality which represent man's fundamental view of himself and of existence. Out of the countless number of concretes—of single, disorganized and (seemingly) contradictory attributes, actions and entities—an artist isolates the things which he regards as metaphysically essential and integrates them into a single new concrete that represents an embodied abstraction.[6]

Guided by his own metaphysical value-judgments (explicit or otherwise), an artist selects, out of the bewildering chaos of human experience, those aspects he regards as indicative of the nature of the universe. Then he embodies them in a sensory-perceptual concrete such as a statue, a painting, or a story (this last is perceptual in that the writer must make certain characters and events real by conveying their visual appearance, sounds, textures, etc.). The result is a universe in microcosm. To be exact, the result is a view of the universe in the form of a deliberately slanted concrete, one shorn of all irrelevancies and thus broadcasting unmistakably to the viewer or reader: "This is what counts in life—as I, the artist, see life."

The artist is the closest man comes to being God. We can validly speak of the world of Michelangelo, of Van Gogh, of Dostoyevsky, not because they create a world ex nihilo, but because they do *re*-create one. Each omits, rearranges, emphasizes the data of reality and thus creates the universe anew, guided by his own view of the essence of the original one.

Suppose, to develop an example of Miss Rand's, one

sought to grasp the difference between an ancient Greek and a medieval Christian perspective on the universe. A philosopher could deliver many lectures covering the difference in regard to the primacy of existence, the relation of soul and body, law vs. miracles, reason vs. faith, choice vs. determinism, and the like. So many issues on so broad a level of abstraction would be involved, however, that one could hardly grasp from such lectures the net import of either view; one would know, in effect, many details of two theories, but not, for either period, the perspective as a whole. But if one then contemplates a statue of Adonis as against a deformed, cowering Adam, one grasps the import: one gets the sum of each vision and the contrast between them directly, in the form of two percepts.

The statues can perform this function because of the philosophical selectivity of their creators. The Greek sculptors knew that some men are sick, grimace in pain, fail; but they did not depict *man* in these terms because they did not ascribe metaphysical significance to these negatives. Similarly, the medieval sculptors knew that some men are healthy, laughing, successful; but to them this was a temporary accident or an illusion. In this vale of tears, Augustine remarked, the person who thinks himself happy "is more miserable still."[7]

An art work does not formulate the metaphysics it represents; it does not (or at least need not) articulate definitions and principles. So art by itself is not enough in this context. But the point is that philosophy is not enough, either. *Philosophy by itself cannot satisfy man's need of philosophy.* Man requires the union of the two: philosophy and art, the broad identifications and their concrete embodiment. Then, in regard to his fundamental, guiding orientation, he combines the power of mind and of body, i.e., he combines the range of abstract thought with the irresistible immediacy of sense perception.

Ayn Rand summarizes in a definitive formulation:

> Art is a concretization of metaphysics. *Art brings man's concepts to the perceptual level of his consciousness and allows him to grasp them directly, as if they were percepts.*

This is the psycho-epistemological function of art and the reason of its importance in man's life (and the crux of the Objectivist esthetics).[8]

Here again we see man's need of unit-economy. Concepts condense percepts; philosophy, as the science of the broadest integrations, condenses concepts; and art then condenses philosophy—by returning to the perceptual level, this time in a form impregnated with a profound abstract meaning.

There is an obvious analogy here between language and art. Both blend parts (whether perceptual units or philosophical principles) into a whole by similar means: both complete a process of conceptual integration by the use of sensuous elements. Both thereby convert abstractions into the equivalent of concretes. As Miss Rand puts it, both convert abstractions "into specific entities open to man's direct perception. The claim that 'art is a universal language' is not an empty metaphor, it is literally true—in the sense of the psycho-epistemological function performed by art."[9]

("Psycho-epistemology" is an invaluable term of Ayn Rand's, albeit one that pertains more to psychology than to philosophy. "Psycho-epistemology" designates "the study of man's cognitive processes from the aspect of the interaction between the conscious mind and the automatic functions of the subconscious."[10] Epistemology, in essence, studies conscious, volitional processes; a "psycho-epistemological" method or function is one that also involves subconscious, automatized elements.)

By converting abstractions into percepts, art performs another crucial (and inseparable) function. It not only integrates metaphysics, but also *objectifies* it. This means: it enables man to contemplate his view of the world in the form of an existential object—to contemplate it not as a content of his consciousness, but "out there," as an external fact. Since abstractions as such do not exist, there is no other way to make one's metaphysical abstractions fully *real* to oneself (or, therefore, fully operative as one's guide). "To acquire the full, persuasive, irresistible power of reality," Miss Rand writes, "man's metaphysical abstractions have to confront him in the form of concretes—i.e., in the form of art."[11]

The above is another expression of the primacy of existence. Since consciousness is not an independent entity, it cannot attain fulfillment within its own domain. In order to satisfy even its own most personal needs, it must in some form always return to its primary task: looking outward. To an entity whose essence is perception, there can in the end be no substitute for perception.

Now let us consider the condensing and objectifying function of art as it applies to another branch of philosophy: ethics.

Ethics (like metaphysics) is a complexity of broad abstractions which, to guide one's actions effectively amid the vicissitudes of daily concretes, must form in one's mind a sum. To grasp and apply a given code of values properly, one must know a series of separately identified moral rules—and also their integration, i.e., the moral character and way of life to which they add up. Such integration requires reduction to a unit: one must be able to summon into the focus of consciousness an image of a man following such a code. This involves a process of objectification; it requires the projection of a specific person. Thus the crucial importance, on a purely philosophical level, of fictional heroes like Howard Roark and John Galt. Without such projections, the Objectivist theory of ethics, however well presented, could not be clearly grasped by a man—just as the Christian code would be vague and floating apart from the stories of Jesus or of the saints. An ethical treatise alone does not give man the moral guidance he needs; nor does the image of a hero do so. But the union of the two does give it. "Art," Miss Rand concludes, "is the indispensable medium for the communication of a moral ideal."[12]

Ethics, she observes, is comparable to theoretical engineering. Both are applied sciences, concerned to guide human action, and both thus demand a form of technology, i.e., the actual creation of values. What the designer of a bridge or a spaceship is to engineering, the artist is to ethics: "Art is the technology of the soul. . . . Art creates the final product. It builds the model."[13]

Not all art works perform this function. The essential field in this context (which can be supplemented by the other arts) is literature, which alone is able to depict the richness of man in action across time, making choices, pursuing goals, facing obstacles, exhibiting not merely an isolated virtue, but a whole code of them. Further, although all art works involve some moral content, at least implicitly, the nature of such content depends on the basic viewpoint of the artist. Some artists' viewpoint leads them not to a vision of ideals to be reached, but to the conclusion that ideals are a chimera. The model-building aspect, therefore, though an eloquent illustration of art's psycho-epistemological function, is not a universal attribute of art; and even where it is present, it is not a primary. The primary concern of art, whatever its medium or viewpoint, is not ethics, but that on which ethics depends: metaphysics.

To a rational man, art that objectifies *his* metaphysics provides a unique kind of inspiration; it is an indispensable source of emotional fuel. A rational man's goals, being demanding and long-range, require a lifetime of effort and action. But a man cannot live only in the future; in Miss Rand's words, he needs a moment of rest, "in which he can experience the sense of his completed task, the sense of living in a universe where his values have been successfully achieved." By virtue of its power selectively to re-create reality (and, directly or indirectly, to project a hero), art can give man "the pleasure of feeling what it would be like to live in [his] ideal world. . . . [The fuel involved is] the life-giving fact of experiencing a moment of *metaphysical* joy—a moment of love for existence." Those who enter and belong in the enraptured universe of Victor Hugo—or of *Atlas Shrugged*—know the emotion to which Miss Rand is here referring.[14]

The irrational man gains *his* form of metaphysical satisfaction from his kind of art. The concretized projection of "What fools these mortals be," for instance, gives him not fuel to act, but consolation, reassurance, a license to stagnate. On a lower level, as our own century's trend illustrates, art may satisfy the lust of the life-hater, giving him the sense of his special brand of triumph: the triumph over all values and, ultimately, over existence as such.

Whether men are good or evil, they characteristically react to art in profoundly personal terms. When an art work does objectify his metaphysics, the reader or viewer experiences a confirmation of his mind and self on the deepest level; the perceptual concrete functions as an affirmation from reality of the efficacy of his consciousness. "Your approach to values is right," the painting or story implicitly tells him, "your grasp of the world is right, *you* are right." When an art work clashes with a man's metaphysics, by contrast, the experience represents a denial of his efficacy or even a war against his consciousness. The implicit message is: "Reality is not what you think, your values are a delusion, you as a person are wrong, wrong in every way that counts, wrong all the way down." To messages fraught with this category of meaning, responses of passionate embrace or violent recoil are inevitable.[15]

So far, I have been considering the *subject* of an art work, or *what* it presents—the perceptual concretes that convey its view of the world. But there is another essential aspect of art: *style,* i.e., *how* the artist presents his subject. "The subject of an art work," writes Ayn Rand, "expresses a view of man's existence, while the style expresses a view of man's consciousness. The subject reveals an artist's *metaphysics,* the style reveals his *psycho-epistemology.*" An artist's style, for example, may express a state of full focus—of clarity, purpose, precision; or a state of fog—of the opaque, the random, the blurred. In either (and any) case, style, like subject, has philosophical roots and meaning. In Ayn Rand's words, style reveals an artist's implicit view of the mind's "proper method and level of functioning," the level "on which the artist feels most at home." This is another reason why men react to art in profoundly personal terms. Like subject, though from a different aspect, style is experienced by the reader or viewer as a confirmation or denial of his consciousness.[16]

(Ayn Rand discusses style in chapters 3, 4, and 5 of *The Romantic Manifesto.* As to literary style in particular, the best source, rich in analyses of actual examples, is her 1958 *Lectures on Fiction Writing,* presently being edited for publication.)

In regard to all its distinctive functions, I must now stress, the role of art is *not* didactic.

Even when art does project a moral ideal, its goal is not to teach men that ideal. The purpose of art is not education or proselytizing, neither in regard to ethics nor to metaphysics. To teach these subjects is the task of philosophy, for which art is not a substitute; an art work is not a textbook or a propaganda vehicle. "The basic purpose of art," writes Miss Rand, "is *not* to teach, but to *show*—to hold up to man a concretized image of his nature and his place in the universe."[17] Since the function of art is to bring man's concepts to the perceptual level, the task of the artist is not to present conceptual information, but to provide man with a definite experience. It is the experience not of thinking, but of seeing, as he contemplates the artistic concrete: *"This* is what reality is like."

One can learn a great deal about life from a work of art (from its philosophy and theme)—just as, Miss Rand notes, one can learn a great deal about flying by dismantling and studying an airplane. But in both cases the knowledge one gains is a fringe benefit, not a primary. The purpose of a plane, as of an art work, is not to provide material for a classroom, but to *do* something. The purpose is to make possible to man a certain kind of action.

Art, one may say, *is* concerned to "teach." What it teaches, however, is not a theory, but a technique, a technique of directing one's awareness, directing it away from the inconsequential and toward the metaphysically essential. Art thereby clarifies a man's grasp of reality. "In this sense," Miss Rand writes, "art teaches man how to use his consciousness. It conditions or stylizes man's consciousness by conveying to him a certain way of looking at existence."[18]

In order to convey it, an art work, as already stated, must be a selective re-creation of reality. The operative word here is *selective*.

Art is not an instrument of literal reproduction. An artist's function is not to observe the data of nature, human or otherwise, then to report neutrally on what he has seen. He is not concerned to transcribe without estimate "the way men act" or "the way things are"; in different forms, this is the job of science, journalism, or photography. Art reports on "the way things are" *metaphysically.* The artist, therefore, has to choose from his observations; he has to slant the data in a calculated manner. This is not an escape from reality, but a unique form of attentiveness to it. Art offers not a competition to scientific fact, but a different kind of focus on reality, the fundamental focus that makes science and all other specialized pursuits possible. "An artist," writes Miss Rand, "does not fake reality—he *stylizes* it. . . . His concepts are not divorced from the facts of reality—they are concepts which integrate the facts *and* his metaphysical evaluation of the facts."[19]

An art work tells man not that something is, but that it is *important*.

"Important" is not synonymous with "good" (an evil may be important). "Important," according to one dictionary, denotes a standing "such as to entitle to attention or consideration"—and the only fundamental entitled to man's attention, Miss Rand holds, is reality. "Important," therefore, is essentially a metaphysical term, which pertains to and demarcates the special province of the artist:

> *Cognitive* abstractions are formed by the criterion of: what is *essential* (epistemologically essential to distinguish one class of existents from all others). *Normative* abstractions are formed by the criterion of: what is *good? Esthetic* abstractions are formed by the criterion of: what is *important.*[20]

An artist does not enunciate in his work his view of what is important; he may not even know his view in conscious terms. He needs merely to re-create reality, and the selectivity inherent in the process does the esthetic job. "His selection," writes Miss Rand, "constitutes his evaluation: everything in a work of art—from theme to subject to brushstroke or adjective—acquires metaphysical significance by the mere fact of being included, of being *important* enough to include."[21]

Thus Ayn Rand's eloquent example of a beautiful woman wearing a glamorous gown, with a cold sore on her lips.[22] In real life, the sore would be a meaningless infection. But a painting of such a woman would make a metaphysical statement. If an ugly little blister, like a demon leering out of the canvas, is important to an artist, if that is what he selects as entitled to men's focus and essential to their nature, then the meaning is: the attempt at beauty is futile and man is ridiculous; he is a worm with delusions of grandeur, at the mercy of a reality that mocks his aspirations.

A similar issue is involved when critics sneer at the heroes of popular novels or TV shows for always finding the murderer, curing the patient, winning the case. The critics invoke "truth," the truth found in statistical tables or in newspapers;

in real life, they say, people, unlike Perry Mason, do not always triumph over obstacles. What actually motivates such criticism is not "truth," but philosophy. No one contests the fact that detectives et al. can fail. The esthetic issue is whether such failure indicates *man's* destiny. The intellectuals' hatred of "happy endings" does not spring from the fact that criminals often go free in real life; it springs from the haters' insistence that when criminals *are* caught or patients cured or values achieved, such an outcome is *metaphysically* insignificant. The similarity between this viewpoint and that of Augustine is obvious.

The popular heroes are popular because the public desperately needs a certain fuel: not statistics about the favorable prospects of police work or the percentage of successful lawsuits, but an affirmation of the human potential. It is this affirmation that the intellectuals resent and seek to negate.

Not all happy endings convey a positive meaning. In Ayn Rand's *We the Living,* for example, the theme is the evil of dictatorship. All the characters of stature (including the heroine, who tries to flee the country) are destroyed—owing to the nature not of life, but, as the story makes clear, of statism. In this context, a happy ending would have declared that freedom is inessential to human life, which would imply that man is a mindless puppet, i.e., the opposite of a hero. Here again journalistic fact—the fact that some men do flee a dictatorship without being caught—is irrelevant. An art work is not a report on how well the borders of a nation are guarded.

No concrete within an art work, such as the type of ending given to a story, can be judged outside the full context of the work. The point is that, within the context, every concrete, simply by virtue of being included, acquires significance.

As a teenager, I told Miss Rand once that it was difficult to live up to the exalted quality of her novels. "If John Galt were out on a date," I said, "he would open a bottle of champagne with the ease of flourishing a cape, and the mood would be highly romantic. But when I do it, the cork sticks, I fumble with the bottle, and the mood is sabotaged. Why can't life be more like art?"

Miss Rand answered that the cork could very well stick for a real-life Galt, too. But if it did, he would brush the distraction aside; he would not let it affect his mood or evening. "In life," she said, "one ignores the unimportant; in art, one omits it."

Most men do not know in explicit terms what they regard as important. They are unfamiliar with philosophy and hold few ideas on the subject; yet they are able to create and/or respond to art. This is possible because all men, whatever their conscious mental content, hold metaphysical value-judgments in a special form, which Ayn Rand calls a *sense of life*. A "sense of life" is "a pre-conceptual equivalent of metaphysics, an emotional, subconsciously integrated appraisal of man and of existence."[23] Such a subconscious appraisal is involved in art of any kind or school.

From early childhood on, an individual continually makes choices and reaches conclusions in regard to concrete problems. These choices and conclusions, along with the feelings they engender, ultimately imply an abstract sum, a sense of oneself and the world. Since the mind *is* an integrating faculty, its contents have to be integrated; a conceptual consciousness—even a concrete-bound one—cannot escape making in some form broad generalizations about life. If a man characteristically chooses to be mentally active, that will lead him, other things being equal, to a sense of efficacy and of optimism (of a benevolent universe). If a man characteristically makes the opposite choice, then he gives himself up to chance; but his mental mechanism still goes on summing up his experiences, instilling in *him* a sense of helplessness and malevolence. In both cases, and in all the mixtures in between, Miss Rand observes,

> [w]hat began as a series of single, discrete conclusions (or evasions) about his own particular problems, becomes a generalized feeling about existence, an implicit *metaphysics* with the compelling motivational power of a constant, basic emotion—an emotion which is part of all his other emotions and underlies all his experiences. *This* is a sense of life.[24]

When they reach adulthood, some men—a handful—work to translate their sense of life into an explicit philosophy. Those who follow the proper development seek to prove their philosophy logically; then, if the evidence requires it, they amend their earlier, implicit metaphysics, thereby bringing into harmony these two aspects of their soul. Other men enter the field of explicit ideas, but default on this task; they do not try to relate the conscious and the subconscious. Such men may live out their days tortured by a clash between philosophy and sense of life, i.e., between their avowed beliefs and their basic feelings. Still other men—the vast majority—hardly conceptualize metaphysical issues at all; they remain at the mercy of their inarticulate sense of life, whatever it happens to be.

In all these cases, however, the element responsible for art is the same. The element is not explicit philosophy, but sense of life, i.e., one's deepest convictions held in emotional form, which (like any automatized integration) function with lightninglike speed.

> It is the artist's sense of life that controls and integrates his work [writes Miss Rand], directing the innumerable choices he has to make. . . . It is the viewer's or reader's sense of life that responds to a work of art by a complex, yet automatic reaction of acceptance and approval, or rejection and condemnation.[25]

Art is inherently philosophical, even if those who create and respond to it are not. Art may not be philosophical explicitly, but it must be so *implicitly;* it must express some sense-of-life emotion. As and when necessary, this emotion can be identified in words; it can be translated into explicit metaphysical value-judgments.

Sense-of-life emotions, being products of a complex cause, can be difficult to identify; and most men regard emotions of any kind as outside the province of the mind. Hence the widespread view that artistic responses are inexplicable and that art is a species of the unknowable. In fact, however, sense-of-life emotions, like all others, are explicable—and alterable, if the facts of reality so demand. Like every phenomenon of human life, the realm of art *is* knowable—if one uses the human means of knowledge.

Objectivism offers a *rational* esthetics. Ayn Rand's theory is not only defensible in reason; it ties art *to* the faculty of reason. It shows that the root of art is not some mystic power which prostrates man's cognitive faculty, but the exact opposite: the root *is* man's cognitive faculty.

Romantic Literature as Illustrating the Role of Philosophy in Art

Let us concretize the above theory by focusing on a specific school of art, Romanticism; and, within it, on a specific art, literature. Out of all the possibilities, I choose Romanticism because it is, in Ayn Rand's view, "the greatest achievement in art history."[26] I choose literature because it is relatively easy to discuss in objective terms, and, above all, because Ayn Rand was concerned as an esthetician predominantly with her own field, the novel.

"Romanticism" denotes an art movement dating from the early nineteenth century; among its greatest writers are Victor Hugo, Dostoyevsky, Friedrich Schiller, and Edmond Rostand. This movement must not be confused with what is called "Romanticism" in philosophy, i.e., the Fichte-Schelling-Schopenhauer brand of mysticism. Judged by essentials, Ayn Rand holds, these two movements are opposites.[27]

The most obvious characteristic of Romanticism, which many critics take as definitional, is its projection of passion, drama, color—i.e., of emotion—as against the formulaic Classicism that preceded it and the bleak Naturalism that followed it. The root of emotion, however, is value-judgments, and the root of value-judgments is man's power of choice. According to the rule of fundamentality, therefore, this last must be taken as the school's essential characteristic. "Romanticism," in Ayn Rand's definition, "is a category of art based on the recognition of the principle that man possesses the faculty of volition."[28]

The Romantic school arose on the heels of the Enlightenment, when medievalism had finally succumbed to the pagan, especially Aristotelian, influence.[29] The result, philosophically, was not Aristotelian ideas—thinkers were turning en masse to Kant—but, culturally, an Aristotelian sense of life. What dominated the culture was a largely subconscious confidence in the power of man's mind; the political corollary was the spread of capitalism. Thus arose an art intoxicated by the discovery of man's unlimited potential, an art centering on choice and freedom, emphasizing the ability of the individual to select his course and to act accordingly.

The Romanticists were generally unphilosophical and did not identify their roots in the above terms. They did not know that Aristotle was their father or that freedom requires capitalism. On the contrary, most believed in loose versions of mysticism and altruism. They were united only on the principle that man is self-directed and goal-directed, that he is an initiator moved by values he has freely accepted. What these artists rejected was a single tenet: determinism (on which Naturalism was later based). They rejected the idea of man as a puppet, whether of God or society.

In the case of the highest exponents of Romanticism, the affirmation of volition affects every attribute of their work. In literature, it affects theme, story, characterization, and style. Historically, the two aspects that most clearly separate Romanticism from Naturalism are type of story and type of characterization.

Turning to the first, Ayn Rand indicates the Romantic approach as follows. If man must choose values, she writes,

> then he must act to gain and/or keep them—if so, then he must set his goals and engage in purposeful action to achieve them. The literary form expressing the essence of such action is the *plot*. A plot is a purposeful progression of logically connected events leading to the resolution of a climax.[30]

For Ayn Rand, "plot" denotes a specific kind of literary structure. To identify it, every term in her definition is necessary.[31]

To begin with, a plot is a progression of *events*—and "events" in this context means actions in the physical world. Values are a guide to action, and art is a re-creation of reality. If a writer regards men's choice of values as important, therefore, he must dramatize their choices *in* reality. A plot writer is not concerned primarily with the depiction of character, psychology, or introspection. All these, in some form, are vital as means; but their end and justification, in art as in life, is that to which they lead men in the realm of existence. The end is what the characters *do*. This is why Ayn Rand regards plot as *"the* crucial attribute of a novel."[32]

Since man is an integration of mind and body, his life is neither thought without action nor action without thought; plot follows the second half of this principle also. Since plot presents men in pursuit of values, the form excludes "pure action," i.e., physical movements devoid of spiritual meaning, such as mindless fist fights, car chases, or spaceship wars. Plot does not depict inner life by itself, however evocative, or bodily motion, however flashy; it is not a vehicle of "mood studies" or of "special effects." The "stream of consciousness" literature revered by our colleges belongs in the same esthetic category as the physicalistic junk coming out of Hollywood. Both variants are debarred by the same principle from the realm of plot (and of reason).[33]

Plot is a progression of *logically connected* events. A chronicle, a memoir, or a Naturalistic "slice of life" usually presents a series of events and may even be suspenseful. But the relationship among the events—their sequence and ending—is largely a matter of chance: this, the author says in effect, is how things happened to happen. A plot story, by contrast, has a definite structure: each major event necessitates the next. In the terminology of logicians, the first type of story represents merely temporal succession; the second represents causal connection. The author of a plot, therefore, must be highly selective in regard to the events he includes. In Ayn Rand's words, he must devise

> a sequence in which every major event is connected with, determined by and proceeds from the preceding events of the story—a sequence in which nothing is irrelevant, arbitrary or accidental, so that the logic of the events leads inevitably to a final resolution.[34]

A writer cannot devise a logical sequence if his characters are goalless. On the contrary, his task is specifically to dramatize purposefulness, i.e., to single it out for artistic emphasis. This requires that he show a purposeful will enduring in the face of obstacles. Since the achievement of goals is not given to man automatically, the plot writer must underscore this fact; he must show man struggling for his goals against antagonistic forces. In other words, the story must be based on *conflict*—either inner conflict, among a character's own values, and/or outer conflict, against the values of other men. The struggle ultimately leads to a climax; the climax is the event(s) that resolves the conflicts, telling the reader who (if anyone) wins out.[35]

For an example of the several features of a plot, let us refer to one brief segment of *The Fountainhead,* its climax, which runs from the dynamiting of the Cortlandt housing project through Roark's trial. (Anyone who has read this far is, I assume, familiar with the novel.)

The dynamiting, first of all, is an event. It is not a theoretical discussion or a bit of soul-searching, but an eminently physical action—with an eminently spiritual meaning: a man's affirmation of *his* ownership of his work. Now consider how this action is related to what went before—and how, as the climax, it resolves the conflicts of all the leading characters.

The thematic conflict in the book, dramatized in the main line of events, pits Roark, the intransigent individualist, against every kind of second-hander, who demand of him selfless service and mindless obedience. In the final showdown, accordingly, each side is led to enact its viewpoint on a grand scale. The second-handers seize Roark's achievement without payment and alter it without reason; he responds by blasting both their claim to his work and their disfigurement of it. Counting on the fact that men survive by reason and, given a chance, will listen to it, Roark then explains his action to the world—and is vindicated.

Keating, the parasite devoid of ego, craves but is unable to carry out the Cortlandt assignment; so he can only beg once again to survive through Roark's effort. This final revelation—to himself, then to the world—of his utter spiritual poverty is the culminating act of his destruction.

Wynand, the man of nobler values who thinks he can protect them by catering to the mob, tries in the crisis to protect the man he loves. His own contradiction, however, defeats him; his newspaper is actually harmful to Roark's cause. Popularity in the realm of fools, he finds, is impotence in the realm of values.

Toohey, the consciously evil power-luster who is now at the height of his power, finds that he cannot exercise his power successfully. *His* contradiction is that he has to count on the very men he is seeking to leash and thus destroy. Once Roark and Wynand, each in his own way, withdraw their creative ability, there is nothing left to or of him.

Dominique, the idealist who loves Roark but thought him doomed by a malevolent universe, observes the logic of the unfolding events. She sees that her inner torture was needless—because the good, including Roark, is not doomed.

The Cortlandt explosion with its aftermath involves all the main characters, follows from their life courses, and resolves their conflicts. Roark does not dynamite Cortlandt capriciously; given his basic values and the facts confronting him, he has to take that kind of action and, in the end, to win out thereby. The same applies *mutatis mutandis* to the other characters. There is nothing irrelevant, arbitrary, or accidental here; what happens is necessitated by all the major events that came earlier.

This is an example of a plot structure, as against a haphazard string of occurrences.

We often hear that plot is "artificial," because the events of real life have no such structure. Ayn Rand replies that they *do* have it. But to grasp the fact, she adds, one must be able to think in terms of principles:

> The events of men's lives follow the logic of men's premises and values—as one can observe if one looks past the range of the immediate moment, past the trivial irrelevancies, repetitions and routines of daily living, and sees the essentials, the turning points, the direction of a man's life. And, from that viewpoint, one can also observe that the accidents or disasters, which interfere with or defeat human goals, are a minor and marginal, not a major and determining, element in the course of human existence.[36]

If the province of art is the "important," then what is important to the plot writer is not the fact of accident, but the *power of values* in human life. Since his story presents an inexorable connection between values, action, and climax, the meaning is not only that men choose goals, but also that this fact is fraught with consequence. The logic of the artist's structure, no matter what particular events or theme he presents, is what speaks volumes here. Plot implies that *life* is logical, in the sense that a man's choices are what shape his fate.

"Contrary to the prevalent literary doctrines of today," Ayn Rand concludes, "it is *realism* that demands a plot structure in a novel. . . . [I]f one is to present man *as he is*—as he is metaphysically, by his nature, in reality—one has to present him in goal-directed action."[37]

If man is regarded as a pawn of society, by contrast, then his choice of values is regarded not as a power in his life, but as an illusion. In this view, man is a reactor, buffeted by whatever forces impinge on him; there is no necessary connection among the events of his days and no logic in the way he ends up. The literary form expressing this theory is "uncontrived" stories or no story, i.e., plotlessness (to which Naturalist writers are committed).

The opponents of Romanticism characteristically denounce plot in terms too angry for a merely literary dispute. Their intensity is not inappropriate, however, because the dispute is not merely literary. Like so many other esthetic controversies, it reduces to an issue of fundamental philosophy. Once again, the Objectivist principle is evident: art is a concretization of metaphysics.

Turning now to characterization: the consistent, top-level Romanticists are committed to the premise of volition in regard both to existence and to consciousness, i.e., both to action and to character.[38] These writers are moralists; they are concerned not only with values in the sense of concrete goals, but also with *moral* values, i.e., with the kinds of choices that shape a man's whole approach to life. The plots of such writers endow physical action with a profound spiritual meaning; their themes deal with fundamental, timeless issues of human existence.

These novels and plays do not merely indicate how men act. They tell us, often down to the level of basic motivation, *why* the characters are pursuing certain goals. Such characters are consistent and intelligible (even when torn by conflict). They have the kind of soul that makes possible intelligible, value-directed action. In other words, they have the inner logic that is the precondition of the logic of plot.

To achieve such characterization, the Romantic writer

once again must be highly selective. Just as he cannot record chance events, so he cannot re-create the eclectic specimens of humanity he sees around him. His characters, in Ayn Rand's words, are "abstract projections, not reproductions of concretes; they are invented conceptually, not copied reportorially from the particular individuals he might have observed." The Romanticist's characterological material, she writes elsewhere, "is not journalistic minutiae, but the abstract, the essential, the universal principles of human nature. . . ." Out of the chaos of contradictions that makes up most people's souls, the author selects and stylizes certain attributes, presenting them in purer form than they exist in average men. The resulting characters are "larger than life"; they are abstractions pertaining to man metaphysically, which can subsume real-life individuals from all places and times. For example, the result is not "a modern architect from New York in the 1930s," but Roark, the individualist.[39]

Metaphysical characterizations and timeless themes are not the exclusive prerogative of Romantic writers; they are possible to many different schools of literature. What the Romanticists alone dramatize, however, is the metaphysical abstraction of man moved by his own choices.

The characters of Romantic fiction are not floating abstractions; they are not the stick or stock figures of a morality play. The Romantic figure "has to be an abstraction," Miss Rand observes, "yet look like a concrete; it has to have the universality of an abstraction and, simultaneously, the unrepeatable uniqueness of a *person.*"[40]

When the era of Naturalism arrived, its exponents soon dropped the abstract approach to characterization. The writer, it was increasingly said, must be "value-free"; he must not project a hero or any other departure from "men as they are"; the latter, being socially determined, are inevitable. But the Naturalists still had to decide which of men's actual traits to record and which to omit. They decided it, as Ayn Rand points out, by

substituting *statistics* for a standard of value. That which could be claimed to be typical of a large number of men, in any given geographical area or period of time, was regarded as metaphysically significant and worthy of being recorded. That which was rare, unusual, exceptional, was regarded as unimportant and *unreal*.[41]

Despite their literary theory, Naturalists have to employ some selectivity; they cannot, therefore, avoid conveying an implicit metaphysical meaning. By entering the field of art, they become subject to its necessities, like it or not. In their conscious attempt, however, as Ayn Rand writes, the Naturalists were "dedicated to the negation of art. . . . In answer to the question: 'What is man?' . . . [they said:] 'These are the folks next door.' Art—the integrator of metaphysics, the concretizer of man's widest abstractions—was shrinking to the level of a plodding, concrete-bound dolt. . . ."[42]

(Given their belief in human helplessness, the Naturalists were drawn to the depiction of negatives: of poverty, wretchedness, ugliness, corruption. In the end, their portrait of doom became so stark that the school broke up. Its remnants merged into the depravity school of literature, which offers not statistical averages, but, once again, metaphysical projections: this time of man not as potential hero, but as inevitable monster.)[43]

To the Romanticist, intoxicated as he is with the possible, it is a virtue, not a flaw, that the men and events he portrays are exceptional, dramatic, heroic, beautiful. It is a badge of honor that he does *not* record "things as they are," but looks beyond them. In his view, the people one sees represent merely the choices that specific individuals happen to have made. Such people do not exhaust that which counts about man: the choices open to him by his nature. In this regard, the Romanticist follows (while the Naturalist denies) what Ayn Rand calls "the most important principle of the esthetics of literature."[44] The principle was first formulated, logically enough, by the father of logic.

"The distinction between historian and poet," writes Aristotle in the *Poetics,* "consists really in this, that the one describes the thing that has been, and the other a kind of thing that might be. Hence poetry is something more philosophic and of graver import than history. . . ." "History," in Ayn Rand's paraphrase of this statement, "represents things as they are, while fiction represents them as they might be and ought to be."[45]

By its nature, Romanticism is an approach to which Ayn Rand's complete theory of art applies—not only art as concretizer of metaphysics, but also art as model builder and thus as the fuel of the soul. To those who reject such art as an "escape," Ayn Rand replies:

> If the projection of value-goals—the projection of an improvement on the given, the known, the immediately available—is an "escape," then medicine is an "escape" from disease, agriculture is an "escape" from hunger, knowledge is an "escape" from ignorance, ambition is an "escape" from sloth, and life is an "escape" from death. If so, then a hard-core realist is a vermin-eaten brute who sits motionless in a mud puddle, contemplates a pigsty and whines that "such is life." If *that* is realism, then I am an escapist. So was Aristotle. So was Christopher Columbus.[46]

Although its essence was the opposite of escapism, however, Romanticism could not fully carry out its intention.[47] The cause was the ethics of altruism. The creation of credible value models requires a certain kind of values; a character is not an inspiring vision of man "as he might be" if the ideals he enacts lead him to contradiction, loss, destruction. Accepting as they did an inverted moral code, the Romanticists were generally unable to project a convincing hero; the self-assertive villains in their stories regularly stole the fire and drama from the anemic embodiments of virtue. Thus the school was led eventually to retreat from characterization—from motivation, psychology, moral values—into stories of purely external action; and to retreat from action dealing with real-life issues into costume dramas or, later, fantasy. Thus, increasingly, the movement did become escapist.

When the Aristotelian sense of life was finally killed by nineteenth-century philosophy, when Naturalism and then "modernism" began to take over the realm of art, the Romanticists (what was left of them) were helpless. They had neither the ideas nor the intellectual seriousness necessary to fight the trend.

Ayn Rand's code of values is what the Romanticists had needed. Her code enables the hero-worshiping artist to project a fully convincing hero, a man living, acting, and succeeding in reality. Ayn Rand calls this approach to art, which is her own approach, *Romantic Realism*. Her novels are true to Aristotle's principle: the world they create truly "might be." "I am Romantic," Ayn Rand has said, "in the sense that I present men as they ought to be. I am Realistic in the sense that I place them here and now and on this earth in terms that apply to every rational reader who shares these values and wants to apply them to himself."[48]

Let me conclude this discussion with a generalized indication of the nature of Romantic literary style, bearing in mind that style is the most complex and idiosyncratic of all artistic attributes.

In regard to style, as to events and characterization, the Romantic writer is highly selective. "Romantic style," Miss Rand once observed, "is description by means of essentials, but giving one the concretes, not floating abstractions."[49] Whether he is describing a sunset, a city, or a human face, the Romantic writer offers not a mass of trivial detail, however true to life, but only the perceptual essentials, the telling facts (down to small touches) that make the object concretely real to the reader. At the same time, the writing is not neutral or detached; it is emotionally slanted. What it conveys is not merely facts, but facts bearing an evaluative meaning of some kind. In the best writers, the evaluation is not superimposed on the description, but seems to flow inevitably from it, by virtue of the compelling inner logic of the writing.

As the above mere hint suggests, Romantic literary style, like the other features of the school (and like any rational human product) depends for its validation on a certain kind of philosophy: a philosophy of integration, not of dichotomy. Here again what men need urgently is the definition of a perspective able to unite percepts and concepts, facts and values, reason and emotion, mind and body.

Without such a philosophy, men *can* create plots, project heroes, and write beautifully, just as they can live successfully—for a while. But if they do not know the deepest meaning and justification of a noble endeavor, they are not in intellectual control of it, and the ignoble soon takes over.

The fall of Romanticism is an eloquent case in point.

Esthetic Value as Objective

As the history of Romanticism indicates, an artist's philosophy can have significant consequences in regard to his esthetic merit. This does not, however, alter the fact that there is a difference between philosophic and esthetic judgment.

In judging an art work's philosophy, one is concerned with a question of truth: are the implicit metaphysical value-judgments guiding the artist's selections true or false, proved or arbitrary, logical or illogical? (Any explicit ideology in a work that clashes with its operative metaphysics is essentially irrelevant to its meaning.)

In judging an art work qua art, by contrast, one enters the domain of a highly personal emotion, sense of life. The goal of art, we have said, is not to prove but to show—to concretize whatever sense of life the artist has, whether it be true or false. "The fact that one agrees or disagrees with an artist's philosophy," Miss Rand concludes, "is irrelevant to an *esthetic* appraisal of his work *qua* art."[50] A false philosophy can be embodied in a great work of art; a true philosophy, in an inferior or worthless one. How then does one judge *esthetic* value?

The standard answer, which Objectivism rejects, is that one judges it by feeling. Even though the task of art is to concretize a certain emotion, Ayn Rand holds, this does not mean that the emotion is a tool of cognition; a sense of life is the source of art, but it is not a means of esthetic judgment. The viewer, reader, or listener can feel that a given work is great, he can even feel that it is a superlative embodiment of profound value-judgments—but feeling doesn't make it so. In this field, as in any other, valid assessment requires a process of reason.

With rare exceptions, estheticians who rejected emotionalism turned instead to authoritarianism. Just as mankind's religious leaders laid down concrete-bound moral commandments, so their equivalents in esthetics laid down concrete-bound decalogues of their own to govern the evaluation of plays, music, and buildings. These esthetic commandments were usually derived from esteemed art works of the past, then upheld as a guide for all future art. In modern times, this approach was represented by Classicism. It is a telling commentary on Western thought that the dogmatic absolutes urged by Classicism are still widely regarded as an example in esthetics of "the cool voice of reason."

A proper esthetic evaluation is neither emotional nor authoritarian. The pattern to follow in this field has been described briefly by Ayn Rand:

> In essence, an objective evaluation requires that one identify the artist's theme, the abstract meaning of his work (exclusively by identifying the evidence contained in the work and allowing no other, outside considerations), then evaluate the means by which he conveys it—i.e., taking *his* theme as criterion, evaluate the purely esthetic elements of the work, the technical mastery (or lack of it) with which he projects (or fails to project) *his* view of life.[51]

To translate a metaphysical feeling into the terms of a perceptual experience is an extraordinarily demanding task. One must know what one wants to express and how to do it within the medium and form one has chosen; so one must know what are the attributes of these latter, their potentialities, their limitations, their requirements. Then one must methodically exploit the attributes to the end of conveying one's meaning in its every shading of nuance.

All human creativity involves focus, purpose, thought. Art is emphatically included in this statement, as the composer Richard Halley makes clear in a well-known speech from *Atlas Shrugged*. The real artist knows, he says, "what discipline, what effort, what tension of mind, what unrelenting strain upon one's power of clarity are needed to produce a work of art . . . [I]t requires a labor which makes a chain gang look like rest and a severity no army-drilling sadist could impose. . . ."[52]

Contrary to today's viewpoint, artistic creation is the opposite of the self-indulgent, the whim-worshiping, the irrational. An artist can choose to objectify any metaphysical value-judgments he wishes; but this fact does *not* imply that he can choose any means he wishes in order to objectify them. On the contrary, he can objectify his viewpoint only by adhering (knowingly or otherwise) to certain rational principles,

principles that apply universally, to art as such, regardless of an individual artist's philosophy. These are the principles that constitute the standard of proper esthetic judgment. To identify them is the task of the science of esthetics (which must also indicate how they apply within the context of the different artistic media and forms).

The source of the principles must be the nature of art itself and its role in man's life. This is the expression in esthetics of the method one follows in ethics. One is able to define a rational code of ethical principles only by first identifying what values are and why man needs them.

Miss Rand does not discuss esthetic evaluation systematically, but she does offer several leads to the field. For illustrative purposes, I have chosen (from different contexts) three esthetic principles that she advocates. The first of these is the requirement of *selectivity in regard to subject.*

Since the subject is what conveys the artist's metaphysics, art by its nature must have a subject, and it must be at least implicitly philosophical. One need not agree with an artist's theme, metaphysics, or choice of subject; he is free to express his viewpoint by choosing the concretes he regards as best suited to the purpose. But "best" may not be determined by caprice. Since art by its nature is selective, the artist must make a conscious, rational choice in this issue, given the sense of life he is seeking to concretize. "It is the selectivity in regard to subject," Miss Rand writes—

> the most severely, rigorously, ruthlessly exercised selectivity—that I hold as the primary, the essential, the cardinal aspect of art. In literature, this means: *the story*—which means: the plot and the characters—which means: the kind of men and events that a writer chooses to portray.[53]

No matter what his sense of life, an artist may not properly choose as his subject the random, the second-handed, or the metaphysically meaningless (e.g., Brillo pads). Since he has a definite perspective on reality to convey, he may not choose his subject by the standard of: "whatever comes along" or "whatever incidents of my adolescence I happen to remember." Since it is *his* perspective, his standard cannot be: "whatever subject others have chosen or the critics ap-

prove." Since he is engaged in an activity with an objective
purpose, his standard cannot be: "whatever appeals to me."

An obvious violation of this first principle would be a
crazy quilt of borrowed elements that add up to nothing, such
as one finds in the typical soap opera, "philosophical" novel,
or Broadway musical. The primary cause of bad art, as Miss
Rand observes, is the fact that it is a product of imitation, not
of creative expression. The imitator is not guided by a sense
of life; he picks up elements from other works instead—
throwing in a love triangle to spice up a lagging story line; or
a windy dissertation on death and infinity "for depth"; or a
splashy production number to ensure a "big finale." A product of this sort, popular or academic, may suggest snatches of
several viewpoints and may even be artful in delimited respects. As a total, however, it is devoid of meaning and therefore of esthetic value.

On a higher level of the same error are serious artists who,
thanks to their theory of art, explicitly forbid selectivity in
regard to subject, insisting that the artist offer an uncritical
"slice of life." While a definite sense of life meaning emerges
from such a work, it does so tangentially and as a rule inconsistently, since any projection of metaphysics conflicts with
the artist's theory and intention. In this context, the artist's
philosophy (e.g., the Naturalist's determinism) *is* relevant to
esthetic judgment. It is relevant not because the philosophy is
false, but only to the extent that it leads the artist to contradict the nature of art and thereby undercuts him qua artist.

Most artists who shrug off selectivity in regard to subject
do it on the grounds that what counts in art is only *style*. Ayn
Rand regards this viewpoint as a fundamental inversion. "The
subject is not the only attribute of art," she writes,

> but it is the fundamental one, it is the end to which all the
> others are the means. In most esthetic theories, however,
> the end—the subject—is omitted from consideration, and
> only the means are regarded as esthetically relevant. Such
> theories set up a false dichotomy and claim that a slob
> portrayed by the technical means of a genius is preferable
> to a goddess portrayed by the technique of an amateur. I
> hold that *both* are esthetically offensive; but while the sec-

ond is merely esthetic incompetence, the first is an esthetic crime.

There is no dichotomy, no necessary conflict between ends and means. The end does *not* justify the means—neither in ethics nor in esthetics. And neither do the means justify the end: there is no esthetic justification for the spectacle of Rembrandt's great artistic skill employed to portray a side of beef. . . .

In art, and in literature, the end and the means, or the subject and the style, must be worthy of each other.[54]

Art is not "for art's sake," but for *man's* sake. One contemplates art for the vision of reality it offers, not because, devoid of vision, it is merely a vehicle of technical virtuosity. The artist's freedom in regard to philosophy is not the freedom to dismember art; it is not the freedom to award significance to a single one of its attributes while dropping the context which gives that attribute its function.

The extreme of the antisubject attitude is the idea that an art work should not depict recognizable entities at all, i.e., that it should have no subject. In Objectivist terms, this hollow irrationalism amounts to the notion that the way to recreate reality is to dispense with it. The same flight from content characterizes modernism in virtually every field. Thus, while artists disdain "representation," philosophers disdain conclusions, priding themselves instead on an activity, "analysis," which is practiced for its own sake and never issues in any system of thought. Just as educators banish subject matter from the classroom so as to teach students techniques of social interaction and of "experimentation." Just as leading physicists declare that they are concerned not with the real nature of the physical world, but only with floating equations that somehow foster successful prediction. Just as the courts are emptying the term "freedom" of substantive meaning—while focussing instead on procedural questions, such as the "due process" necessary to deny to some poor soul his inalienable rights.

The modern cultural approach was epitomized fifty years ago in the Nazi concentration camps where competent surgeons performed expert operations on the inmates—removing perfectly healthy organs or limbs. This is a fictionlike example

of elevating technique above content, process above substance, means above ends. It may be taken as a gruesome symbol of the mentalities in any field who enjoy exercising skill
in a vacuum, without being "tied down" by absolutes, purpose, or *values*.

Since Ayn Rand represents the antithesis of these mentalities, her view of the proper subject of an art work reflects
the fact. "That which is not worth contemplating in life," she
writes, leading up to the model-building function of art, is not
worth re-creating in art.

> Misery, disease, disaster, evil, all the negatives of human
> existence, are proper objects of *study* in life, for the pur-
> pose of understanding and correcting them—but are not
> proper objects of *contemplation* for contemplation's sake.
> In art, and in literature, these negatives are worth re-
> creating only in relation to some positive, as a foil, as a
> contrast, as a means of stressing the positive—but *not* as
> an end in themselves. . . .
>
> That one should wish to enjoy the contemplation of
> *values*, of the *good*—of man's greatness, intelligence, abil-
> ity, virtue, heroism—is self-explanatory. It is the contem-
> plation of the *evil* that requires explanation and
> justification; and the same goes for the contemplation of
> the mediocre, the undistinguished, the commonplace, the
> meaningless, the mindless.[55]

The above passage comes from Ayn Rand's personal artistic manifesto, "The Goal of My Writing." I take her to be
speaking here as an Objectivist, defining a crucial esthetic implication of her view that evil is impotent, but not as an esthetician prescribing standards of judgment for art as such,
regardless of the artist's philosophy. An artist, as she often
suggests elsewhere, does not have to depict the good. Depending on his sense of life, he may depict heroes or average
men or even "crawling specimens of depravity."[56] He may do
it and still create good art—so long as, within his own context, he adheres to all the principles of good art, including the
principle of selectivity in regard to subject.

A second principle of esthetic judgment, which pertains
to style, is the requirement most simply described as *clarity*.
In the broad sense applicable here, "clarity" denotes the

quality of being distinct, sharp, evident to the mind, as against being obscure, clouded, confused. This is a requirement of any human product that involves a conceptual meaning. Art, like science, philosophy, and cooking instructions, must be "fully intelligible" (one of the *Oxford English Dictionary*'s definitions of "clear"). Of course, an artist can choose to present the universe as an incomprehensible jungle—but only if the presentation itself is intelligible.

Today's mystics and skeptics demand "ambiguity" in art; they assert as a self-evidency the virtue of the elusive, the enigmatic, the indeterminate, the opaque. Although these qualities would represent failure in any conceptual product, they are especially deadly in the field of art. The function of the artist is to overcome the opacity of human experience— to confront a universe that does often seem baffling and, by judicious selectivity, to reveal its true essence. The purpose of art, in other words, is the opposite of today's bromide. The purpose is not to revel in life's "ambiguity," but to eliminate it.

"Predominantly (though not exclusively)," writes Miss Rand,

> a man whose normal mental state is a state of full focus, will create and respond to a style of radiant clarity and ruthless precision—a style that projects sharp outlines, cleanliness, purpose, an intransigent commitment to full awareness and clear-cut identity—a level of awareness appropriate to a universe where A is A, where everything is open to man's consciousness and demands its constant functioning.
>
> A man who is moved by the fog of his feelings and spends most of his time out of focus will create and respond to a style of blurred, "mysterious" murk, where outlines dissolve and entities flow into one another, where words connote anything and denote nothing, where colors float without objects, and objects float without weight—a level of awareness appropriate to a universe where A can be any non-A one chooses, where nothing can be known with certainty and nothing much is demanded of one's consciousness.[57]

The nemesis of all the champions of "blurred murk" in art is the science of epistemology. Since art satisfies a need of man's cognitive faculty, *it must conform to the requirements of that faculty.* These requirements are precisely what is identified by epistemology, and they are not malleable to anyone's desires. A writer, for example, must obey the rules of using concepts; if he does so, his work, however otherwise flawed, is at least intelligible. If, however, a writer decides to dispense with the rules—if he jettisons definition, logic, and grammar in order to offer neologisms, contradictions, and word salads—then he objectifies, concretizes, and communicates nothing. The same principle applies to every art form, whatever the nature of its medium.

The above is the answer to "nonobjective art." The latter deliberately flouts the rules of the human mind, perceptual and conceptual; it is addressed to man as he *does not* perceive and *cannot* think. Such a product is not open to human cognition; it is defiantly senseless. One errs if one sanctions these manifestations by the effort of interpretation; they can be given "meaning" only by devotees of the arbitrary who purport to decode "symbolism" hidden from the normal (nonmystical) mind.

Stuff of this sort is not "art with a new viewpoint" or even "bad art"; it is to art what the arbitrary is to cognition; it is *anti-art*. Metaphysically, it is the attempt not to re-create, but to annihilate reality. Epistemologically, it is the attempt not to integrate, but to disintegrate man's consciousness—in Ayn Rand's words, to "reduce it to a pre-perceptual level by breaking up percepts into mere sensations." This, she writes, "is the intention behind the reducing of language to grunts, of literature to 'moods,' of painting to smears, of sculpture to slabs, of music to noise."[58]

An *objective* art work respects the principles of human epistemology; as a result, it is knowable by the normal processes of perception and logic. The nature and meaning of such art is independent of the claims of any interpreter (including the artist himself). Objective art is not necessarily good; but it *is* graspable by a rational being. To this extent, it at least qualifies as a legitimate human product.

A third principle of esthetic judgment, which can make the difference between good and great art, is the requirement that Ayn Rand calls "the hallmark of art": *integration.*[59]

Since art is selective, the artist must be so, too—in *every* aspect of his function. Taking as the standard of selection his theme, he must weigh the need and implications of every item, major or minor, which he considers including in his work. He must regard and present the items he chooses not as isolated ends-in-themselves, but as attributes of an indivisible whole. This is the only way to achieve the kind of whole which is art, i.e., a slanted concrete, embodying, objectifying, flaunting a definite sense of life.

Here is an excerpt from Ayn Rand's description of a movie whose malevolent sense of life she rejects: *Siegfried,* directed by Fritz Lang.

> Every action, gesture and movement in this film is calculated. . . . Every inch of the film is *stylized,* i.e., condensed to those stark, bare essentials which convey the nature and spirit of the story, of its events, of its locale. The entire picture was filmed indoors, including the magnificent legendary forests whose every branch was man-made (but does not look so on the screen). While Lang was making *Siegfried,* it is reported, a sign hung on the wall of his office: "Nothing in this film is accidental." *This* is the motto of great art.[60]

Since everything included in an art work acquires significance by virtue of being included, the inclusion of anything insignificant produces a lethal contradiction: by the nature of art, the item must mean something—yet it doesn't. In a scientific report, irrelevancy can often be bracketed and ignored; it need not affect cognition or communication. In a work of art, however, irrelevancy redounds on the total. The contradiction involved is lethal because it destroys the spell, i.e., the integrity and power of the stylization. Since art is a re-creation of the universe from a personal perspective, it offers man, in effect, a new reality to contemplate; anything accidental works to make the new reality unreal.

In a proper art work, the whole implies the parts, down to the smallest ones; just as the parts imply one another and the whole. A proper story, noted Aristotle, who upheld a similar esthetic principle, must have "all the organic unity of a living creature."

"A good novel," writes Miss Rand, illustrating the point in her own field, "is an indivisible sum: every scene, sequence and passage of a good novel has to involve, contribute to and advance all of its major attributes: theme, plot, characterization." If a good novelist sends his characters to the country for a weekend, he does not interrupt the action in order to offer a needless description, however loving, of the countryside; if he offers it, he needs it, and an intelligent reader can know why. Nor does a good writer tell us about a character's parents, dress, facial expressions, or slightest movement—not until and unless a complex set of factors dictates that he do so. The kind of detail he *does* tell us is eloquently illustrated by the last sentence of the following, taken from the end of Roark's trial in *The Fountainhead:* " 'The prisoner will rise and face the jury,' said the clerk of the court. Howard Roark stepped forward and stood facing the jury. At the back of the room, Gail Wynand got up and stood also."[61]

On one level, the fact of Wynand's standing up pertains to the plot; it underscores the intensity of his concern for Roark. But, in brilliantly visual terms, the action also dramatizes a deeper meaning, pertaining to the theme. By rising to hear the verdict, Wynand is acknowledging that his life, too, has been on trial in this case; he rises, in effect, as a prisoner awaiting conviction, prepared to hear a formal statement of his guilt. He reveals thereby an aspect of his character: the courage that can face such a verdict openly, without flinching or defense.

This is a *non*accidental detail. This is purpose and integration in literature—and a magnificent simplicity, i.e., economy of artistic means.

For its proper elaboration, our discussion so far, which itself is merely a lead to some broad esthetic principles, would have to be applied specifically to the major arts. Ayn Rand does indicate her approach to each of them. In "Art and Cognition," she explains (to my knowledge, for the first time) what the valid forms of art are and why only these qualify (they derive from the nature of man's cognitive faculty). Then she surveys the field, including painting, sculpture, music, and the performing arts, from the perspective of her own esthetics. Her hypothesis concerning the nature and meaning of music, the most difficult of the arts to conceptualize, is especially

noteworthy; it offers an unprecedented integration of epistemology and esthetics with the physiology of hearing.[62]

Regrettably, all of this fascinating material belongs in a
treatise on art. My concern is only to draw the philosophic
conclusion from the esthetic leads already indicated.

Art *can* be judged rationally. Esthetic appraisal does not
involve an "esthetic sense" that divines qualities inherent in
an art work apart from any relation to human consciousness.
It does not involve the equivalent of a mystic "conscience"
in ethics, which "just knows" the right estimates. Nor does
the rejection of such a faculty entail a retreat to the notion
that art is a matter of taste, personal or social, about which
there is no disputing. Here again we see the false alternative
of intrinsicism vs. subjectivism.

As in ethics, so in esthetics: value is an aspect of reality
in relation to man. Value means the evaluation of a fact (in
this case, of a certain kind of human product) in accordance
with rational principles, principles reducible to sense perception. This is precisely the pattern one follows in esthetic evaluation. One reduces esthetic principles to the nature of art, and
art to a need of human life, i.e., to the primary of ethics; which
in turn reduces to one's acceptance of the axiom of existence.

Like goodness, therefore, beauty is not "in the object" or
"in the eye of the beholder." It is *objective.* It is in the object—as judged by a rational beholder.

Esthetic principles, let me add, are not the only standards
relevant to evaluating a work of art. Objective evaluation must
recognize that art includes both esthetic means and metaphysical content. Full objectivity consists in identifying both
elements, judging each rationally, then integrating one's judgments into an estimate of the total. As in regard to judging
people, the emotional effect produced by the total may range
across the spectrum, from revulsion to indifference to delimited appreciation to a profound embrace of substance and
form, the equivalent in the art realm of romantic love.

Esthetic quality alone, therefore, is not sufficient to make
a work of art a value to a rational man. "Since art is a philosophical composite," Miss Rand writes,

> it is not a contradiction to say: "This is a great work of
> art, but I don't like it"—provided one defines the exact

meaning of that statement: the first part refers to a purely esthetic appraisal, the second to a deeper philosophical level which includes more than esthetic values.[63]

It is by the standards of this deeper level—of truth and mastery combined—that Ayn Rand evaluates Romanticism, in the hands of its top practitioners, as being, *objectively,* the greatest achievement in art history.

• • • •

The fact that esthetics is a consequence of an entire philosophy is most obvious in the systems of Aristotle and Kant. Aristotle may be regarded as the father of Romanticism. His epistemological antipode, Kant, is the father of modern art (see Kant's *Critique of Judgment).*

Unfortunately, the concept of "philosophic consequence" has not been grasped by historians—neither in regard to politics nor to esthetics. Developments in both fields are regularly ascribed to irrelevant factors; or, worse, the causes are identified in reverse. Thus we hear that capitalism derived from religious faith—and Romanticism, from subjective feeling; the mantle of reason is then awarded to socialism and Naturalism. In both cases, Miss Rand observes, the destruction of the good "was made possible by philosophical default. . . . The issues were fought in terms of non-essentials, and the values were destroyed by men who did not know what they were losing or why."[64]

The defenders of capitalism defaulted by staking everything on the principle of rights by itself, just as the Romanticists staked everything on the principle of volition. Both groups accepted their defining principle out of context, without understanding its relation to the rest of philosophy or to reality. They did not know that their principle was thereby doomed, because ideas such as rights or volition depend ultimately on a vast complexity. They depend on an *integrated* philosophy of reason, including a rational code of values.

Such is precisely the historic lifeline that Objectivism throws to both approaches. The lifeline consists in demonstrating what kind of movement in each field *does* represent reason and what kind does not.

In her novels, Ayn Rand concretized, in masterly form,

her own vision of the world and of man. In her philosophic and esthetic essays, she defined the nature and deepest roots of great art. She was explaining such art while creating it. She was making possible a rebirth of Romanticism, while starting the rebirth herself.

Ayn Rand identified, all the way down to fundamentals, why man needs the unique form of nourishment which is art. Then, to a starving century, she provided a banquet.

Epilogue

THE DUEL BETWEEN PLATO AND ARISTOTLE

The following is an application of Objectivism to a specialized field, history. I am offering this conclusion as a further indication of the power of ideas in man's life. The material touched on below is discussed in the title essay of Ayn Rand's *For the New Intellectual.* A detailed treatment is presented in my book *The Ominous Parallels.*[1]

* * * *

Ayn Rand's theory of man leads to a distinctive interpretation of history. By identifying the cause of human action, her theory enables us to discover the factor that shapes men's past—and future.

If man is the conceptual being, philosophy is the prime mover of history.

A conceptual being is moved by the content of his mind—ultimately, by his broadest integrations. Man's actions depend on his values. His values depend on his metaphysics. His conclusions in every field depend on his method of using his consciousness, his epistemology. In the life of such a being, fundamental ideas, explicit or implicit, are the ruling power.

By their nature, fundamental ideas spread throughout a society, influencing every subgroup, transcending differences in occupation, schooling, race, class. The men who are being influenced retain the faculty of volition. But most are innocent of explicit philosophy and do not exercise their power to judge ideas. Unwittingly, they take whatever they are given.

Philosophy first shapes a small subgroup: those whose occupation is concerned with a view of man, of knowledge, of values. In modern terms, these are the intellectuals, who move philosophy out of the ivory tower. The intellectuals count on and use philosophy to create its first concrete expression, a society's culture, including its art, its manners, its science (if any), and its approach to education. The spirit of a culture, in turn, is the source of the trends in politics. Politics is the source of economics.

Objectivism does not deny that "many factors" are involved in historical causation. Economic, psychological, military, and other forces play a role. Ayn Rand does not, however, regard all these forces as primaries.

There is no dichotomy between philosophy and the specialized factors. Philosophy is not the only cause of the course of the centuries. It is the *ultimate* cause, the cause of all the other causes. If there is to be an explanation of so vast a sum as human history, which involves all men in all fields, only the science dealing with the widest abstractions can provide it. The reason is that only the widest abstractions can integrate all those fields.

The books of philosophers are the beginning. Step by step, the books turn into motives, passions, statues, politicians, and headlines.

Philosophy determines essentials, not details. If men act on certain principles (and choose not to rethink them), the actors will reach the end result logically inherent in those principles. Philosophy does not, however, determine all the concrete forms a principle can take, or the oscillations within a progression, or the time intervals among its steps. Philosophy determines only the basic direction—and outcome.

In order to grasp the role of philosophy in history, one must be able to think philosophically, i.e., see the forest. Whoever sees it knows that history is not the domain of accident.

▪   ▪   ▪   ▪

For two millennia, Western history has been the expression of a philosophic duel. The duelists are Plato and Aristotle.

Plato is the first thinker to systematize other-worldliness. His metaphysics, identified in Objectivist terms, upholds the primacy of consciousness; his epistemology, intrinsicism and its corollary, mysticism; his ethics, the code of sacrifice. Aristotle, Plato's devoted student for twenty years, is the first thinker to systematize worldliness. His metaphysics upholds the primacy of existence; his epistemology, the validity of reason; his ethics, the ideal of personal happiness.

The above requires qualifications. Plato himself, thanks to the influence of paganism, was more worldly than his followers in Christendom—or in Königsberg. Aristotle, thanks to the influence of Plato, never became completely Aristotelian; although his discoveries made possible all future intellectual progress, his system in every branch retained a sizable remnant of intrinsicism. Plato's followers included philosophers of genius, who finally stripped from his ideas every form of inconsistency and cover-up. Aristotle's followers—aside from Thomas Aquinas, who wrote as a faithful son of the Church— were lesser men, unable to purify or even fully to grasp the master's legacy.

The first battle in the historical duel was won decisively by Plato, through the work of such disciples as Plotinus and Augustine.

The Dark Ages were dark on principle. As the barbarians were sacking the body of Rome, the Church was struggling to annul the last vestiges of its spirit, wrenching the West away from nature, astronomy, philosophy, nudity, pleasure, instilling in men's souls the adoration of Eternity, with all its temporal consequences.

"The early Christian fathers," writes one historian,

> delighted in such simple self-tortures as hairshirts, and failing to wash. Others proceeded to more desperate extremes, such as Ammonius who tortured his body with a red-hot iron until it was covered with burns. . . . It would not be necessary to dwell on these depressing details if it were not for the fact that the Church erected these appalling practices into a virtue, often canonizing those who practiced them. . . . [St. Margaret Marie Alacoque] sought

out rotten fruit and dusty bread to eat. Like many mystics she suffered from a lifelong thirst, but decided to allow herself no drink from Thursday to Sunday, and when she did drink, preferred water in which laundry had been washed. . . . She cut the name of Jesus on her chest with a knife, and because the scars did not last long enough, burnt them in with a candle. . . . She was canonized in 1920. . . . St. Rose ate nothing but a mixture of sheep's gall, bitter herbs and ashes. The Pazzi, like the Alacoque, vowed herself to chastity at an incredibly early age (four, it is said).[2]

Neither serf nor lord emulated these eloquent expressions of the medieval soul. But both admired them from afar—as pious, profound, moral. No amount of "practical" considerations can explain this admiration. Nothing can explain it, or the culture, politics, and starvation to which it led, except a single fact: men took religion seriously. This is a state of mind most moderns can no longer imagine, even when they see it on the rise again.

For centuries, Aristotle's works were lost to the West. Then Thomas Aquinas turned Aristotle loose in that desert of crosses and gallows. Reason, Aquinas taught, is not a handmaiden of faith, but an autonomous faculty, which men must use and obey; the physical world is not an insubstantial emanation, but solid, knowable, real; life is not to be cursed, but to be lived. Within a century, the West was on the threshold of the Renaissance.

The period from Aquinas through Locke and Newton was a transition, at once gingerly and accelerating. The rediscovery of pagan civilization, the outpouring of explorations and inventions, the rise of man-glorifying art and of earthly philosophy, the affirmation of man's individual rights, the integration of earlier leads into the first system of modern science—all of it represents a prodigious effort to throw off the medieval shackles and reorient the Western mind. It was the prologue to a climax, the first unabashedly secular culture since antiquity: the Enlightenment. Once again, thinkers accepted reason as uncontroversial.

The God of the Scriptures became the passive observer mentioned by deism; the miracle-mongers could not compete any longer with the spokesmen of nature, who were sweeping the world with their discovery of causality, in the form of *temporal* laws that are "eternal and immutable." Revelation became an embarrassment; the educated had discovered "the only oracle of man": observation and the unaided intellect. Salvation as men's goal gave way to the pursuit of happiness on earth. Humility gave way to an all-but-forgotten emotion, pride: men's pride in the unlimited knowledge they expected to achieve and the unlimited virtue (human "perfectibility," this last was called).

In regard to every philosophic essential, the ruling spirit was the opposite of intrinsicism—and of subjectivism. The spirit was worldliness without skepticism. This means that, despite the period's many contradictions, the spirit was Aristotle's.

Faith and force, as Ayn Rand observed, entail each other, a fact exemplified in the feudalism of the medieval centuries. But reason and freedom entail each other, too. The purest example of this fact was the emergence of a new nation in the New World. It was the first time a nation had ever been founded consciously on a philosophic theory. The theory was the principle of rights.

Man, America's Founding Fathers said in essence, is the rational animal. Therefore the individual, not the state, is sovereign; man must be left free to think, and to act accordingly. Unlike Plato, whose political ideas followed from his basic premises, Aristotle's political ideas were mixed; they were a blend of individualistic and Platonic elements (the concept of "rights" had not yet been formulated). In the Declaration of Independence and the Constitution that implements it, we see at last the full expression, in *political* terms, of the Aristotelian fundamentals.

Despite the claims, then and since, about its Judeo-Christian roots, the United States with its unique system of government could not have been founded in any philosophically different period. The new nation would have been inconceivable in the seventeenth century, under the Puritans, to say nothing of the twelfth—just as, the power of tradition apart, its selfish, absolutist individualism would never survive a vote today (which is why a second Constitutional convention would be a calamity). America required what the Enlightenment alone offered: enlightenment.

The combination of reason and freedom is potent. In the nineteenth century, it led to the Industrial Revolution, to Romantic art, and to an authentic good will among men; it led to an unprecedented burst of wealth, beauty, happiness. Wherever they looked, people saw a smiling present and a radiant future. The idea of continuous improvement came to be taken for granted, as though it were an axiom. Progress, people thought, is now automatic and inevitable.

The last thing the nineteenth century imagined was that the next stop in the human express would be Sarajevo and the metaphysics of "nausea."

The whole magnificent development—including science, America, and industrialization—was an anomaly. The ideas on which the development rested were on their way out even as they were giving birth to all these epochal achievements.

Since the Renaissance, the anti-Aristotelian forces had been regrouping. In the seventeenth century, Descartes planted Platonism once again at the base of philosophy. Thanks to their intrinsicist element, the Aristotelians had always been vulnerable to attack; above all, they were vulnerable in two crucial areas: the theory of concepts and the validation of ethics. (Ethics, Aristotle had taught, is not a field susceptible to objective demonstration.) These were the historic openings, the double invitation that the better intellectuals unknowingly handed to the Cartesian trend. In the penultimate decade of the eighteenth century, just when America was being born, that trend, unopposed, bore its fruit.

The fruit was the end of the West's *philosophical* commitment to reason, the conscious changeover in the ivory tower from the remnants of Aristotle to his antithesis. The thinker who ended the Enlightenment and laid the foundation for the twentieth century was Kant.

In order to solve the problem of concepts, Kant held, a new metaphysics and epistemology are required. The metaphysics, identified in Objectivist terms, is the primacy of consciousness in its social variant; the epistemology is social subjectivism and its corollary, skepticism. This approach left Kant free to declare as beyond challenge the essence of the intrinsicist ethics: duty, i.e., imperatives issued by (noumenal) reality itself. When Kant's new approach took over Western philosophy fully, as it did within decades, duty to the noumenal world became duty to the group or the state.

Kant's Copernican Revolution reaffirmed the fundamental ideas of Plato. This time, however, the ideas were not moderated by any pagan influence. They were undiluted and thus incomparably more virulent.

Plato and the medievals denied Existence in the name of a fantasy, a glowing super-reality with which, they believed, they were in direct, inspiring contact. This mystic realm, they said (or at least its lower levels) can be approached by the use of the mind, even though the latter is tainted by its union with the body. Man, they said, should sacrifice his desires, but he should do it to gain a reward. His proper goal, even the saints agreed, is happiness, his own happiness, to be attained in the next life.

Kant is a different case. He denies Existence not in the name of a fantasy, but of nothing; he denies it in the name of a dimension that is, by his own insistent statement, unknowable to man and inconceivable. The mind, he says, is cut off not merely from some aspects of "things in themselves," but from everything real; any cognitive faculty is cut off because it has a nature, *any* nature. Man's proper goal, says Kant, is not happiness, whether in this life or the next. The "radically evil" creature (Kant's words) should sacrifice his desires *from* duty, as an end in itself.

Occasional fig leaves aside, Kant offers humanity no alternative to the realm of that which is, and no reward for renouncing it. He is the first philosopher in history to reject reality, thought, and values, not for the sake of some "higher" version of them, but *for the sake of the rejection*. The power in behalf of which his genius speaks is not "pure reason," but pure destruction.

The result of Plato's approach was a form of adoration. The result of Kant, in Ayn Rand's words, was "hatred of the good for being the good." The hatred took shape in the culture of nihilism.

Modernist intellectuals are comparable to a psychopath who murders for kicks. They seek the thrill of the new; and the new, to them, is the negative. The new is obliteration, obliteration of the essential in every field; they have no interest in anything to take its place. Thus the uniqueness of the century behind us: philosophy gleefully rid of system-building, education based on the theory that cognition is harmful, science boastful of its inability to understand, art which expelled beauty, literature which flaunted *anti*heroes, language "liberated" from syntax, verse "free" of meter. *non*representational painting, *a*tonal music, *un*conscious psychology, *de*construction in literary criticism, *in*determinacy as the new depth in physics, *in*completeness as the revelation in mathematics—a void everywhere that was acclaimed by the avantgarde with a metaphysical chuckle. It was the sound of triumph, the triumph of the new *anti*-ideal: of the unknowable, the unreachable, the unendurable.

In a Kantian reality, nothing else was possible.

Kant, surrounded by the Enlightenment, did not develop the political implications of his philosophy. His followers, however, had no trouble in seeing the point; from the premises he supplied, Fichte, Hegel, Marx (and Bismarck) drew the conclusion. Thus the two most passionately antifreedom movements in history, Communism and Fascism, along with all their lesser, welfare-statist antecedents and kin.

Modern statism emanated, as it had to, from the "land of poets and philosophers." The reason is not the "innate depravity" of the Germans, but the nature of their premier philosopher.

Statism cannot sustain an industrial civilization. Nihilism cannot abide it. Hence, in due course, another manifestation: the growing attacks on technology, i.e., the *anti*-Industrial Revolution. It was the vow of poverty over again, not as a gateway to Heaven this time, but as a means to the welfare of water, trees, and "endangered species." The latter could be any species—except the human.

So much has been lost so fast. In no time at all, the West moved from "perpetual peace" to perpetual war; from the rapture of Victor Hugo to the tongue in the asshole of Molly Bloom; from progress taken for granted to Auschwitz taken for granted.

■ ■ ■ ■

Ayn Rand is to Aristotle what Kant is to Plato. Both sides of the perennial duel, in their pure form, have finally been made explicit. Kant's philosophy is Platonism without paganism. Ayn Rand's philosophy is Aristotelianism without Platonism.

At this moment in history, the West is mutating again. The reason is that Kant as a cultural power is dead.

Kant is dead in academic philosophy; the subject has effectively expired under his tutelage. He is dead among the intellectuals, whose world view is disillusionment (they call it the "end of ideology"). He is dead in the realm of art, where nihilism, with little left to defy, is turning into its inevitable product: nihil (this is now being called "minimalism" and "postmodernism").

Kant is dead even in Berlin and Moscow. As of this writing, although it is too early to know, communism seems to be disintegrating.

The collapse of a negative, however, is not a positive. The atrophy of a vicious version of unreason is not the adoption of reason. If men fail to discover living ideas, they will keep moving by the guidance of dead ones; they will keep following, by inertia, the principles they have already institutionalized. For the nations of East and West alike today, no matter what their faddish lipservice to a "free market," the culmination of these principles is some variant of dictatorship, new or revised—if not communist, then fascist and/or religious and/or tribal. Force and faith on such a scale would mean the fate of the ancients over again.

The only man who can stave off another Dark Ages is the Father of the Enlightenment.

It is true that Aristotle has flaws, which always gave his enemies an opening. But now the opening has been closed.

The solution to the crisis of our age *is* love, as everyone says. But the love we need is not love of God or the neighbor. It is love of the good for being the good. The good, in this context, includes reality, man the hero, and man's tool of survival.[3]

Some remnant of such love still survives in the West. Above all, it survives in the people of America—which, despite its decline, is still the leader and beacon of the world. This is the grounds for hope. A nation, however, is shaped ultimately not by its people, but by its intellectuals. This is the grounds for fear, unless some "new intellectuals," as Ayn Rand called them, can be created.

A philosophy by its nature speaks to all of humanity, not to a particular time or place. A certain kind of philosophy, however, cries out to be heard by a certain place first.

Objectivism is preeminently an American viewpoint, even though most people, here and abroad, know nothing about it. It is American because it identifies the implicit base of the United States, as the country was originally conceived.

Ayn Rand's ideas would resolve the contradiction that has been tearing apart the land of the free, the contradiction between its ethics and its politics. The result would be not America as it is or even as it once was, but the grandeur of a Romantic pinnacle: America "as it might be and ought to be."

If one judges only by historical precedent, this kind of projection is the merest fantasy; we are arguably past the point of no return. America, however, is a country without precedent, and man has the faculty of volition.

To the end of her life, Ayn Rand upheld her distinctive "benevolent-universe" premise. The good, she maintained, *can* be achieved; "it is real, it is possible, it's yours."[4] So long as there is no censorship, she taught, there is a chance for persuasion to succeed.

If no definite prediction can be made, she taught, then in reason only one action is proper: to go on fighting for reason.

■   ■   ■   ■

"All things excellent," said Spinoza, "are as difficult as they are rare." Since human values are not automatic, his statement is undeniable.

In another respect, however—and this is Ayn Rand's unique perspective—the task ahead is not difficult.

To save the world is the simplest thing in the world.

All one has to do is think.

New York City—South Laguna, CA
1984–1990

REFERENCES

$\mathbf{A}$yn Rand's complete works in book form (including posthumous material as of 1991) are as follows. Where applicable, the original hardcover data are supplied in parentheses, although *page numbers in these notes refer to the specific paperback editions* cited below, which are widely accessible.

Anthem (Caldwell, Idaho: Caxton, 1946) New York: Signet, 1961.

Atlas Shrugged (New York: Random House, 1957) New York: Signet, 1959.

The Ayn Rand Lexicon: Objectivism from A to Z (New York: NAL Books, 1986) New York: Meridian, 1988.

Capitalism: The Unknown Ideal (New York: New American Library, 1966) New York: Signet, 1967.

The Early Ayn Rand: A Selection from Her Unpublished Fiction (New York: NAL Books, 1983) New York: Signet, 1986.

For the New Intellectual (New York: Random House, 1961) New York: Signet, 1963.

The Fountainhead (Indianapolis: Bobbs-Merrill, 1943) New York: Signet, 25th anniv. ed., 1968.

Introduction to Objectivist Epistemology, expanded 2nd ed. (New York: NAL Books, 1990) New York: Meridian, 1990.

The New Left: The Anti-Industrial Revolution. New York: Signet, 2nd rev. ed., 1963.

Night of January 16th (Cleveland: World Publishing, 1968) New York: Plume, 1987.

Philosophy: Who Needs It (New York: Bobbs-Merrill, 1982) New York: Signet, 1984.

The Romantic Manifesto (Cleveland: World Publishing, 1969) New York: Signet, 2nd rev. ed., 1971.

The Virtue of Selfishness (New York: New American Library, 1964) New York: Signet, 1964.

The Voice of Reason: Essays in Objectivist Thought (New York: NAL Books, 1989) New York: Meridian, 1990.

We the Living (New York: Macmillan, 1936) New York: Signet, 1960.

The Ayn Rand Letter (1971–1976) San Diego: Second Renaissance Books, 1990.

The Objectivist (1966–1971) San Diego: Second Renaissance Books, 1990.

The Objectivist Newsletter (1962–1965) San Diego: Second Renaissance Books, 1991.

Because *The Ayn Rand Lexicon* refers to all of Ayn Rand's nonfiction, offering alphabetized citations covering hundreds of topics, my own references in the notes to additional source material by Miss Rand have been brief.

The following abbreviations are used for frequently cited books.

AS	*Atlas Shrugged*
CUI	*Capitalism: The Unknown Ideal*
IOE	*Introduction to Objectivist Epistemology*
RM	*The Romantic Manifesto*
VOS	*The Virtue of Selfishness*

Chapter One

1. *Philosophy: Who Needs It,* p. 5.
2. Ibid.
3. Ayn Rand discusses the underscoring function of axioms in *IOE,* pp. 58 ff.
4. See ibid., Appendix, pp. 245–49.
5. *AS,* p. 942.
6. Ibid.
7. Ibid.
8. *IOE,* p. 55.
9. Ibid., pp. 55–56, 6. Ayn Rand does not deny that a child learns the axiomatic concepts, even on the implicit level, in a definite order (see below, pp. 12–18). For further discussion of her concept of "implicit," see *IOE,* Appendix, pp. 159–62.
10. *AS,* p. 965.
11. See *IOE,* pp. 5–6.
12. "Entity" is a specification or narrowing of "existent." As such, it is not a starting point of *all* knowledge in the way the universals "existence," "consciousness," and "identity" are.
13. For a discussion of the concept "entity," see *IOE,* Appendix, pp. 264–79.
14. *AS,* p. 962.
15. *Philosophy: Who Needs It,* "The Metaphysical Versus the

Man-Made," p. 25. This article contains Ayn Rand's fullest discussion of the primacy of existence.

16. Ibid., p. 27. It is, of course, proper to evaluate physical concretes in relation to a human goal, assuming that the goal is rational and that the concretes are alterable by human action. For example, it is valid to estimate a barren desert as "bad," not in the sense of its being "wrong," but of its being "inhospitable to human life." Such estimation is *not* an example of evaluating or condemning metaphysical reality. For further discussion, see my article "Fact and Value," in *The Intellectual Activist,* V (1), New York, May 18, 1989.

17. Ibid.

18. See *The Voice of Reason,* "Review of Randall's *Aristotle,*" pp. 10–11.

Chapter Two

1. See *AS,* p. 966.
2. Ibid., p. 942.
3. See *IOE,* Appendix, pp. 279–82. Ayn Rand accordingly rejects the primary-secondary quality distinction, along with the Cartesian contention that the essence of matter is spatiality or extension. Leaving aside its other problems, this latter theory is at best premature: the primary attributes of matter cannot be identified as such until physics reaches its culmination. As long as there is a further stage of physical knowledge still to come, there is no way to establish that a given physical attribute *is* irreducible.
4. See ibid., ch. 8.
5. *For the New Intellectual,* title essay, p. 32.
6. See *IOE,* pp. 78–79.
7. *VOS,* p. 19.
8. See *IOE,* p. 5.
9. See ibid., p. 29.
10. *AS,* p. 939.
11. Ibid., p. 944.
12. See ibid., pp. 961–62.
13. An item of knowledge, though initially acquired by a vo-

litional process, often becomes automatized. The full use of this knowledge within a process of new cognition involves mental work, however, and is not automatic.

Chapter Three

1. *IOE,* p. 6.
2. Ibid.
3. Ibid.
4. Ibid., pp. 6–7.
5. Ibid., p. 5.
6. Ibid., pp. 17–18.
7. Ibid., p. 10.
8. Ibid., p. 11.
9. Ibid., p. 7.
10. Ibid., p. 8.
11. This is the revolutionary principle elaborated in detail in *IOE.*
12. Ibid., p. 11.
13. Ibid., p. 12.
14. Ibid.
15. Ibid., p. 13.
16. See ibid., p. 14.
17. Ibid., p. 15.
18. Ibid., p. 13. This statement is italicized in the original text.
19. Ibid., p. 17.
20. Ibid., p. 18.
21. The problem of defining which concepts are *objectively* first-level, regardless of any options that exist in the order of learning concepts, is discussed in *IOE,* Appendix, pp. 204–17.
22. Ibid., p. 31.
23. Ibid., pp. 31–32.
24. Ibid., p. 36.
25. Ibid., p. 40.
26. Ibid., p. 43.
27. Ibid., pp. 43–45.
28. Ibid., p. 46.
29. See ibid., pp. 45 ff.

30. Ibid., p. 48.
31. Ibid. This statement is italicized in the original text.
32. Ibid., p. 49. This statement is italicized in the original text.
33. For fuller discussion, see my article "The Analytic-Synthetic Dichotomy," reprinted in *IOE,* especially pp. 94–106.
34. Ibid., pp. 66–67.
35. See ibid., pp. 62–63.
36. Ibid., p. 63.
37. Ibid., p. 64.
38. Ayn Rand's philosophical notes will be published in due course.

Chapter Four

1. See *IOE,* pp. 52–54.
2. Ibid., p. 70.
3. Ibid., p. 71.
4. Ibid., pp. 70–74.
5. See ibid., pp. 72–74.
6. See *Voice of Reason,* "Who Is the Final Authority in Ethics?" pp. 17–19; *IOE,* pp. 81–82.
7. *AS,* p. 943.
8. Ibid., p. 942.
9. Ibid., p. 943.
10. Ibid.
11. See *IOE,* pp. 42–43.
12. Ayn Rand discusses Rawls in *Philosophy: Who Needs It,* "An Untitled Letter," pp. 108–19.
13. See *IOE,* p. 39.
14. See *VOS,* "The Objectivist Ethics," p. 26.
15. This principle, inherent in Ayn Rand's theory of concepts, runs throughout *IOE.* It is also expressed in *RM,* pp. 19, 26–27, 57, 64, 77.
16. See *IOE,* p. 74.
17. See *AS,* p. 964.
18. *IOE,* p. 49.
19. See *IOE,* pp. 250–51.
20. W. Gerber reviewing P. Unger, *Ignorance: A Case for*

Skepticism in *Review of Metaphysics,* XXIX (4), June 1976, p. 751.

21. See *IOE,* pp. 52–54, 79.

22. Quoted in W. Windelband, *A History of Philosophy,* 2nd ed., trans. J. H. Tufts (New York: Macmillan, 1901), p. 223.

23. Kant's deduction of the categories turns on the attempt to ground necessity. But this attempt itself reflects an invalid theory of concepts. In the traditional realist approach, necessity is viewed as a relation between universals; like universals, therefore, it can be grasped only by "intuition"—a theory the moderns easily demolish. Kant then purports to save necessity through his Copernican revolution. Kant's theory of concepts, accordingly, though not nominalistic, is akin to nominalism in the respect relevant here: both theories represent subjectivist reactions to the deficiencies of intrinsicism. In form and scale, of course, Kant's subjectivism is unprecedented. This is what makes Kant a turning point, not merely another skeptic.

24. See *Philosophy: Who Needs It,* "Philosophical Detection," pp. 14–15.

25. *IOE,* pp. 81–82.

Chapter Five

1. *VOS,* "The Objectivist Ethics," p. 20.

2. See ibid., pp. 27–28; *Philosophy: Who Needs It,* title essay, pp. 5–6.

3. Infants and animals experience certain emotions because they can evaluate objects on the sensory or perceptual level of consciousness. Philosophy, however, is concerned with man qua rational being, not with perceptual-level analogues of his attributes (which are studied by psychology or biology).

4. See *Philosophy: Who Needs It,* title essay, pp. 5–6; *The New Left: The Anti-Industrial Revolution,* "The Comprachicos," p. 192.

5. See *Philosophy: Who Needs It,* "Philosophical Detection," p. 17.

6. *For the New Intellectual,* title essay, p. 55, emphasis added.

7. *AS,* p. 962.

8. Ibid., p. 943; see also *IOE,* p. 48.

9. See *AS,* p. 983.

10. For further comments on the problem of error, see my article "Maybe You're Wrong," in *The Objectivist Forum,* II (2), April 1981, pp. 8–12.

11. *IOE,* p. 35.

12. See *For the New Intellectual,* title essay, pp. 17–18; *IOE,* p. 79.

13. For a criticism of some of these false alternatives, see my essay "The Analytic-Synthetic Dichotomy," in *IOE,* pp. 88–121.

Chapter Six

1. *VOS,* "The Objectivist Ethics," p. 16.

2. Ibid.

3. *AS,* p. 939.

4. H. Binswanger, *The Biological Basis of Teleological Concepts* (Marina Del Rey, CA: Ayn Rand Institute Press, 1990), p. 63.

5. See *VOS,* "The Objectivist Ethics," p. 16.

6. See ibid., pp. 18–19.

7. See *AS,* pp. 938–39; *VOS,* "The Objectivist Ethics," pp. 19–20; *For the New Intellectual,* title essay, p. 15.

8. See *VOS,* "The Objectivist Ethics," pp. 23–24.

9. See ibid., p. 21.

10. See *AS,* pp. 938–39; *VOS,* "The Objectivist Ethics," p. 21; *The Fountainhead,* p. 680.

11. *AS,* pp. 945, 952 ff.

12. Ibid., p. 952.

13. *The Fountainhead,* p. 680.

14. Ibid.

15. Ibid., pp. 680–81.

16. *The Rational Faculty,* p. 4. This essay, an excerpt from Ayn Rand's private journal dated April 22, 1945, was published posthumously by *The Intellectual Activist* (New York, 1986). See also *The Fountainhead,* p. 680.

17. *The Rational Faculty,* pp. 7, 6.
18. Ibid., p. 7.
19. See *AS,* pp. 471 ff.
20. Ibid., pp. 946–47.
21. Although one clause of this sentence is reminiscent of a line from Sartre, the idea is the opposite of his viewpoint. Existentialism, as an orgy of voluntarism, necessarily implies man's utter helplessness, regardless of any out-of-context remarks by Sartre intended to make it "humanistic."

Chapter Seven

1. *VOS,* "The Objectivist Ethics," p. 13.
2. Ibid.
3. Ibid., p. 15.
4. Ibid.
5. *AS,* p. 939.
6. *VOS,* "The Objectivist Ethics," p. 16.
7. Ibid., p. 17. *AS,* p. 939.
8. Ibid.
9. Ibid., p. 940; see also *VOS,* "The Objectivist Ethics," p. 22.
10. *AS,* p. 940.
11. *The Random House Dictionary of the English Language,* College Ed., ed. L. Urdang (New York: Random House, 1968).
12. *VOS,* "The Objectivist Ethics," p. 24.
13. Ibid.
14. Ibid.
15. See *CUI,* "The Anatomy of Compromise," p. 144.
16. *AS,* p. 940.
17. *VOS,* "The Objectivist Ethics," p. 24.
18. *AS,* p. 940.
19. Ibid.
20. *VOS,* "The Objectivist Ethics," p. 25; *AS,* p. 944.
21. Ibid., p. 982.
22. Ibid., p. 939.
23. *VOS,* "The Objectivist Ethics," p. 25.
24. *For the New Intellectual,* title essay, p. 15.

25. *VOS,* "The Objectivist Ethics," p. 20.
26. See *AS,* p. 731.
27. Ibid., p. 944.
28. Ibid., pp. 945, 962.
29. See *VOS,* "The Objectivist Ethics," pp. 25–26.
30. See *AS,* p. 961.
31. Ibid., p. 963.
32. *VOS,* "The Objectivist Ethics," p. 14.
33. Ibid., p. 25.
34. See *VOS,* Introduction, pp. vii–x.
35. Ibid., p. x.
36. See *AS,* pp. 953 ff.; *VOS,* "The Ethics of Emergencies," p. 44.
37. *AS,* pp. 955–56.
38. Ibid., p. 993. Ayn Rand's view here is the opposite of Kant's principle of "treating humanity . . . always as an end." Kant bars the exploitation of one man by another, while demanding of everyone a life of total self-sacrifice. For a discussion of Kant's ethics, see my book *The Ominous Parallels* (New York: Mentor, 1983), pp. 74–84.
39. See *The Fountainhead,* pp. 606–9, 682 ff.
40. See *AS,* pp. 741–42, 713–14; *VOS,* "The 'Conflicts' of Men's Interests," pp. 50–56.
41. *VOS,* "The Objectivist Ethics," p. 32.
42. Ibid., pp. 31–32.
43. Ibid., "The Ethics of Emergencies," p. 44; *The Fountainhead,* p. 377.
44. See *VOS,* "The Ethics of Emergencies," pp. 43–49.
45. Ibid., p. 45.
46. Ibid., pp. 47–49.
47. See *CUI,* "What Is Capitalism?" pp. 21–22.
48. Ibid., p. 22.
49. *Philosophy: Who Needs It,* "Causality Versus Duty," p. 99.
50. Ibid., pp. 99–101.
51. See *AS,* p. 941.
52. *Philosophy: Who Needs It,* "Causality Versus Duty," p. 96.
53. Ibid., pp. 97–98.

Chapter Eight

1. The same material is organized somewhat differently in *VOS*, "The Objectivist Ethics," pp. 25–27.
2. Ibid., p. 26.
3. *The Fountainhead*, p. 681.
4. Ibid., p. 683.
5. Ibid., p. 609.
6. See especially pp. 606–9.
7. See *VOS*, Introduction, p. x.
8. *AS*, p. 389.
9. *The Fountainhead*, p. 679.
10. See *VOS*, "The Ethics of Emergencies," p. 46.
11. *AS*, p. 945.
12. Ibid.
13. See *VOS*, "Doesn't Life Require Compromise?" p. 69.
14. Ibid., p. 68.
15. Ibid.
16. *AS*, p. 979.
17. *CUI*, "The Anatomy of Compromise," p. 147.
18. Ibid. The moral fact that evil has to count on some element of good is what makes plausible Kant's "universalizability" principle. The fact, however, is incompatible with any intrinsicist dogma; it rests on an ethics of life, rationality, and egoism.
19. See *AS*, p. 945; *VOS*, "The Objectivist Ethics," p. 26.
20. *AS*, p. 945.
21. See *Philosophy: Who Needs It*, "Philosophical Detection," p. 16.
22. Ibid., "What Can One Do?" p. 201.
23. See ibid., "Philosophical Detection," p. 16.
24. *AS*, p. 945.
25. Like the Greeks, Ayn Rand validates virtue by its effects on the actor's well-being. In identifying these effects, however, her approach is unique. Plato, e.g., regards dishonesty as self-defeating ultimately because of its other-worldly consequences. Aristotle regards it as self-defeating because of its clash with the (undemonstrable) principle of the mean. Ayn Rand regards it as self-defeating *objectively*, because it leads to a head-on clash between the culprit and (this) reality.

26. See *IOE*, p. 55; *AS*, pp. 945–46; *VOS*, "The Objectivist Ethics," p. 26.
27. See ibid., "How Does One Lead a Rational Life in an Irrational Society?" pp. 71–74.
28. Ibid., pp. 71, 72; *AS*, p. 946.
29. *VOS*, "How Does One Lead a Rational Life in an Irrational Society?" p. 72. This statement is italicized in the original text.
30. See *AS*, p. 945; *VOS*, "How Does One Lead a Rational Life in an Irrational Society?" pp. 72–73.
31. See *The Voice of Reason*, "The Psychology of Psychologizing," pp. 23–31.
32. See *VOS*, "The Cult of Moral Grayness," pp. 75–79.
33. *AS*, pp. 686, 945.
34. See *VOS*, "How Does One Lead a Rational Life in an Irrational Society?" p. 73.
35. See *AS*, p. 948; *VOS*, "The Objectivist Ethics," pp. 31–32.
36. *AS*, p. 948.
37. Ibid., p. 530.
38. Ibid., p. 959. See also *VOS*, "The Objectivist Ethics," pp. 31–32.
39. See *The New Left: The Anti-Industrial Revolution*, "The Age of Envy," pp. 164 ff.; *Philosophy: Who Needs It*, "An Untitled Letter," pp. 103 ff.
40. *AS*, p. 946.
41. *The New Left: The Anti-Industrial Revolution*, "The Age of Envy," pp. 152–86.
42. *For the New Intellectual*, title essay, p. 15. See also *VOS*, "The Objectivist Ethics," p. 26.
43. See George Reisman, *The Government Against the Economy* (Ottawa, IL: Caroline House, 1979), pp. 15 ff.
44. See *AS*, pp. 387–91.
45. Ibid., p. 946.
46. See ibid., p. 946; *VOS*, "The Objectivist Ethics," p. 26.
47. *AS*, pp. 728–29.
48. Ibid., p. 946; *VOS*, "The Objectivist Ethics," p. 25.
49. See "*Playboy*'s Interview with Ayn Rand," 1964, quoted in *The Ayn Rand Lexicon*, pp. 62–63.
50. *AS*, pp. 569–70.

51. Both Aristotle and Nietzsche in their own terms make a similar point.
52. See *The Ayn Rand Letter*, "From My 'Future File,' " III (26), September 1974, p. 373.
53. *The Fountainhead*, p. 253.
54. See *VOS*, "The Objectivist Ethics," p. 27; *AS*, pp. 946–47.
55. *RM*, "The Goal of My Writing," p. 169.
56. See *AS*, p. 983.
57. Ibid.
58. See ibid.
59. *VOS*, "The Objectivist Ethics," p. 27.
60. *AS*, p. 984.
61. See ibid., pp. 947, 981–82.
62. Ibid. p. 981.
63. Ibid. This statement is in the second person in the original text.
64. Ibid., p. 982.
65. Ibid., p. 981.
66. See ibid., pp. 949–50; *VOS*, "The Objectivist Ethics," pp. 32–33.
67. *CUI*, "What Is Capitalism?" p. 17.
68. *AS*, p. 949.
69. Ibid.
70. Ibid.
71. Ibid., p. 390.
72. *CUI*, "What Is Capitalism?" p. 23.
73. See *VOS*, "The Nature of Government," p. 111.
74. *AS*, p. 950.
75. See *CUI*, "What Is Capitalism?" pp. 22–23.

Chapter Nine

1. *AS*, p. 983.
2. See ibid., pp. 977–78.
3. See ibid., pp. 972–73.
4. *The Fountainhead*, p. 493; *We the Living*, pp. 358, 357.
5. *CUI*, "The Anatomy of Compromise," pp. 148–49.
6. See *AS*, p. 973.
7. See ibid., pp. 399 ff., 437 ff., 687–89, 915–16, 972–73.

8. See ibid., p. 947; *VOS,* "The Objectivist Ethics," pp. 17–18, 27–28.

9. *AS,* p. 940.

10. See *VOS,* "The Objectivist Ethics," p. 28.

11. See *AS,* pp. 941, 948; *VOS,* "The Objectivist Ethics," pp. 28–29.

12. *AS,* p. 948.

13. See ibid., p. 950.

14. Ibid., p. 950.

15. See *VOS,* "The Objectivist Ethics," p. 29.

16. *The Fountainhead,* p. 344.

17. In *The Fountainhead,* p. 195, a character's voice is described as "radiantly premonitory."

18. See *VOS,* "The Objectivist Ethics," pp. 29–30.

19. *AS,* p. 706.

20. *The Voice of Reason,* "Of Living Death," pp. 54 ff.; see also *AS,* pp. 460–63.

21. See ibid., p. 461.

22. *The Fountainhead,* p. 518.

23. *AS,* p. 461.

24. See ibid., pp. 462–63.

25. Ibid., p. 241.

Chapter Ten

1. *VOS,* "Man's Rights," p. 92.

2. Ibid., p. 93. "Textbook of Americanism," a 1940s pamphlet by Ayn Rand, p. 5; quoted in *The Ayn Rand Lexicon,* p. 214.

3. See *VOS,* "Man's Rights," pp. 93–94.

4. *AS,* p. 986.

5. *For the New Intellectual,* title essay, p. 25.

6. *VOS,* "Man's Rights," p. 94.

7. See "Textbook of Americanism," p. 7; quoted in *The Ayn Rand Lexicon,* p. 215.

8. *VOS,* "Man's Rights," pp. 96–99. The political theorist is Isabel Paterson in *The God of the Machine.*

9. See *VOS,* "Collectivized Rights," pp. 101–6.

10. Ibid., pp. 102, 101.

11. See *The Voice of Reason,* "Of Living Death," pp. 58 ff.

12. See "A Last Survey," *The Ayn Rand Letter,* IV (2), November–December 1975, p. 383. Miss Rand is speaking here of an embryo.
13. See *VOS,* "Man's Rights," p. 95, and "The Nature of Government," p. 108.
14. *AS,* pp. 985–86.
15. *VOS,* "The Nature of Government," p. 107.
16. See ibid., pp. 108–9.
17. Ibid.
18. Ibid., p. 109.
19. See ibid., p. 110.
20. Ibid., pp. 110–11.
21. Ibid., p. 112.
22. See *AS,* p. 950.
23. See *VOS,* "The Nature of Government," p. 110.
24. See *The New Left: The Anti-Industrial Revolution,* especially "The Left: Old and New," pp. 82–95, and "The Anti-Industrial Revolution," pp. 127–51.
25. *The New Left: The Anti-Industrial Revolution,* "The Left: Old and New," p. 91.
26. See *VOS,* "The Nature of Government," pp. 112–13.
27. See *CUI,* "The New Fascism: Rule by Consensus," pp. 206–7.
28. *Philosophy: Who Needs It,* "Censorship: Local and Express," p. 187.
29. Ibid. The first sentence of this passage is italicized in the original text.

Chapter Eleven

1. *CUI,* "What Is Capitalism?" p. 19. This statement is italicized in the original text.
2. See *VOS,* "The Objectivist Ethics," p. 33.
3. See *CUI,* "What Is Capitalism?" pp. 20 ff.
4. See ibid., "Antitrust," by Alan Greenspan, especially p. 68.
5. *AS,* p. 992.
6. New York: Putnam, 1943, p. 221.
7. *AS,* p. 974.
8. Ibid., p. 452.

9. See *CUI,* "What Is Capitalism?" pp. 21 ff.
10. Ibid., p. 23.
11. Ibid., pp. 24–25.
12. Ibid., pp. 25–26; 25.
13. Ibid., p. 26.
14. *AS,* p. 388.
15. Ibid., pp. 387, 391.
16. Ibid., p. 391.
17. *CUI,* "America's Persecuted Minority: Big Business," p. 48.
18. *AS,* pp. 988–89.
19. Darwin's theory, Ayn Rand held, pertains to a special science, not to philosophy. Philosophy as such, therefore, takes no position in regard to it.
20. *AS,* p. 412.
21. Most of these charges against capitalism (and many others) receive separate discussions in *CUI* or *VOS.*
22. *CUI,* "The Roots of War," p. 37.

Chapter Twelve

1. *RM,* "The Psycho-Epistemology of Art," p. 17.
2. Ibid., p. 19.
3. Ibid.
4. Ibid.
5. Ibid. This statement is italicized in the original text.
6. Ibid., pp. 19–20.
7. See ibid., "Art and Sense of Life," pp. 36–37.
8. Ibid., "The Psycho-Epistemology of Art," p. 20.
9. Ibid.
10. Ibid., p. 18.
11. Ibid., p. 23.
12. Ibid., p. 21. This statement is italicized in the original text.
13. Ibid., "The Goal of My Writing," p. 169.
14. Ibid., "Art and Sense of Life," pp. 38–39.
15. See ibid., p. 38.
16. Ibid., pp. 40–42.
17. Ibid., "The Psycho-Epistemology of Art," p. 22.
18. Ibid., "Art and Cognition," p. 45.

19. Ibid., "Art and Sense of Life," p. 36.
20. Ibid., "Philosophy and Sense of Life," p. 28, and "Art and Sense of Life," p. 36.
21. Ibid., "Art and Sense of Life," p. 36.
22. See ibid., pp. 34–37.
23. Ibid., "Philosophy and Sense of Life," p. 25.
24. Ibid., p. 26.
25. Ibid., "Art and Sense of Life," pp. 34–35.
26. Ibid., Introduction, p. viii.
27. See ibid., "What Is Romanticism?" p. 106.
28. Ibid., p. 99.
29. See ibid., p. 103.
30. Ibid., p. 100.
31. See ibid., "Basic Principles of Literature," pp. 82–83.
32. Ibid., p. 82. Aristotle held a similar view; see *De Poetica* 1150a 18–24.
33. See ibid., "Basic Principles of Literature," pp. 86–87.
34. Ibid., p. 82.
35. Ibid., pp. 82, 86.
36. Ibid., p. 83.
37. Ibid.
38. See ibid., "What Is Romanticism?" p. 107, and "Basic Principles of Literature," pp. 87–89.
39. Ibid., "What Is Romanticism?" p. 100, and "Bootleg Romanticism," p. 132.
40. Ibid., "Basic Principles of Literature," p. 87.
41. Ibid., "The Esthetic Vacuum of Our Age," p. 124.
42. Ibid., pp. 124–25.
43. See ibid., p. 126.
44. Ibid., "Basic Principles of Literature," p. 80.
45. *De Poetica*, 1451a36–b7; *RM*, "Basic Principles of Literature," p. 80.
46. Ibid., "The Goal of My Writing," pp. 167–68.
47. See ibid., "What Is Romanticism?" pp. 107–15.
48. Ayn Rand's *Lectures on Fiction Writing*, unpublished. Lecture II.
49. Ibid., Lecture X.
50. *RM*, "Art and Sense of Life," p. 42.
51. Ibid., p. 42.
52. *AS*, p. 728.
53. *RM*, "The Goal of My Writing," p. 166.

54. Ibid.
55. Ibid., pp. 166–67.
56. Ibid., "Art and Sense of Life," p. 40.
57. Ibid., pp. 40–41.
58. Ibid., "Art and Cognition," pp. 76–77.
59. Ibid., p. 65.
60. Ibid., p. 72.
61. Ibid., "Basic Principles of Literature," p. 93; *The Foun-tainhead,* p. 687.
62. "Art and Cognition" is chapter 4 of the 2nd ed. of *RM.*
63. *RM,* "Art and Sense of Life," p. 43.
64. Ibid., "What Is Romanticism?" p. 102.

Epilogue

1. New York: Mentor, 1983.
2. G. Rattray Taylor, *Sex in History* (New York: Thames and Hudson, 1954), p. 44.
3. See *The New Left: The Anti-Industrial Revolution,* "The Age of Envy," p. 186.
4. *AS,* p. 993.

INDEX

NOTE: Under each main entry, the subtopics and cross-references are not arranged in alphabetical order. Rather, they are arranged in the order in which they first occur in the book. This has the advantage of placing them, as a rule, in the order from more fundamental to more derivative.

A

Identity *(continued)*
　law of, 6–7; and causality,
　　14–17; and metaphysically
　　given facts, 24–30; and
　　consciousness, 48–52; and
　　objectivity, 118–119
　concept of, 12–14, 74–75
　See also Axioms;
　　Contradiction, law of.
Independence, 251–253
　defined, 251
　philosophic basis of, 253–255
　intellectual side of, 255–257
　existential side of, 257–259
　and honesty, 271–272
　as contextual, 274–275
　and capitalism, 381–384
　See also Egoism; Virtue.
Individualism
　basis of in nature of reason,
　　198–205
　defined, 361
　application to politics of,
　　361–363
　See also Egoism.
Induction, and measurement-
　omission, 90–91
Industrial Revolution, 195,
　294–295, 380
Infinity, 31–32
"Instinct," 193–194
Integration, 77
　as essential to philosophy
　　(and vice versa), 1–4, 128
　perceptual, 52–53
　as a requirement of
　　objectivity, 119, 125–128,
　　138
　evasion as non-integration,
　　224–225
　of values as requiring a
　　central purpose, 298–300
　as the hallmark of art, 416–
　　417, 445–447

　See also Context.
Integrity, 259–261
　defined, 259
　intellectual side of, 261
　existential side of, 261–262;
　　and evil of compromise,
　　262–267
　why the good demands
　　consistency, 265–266
　as impossible under statism,
　　388–389
　See also Virtue.
Intrinsicism
　in regard to concepts, 142–
　　144
　in regard to knowledge,
　　145–146, 147–150
　mysticism a consequence of,
　　182
　in regard to values, 245–
　　246, 247
　assault on virtue by, 267,
　　275, 283–284, 308–310
　leads to the initiation of
　　physical force, 321–323
　leads to moral-practical
　　dichotomy, 334–335
　assault on happiness and sex
　　by, 341–342, 346–348
　assault on individual rights
　　by, 361
　in regard to art, 448
　See also Supernaturalism;
　　Objectivity; Mysticism.

J

Justice, 276–279
　defined, 276
　intellectual side of, 279–282
　existential side of, 282–286;
　　and trader principle, 286–
　　290

based on primacy of
existence, 149–150
of values, 241–248
as basis of mind-body
integration, 334–335
of individual rights, 360–
361
objective law, 364–365
relationship to virtue, 395–
396
of capitalism, 395–396
of economic value, 396–402
of esthetic value, 438–450
See also Context; Hierarchy;
Intrinsicism; Subjectivism;
Reason.
Options
in concept-formation, 114–
116
in the order of knowledge,
131–132
moral, 323–324

P

Parmenides (b.c. 515 B.C.), 4,
23
Philosophy
man's need of, 1–3, 128,
156–157, 414–420
systematic nature of, 1–4
branches of, 3
starting points of, 4, 139–
141
subject matter of, 413–414
as the ultimate cause of
history, 451–460
Physical force, initiation of
defined, 310, 318–320
as a negation of reason,
310–315
as a negation of value, 315–
318

philosophic premises of its
advocates, 320–323
and individual rights, 359–
360
Plato (427?–347 B.C.)
primacy-of-consciousness
viewpoint of, 21, 30
mind-body dichotomy of,
29, 35, 158
intrinsicism of, 142, 144,
145–146
collectivism of, 202
ethics of, 471n25
role in history of, 453–454,
456–459
Pleasure and pain, 193, 335–336
Politics, 3, 350–351
relationship to economics
of, 378–379
Possibility and probability,
175–179
Pragmatism, as a form of
subjectivism, 146
Pride, 303–304
defined, 303
intellectual side of, 304–305
existential side of, 305
and self-esteem, 305–310
See also Virtue.
Primacy of existence, 17–23,
35–36
epistemological implications
of, 20
as opposed to primacy of
consciousness, 19, 20;
defined, 18; three versions
of, 21–23; leads to
intrinsicism, 145–146;
leads to collectivism, 201–
202
as a basis of the need for
epistemology, 37–38
applied to sensory form,
46–47

THE EARLY AYN RAND

A Selection from her Unpublished Fiction

Edited and with an Introduction and Notes by Leonard Peikoff

Selected by Leonard Peikoff, Ayn Rand's longtime associate and literary heir, this collection of previously unpublished short fiction and plays—predating her masterpiece, *The Fountainhead*—provides a revealing and provocative view of her evolution as artist and philosopher.

The eleven pieces range from beginner's exercises remarkable for their honesty and depth of feeling, to the poetry and power of excerpts from early versions of *We the Living* and *The Fountainhead*. In his extensive Introduction and commentary, Leonard Peikoff relates each selection to the body of Ayn Rand's work and places each in the context of her life. This volume will be eagerly welcomed by all admirers of her great mature works.